Bilingualism
In
Early
Childhood

Bilingualism In Early Childhood

Papers from a Conference on Child Language, *Chicago, 1971*

edited by

WILLIAM F. MACKEY
International Center for Research on Bilingualism
Laval University, Quebec

and

THEODORE ANDERSSON
University of Texas at Austin
Austin, Texas

NEWBURY HOUSE PUBLISHERS / ROWLEY / MASSACHUSETTS

Library of Congress Cataloging in Publication Data

Conference on Child Language, Chicago, 1971.
  Bilingualism in early childhood.

  (Series on studies in bilingual education)
  Bibliography: p.
  Includes index.
  1. Education, Bilingual—Addresses, essays, lectures.
2. Bilingualism—Addresses, essays, lectures.
3. Children—Language—Addresses, essays, lectures.
I. Mackey, William Francis, 1918-   II. Andersson,
Theodore, 1903-   III. Title.   IV. Series.
LC3719.C66 1971   371.9'7   77-941
ISBN 0-88377-075-X

Cover design by Cynthia Crowley

This book was typeset at the International Center for
Research on Bilingualism, Laval University, Quebec

NEWBURY HOUSE PUBLISHERS, Inc.

Language Science
Language Teaching
Language Learning

ROWLEY, MASSACHUSETTS 01969

Printed in the U.S.A.   First printing: June 1977
                                                   5   4   3   2   1

NEWBURY HOUSE SERIES

STUDIES IN BILINGUAL EDUCATION

Sponsored by
The International Center for Research on Bilingualism
Laval University
Quebec City, Canada

BILINGUAL EDUCATION IN A BINATIONAL SCHOOL
by William F. Mackey

THE LANGUAGE EDUCATION OF MINORITY CHILDREN
Selected Readings
Edited by Bernard Spolsky

BILINGUAL EDUCATION OF CHILDREN: The St. Lambert Experiment
by Wallace E. Lambert and G. R. Tucker

A SOCIOLINGUISTIC APPROACH TO BILINGUAL EDUCATION
by Andrew D. Cohen

BILINGUAL SCHOOLING AND THE SURVIVAL OF SPANISH
IN THE UNITED STATES
by A. Bruce Gaarder

THE AMERICAN BILINGUAL TRADITION
by Heinz Kloss

BILINGUALISM IN EARLY CHILDHOOD
Edited by William F. Mackey and Theodore Andersson

BILINGUAL SCHOOLS FOR A BICULTURAL COMMUNITY
William F. Mackey and Von N. Beebe

CONTENTS

FOREWORD

The idea of this Conference on Child Language had its origin in Stockholm in August of 1970, when Dr. Max Gorosch, Executive Secretary of the International Association of Applied Linguistics (IAAL), asked me whether I would help activate the Association Commission on Child Language (CCL). I agreed to help Mr. R. W. Rutherford, Organiser of the Child Language Survey, York, England, to whom the Executive Committee looked for leadership. It was agreed that I would take main responsibility for organizing this Conference and leave to Mr. Rutherford the task of arranging a possible follow-up conference in Europe.

The Center for Applied Linguistics (CAL), the United States affiliate of the IAAL, readily agreed, through Dr. John Lotz, then Director, and Dr. Albert H. Marckwardt, who succeeded as Acting Director in July, 1971, to co-sponsor the Conference.

Mr. C. Edward Scebold, Executive Secretary of the American Council on the Teaching of Foreign Languages (ACTFL), offered not only to co-sponsor the Conference but to assist materially with the arrangements if the Conference could be held at the same time and place as the Fifth Annual Meeting of ACTFL. It was therefore decided to schedule the Conference in the Conrad Hilton Hotel in Chicago on November 22, 23, and 24, 1971.

A final generous offer of co-sponsorship came from Professor Henri Dorion, Director of the International Center for Research on Bilingualism (ICRB), Quebec, Canada, who offered to have the Center prepare a Preprint of papers received in time as well as to undertake publication of the Conference Proceedings.

Calling on colleagues for help—who responded most generously—I tried in my spare time to identify as many as possible of those who were actively engaged in research on child language and willing and ready to prepare papers. Several outstanding investigators were unable on short notice to collaborate, but the response was nevertheless most gratifying. In fact, so active is research in this field that it was considered advisable to restrict the subject to "the learning of two or more languages or dialects by young children, especially between the ages of three and eight, with particular attention to the social setting." The reader will note that not all papers conform strictly to this subject, but the majority reflect the dual language interest of the sponsoring organizations.

Twenty-six papers out of a final total of twenty-nine were submitted in time for inclusion in the Preprint. It had been planned that Preprint would reach all writers, panel chairmen and recorders, and preregistrants in time to be read before the Conference, thus eliminating the reading of papers and permitting extensive discussion in plenary sessions. Owing to unforeseen delays, this plan miscarried in part. However, panelists cooperated fully by trying to summarize briefly important points in their papers in order to leave maximum time for discussion.

A transcript of the discussion, however, proved too lengthy to be included within the covers of the present book. This transcript, along with other relevant material will, it is hoped, be included in a subsequent volume.

As explained by William Mackey in his Introduction, we have rearranged the papers in an effort to create a more logical sequence and to produce a more readable book.

I should like to thank all those who made possible this meeting of researchers in the field of child language and child bilingualism, especially those who contributed papers to the Conference. Let me thank the chairmen and recorders of the various panel sessions, who also constituted the Committee on Planning for the Future. They worked hard and quickly to digest and arrange the suggestions and recommendations of the conferees. A particular word of thanks is due Richard Tucker for graciously responding to my last-minute request to preside at the final session, a task he carried off with characteristic *brio.*

If the Conference was, as Edward Scebold pointed out, indebted to Dr. Max Gorosch for the original suggestion, it could not have taken place without the strong support of those who were able to bring the prestige of their organizations to the support of the Conference: Edward Scebold of ACTFL; John Lotz and Albert Marckwardt of CAL; and Henri Dorion, Jean-Guy Savard, and William Mackey of ICRB.

I should also like to mention with thanks the help of associates in Edward Scebold's office: Mrs. Inge Savelsberg, who was most helpful throughout the preparatory stage and throughout the Conference; Mrs. Carol Sherman; and Miss Barbara McKeckney.

A special word of thanks goes to William Mackey, who cheerfully agreed to share with me the editing of these Proceedings and has in fact done the major part of the task in addition to contributing a critical Introduction which places this Conference on Child Languages in its proper international perspective.

And now finally let me say that in casting a backward glance over this Conference I am reminded of that common type of book review in which the critic fails to review the book at hand and instead deplores the fact that another kind of book was not written. As Dr. Els Oksaar very aptly put it, "There is no way of pleasing everyone." I hope that, though many conferees would have liked a different kind of conference, all will have found some profit in the Conference and that they and other readers of this book will be able to consider it a report of not altogether insignificant progress.

Theodore Andersson
The University of Texas at Austin,
Conference Chairman

Austin, Texas
July, 1972

Bilingualism
In
Early
Childhood

INTRODUCTION
William F. Mackey

The proceedings of this conference bring together two fields of enquiry — child language and bilingualism — which have attracted a rapidly increasing public. As a perusal of the recent collections and bibliographies in these two areas would indicate, there has been a great deal of activity since the early 1950's, both in the field of child language[1] and in the study of bilingualism.[2]

Interest in the problems of early childhood bilingualism however is by no means confined to the second half of our century: the very title of this book is almost a literal translation of that of an article published in 1923 — *"Uber Zweisprachigkeit in der frühen Kindheit."* [3] Nor is the phenomenon limited to the ethnic minorities of the New World. European documents on bilingual schooling go back at least three centuries; the French-German bilingual school in Berlin is headed for its tricentennial in the late 1980's.[4]

Held in the heartland of the United States it is understandable that this conference has produced papers and discussions based largely on North American experience and reflecting the growing concern with the problems of underprivileged ethnic minorities — problems which the U.S. Bilingual Education Act of 1968 was designed to help solve. If childhood bilingualism or bidialectalism is a problem for minorities in the United States, however, it is often a matter of national survival in other countries.

It would be prudent, therefore, to approach these proceedings with some reference to similar meetings held at other times and in other places. It seems that the problems of early childhood bilingualism became questions of public concern after the beginning of mass universal education. In 1847 a series of reports of the Commission of Inquiry into the state of education in Wales treats of the attitude of parents on the teaching of the two languages to children.[5] And a later report, of 1887, of the Royal Commission on Education documents evidence of bilingual teaching in Welsh elementary schools.[6] About a decade later we find the American Philological Association at its 1898 meeting discussing language rivalry in cases of "race-mixture".[7] Problems of bilingualism in education also appeared in the proceedings of the 1911 Imperial Education Conference.[8]

It was not until after the First World War, however, that we find an international conference devoted exclusively to problems of childhood bilingualism. This conference was held during the heyday of the League of Nations and its affiliated International Office of Education which organized an international meeting in Luxembourg on the problems of bilingualism and education.[9]

1

In the 1930's the problem was the subject of interchanges within the New Education Fellowship[10] and the World Federation of Educational Associations;[11] it was also debated and described in such periodicals as the *Yearbook of Education* and *Overseas Education*.[12]

After the Second World War, the world-wide interest in a lasting peace and in international understanding created a new interest in bilingual education. The 1950's saw the rise of the *monde bilingue* movement, supported by such organizations as the United Towns Federation[13] and a growing interest in bilingualism on the part of a number of international organizations.

In 1960, UNESCO, through its United Kingdom National Commission, organized an international seminar on bilingualism in education which included wide-ranging discussions on the relation of bilingualism to school and society and well-documented papers on the educational, linguistic, social, psychological, and cultural aspects of childhood bilingualism.[14] Two years later, the Committee for Technical Cooperation in Africa, in conjunction with the Inter-African Committee on Linguistics, held a week-long symposium on multilingualism.[15] Fully half of the papers and discussions of this symposium were devoted to the educational problems of bilingualism, including the use of a foreign language as a medium of instruction — especially the use of English and French in African schools.

Also during this period and at the time of the FLES movement in the United States and in Europe[16] there were meetings on early childhood language learning — many organized under the auspices of UNESCO. Notable among these are the meetings held at the UNESCO Institute of Education in Hamburg — one in 1962,[17] and another in 1966. At this latter meeting there were reports of bilingual education in elementary schools in Asia, Africa, the United States, France, and Germany.[18] The following year — also under the auspices of UNESCO and through its Canadian Commission, an international seminar on the description and measurement of bilingualism was held in Moncton. Here early childhood bilingualism was given a prominent place in the papers describing how and when persons become bilingual and also in those on the measurement of bilingual proficiency.[19]

After the enactment of the Bilingual Education Act in the United States, the U.S. Office of Education organized in 1969 a national conference on bilingual education, with particular emphasis on the language skills. There were reports both on the early childhood acquisition of two languages in the home and on the more formal setting of the school program.[20] Regional conferences were also held in different parts of the United States to discuss local problems of bilingual education.

In Canada, there had been smaller meetings of experts organized by the Royal Commission on Bilingualism and Biculturalism during the preparation of its report[21] and later by the Commission on the French Language in Quebec for a similar purpose. Bilingual education was given an important place in two of the Round Table Conferences on languages and linguistics organized by Georgetown University — one in 1954 and another in 1970.[22]

In 1971 the Modern Language Centre of the Ontario Institute for Studies in Education organized a conference on bilingual schooling at which there were a number of reports of experiences from various parts of Canada and the United States.[23] Later the same year, UNESCO, which had somewhat shifted its main emphasis from language teaching to language policy, held two meetings in Paris on the contribution of educational anthropology and sociolinguistics to language education and policy in which a section was devoted to the special problems of multilingual education.[24]

The following year, the *monde bilingue* movement which had flourished during the 1950's bloomed again in the form of an international symposium on bilingual education as an opportunity for municipal and regional governments throughout the world; the conference, held in Aoste, Italy, was the occasion for the launching of a World Information Center on Bilingual Education.[25]

The present proceedings are therefore a contribution to the growing conference literature on bilingual education, particularly to the study of early childhood bilingualism.

In presenting these proceedings, the editors felt that the papers could preferably be grouped differently from the order of oral presentation at the Conference. It appeared that some of the contributions had more in common than had first been anticipated. Some of the papers were of a more general or theoretical nature and were therefore grouped under the heading of "theory and method." Others were devoted to the language problems of the very young (early language learning) or language learning in the home (family bilingualism). Seven papers treated the problem in its social context (bilingualism and society). About a dozen of the papers were, on the other hand, related to the educational context. Some of these were programmatic; others were descriptive. We divided the first category into two sections — preschool language learning, and the primary curriculum. The purely descriptive studies were grouped into another section (case studies of school bilingualism). Finally, there were papers oriented toward future policy or research; these were grouped into a concluding section immediately preceding the report of the final general discussion on planning for the future.

Each of these sections can of course be read separately within the context of its own literature. The first section (theory and method) is related to a growing theoretical literature on the nature of language learning. These are here related to the problems of bilingualism, bidialectalism, and bilingual education and can be handled within the context of the theoretical literature on child bilingualism.[26]

The second section (early language learning) starts with a paper which, although not related directly to bilingualism, throws much light on the issues of early language acquisition in the controversial context of child language pathology; since pathology was not the main concern of the conference, however, there are no papers from other schools. The section includes case studies of individual preschool children and could profitably be read in the context of the full-length studies of such great pioneers as Werner Leopold.[27] Related to this is the third section (family bilingualism) which must take its data from the same or similar case studies,[28] combined with statistical treatment of the strategies most commonly adopted in different areas and their social consequences. The fourth section (bilingualism and society) deals with special problems of child bilingualism and bidialectalism in different sorts of communities — immigrant, aboriginal, or national minority. It can be placed in the general context of the study of interaction between languages and their environments.[29]

The fifth and sixth sections (planning preschool language learning and planning the primary curriculum) have to do with planned early childhood bilingualism. There are few basic studies on formal preschool bilingualism as such, but there is a wide-ranging survey of the problems in the book of Renzo Titone, which covers the entire field of early childhood bilingualism.[30]

The seventh section is devoted to bilingual schooling proper. This section can be placed within the context of the survey by Andersson and Boyer,[31] especially as it relates to contemporary American practice; it can also be placed within an historical context of bilingual education in America.[32] But since only four cases are here described, it would be wise for the reader to compare them with other studies done in such countries as South Africa,[33] Sweden,[34] Ireland,[40] Finland,[35] and Wales[39] — even with some of the earlier studies done in that country.[36]

The final section (policy and research) and the conclusion (planning for the future) relate to the general problems of language loyalty in the United States[37] and elsewhere, and to research into the problems of bilingualism in general.[38] It also relates to the vaster area of national language policy and language planning.[41]

In sum, the following papers should be placed not only within the conference literature on bilingualism and child language, but also within the context of the main works on each of the aspects of the study of childhood bilingualism to which this conference was designed to contribute.

NOTES

[1] Aaron Bar-Adon and Werner F. Leopold. *Child Language: A Book of Readings.* Englewood Cliffs: Prentice-Hall, (1971).

[2] William F. Mackey. *An International Bibliography of Bilingualism.* Quebec: Presses de l'Université Laval, (1972).

[3] Wilhelm Stern. "Über Zweisprachigkeit in der frühen Kindheit." *Zeitschrift für angewandte Psychologie,* 30 (1932), pp. 168-172.

[4] Willy Brandt, Pierre Moisy, *et al. Festschrift zur Feier des 275 jährigen Bestehens des Französischen Gymnasiums (Collège français fondé en 1689).* Berlin: Erich Pröh, (1965).

[5] Glyn Roberts, *et al. A Bibliography of the History of Wales.* Cardiff: University of Wales Press, (1962), pp. 235-237.

[6] *Report of the Royal Commission on Education.* Newport: Southall, (1888).

[7] George Hempl. "Language-rivalry and Speech-differentiation in the case of Race-mixture." *Transactions of the American Philological Association,* 29 (1898), pp. 31-47.

[8] *Imperial Education Conference Report.* London: HMSO, (1911, 1923).

[9] Bureau International d'Education. *Le bilinguisme et l'éducation. Travaux de la conférence internationale tenue à Luxembourg.* Geneva: BIE, (1928).

[10] Michael West. "The Bilingual Problem." Wyatt Rawson, ed., in *Education in a Changing Commonwealth.* London: New Education Fellowship, (1931), pp. 106-116.

[11] *Proceedings of the World Federation of Educational Associations,* 5 (1933): The Dublin Meeting.

[12] *Overseas Education* (London: HMSO): Vols. 1 (pp. 22, 44), 2 (pp. 142, 190), 3 (pp. 33, 78, 129, 207), 7 (p. 59), 13 (p. 355), 15 (p. 82), 16 (p. 60), 27 (p. 153), 28 (pp. 17,72), 31 (p. 50).

[13] E.R. Briggs. "New Light on the Problem of Acquiring a Second Language." *Cités Unies,* 9 (1958), pp. 26-27).

[14] United Kingdom National Commission for UNESCO. *Report on an International Seminar on Bilingualism in Education* (Aberystwyth, Wales) London: HMSO, (1965).

[15] Scientific Council for Africa. *Symposium on Multilingualism: Second Meeting of the Inter-African Committee on Linguistics (Brazzaville, 16-21, VII, 1962).* CSA Publication No. 87. London: CSA Publications Bureau, (1964).

[16] Heinz Kloss. *FLES: zum Problem des Fremdsprachenunterrichts an Grundschulen Amerikas und Europas.* Godesberg: Verlag Wissenschaftliches Archiv, (1967).

[17] H.H. Stern (ed.). *Foreign Languages in Primary Education.* London: Oxford University Press, (1967).

[18] H.H. Stern (ed.). *Languages and the Young School Child.* London: Oxford University Press, (1969).

[19] L.G. Kelly (ed.). *Description and Measurement of Bilingualism: An International Seminar, University of Moncton, June 6-14, 1967.* Toronto: University of Toronto Press (Published in association with the Canadian National Commission for UNESCO), (1969).

[20] Educational Services Corporation. *National Conference on Bilingual Education: Language Skills.* Final Report for Bureau of Research of the United States Office of Education: Contract No. OEC-3-9-180346-0044 (010) Washington: ESC, (1969).

[21] André Laurendeau, *et al. Report of the Royal Commission on Bilingualism and Biculturalism: Vol. 2, Education.* Ottawa: Queen's Printer, (1968).

[22] James E. Alatis (ed.). *Monograph Series on Languages and Linguistics,* 23 (1970). Washington: Georgetown University Press. See also No. 7, (1954).

[23] Merrill Swain (ed.). *Bilingual Schooling: Some Experiences in Canada and the United States. A Report on the Bilingual Education Conference, Toronto, March 11-13, 1971.* Toronto: Ontario Institute for Studies in Education (Symposium Series/1), (1972).

[24] UNESCO. *The Role of Linguistics and Sociolinguistics in Language Education and Policy,* and *The Contribution of Educational Anthropology and Sociolinguistics to Educational Development.* Paris: UNESCO (Documents ED/WS/283 + 286), (1972).

[25] Jean-Maurice Chevalier. "A propos du Colloque d'Aoste." *Cités Unies,* 68-69 (1972), pp. 38-41.

[26] Robert Maynard Jones. *System in Child Language,* Cardiff: University of Wales Press (Welsh Studies in Education, 2), (1970). (See also W.F. Leopold's bibliography.)

[27] Werner F. Leopold. *The Bilingual Child,* (4 vols.). Evanston: Northwestern University Press, (1939-49, reprinted 1972).

[28] Velta Rūķe-Draviņa. *Mehrsprachigkeit im Vorschulalter.* (Travaux de l'Institut de Phonétique de Lund) Lund: Gleerup, (1967).

[29] Einar Haugen. *The Ecology of Language* (Essays by Einar Haugen selected and introduced by Anwar S. Dil) Stanford: Stanford University Press, (1972).

[30] Renzo Titone. *Bilinguismo precoce e educazione bilingue.* Rome: Armando Armando Editore (Serie di psicologia, 7), (1972).

[31] Theodore Andersson and Mildred Boyer. *Bilingual Schooling in the United States,* (2 vols.). Washington: U.S. Government Printing Office, (1970).

[32] Heinz Kloss. *The American Bilingual Tradition.* Rowley, Mass.:

Newbury House (in press).

[33] E.G. Malherbe. *The Bilingual School: A Study of Bilingualism in South Africa.* London: Longmans, (1946) (1st ed., Johannesburg, 1934).

[34] Tore Österberg. *Bilingualism and the First School Language: An Educational Problem Illustrated by Results from a Swedish Dialect Area.* Umeå: Västerbotten, (1961).

[35] Wilhelm Wieczerkowski. *Bilinguismus im frühen Schulalter: Gruppenprüfungen mit Intelligenztests und mit dem Helsingforstest.* Helsinki: Societas Scientiarum Fennica (Commentationes Humanarum Litterarum XXXIII.2), (1963).

[36] J. Hughes, D.J. Saer, and F. Smith. *The Bilingual Problem.* Wrexham: Hughes & Son (for the University College of Wales, Aberystwyth), (1924).

[37] Joshua A. Fishman, *et al. Language Loyalty in the United States: The Maintenance and Perpetuation of Non-English Mother Tongues by American Ethnic and Religious Groups.* The Hague: Mouton, (1966).

[38] Einar Haugen. *Bilingualism, Language Contact and Immigrant Languages in the United States: A Research Report 1956-1970* (Current Trends in Linguistics, Vol. 10) The Hague: Mouton (1973). See also Einar Haugen, *Bilingualism in the Americas: A Bibliography and Research Guide* (Publication of the American Dialect Society, 26) University, Ala.: University of Alabama Press, (1956) (Reprinted 1964).

[39] United Kingdom Ministry of Education (Central Advisory Council for Education: Wales. *The Place of Welsh and English in the Schools of Wales.* London: HMSO, (1953).

[40] John Macnamara. *Bilingualism in Primary Education.* Edinburgh: Edinburgh University Press, (1966).

[41] J.A. Fishman, C.A. Ferguson, and J. Das Gupta (eds.). *Language Problems of Developing Nations.* New York: Wiley, (1968). See also: Robert LePage, *The National Language Question.* London: Oxford University Press, (1964).

T.A.

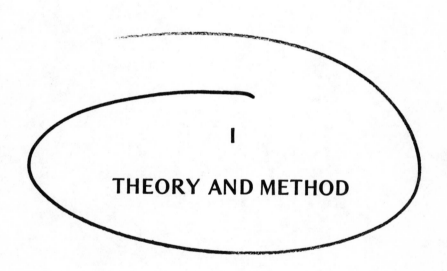

I

THEORY AND METHOD

A model for bilingual policy description will be examined first, namely derived from my paper on "National Languages and Languages of Wider munication in the Developing Nations" (Fishman, 1969). In its initial mulation the model proved to be useful to me and to some others lman, 1971; Whitely, 1970) for the purpose of discussing national language policies in general. On further examination, this model may hold forth me promise also for the purposes to be discussed here.

Type A policy formulations with respect to bilingual education transpire in those settings in which educational authorities feel compelled to select for educational use a language which is *not* a mother tongue within the administrative unit of educational policy decision (a country, a region, a district, etc.). This is done when none of the varieties natively available within such units is considered to be integratively school-worthy, i.e., to correspond to a great tradition of past, present, and future integrative authenticity and integrative greatness. Under such circumstances an outside language of wider communication (LWC) is selected (at times by popular demand) to fulfil most educational functions.

The immediate practical consequences of conducting a school system in a language which is not the mother tongue of (the vast majority of) the students are many. The first consequence is that the Type A policy itself must initially be set aside for the earliest period of education, no matter how brief this may be, so that at least a minimum of one-way communication (from pupils to teachers) is possible from the outset. A frequent further consequence is that teachers too must begin by using the mother tongue (MT) of their pupils or at least by being receptively familiar with it and with some of its contrastive features vis-à-vis the LWC which they must implement. All in all, however, the bilingual education that results from Type A policy decisions is minimal and transitional. Even if this stage is recognized in teacher training or in the preparation of learning and teaching materials, the goal is to leave bilingualism behind as soon as possible in order to transfer all educational efforts to the selected external LWC. Several countries of West Africa (e.g., Gambia, Sierra Leone) have made national policy decisions of this type, as have Latin American countries with respect to the education of indigenous regional Indian populations, and most host countries with respect to the education of regionally concentrated immigrant groups, particularly those of low social standing.

Further consequences of Type A policy decisions re bilingual education also inevitably flow from the adoption of an external LWC. Since the language adopted is a mother tongue elsewhere (outside of the administrative unit under consideration), it must be decided whether the curriculum and standards in effect "there" should also be implemented "here," or whether indigenously determined content, methods, and standards are to be employed. Frequently the former view has prevailed at the outset and the latter view has been accepted only later and reluctantly. Finally the con-

1

A Model for Bilingual and Bidialectal Educat

Joshua A. Fishman

A basic conceptual premise of modern sociology of language/soc
guistics is that the functional diversification of the language repertoire
speech community can be analyzed along essentially identical dimensic
regardless of the societal views or the nature of the codes or varieti
involved therein. Thus, whether it consists of several "languages," or whethe
it consists of several "dialects" or "sociolects," or whether it consists of both
different "languages" and different "dialects/sociolects," the functional allocation of varieties within the community is felt to be describable in much
the same way. Whether the analysis is in terms of situations and their counterparts or in terms of domains and their counterparts is related not to any
distinction between "languages" on the one hand and "dialects" on the
other, but, rather, at best, to the level of analysis required by the researcher
for the particular problem under study, or, at worst, to the level indicated by
the limits of his own professional indoctrination. In either case the distinction between "languages" and "dialects" is considered to be basically a
within-community, functional-evaluative distinction, rather than one that
can be made primarily on the basis of objective external criteria. Certainly a
diachronic view amply supports this approach (revealing any number of once
"mere" dialects, that were subsequently functionally, evaluatively, and struc-
turally "elevated" to the position of languages as well as many cases of the
reverse progression), however much a synchronic view may reveal objective
differences between coexisting languages and dialects with respect to such
matters as extent of elaboration and codification.

Given the foregoing view that all varieties in a community's repertoire
can be subjected to sociolinguistic analysis along identical dimensions —
regardless of the functional-evaluative-structural differences that may characterize them — this paper attempts to examine the further question as to
whether a single integrative model is also possible with respect to educational
policy description when such policy deals with separate languages on the one
hand and with separate dialects on the other.

sequences for adult literacy of Type A policy decisions are clearly far-reaching. Those beyond school age have even greater difficulty in achieving and retaining literacy in a foreign language than do those who are still of school age. Even the latter experience difficulty in both of these respects given the high drop-out rates and the lack of post-school functional exposure to or reliance upon the school language which mark most settings in which Type A policy decisions are reached.

Do Type A policies (which, in effect, restrict bilingual education to the barest minima consistent with transitional goals) have their counterparts in the area of bidialectal education? Obviously there are many similarities, particularly where social mobility is low and role repertoires are narrow. Under such circumstances dialects/sociolects that are common in other parts of the country/region/district may be generally unmastered and nonfunctional within particular administrative units. To the extent that the transition to the school variety, or dialect (D), is unreasonably hurried, and to the extent that use of other varieties, or dialects (d1, d2, d3), are considered contra-educational (contra-cultural, contra-integrative) at the same time that role expansion is restricted or nonexistent, then obviously an educational burden is being placed upon those least equipped to carry it and a barrier to future mobility is being erected against those least likely to scale it successfully. Such an approach to "nonstandard" dialects is still common in connection with the view of Black English and Chicano Spanish held by many American school districts, as well as the views of nonstandard French, Spanish, Russian, Hebrew, and Arabic still common in the countries for which the standard (or classical) versions of these languages are the only ones administratively recognized.

In none of the above cases is the view widespread that whereas all schools should teach all students something in D and some students many things in D, there are also at least some things that should be taught to all students in d and some students most of whose education may well be in d rather than in D. The insistence on D and D only (for all students for all subjects) is potentially nonfunctional in many ways even though it may be a widely shared view rather than one imposed from without. It artificializes education to the extent that it identifies it with a variety that is not functional in the life of the community. It threatens the viability of the student's primary community and of its primary networks to the extent that it implies that only by leaving his native speech repertoire behind can the student enter a new role repertoire (and a new reward schedule). It often causes education to depend upon outsiders to the community — a veritable army of occupation and pacification on occasion — rather than permitting it to be a partially shared function across communities or a community-controlled function. It tends to impose educational content and methods and standards upon communities that are not as meaningful or as indigenous or as appealing to pupils as would be the case if the native life patterns (including the native speech) of the community were also viewed as school-worthy.

All in all, the similarities between Type A policies when L1, L2, L3, and LWC are concerned, and Type A policies when d1, d2, d3, and D are concerned are both great and disturbing. In both cases local populations are relatively unconsulted, and decisions are commonly made for them by elites marked by broader integrative philosophies and also by self-status protective interests.

Type B policies at the interlanguage level pertain to bilingual education of a somewhat more permissive sort. Type B policies hold that an internally integrative great tradition does exist at the unit level. Nevertheless, for one reason or another, additional traditions too must be recognized. On the one hand, there may be smaller traditions (i.e., smaller than those that are unit-wide), one or more of which are believed to have their own place and deserve some acknowledgment in the cultural-educational sphere. On the other hand there may (also) be certain larger traditions than those that are unit-wide and these (too) may require (or demand) recognition. All in all, therefore, Type B policies obtain where administrative units do recognize an overriding and indigenous integrative principle but yet provide for local variation under and beneath or over and above it.

Such might be considered the between-language situation in the Soviet Union vis-à-vis Russian and (at least) the larger local national languages, in Mainland China vis-à-vis common spoken and written Mandarin and at least larger regional languages, in Yugoslavia vis-à-vis Serbian and the various larger regional languages, in the Philippines vis-à-vis Pilipino and the various larger regional languages, and, perhaps, within time, in the USA vis-à-vis English and the more entrenched minority languages. Certainly such policies result in a series of practical problems of their own. How many and which languages should be recognized and what should be taught in them and for how many years? The fact that bilingualism is not viewed as being merely transitional in nature does not, in and of itself, provide a single answer to such questions. As indicated elsewhere, bilingual education in the monocentric context (and, therefore, normally for the minority child alone) may still be merely oral or partial rather than full (Fishman and Lovas, 1970).

At the level of between-dialect policy decisions Type B policies certainly also obtain. Once again these policies have a distinct similarity to those that exist at the between-language level. Once again there is one variety, or dialect (D), which is viewed as having indigenous cross-unit validity. Some subjects, it is believed, should be taught in this variety everywhere and to everyone. However, in addition, and particularly in the elementary grades, it is believed that there are also other subjects that may well be taught in various parts of the polity in the local d's that parents, children, and school teachers alike share as the everyday varieties of various social functions. Only in the upper grades — in schools which are likely to be regional rather than local in nature — is it expected that almost everything will be taught in D, but then such schools are either not expected to serve everyone to begin with, or, in addition, by the time students reach them, they will have had eight or more years of time to master D, at least in writing if not fully in speech.[1]

The foregoing approach to bidialectal education is encountered in most parts of Germany (see Fishman and Lueders, in press), in most parts of Italy, in most parts of the Netherlands, in many parts of Norway and Great Britain, in various sections of German Switzerland, and elsewhere. The burden of acquiring and mastering D is primarily reserved for the written language and falls primarily upon those best able to handle it, namely, those with the most education and, therefore, with the expectation of the widest role-repertoire and with the best chances for real social as well as geographic mobility. Teachers (particularly elementary school teachers) and pupils are commonly members of the same speech community. The school is not viewed as a foreign body thrust upon an unwilling local populace, but rather as a place in which local speech, local folklore, local history, and local authenticity have their rightful place. However, the local who aspires to the wider role repertoire that is the mark and the distinction of the professional and the intellectual must also prepare to rub shoulders with peers from other localities than his own, and, therefore, he must master D, as well as d1 (or socially differentiated d1, d2, d3). All communities recognize and respect D, but all communities also feel themselves to be respected and consulted partners in the overall enterprise which D symbolizes.

Finally we come to *Type C* policies with respect to between-language relationships. In this connection we find that no single integrating indigenous tradition exists, but, rather, several competing great traditions each with its numerous and powerful adherents. Thus, regional differences, far from needing protection or recognition, need instead to be bridged or momentarily set aside if the polity is to survive. It is well recognized that pupils will be educated in their own mother tongues. The only question is whether they will also be sufficiently educated in some other tongue that they can use for communicating with fellow citizens of another mother tongue. Here bilingual education is of two kinds: sometimes in one or another of the several coequal (and often mutually sensitive) regional languages, and sometimes in an exterior LWC that may appear non-threatening to all concerned. Such bilingual education is common in Belgium, in Canada, in Switzerland, in India. Sometimes such polities lack a real link language, and only a small bilingual elite exists to hold together their multicentricity. Switzerland is an example of how stable even such arrangements can be (although German probably functions as an overall link language more frequently than is officially recognized to be the case).

---

[1] The rejection of this belief underlies all decisions on behalf of exclusively monodialectal education.

Type C polities also have their counterparts at the between-dialect level although these are few in number. Just as there are several polities with locally well-entrenched languages, such that each locality must be educationally concerned with teaching a link language for communication with the other localities of the same polity, so there are (or, at least, have been) counterparts of this situation at the between-dialect educational policy level. There are, of course, also polities in which each region teaches in its own dialect without any concern at all for a link dialect, owing to the fact that the dialects themselves are of high mutual understandability and of roughly similar social standing. The United States and several Latin American countries may be said to be in this situation.

In recent years, a noteworthy Type C policy at the interdialectal level existed at the height of Norway's efforts to link Riksmaal and Landsmaal via a manufactured Samnorsk. However, if we go back earlier in history we can find a few more instances of this same type. These are instances from settings in which language standardization was not yet well advanced and vernacular education was primarily regional rather than national. Indeed, wherever vernacular education became well established in advance of unifying political or industrial development (Germany, Italy, Ireland) it was the unifying standard that had to fight for a place in education rather than the regional variant. Nevertheless, such cases tend to be self-liquidating in developing settings. Where a single standard becomes accepted, it tends to lead to Type B policies in the bidialectal education field. Where no such standard becomes accepted, bidialectalism in education is not a meaningful problem.

Conclusions

Generally speaking, the same theoretical model of educational policy decisions may be said to be useful for the description of bilingual as well as for bidialectal education. Indeed, use of such a model indicates that the same administrative units may well vary with respect to their policies at these two levels. Some units may be very permissive at one level but entirely nonpermissive at others. Thus, some units are more permissive with respect to dialects than they are with respect to languages (e.g., German Switzerland, Italy), whereas others are more permissive with respect to languages (e.g., India, where only standard Hindi may be taught, even though there are tens of millions of speakers of regional varieties of Hindi). In addition, the use of a similar model for both kinds of variation renders more easily comparable any data pertaining to questions re degree (e.g., number of years), curricular content, etc. Once again, educational units vary widely in these respects when their bilingual and bidialectal policies are compared. Finally, the use of a single model for both levels of analysis facilitates comparisons at differing administrative levels and may make it possible to more quickly compare not only polities with polities and districts with districts, but also to undertake simultaneous between-polity and within-polity studies in order to compare both of these sources of policy variations.

Summary

Given the view that all varieties of language or dialect in a community's repertoire can be subjected to sociolinguistic analysis along identical dimensions, this paper attempts to examine the further question as to whether a single integrative model is also possible with respect to educational policy description when such policy deals with separate languages on the one hand and with separate dialects on the other.

A model for bilingual policy description, derived from my paper on "National Languages and Languages of Wider Communication in the Developing Nations," will first be described and discussed; then a comparison will be made with a parallel model for bidialectal policy description.

Under Type A are considered those settings in which educational authorities feel compelled to select for educational use a language (or dialect) which is not a mother tongue.

Type B pertains to policies which hold that, although an internally integrative great tradition does exist, for one reason or another additional traditions too must be recognized.

Under Type C we consider the situation where several competing great traditions exist, each with its numerous and powerful adherents.

And we conclude that, generally speaking, the same theoretical model of educational policy decisions may be said to be useful for the description of bilingual as well as for bidialectal education.

Bibliography

Fishman, Joshua A. "National Languages and Languages of Wider Communication in the Developing Nations." *Anthropological Linguistics*, XI, No. 11 (1969), pp. 111-135.

Fishman, Joshua A. and John Lovas. "Bilingual Education in Sociolinguistic Perspective." *TESOL Quarterly*, IV, No. 4 (1970), pp. 215-222.

Fishman, Joshua A. and Erika Lueders. "What Has the Sociology of Language to Say to the Teacher? (On Teaching the Standard Variety to Speakers of Dialectal or Sociolectal Varieties)." In Courtney B. Cazden, Vera John, and Dell Hymes, eds., *Functions of Language in the Classroom*. New York: Teachers College Press (1972).

Kelman, Herbert. "Language as Aid and Barrier to Involvement in the National System." In Joan Rubin and Björn Jernudd, eds., *Can Language be Planned?* Honolulu: East-West Center and University of Hawaii Press, (1971).

Whiteley, W.H. *Language Use and Social Change*. London: Oxford University Press, (1970).

2

Cognitive Strategies of Language Learning
John Macnamara

Some things children seem to learn naturally; others they have to be taught. Unaided, they seem to learn to walk and to perceive the world visually; on the other hand, nearly all children have to be taught arithmetic. Language is a peculiar embarrassment to the teacher, because outside school children seem to learn language without any difficulty, whereas in school with the aid of teachers their progress in languages is halting and unsatisfactory. It is common experience that when translated to a town where their native language is not spoken children will become reasonably proficient in the new language in the space of six months. It is equally common experience that after six years of schooling in a second language, whatever the teaching method, most children emerge with a very poor command of the language. The first set of experiences shows that children are possessed of a very powerful device for learning languages; the second set of experiences shows that the school harnesses this device only in a most inadequate manner. This in turn argues that we have a poor understanding of the natural device for learning languages. My paper is about this device, about common beliefs as to its scope, and about the implications of what we know of the device for the language classroom.

The function of the human language learning device is defined with reference to a natural language such as English or French. If we could specify exactly the code which we call English, we would have taken the first and most important step in the direction of specifying the nature of the language learning device. The second step would be to specify the actual learning process whereby a person grapples with the code and masters it. The trouble with this approach is massive, however: we are very far indeed from being able to specify a code like English, and we are even farther from being able to specify the language learning process. Of any natural language we know that it has a lexicon, a sound system, and a set of structural rules. But anyone who is even vaguely familiar with linguistics knows that each is the subject of vigorous controversy. Katz and Fodor (1963) have made an interesting beginning in the description of the sort of lexicon which English users carry about in their head; Quillian (1967, 1968, and 1969) has gone further than they did and attempted to build a computer model of a human lexicon; but I (Macnamara, 1971) have argued elsewhere not only that their work is defective in detail but that they have taken the wrong direction. The obscurities of phonology and syntax are acclaimed in every book and paper one reads on these subjects. The work of structural and transformational linguists amounts to a very considerable deepening of our understanding of the rules of phonology and syntax. However, every linguist would, I think, agree with Professor Lakoff's (1970) statement in a recent paper that we can scarcely claim to have done more than introduce the subjects.

The essential obscurity of language is in its loose relationship to that elusive and inapprehensible process which we call thought. A single word, like *back*, can have many meanings (e.g., rear part of a body, to wager), while a single object or idea can be expressed by several words (e.g., *drunk*, *intoxicated*). A single syntactic device can have quite different semantic functions (e.g., *I have a pin; I have a pain*), whereas a single semantic relationship can be signalled by means of a variety of syntactic devices (e.g., *My hair is black; I have black hair*). To make matters even worse, many ideas are conveyed without the use of any explicit linguistic device. For example, the directive, *close the door*, does not carry any explicit indication that *you* has been deleted and is understood. The problem is even more deep-rooted than this example implies. The command, *put on your shoes*, does not express the *you*, but neither does it specify where the shoes are to be put (on the feet, not on the hands), nor even on whose feet (yours rather than mine). So rich and powerful is the human interpretative system that much can be left unsaid. To express everything one intends is to be a bore — it may even be impossible in principle. One result of all this is that the line which divides language and thought is a very thin one, and there is usually doubt about where it should be drawn. In this connection see Uriel Weinreich's (1966) reintroduction of the medieval problem of relating semantic and grammatical categories. He raises serious doubts about whether one can usefully call categories such as "noun" and "verb" grammatical, while one calls categories such as "animate" and "inanimate" semantic. On the other hand, Noam Chomsky (1965) had great problems deciding whether to treat the selection restrictions on lexical items as grammatical or semantic. In other words, should we regard *The stone loved* as ungrammatical or just nonsense. All in all, then, it is difficult to say what we learn when we learn a language.

It is even more difficult to specify the learning process. Several factors which have an effect on certain types of learning have been isolated by psychological research. But I think it fair to say that the core of the process still eludes us. However, I will return to this topic later in my paper.

Cognitive basis of language learning

If we were to ask teachers, as I have often done, what is the essential difference between the classroom and the street as a place in which to learn a language, they would answer "motivation". I am sure that the teachers are right; we do not seem to have adequately motivated children in classrooms to learn a language. Notice, however, that in so answering, teachers avoid the problems with which we have been dealing. They do not seek in the essential nature of language or language learning for the difference between the classroom and the street. Neither do they attribute the difference to the essential nature of the language learning device. They seem to say, rather, that whatever the nature of that device, it does not function properly unless a person is highly motivated to make it function.

I have argued elsewhere (Macnamara, 1972) that infants learn their mother tongue by first determining, independent of language, the meaning which a speaker intends to convey to them, and then working out the relationship between the meaning and the expression they heard. In other words, the infant uses meaning as a clue to language, rather than language as a clue to meaning. The argument rests upon the nature of language and its relation to thought, and also upon the findings of empirical investigations into the language learning of infants. The theory is not meant to belittle the child's ability to grapple with intricate features of the linguistic code. These must be grasped even if the clue is usually — though by no means always — to be found in meaning. The theory claims that the main thrust in language learning comes from the child's need to understand and to express himself.

Contrast, now, the child in the street with the child in the classroom. In the street he will not be allowed to join in the other children's play, not be allowed to use their toys, not even be treated by them as a human being, unless he can make out what they say to him and make clear to them what he has to say. The reward for success and the punishment for failure is enormous. No civilized teacher can compete. But more to the point, the teacher seldom has anything to say to his pupils so important that they will eagerly guess his meaning. And pupils seldom have anything so urgent to say to the teacher that they will improvise with whatever communicative skills they possess to get their meaning across. If my analysis of infant language learning is correct, as I believe it to be, it can surely explain the difference between the street and the classroom without placing any serious strain on the analogy between first and second language learning.

The solution then is to make the language class a period of vital communication between teacher and pupils. How simply that is said! Of course I have no practical hints. Though I was a language teacher for several years myself, that was a long time ago, and in any case I was a slave to public examinations. Moreover, there is no point in my entering into competition with talented teachers who did not surrender their minds to the last half century's talk about methods and always saw language as essentially linked to communication. Nevertheless, the theory I am proposing does suggest some broad strategies which I may mention with impunity.

An infant could not guess what his mother was saying to him unless there were a good many surrounding clues. Mother usually talks to a small child only about those things which are present to the senses, things that the child can see, feel, smell, taste, hear, things which are happening or which the child or she herself is doing. Nearly always, too, a mother's speech carries exaggerated intonational patterns. Indeed a mother's speech to an infant is intonationally often quite distinct from her speech to others. All of this together with the mother's facial expressions is a strong clue to her meaning or intention. It enables the child to determine her meaning and use it as the key to the code she uses to express her meaning in. The teacher, then, would be wise to provide as many aids as possible to his meaning. And he should encourage the pupils to guess. This probably implies that he should be slow to give the child the meaning in the child's native tongue.

Parents are proud of any effort which a small child makes to express himself in words. They welcome his phonological innovations; they accept his bits of words; and they understand his telegraphese. As a matter of fact, parents seldom correct a small child's pronunciation or grammar; they correct his bad manners and his mistakes on points of fact (see Gleason, 1967). Somehow, when a child is vitally concerned with communication he gradually gets over his difficulties and eradicates errors, at least to a point where society accepts his speech. That is, vitally engaged in the struggle to communicate and supported by the approval of his parents, he makes steady progress. His parents' attention is on his meaning not on his language, and so probably is his own. And curiously he and his parents break one of psychology's basic learning rules. Psychology would advise that he should be rewarded only for linguistically correct utterances, whereas parents reward him for almost any utterance. But then the folk wisdom of the Italians, which is older than experimental psychology has created a proverb which gives the lie to psychology and agrees with parent and child — *sbagliando s'impara* ("by making mistakes we learn"). Perhaps in all this there is a lesson for the the schoolmaster. Perhaps he should concentrate more on what the child is saying and less on how he says it. Perhaps the teacher should lay aside the red pencil with which he scored any departure from perfection, and replace it with a word and a smile of encouragement. The Irish too — not to be outdone by the Italians — have their folk wisdom: *mol an óige agus tiochfaid sí* ("praise youth and it will come").

Some dubious folklore

Just to show I'm not a complete reactionary who accepts everything from the bosom of the race, I will devote the remainder of my paper to a critical analysis of two common beliefs: (1) the child learns a language informally, whereas the adult learns it formally; (2) the adult is a much poorer language learner than the child.

From what I have said about the possibility of specifying the elements and rules of a language, it follows that the term formal learning can be applied to language in only the loosest sense. If we cannot reduce language to formula, we cannot learn it by formula. The extent to which we cannot formulate a language is the extent to which our learning of it cannot be formal, and this is to a very great extent. On the other hand there are useful rules or formulas which capture some of the regularities of a language. It is the case that these are often explicitly taught to adults, and they are never taught to infants. May we not speak of the adults' learning as being to this extent formal, and that of the infant as informal? And if so, is this an important difference? A firm answer is of course impossible, but the issue is an interesting one which merits close attention.

We are familiar with all sorts of rules which will serve to illustrate the problem. The beginner at chess is taught the rules of the game and when asked he is usually able to state them. On the other hand the boy who is learning to cycle is usually not taught the rules of balancing the bicycle, nor does anyone explain to him the complications of following curvilinear paths at different speeds as he alternately presses on the left and right pedals. Furthermore the cyclist cannot normally state the rules he applies. Rules, then, can be possessed in an explicit or stateable form, or they may not. Take now the man who is learning to ski. His tutor gives him many rules to follow, but he also tells him that he must not be satisfied until he has formed the rules in his legs. As he makes progress he begins to feel the rightness of the rules; they take on a new existence in him, though he still can state them in the explicit form in which he learned them.

It is my belief that in the skilled performer all rules must exist in a nonexplicit form; they may exist in an explicit form as well. It is further my belief that, in the initial stages of learning, explicit rules can guide the construction of structures which implicitly incorporate the rules. It is these structures, not the explicit rules, which control skilled performance. This I believe to be true even of the chess player: he does not when playing recall explicitly all the rules which inform his perception of the board. However, the gap between explicit rules and performance is less in chess than in skiing. From my earlier remarks on language it follows that language is closer to skiing than to chess, at least in the relationship between rules and performance.

Though we cannot be certain that infants are unconscious of all the linguistic rules which they develop, they certainly must be unconscious of many of them. Similarly, the successful learner of a second language has a great many implicit rules which he is unable to formulate. And only when he has developed structures which implicitly incorporate those rules which he learned in an explicit form will he be able to apply them with mastery.

What I want to say is this. The human language learning device serves to construct in a nonexplicit form a set of nonconscious rules which guide listening and speaking. The device can either extract the nonexplicit rules from the corpus of the language which is to be learned, or it can construct them on the basis of explicitly stated rules of the sort one finds in grammar books. The whole process is very obscure indeed, but I don't see anything against explicit rules and, with two provisos, they are probably a great help. First, the student must not expect to find rules for everything; he must trust his common sense or linguistic intuition. Second, he must learn to get on as soon as possible without explicit rules; he must be prepared to surrender himself to their automatic operation. I imagine that the only reason for distrusting explicit rules is the fact that some people have difficulty in abiding by these two counsels.

The second common belief which I wish to discuss is that one's language learning device atrophies rather early in life. The evidence for this is that babies pick up their mother tongue with what seems like great ease, and young children in suitable environments pick up a second language with little trouble, whereas adults seem to struggle ineffectively with a new language and to impose the phonology and syntax of their mother tongue on the new language. The argument has been supported with some evidence from neurophysiology (Penfield and Roberts, 1959), but the value of this evidence is dubious, to say the least.

I suspect that the evidence which most supporters of the theory draw upon confounds two phenomena, the child in the street and the child in the school. Small children don't go to school; older ones usually learn languages in school rather than in the street. We have already seen that these two phenomena must be distinguished. But besides all this many families have the experience of moving to a new linguistic environment in which the children rapidly learn the language and the adults don't. This happened frequently to English families which moved to one of the colonies, such as India. In such cases, the linguistic experience might well be attributed to unfavorable attitudes towards the new language which the parents but not the children adopted. However, Italian families which migrated to the United States often met with a similar linguistic fate — the children learned English, and the parents, despite favorable attitudes, did not. Is this conclusive evidence that language learning ability atrophies?

No! Let us take clear examples; let us compare a man of forty with an infant. We could not prove that the man was less skilled in language learning unless we gave the man an opportunity equal to that of the child to learn a language. We would need to remove the man from the preoccupations of his work and supply him with a woman who devoted a large part of her time and energy to helping him to learn the language. Further, the woman would have to behave just like the mother of a small baby, which among other things would include treating anything the man said in his mother tongue as she would treat a child's babbling. Naturally such an experiment has never been carried out, and for that reason there are almost no grounds for the general fatalism about adults' ability to learn languages. On the contrary, what experimental evidence we have suggests that adults are actually better than children. Smith and Braine (in press) found adults superior in the acquisition of a miniature artificial language, while Asher and Price (1967) found adults superior at deciphering and remembering instructions given in what to them was a foreign language. Thus there are grounds for optimism in this area.

However, there is evidence that adults and even teenagers generally have difficulty in mastering the pronunciation and intonational patterns of a new language, or even a new dialect. Labov (1966) found that persons who moved to Manhattan after the age of twelve seldom came to sound exactly like persons who grew up there. Similarly, persons who learn a language after adolescence usually sound a little bit foreign. But this does not mean that they do not communicate in that language very effectively and even quite normally. It is unwise to overemphasize their phonological difficulties. Apart from this there is no evidence that after adolescence one cannot learn a language as rapidly and as well as a small child.

Conclusion

One of the main tasks of linguists and psycholinguists is to make a systematic assault on the language learning device which is so remarkable in man. At present we know nothing of it in detail. We do, however, know that it is essentially geared to human thought and to its communication. It does not seem to function at all well unless the learner is vitally engaged in the act of communicating. This seems to be the reason why language teachers have laid such stress on motivation. It is my belief, however, that there has been quite a lot of confusion about the nature of such motivation. It has commonly been conceived (see for example Lambert, 1967) as a general desire to learn a language, and some attention has been paid to different grounds, "instrumental" or "integrative," for such a desire. This approach has led to interesting results. However, the logic of my paper demands a quite different emphasis; it demands that we look for the really important part of motivation in the act of communication itself, in the student's effort to understand what his interlocutor is saying and in his effort to make his own meaning clear. All this is not of course unrelated to a more general motivation to learn a language. The fact that superior attainment in language is associated with integrative motivation argues for a close relationship; after all the integrative attitude is defined as a general desire to communicate with speakers of the new language. But more pressing for most students than a general desire to be able to communicate at some future date is a specific desire to be able to communicate in some actual situation where what is being communicated is of vital concern to the persons involved. It is in the exploration of such specific motivation that I look for substantial advances in language teaching.

Summary

I have been working for some time on the nonlinguistic strategies which children bring to bear on the task of learning their mother tongue. My work has taken the form of analyzing the task and following up with some empirical probes. I feel that what I have been doing has some relevance to the learning of second languages. My major point is that a person's language learning abilities are brought into play only when he is either trying to make out what someone is saying to him in the new language or trying to tell someone something in that language. This in turn suggests a radical revision of approaches to language teaching.

Bibliography

Asher, J.J. and B.S. Price "The Learning Strategy of the Total Physical Response: Some Age Differences." *Child Development*, 38 (1967), pp. 1219-1227.

Chomsky N. *Aspects of the Theory of Syntax*. Cambridge, Mass.: M.I.T. Press, (1965).

Gleason, J.B. "Do Children Imitate? " Paper read at International Conference on Oral Education of the Deaf, Lexington School for the Deaf, New York City, June (1967).

Katz, J.J. and J.A. Fodor "The Structure of a Semantic Theory." *Language*, 39 (1963), pp. 170-210.

Labov, William *The Social Stratification of English in New York City*. Washington: Center of Applied Linguisties, (1966).

Lakoff, G. "Linguistics and Natural Logic." *Synthèse*, 22 (1970), pp. 151-271.

Lambert, W.E. "A Social Psychology of Bilingualism." *Journal of Social Issues*, 23 (1967), pp. 91-109.

Macnamara, J. "Parsimony and the Lexicon." *Language*, 47 (1971), pp. 359-374.

——. "The Cognitive Basis of Language Learning in Infants." *Psychological Review*, 71 (1972), pp. 1-13.

Penfield, W. and L. Roberts. *Speech and Brain Mechanisms*. Princeton: Princeton University Press, (1959).

Quillian, R.M. "Word Concepts: A Theory and Simulation of Some Basic Semantic Capabilities." *Behavioral Science*, 12 (1967), pp. 410-430.

——. "Semantic Memory." In M. Minsky, ed., *Semantic Information Processing*. M.I.T. Press, (1968), pp. 216-270.

——. "The Teachable Language Comprehender: A Simulation Program and Theory of Language." *Communications of the ACH*, 12 (1969), pp. 459-476.

Smith, K.H. and M.D.S. Braine "Miniature Language and the Problem of Language Acquisition." In T.G. Bever and W. Weksel, eds., *Miniature Languages and the Problem of Language Acquisition*. Holt, Rinehart & Winston (in press).

Weinreich, U. "Explorations in Semantic Theory." In T.A. Sebeok, ed., *Current Trends in Linguistics*, Vol. 3. The Hague: Mouton, (1966), pp. 395-477.

3

Bilingualism, Monolingualism and Code Acquisition[1]
Merrill Swain

On a snowy night in Old Québec a couple of years ago, a number of friends gathered for coffee and conversation. Two of them happened to be writing books. One, fluently bilingual, complained, "It is really terrible. I search my mind for a good synonym, and when one pops up, it's just as likely to be in the wrong language. A damn nuisance! " His monolingual friend replied, "I know just what you mean. My book's supposed to be for the layman, and the technical jargon keeps trying to force its way in."

Two similar experiences? But one man spoke two languages, alternately and effectively, and the other spoke one. Yet, their comments suggest that processes of storage and retrieval of lexical material may be alike for monolinguals and bilinguals. Other stories could be cited at length to illustrate a common core of cognitive-linguistic experience. The point I wish to make is that bilingualism and monolingualism are not unrelated entities, each demanding a separate explanation, but are realizations of a single phenomenon, in which varying aspects are observable in different degrees. As such, they should be incorporated into a unitary theoretical framework.

Portents and Precedents

Weinreich (1953, pp. 1-2) commented on the artificiality of the distinction between bilingualism and monolingualism in his study of the interference mechanisms resulting from language contact within a single individual. In this context, he noted that

> . . .it is immaterial whether the two systems are 'languages,' 'dialects of the same language,' or 'varieties of the same dialect,'. . .the mechanisms of interference would appear to be the same whether the contact is between Chinese and French or between two sub-varieties of English used by neighboring families. And while control of two such similar systems is not ordinarily called bilingualism, the term in its technical sense might easily be extended to cover these cases of contact as well.

Recent work by anthropologists (e.g., Gumperz, 1964, 1967; Hymes, 1967) and sociolinguists (e.g., Labov, 1966) makes it clear that most members of communities control several varieties of their language. According to Hymes (1967, p. 9),

> No normal person, and no normal community is limited in repertoire to
> a single variety of code, to an unchanging monotony which would
> preclude the possibility of indicating respect, insolence,
> mock-seriousness, humor, role-distance, etc. by switching from one
> variety to another.

In Weinreich's "technical sense" then, all people are at least bilingual,
and most are multilingual. Bilingualism in its traditional sense may thus be
seen as an obvious case of a general ability to store and switch among
linguistic codes.

Coming to Terms with Terms

Henceforth, *code* will denote any linguistic system used for
interpersonal communication. As such, its various levels of structure —
semantic, grammatical, and phonological — interact in a rule-governed
manner. Languages, dialects, and varieties of dialects are thus all examples of
codes. Further, a speaker's substitution of one language for another, or one
dialect for another, or one variety of a dialect for another, are all examples
of code switching. Insofar as Hymes' premise holds, this is equivalent to
saying that code switching is a normal part of all linguistic activity.

At this point it is unclear what, or even if, new terms should be
introduced. If *bilingual* and *monolingual* really symbolize some insight into
the processes of linguistic functioning, then they should be retained for use
in a psychological theory of code switching. However, it is not at all clear
that distinguishing the speaker who controls two languages from the speaker
who controls two dialects or varieties of dialects leads to psychologically
meaningful insights. Regarding the "complexity of switch,"[2] for example,
Gumperz (1967, p. 54) suggests that language-to-language switching is not
necessarily more complex than variety-to-variety switching. Gumperz'
observations were carried out in situations in which the language switches
(Hindi to Punjabi, and Kannada to Marathi) involved only the substitution of
morphemes. Grammatical structures remained unchanged.

> If we contrast this form of bilingual communication with the rather
> complex selection among phonological, syntactic and lexical variables,
> which Labov's recent work in New York has revealed (1966), it seems
> clear that there are at least some circumstances where bilingualism may
> require less skills than the normal process of communication in some
> monolingual societies.

Summarizing the argument so far, I question the utility of the
bilingual/monolingual distinction in the development of a psychological
theory of code. If, on further investigation, these terms are shown to be
arbitrary and empty of meaning within a psychological framework, they
should be discarded.

The Acquisition of Codes

To suggest that the bilingual/monolingual distinction is an arbitrary one
is to imply that learning two or more languages does not differ in any
significant way from learning one language: both involve the acquisition of

two or more codes. One advantage of studying the child learning two languages simultaneously is that at least some aspects of linguistic development are more easily observed. For example, studies of such children (e.g., Imedadze, 1966; Leopold, 1939-49) have revealed that they first pass through a 'mixed speech' stage wherein sentences include elements of both languages. It would be difficult to find a better demonstration of the fact that language acquisition and sentence construction are not merely realizations of an imitative process, but of a constructive, creative one. Moreover, although this initial stage of code mixing has been identified in the case of the child learning varieties of a language (Weeks, 1970), instances of mixing are so clearly observable in the case of the child learning two languages, that statements about them can be made with greater confidence.

The initial mixed-code stage must necessarily be followed by a period of differentiation. In the case of a child learning several varieties of a language, it hardly seems plausible that entirely separate sets of rules, one to generate each code would be developed (see Figure 1). Such an organization seems quite inefficient merely from the point of view of memory storage. More efficient would be a common core of rules with those specific to a particular code tagged as such through a process of differentiation (see Figure 2).

In Figures 1 and 2 the codes shown as output each require the operation of rules C and D. The model represented by Figure 1 demands that rules C and D be stored in two different locations. In the model represented by Figure 2, however, rules C and D each need only be stored in one location. In the first model, each rule must be marked according to its code. In the second model, only those rules specific to a particular code need to be tagged.

The separate storage model suggests that a rule in common to the codes being learned may be acquired separately for each code. Rules not in common will immediately be tagged according to their respective code. In other words, each code is learned independently of the other. The common storage model implies that a rule in common to the codes being learned will be acquired only once. Further, a rule not in common to the codes may first be considered as a rule in common, later to be tagged as appropriate to a particular code through a process of differentiation.

The Learning of Yes/No Questions

Consider the child whose linguistic environment includes both French and English. Consider further the number of alternatives he has available just for asking a yes/no question. Suppose, for example, that he wants to ask his mother if his friend is coming over. He could say: 1. *He's coming?* 2. *Il vient?* 3. *Est-ce qu'il vient?* 4. *Il vient ti?* 5. *He's coming, eh?* 6. *Il vient, eh?* 7. *He's coming, isn't he?* 8. *Is he coming?* 9. *Vient-il?*

Figure 1

Separate Storage Model

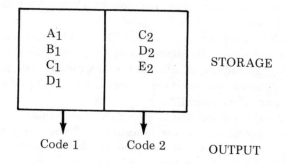

Figure 2

Common Storage Model

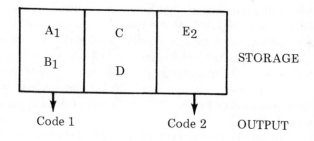

There are two points to note about the questions listed above. First, they represent structures that might be heard from speakers of some Canadian dialects of French and English. Therefore, the question *Il vient, n'est-ce pas?* has been omitted because although it is common in some French dialects, it is rarely used by French Canadians. Throughout the remainder of this paper, any mention of French and English refers to Canadian dialects.

Secondly, there are other ways the child could express the same question. For example, he might choose to use his friend's name. With the exception of question 9, this would not involve any structural change: the name would occur wherever the pronoun now is. Question 9, however, would become, *Jean vient-il?*

The questions listed above exemplify the various means available for signaling the asking of a yes/no question in French or English. A formal characterization of these devices can be found elsewhere (e.g., Klima and Bellugi, 1966; Langacker, 1965; Swain, 1972). Space forbids it here. Generally speaking, however, a yes/no question can be signaled by: an intonation contour which rises at the end of the sentence (questions 1 and 2); the morphemic sequence *est-ce que* located at the beginning of the sentence (question 3); the morpheme *ti* located after the first verbal element in the sentence (question 4);[3] the morpheme *eh* located at the end of the sentence (questions 5 and 6); the complex tag[4] (question 7); a particular ordering of subject and verbal constituents (questions 8 and 9).

What does the child do when he is faced with the task of learning this set of alternatives? In order to answer this question, speech samples of four children who had heard English and French from birth were recorded over a period of six to eight months. At the time when data collection began, the ages of the children were two years, ten months (2.10); three years, two months (3.2); three years, eight months (3.8); and four years (4.0). Therefore, the acquisition sequence we will see is not that of one child followed over two years, but is instead a developmental sequence inferred from the combined data of four children. A longitudinal study of one child was impractical.

A detailed statement of the results is reported elsewhere (Swain, 1972). Here, I will only summarize the basic findings.

At the time the recording sessions began, the youngest child, Monica, was already using two devices to signal yes/no questions: rising intonation and the morpheme *eh*. Her questions included *Café est hot?*, *Ça va commencer?*, *Tu veux la cigarette?*, *You go home?*, and *Ça va don't fall, eh?* Interestingly, these two devices are those the two languages have in common.

When the recording sessions began, the second youngest child, Michael, used not only rising intonation and the morpheme *eh*, but the morpheme *ti*. The latter category included such questions as *T'as ti douzaine d'oeufs?* and

Marcel il vient ti? At this same age (3.2), Monica began to produce questions with *est-ce que*. By 3.4, *est-ce que* began many of her yes/no questions. It was not until age 3.8 that a sudden increase in the frequency of production of *est-ce que* was observed in Michael's yes/no questions. At that time, *est-ce que* was not only correctly added to form questions like *Est-ce que tu sais où les souliers à Merrill ils sont?*, but was incorrectly added to questions containing the question morpheme *ti*, as in *Est-ce qu'on joue ti au magasin?*; and to English questions as in *Est-ce que you give it to her?*

Between 3.3 and 3.8, Michael produced yes/no questions in which the subject followed the first verbal element. For example, he asked *Do you see the glasses?* and *Veux-tu un bonbon?* However, this order of constituents did not occur with other forms of *do* such as *does* or *did*; with other auxiliaries such as *can*, *is*, etc.; or with other subjects than *you* and *tu*. It is suggested that at this point in Michael's linguistic development *do* was a question morpheme, and that sequences like *veux-tu* were simply reduced versions of sequences like *tu veux ti*.

When the recording sessions with Michael ended, he was 3.9. At this time, Michael produced several questions in English which suggest that he could use order to signal yes/no questions. For example, he asked *Can I have that purse?* and *Did you fall this morning?* However, if the questions were negative, or included some form of *to be*, they were produced without rearrangement of subject and verbal constituents, for example, *You don't have any necklace?*, *You're going now?*, and *It's in your purse?* The questions Michael produced in French, in which a rearrangement of subject and verbal constituents appeared, continued to be produced only with *tu* following the first verbal constituent. It was, therefore, impossible to determine if the questions represented a rearrangement of constituents or simply a reduction of sequences like *tu veux ti*.

On the other hand, Douglas, at this age (3.9), produced questions in both French and English suggesting that he could use order to signal yes/no questions. For example, he asked *Es-tu capable de faire un bateau?*, *Veux-tu du lait?*, *Did you see my little maman. . .my big maman bird?*, and *Are we going to watch TV?* Negative yes/no questions were uninverted.

From 3.9 through 4.5, the verbal system was further developed and refined. Numerous questions in which the subject and verbal constituents were rearranged appeared in the data. Examples of such questions, produced by Douglas and Martin, during this period are *Is it a coloring book?*, *Has it been long when you get here?*, *Is one of your friends coming with you?*, *As-tu dormi bien?*, and *Sais-tu que j'ai envie de jouer avec Pascal?* All negative questions and all questions which included the direct pronoun objects *le*, *la*, *les*, or the indirect pronoun objects *lui*, *leur*, were not inverted. Examples are *You can't see anything?*, *Tu sais pas lire en français?*, and *Tu l'as coloré ça?*, *Tu lui envoies?*

If we look very generally at these results, the following developmental pattern emerges in the use of devices to signal yes/no questions. Intonation and the question morpheme *eh* are the first devices to be used. Second are the other special-purpose question morphemes, first *ti*, and then *est-ce que*. Third is the rearrangement of constituents within the sentence. This order is in general agreement with the universal order suggested by Slobin (1970) concerning the emergence of linguistic means for expressing semantic notions. Given the thesis that the same processes are involved in the acquisition of codes, whether the codes are languages or varieties of a language, this is to be expected.

The results also provide some evidence to support the notion of a common storage model. At the time data collection began with the youngest child, only the linguistic means for signaling yes/no questions that are the same for both languages had been learned. To know whether they were acquired separately for each code, one would have to collect data from an earlier period. However, the one device whose acquisition was unmistakably observed — *est-ce que* — suggests that it was first considered as a rule common to both codes. Only later was it tagged as appropriate solely to French. On the other hand, rules for the rearrangement of verbal and subject constituents may have been acquired independently for each code.

Summary

Bilingualism is considered not as a unique phenomenon, but as an obvious or salient case of the use by an individual of his acquired code repertoire. The relevance of this view to the study of the concurrent acquisition of two or more languages is considered. In particular, the learning of yes/no questions by children who had heard French and English from birth is examined.

NOTES

[1] The author whishes to express her thanks to her brother, Dr. H.S. Swain, and to Dr. John Macnamara, who read and commented on an earlier draft of this paper.

[2] A hypothetical dimension. Clearly both psychological and linguistic factors would have to be considered in any measure of complexity. The extent to which it would turn out to be a single dimension is unknown.

[3] *Ti* is often pronounced as *tu*; that is, the two pronunciations are in free variation. Only one child in our sample, Michael, regularly heard the dialect in which *ti* is used as a question morpheme.

[4] This is a complex structure dependent in its form on the main part of the sentence. As no examples of complex question tags were found in our data, further mention of it is omitted.

Bibliography

Gumperz, J.J. "Linguistic and Social Interaction in Two Communities." In J.J. Gumperz and D. Hymes, eds., *The Ethnography of Communication. American Anthropologist*, 66 (1964), pp. 137-153.
——. "Linguistic Markers of Bilingual Communication." *Journal of Social Issues*, 23 (1967), pp. 48-57.

Hymes, D. "Models of the Interaction of Language and Social Setting." *Journal of Social Issues*, 23 (1967), pp. 8-28.

Imedadze. "On the Psychological Nature of Early Bilingualism." Translated by D.I. Slobin. Translation and Abstract Series, Department of Psychology, University of California, Berkeley, June, 1966.

Klima, E.S., and U. Bellugi. "Syntactic Regularities in the Speech of Children." In J. Lyons and R.J. Wales, eds., *Psycholinguistic Papers*. Edinburgh: Edinburgh University Press, 1966.

Labov, W. *The Social Stratification of English in New York City*. Washington, D.C.: Center for Applied Linguistics, 1966.

Langacker, R.W. "French Interrogatives: A Transformational Description." *Language*, 41 (1965), pp. 587-600.

Leopold, W.F. *Speech Development of a Bilingual Child* (4 vols.). Evanston: Northwestern University Press, 1939-1949.

Slobin, D.J. "Suggested Universals in the Ontogenesis of Grammar." Working Paper No. 32, Language-Behavior Research Laboratory, University of California, Berkeley, April, 1970.

Swain, M. *Bilingualism as a First Language*. Doctoral dissertation, University of California, Irvine, 1972.

Weeks, T. "Speech Registers in Young Children." *Papers and Reports on Child Development*, Stanford University, Vol. 1 (1970), pp. 22-42.

Weinreich, U. *Languages in Contacts*. New York: Linguistic Circle of New York, 1953.

4

Assumptions for Bilingual Instruction
in Primary Grades of Navajo Schools

Robert D. Wilson

I.   INTRODUCTION: THE BIRTH OF AN OPPORTUNITY

This paper is a review of some of the assumptions I have made in the development and implementation of a bilingual-bicultural curriculum for Navajo students in the early primary grades.[1] It is unlike any other curriculum in its design, in the breadth of its comprehensiveness, and in the depth of its integration; yet in some way or another it is like many other courses of study both recent and ancient.

My original assignment was to develop an ESL course similar to *Teaching English Early*, (Wilson et al., 1967) one that would be appropriate to the Navajo situation. I soon realized however that what was needed was a total curriculum (all day, all subject areas, plus learning itself), needed not only for teaching English more effectively[2] but also to provide the Navajo student with the abilities for coping with the school situation, with the two cultures, and with change — the one predictable feature of the future. This realization resulted in a change of assignment: develop and implement a total curriculum — with no restrictions on the design.[3]

Simply stated, the curriculum set out to develop and expand the students' abilities for learning, teaching them how to learn, so they could cope with change. It set out to sensitize them to the two cultures, teaching them to be aware of the underlying human nature shared by the two cultures, so they could cope with the two cultures. It set out to structure what the teachers taught and to generalize how they taught, tailoring the curriculum to the children's needs as humans and as Navajos, so they could cope with the school situation. And it wove all three objectives into one design, so that in the process of achieving one objective, the students were getting ready to achieve another objective; for example, cultural and human awareness predisposed them to learning, learning how to learn predisposed them to schooling, structured (alternating with unstructured) schooling predisposed them to more learning, generalized teaching methods taught them how to learn, how to learn predisposed them to learning the new culture and understanding their own, etc., etc., etc.

Making students aware of how to learn assumes their innate abilities for learning. Making them aware of the human condition that underlies the two cultures assumes a common humanity, theirs and everybody else's. Making them aware of structure in subject matter assumes their basic predisposition towards pattern — for pattern takes less storage space than lists and generates knowledge (de Bono, 1969). Innate abilities, common humanity, structure in subject matter are all inherent. This is the basic heuristic of the curriculum, to find the inherent qualities and make them pervasive like growing veins in the organism. The inherent generates. Innate learning abilities process knowledge into structure. Structured knowledge accommodates knowledge beyond itself. (Bruner, 1960: Ch.2) Humanity makes room for all cultures. And the inherent regenerates. Awareness of one's innate learning abilities, if appreciated and used, consciously used, brings about a stronger grasp of one's innate learning abilities. Awareness of structured knowledge, if appreciated and used, consciously used, brings about a greater familiarity with structured knowledge. Awareness that humanity makes room for more than one culture, the two cultures, if appreciated and (given the opportunity) used, consciously used, brings about a deeper sense of humanity. It is what the curriculum considers inherent, and what the curriculum has done with the inherent, that will characterize the assumptions reviewed in this paper.

One of the suspicious exercises of program writers is to claim assumptions without specifying how, specifically, they are made manifest in the program. (What, in other words, the curriculum has done with the inherent.) I will avoid this by giving examples from the methodology of the curriculum, but two things should be kept in mind. First, that one example of how an assumption is expressed in the curriculum does not list all of the ways in which the assumption is expressed in the curriculum. Second, that the derivation of a curricular expression of an assumption from the assumption is not an exercise in logic, where an expression is the only necessary derivation from a particular assumption. Rather, such derivation is the bold act of an intuition, a decision based on insufficient evidence. This second caveat is the motivation for the following section.

II. CLARIFICATION: THE TERMS OF A SCHEMA FOR INSIGHTS

It took quite a while for practitioners of TESL to detach themselves from absolute faith in pattern practice. The growing concern with pattern practice finally succeeded in breaking with the faith when Clifford Prator saw pattern practice as manipulation, pointing out at the same time that all that practice was not altogether appropriate practice for a terminal objective of language, communication (Prator, 1965). Prator's insight was based on implicitly seeing two levels of the pedagogical schema: manipulation as a term in a learning assumption, and pattern practice as a term in an instructional hypothesis. Insights like his are more easily come by when a proper schema is explicitly available. It is the purpose of this section to propose a schema that will provide the analytical clarity needed for generating insights into pedagogical issues and, consequently, for efficiently developing curriculum, any curriculum — and provide, as well, the terms and framework for discussing a few of the assumptions for instruction in the primary grades of Navajo schools.

The schema has four terms: learning assumption, instructional hypothesis, teaching technique, and teacher performance. A learning assumption postulates that an interpretation on the part of the learner will generate learning of some kind. An instructional hypothesis predicts the condition under which the learner's (appropriate) interpretation is likely to be secured. A teaching technique determines and projects the condition-corresponding behavior on the part of the teacher that is likely to trigger the intended interpretation on the part of the learner. A teacher's performance actualizes the technique and makes it believable, as an actor makes a role believable.

There are two theses to the schema. First, that it is the teacher's creative act in making the performance of the technique believable that triggers the intended interpretation, and the interpretation — itself a kind of learning — generates the learning promised by the assumption. Second, that each level of the schema (i.e., each term) is a system: a system of assumptions, a system of hypotheses, a system of techniques, and, even, a "system" of performance.[4]

The caveat from the preceding section bears repeating. The chain of events from the teacher's creative act to the learning promised by the assumption is as strong as the weakest link in the derivations from term to term in the schema. A derivation, say of an instructional hypothesis from a learning assumption, is not an exercise in logic, where one instructional hypothesis is the only necessary derivation from a particular learning assumption. Rather, derivation is the bold act of an intuition, a decision based on insufficient evidence.

Learning assumptions vs. instructional hypotheses

The confusion of learning assumptions with teaching hypotheses is apparently quite common in education, taking the form of doctrinaire instructional hypotheses. This happens because it is apparently presumed that the derivation of instructional hypotheses from learning assumptions is an exercise in logic, where one instructional hypothesis is the only logical derivation from a particular assumption. This is well exemplified in statements that inform both assumption and hypothesis as one and the same claim. For example, it is claimed that learning increases with the increase of individual attention provided in smaller classes, in smaller groups within a class, or ideally in a one-teacher-one-pupil ratio in a tutorial situation. The assumption: learning increases with the increase of individual attention. The hypothesis: this increase in individual attention is effected through smaller classes, smaller groups within a class, or a tutorial situation. The doctrine: only this hypothesis will bring about the increased learning promised in the assumption.

One source of the confusion between learning assumptions and instructional hypotheses is the failure to take note that while a learning assumption is, as a rule, held true for an individual, an instructional hypothesis, in the social context of today's education, is predicted to hold true for a classroom full of pupils. So, learning increases with increase of individual attention — for the individual so attended, according to the instructional hypothesis that opts for, say, small groups in a class, in which individual attention is expressed as something physical or geographical. Thus, in a classroom full of pupils where a teacher has subdivided his class into five smaller groups, group A is getting more of the teacher's attention at any given time. Presumably, group A is increasing its learning. However, groups B, C, D, and E are meanwhile not getting the teacher's attention as implied by the hypothesis. Presumably, these groups do not receive increased learning. Indeed, these four groups derive less learning than if the teacher attended to the class as a whole, distributing what little of his attention is available to each in such a large class.[5] An important question is raised. Is the increased learning in group A alone greater or less than the increased learning for the whole class if attended to as a whole? The point here is the question, not the possible answer to the question. The question suggests that the proposed instructional hypothesis, teacher-pupil ratio, might not be adequately expressing the assumption of increased learning from increased individual attention. It implies that there might be another instructional hypothesis which would be adequate.

If individual attention is not to be expressed as something physical or geographical in the specific form of teacher-pupil ratio, how else might individual attention be expressed? Note, first, that attention implies attention felt by the students (since ineffective attention would promise no increase in learning). Note, second, that individualized attention implies attention felt by each and every student as applying to himself. Given these two observations, individual attention might simply mean that each and every child in the class believes that he has a secure place in the mind (and heart?) of the teacher. Secure. . .a guarantee that nothing, but nothing, will threaten that security, not failure to succeed, not failure to behave, not failure to conform, nothing. Such a feeling of security does not occasion remarks like "The teacher doesn't like to call on me" or the compulsive "Teacher likes to call on me first." Appreciate the challenge of these remarks, considering that even some of the best intentioned teachers fall into patterns of calling on mostly one category of pupils in the class. For example: mostly the brightest pupils or mostly the slowest ones because the teacher likes to provide challenge; mostly the best behaved ones or mostly the most troublesome because the teacher means to keep control; mostly the well adjusted or mostly the maladjusted because the teacher wishes to be a parent. The challenge: "Call on me to participate on the same chance that anyone and everyone of my classmates has. Do not select among us, not even me, on the basis of any criterion whatsoever. Don't make me dependent on any criterion for a place in your mind and heart. Such dependency makes me insecure, distracting me from the objective of the lesson, from learning, and eventually from caring about learning — caring, and attending only to the criterion you have set up."

To meet such a challenge, I have provided the curriculum with an instructional hypothesis: *randomization* of pupil participation assures individual attention for all members of the class. Randomization of pupil participation means that every child in the class has equal chances of participation equal to every other child, virtually all the time.[6] It means, further, that every child in the class believes he has an equal chance of participation because he recognizes randomization for what it is, a game of chance. If the hypothesis is found to hold true, then, on the basis of the learning assumption that increased individual attention brings about increased learning, it may be inferred that to the degree that the pupils feel assured of individual attention, they will profit by increased learning. The difference between this instructional hypothesis and that of teacher-pupil ratio is the degree to which they can assure individual attention to each and every child in the class. Whatever the difference and whichever assures greater individual attention, it has been demonstrated that more than one instructional hypothesis can be derived from one and the same learning assumption.

Instructional hypotheses vs. teaching techniques

However, neither the teacher-pupil ratio nor randomization is a hypothesis in the sense of being testable, at least not by current experimental methods in pedagogy. Both of them need to be behaviorally defined. And both of them should be placed in very specific contexts, also behaviorally defined. If they are to be compared, their contexts should be identical or near identical, depending on the rigor required.

The behavioral form of an instructional hypothesis is a teaching technique, and the technique is tested in a specific teaching situation which, itself, includes other teaching techniques.

An experiment attempts to determine the effect of the teaching technique in the teaching situation. Confusion arises when the experiment is believed to have determined the effect of the instructional hypothesis rather than of the teaching technique. This is generally due to the behavioral orientation of interpreters of experiments: disinclined as they are to recognize a more general, nonbehavioral, yet insightful instructional hypothesis underlying the more specific, behavioral, also insightful teaching technique, they make the teaching technique the underlying principle itself. This confusion of technique for the more general hypothesis reveals itself among some educators in their obsession with particular media — either for or against them — for example, color coding, workbooks, primers.

The confusion of teaching technique and instructional hypothesis is sometimes traceable to the presupposition that there is only one technique for an instructional hypothesis. But this is just not the case. For example: one technique for effecting the instructional hypothesis of randomization is to have the teacher select students for participation by picking out a card from a deck of cards (as an honest card dealer would), each card with a pupil's name on it; another would be to pull out a slip of paper from a paper sack full of slips of papers with the pupils' names on them; still another would be for a blindfolded student in the middle of a circle of his peers to turn several times with one hand outstretched, stopping to point, unpredictably, to one of them; and why not a crap game between each pupil of a pair, the winner of each pair playing against another winner, and so on, until only one winner remains. All of these techniques but the last one have the advantage of brevity, leaving enough time in the period for the objective to be learned. The last one, however, will take most of the class period, leaving very little time for learning. Should the last technique be the one used in a pedagogical experiment, the effect of randomization on learning would be minimal, that is, nonsignificant. Should such an experiment be interpreted as a demonstration of the ineffectiveness of the instructional hypothesis? Or of the teaching technique?

On the other hand, a technique that is demonstrably effective in an experiment elicits a degree of confidence in the underlying instructional hypothesis — but not to the exclusion of other representative techniques that may also be demonstrably effective. The exclusion of other techniques as representative of one and the same instructional hypothesis when one technique has already been demonstrated effective probably arises when the experiment is believed to be generalizable to other contexts: that is, the same technique that proved more effective[7] in a specific context is applicable, unchanged, to another context. The same technique may prove effective in the next context, but then again it may not. Stated this way, hypothetically, the non-generalizability of a technique elicits academic agreement to the thesis. The demonstrable effectiveness of the technique of written texts for the instructional hypothesis of programmed instruction among able readers does not turn out as effective a technique among weak readers, for example, beginning ESL learners in high school classes where number systems are taught through programmed texts in English.

The tasks of formulation and reformulation

One can begin to appreciate the tasks of formulating and reformulating teaching techniques, instructional hypotheses, and learning assumptions by realizing the implications of the thesis that there is more than one possible derivation from term to term in the schema. This is the thesis that has been argued so far in this paper. An example of the implications of this thesis in the formulation of a teaching technique from an instructional hypothesis is here presented to plant the seed of appreciation.

The questions below are relevant to the formulation of a technique (or set of techniques — depending on one's unit of behavior) for the instructional hypothesis recommending a smaller teacher-pupil ratio in a classroom, specifically smaller groups within a class.

(a) Will the class be divided into two, three, four, five, or more groups?

(b) What criteria will be used to determine the groups?

(c) Will the pupils be informed of the criteria for the grouping? If so, how will the criteria be presented?

(d) Which subgroup will the teacher attend to first on any given unit of time, say, during a day, which second, which third (etc.)? Will different groups be attended to first on different days? If so, how will this be determined?

(e) Will the teaching differ for each group or only for some of the groups, or not differ at all?

(f) Will the groups not directly attended to by the teacher at any given time be self-teaching? Or will busy work be allowed? How will self-teaching be distinguished from busy work?

Still more questions come to mind should the division of the class into small groups be changeable:

(g) Will the different groups be formed daily, weekly, or monthly? Or will some particular behavior, like a symptom, signal the need for a new division of the class?

(h) Will the same criteria to determine the groups be used each time a new division is formed? Or different criteria?

(i) Will the time taken to determine the groups at different times be significant enough to affect, negatively, the promises of increased learning? If so, how can this be avoided?

(j) Will teaching change as different groups are determined according to different criteria?

Appreciation of the tasks of formulating and reformulating the components of each level (i.e., each term) of the schema deepens with a consideration of a second thesis of the schema, that each level is a system — a system of techniques, a system of hypotheses, and a system of assumptions. For example, take questions (e) and (j) above, both of which ask about teaching itself. If the teaching will differ for the different groups, or if the teaching will change as the groups change, how will the teaching change? An entire spectrum of teaching techniques becomes a kaleidoscope of questions. And the answers to these questions, a specific set of techniques, can make or break the previously determined technique (whatever it was) for implementing the teacher-pupil ratio hypothesis. Thus, the formulation of a technique requires the formulation of other techniques related to it, that is, the task is one of formulating a system of techniques. It is easy to believe that if the teaching techniques are all of a system, the instructional hypotheses from which they are derived are quite likely to be all of a system themselves — *pari passu* for learning assumptions.

On the level of instructional hypotheses, relatedness between hypotheses can also be shown. Take the instructional hypothesis of randomization explained earlier. It gives everyone in class an equal chance to participate, yes, those who feel ready as well as those who do not feel ready. When the latter are called to participate, an important learning assumption is violated: a student must feel ready to participate if he is to improve his learning, perhaps even if he is to learn at all. What is needed, then, is an instructional hypothesis derived from the learning assumption of felt readiness. So, I have provided the curriculum with an instructional hypothesis that purports to reflect that assumption: *volunteering* to participate. This hypothesis requires the teacher to permit a student to refuse to participate when, as a result of randomization, he is expected to participate. (It also requires the teacher to call on only those students who are volunteering to participate in the situation where only the teacher's sense of randomization is the means of selection — but this aspect of volunteering is not relevant here.) On the other hand, volunteering without randomization would make boldness a criterion for belonging, violating the learning assumption that learning comes more readily when the student feels like an individual: that he belongs simply because he is he.

The learning assumptions are systemic in that they form a hierarchy of categories. First, there are those learning assumptions which postulate the interpretations that make it possible for learning to take place: its initiation, its continuance, and its termination. Learning might be said to be initiated by interpreting a phenomenon, say, something heard, as having a particular feature, for example, a car engine with a noise pattern like that of a neighbor's. The learning might be said to be continued by evaluating the feature as worthy of checking, for example: if it is the neighbor's car, he is home earlier than usual. The learning might be said to be terminated by checking the hypothesis that it is the neighbor's car or by deciding not to check the hypothesis. The latter decision leaves the individual with only an hypothesis, the former with a conclusion; in either case, learning has occurred.

Then there are those learning assumptions which postulate the interpretations that make it possible for learning of a certain kind to take place. For example, what interpretation might be postulated for product-learning that is capable of generating more learning of the product, for example, for counting 1, 2, 3, 4, etc? Possibly, it might be assumed that the interpretation of the product, the subject matter, as having structure, a principle, a generalization (and a particular one at that) is the interpretation that would make product-learning capable of generating more learning of the product; for example, to interpret counting 1, 2, 3, 4, etc. as an instance of addition by 1 (or, even more generally, of addition) would make the student capable of counting with numbers he is not familiar with, say 194, 328, 576.

There is a relationship between the two kinds of learning assumptions above. Learning assumptions that postulate interpretations which make it possible for learning to take place are prerequisites to the learning assumptions that postulate interpretations which make it possible for learning of a certain kind to take place. This seems like an obvious relationship, and it is, but it is apparently not kept in mind by some practicing educators when formulating (implicitly, probably) their instructional hypotheses (and the condition-corresponding techniques). Take the professor who describes structure XYZ of his subject matter in a lecture but fails to point out that he is describing structure XYZ or at what point in his lecture he is describing it — to initiate learning. Or take the professor who does point out structure XYZ but fails to justify, interest, or motivate the students to consider structure XYZ as worthy of checking out — to continue learning. Or the professor who does both of the preceding but fails to provide an opportunity for checking out the accuracy of the students' understanding of the structure, say, by providing examples which the students have to identify as having or not having structure XYZ — to terminate learning. In any case, the relationship suggests the systemic character of the learning assumptions.

The reformulation of the components on each level may start with the learning assumptions. A new assumption may suggest itself, an established assumption may be seen in a different light, a former and rejected assumption may now appear valid. What follows is a reexamination of the system of instructional hypotheses, sometimes resulting in a modification. This, in turn, prompts a reexamination of a specific technique and the rest of the system of techniques, sometimes resulting in a new design. Or the reformulation may start with an instructional hypothesis. A particular hypothesis may be inadequate, failing to provide the stated interpretation. Or it may be superfluous, another instructional hypothesis already supplying the stated interpretation. Or one instructional hypothesis may be inconsistent with another, one nullifying the effects of the other. What follows is a reexamination of the system of assumptions and the system of techniques.

The motivation for reformulating techniques is empirical, or should be. This is the level of the schema which is testable. As the techniques of a curriculum get tested, whether rigorously or loosely, a pattern for modification may be revealed. The key to discovering a pattern and selecting the most promising new design of techniques is a familiarity with the system of instructional hypotheses from which the system of teaching techniques has been derived. Modifying the system of techniques means a reexamination of the system of instructional hypotheses, making it, in turn, subject to possible modification itself, with possible ramifications for the system of learning assumptions.

The task of improving performance

Awesome as the task of formulating and reformulating is in the development of a curriculum, even more challenging is the task of training teachers (or of teachers training themselves) in the performance of the techniques. It is obvious, but the parallelism should be noted, that just as there may be more than one instructional hypothesis to express a learning assumption and more than one teaching technique to give form to an instructional hypothesis, there may be more than one teacher performance for implementing a teaching technique.

Teaching performance varies from teacher to teacher and from day to day for the same teacher. It is dependent on the teacher's ability to act, to play a role more challenging than that of an actor or actress on a stage if only for the fact that the teacher's acting involves audience participation, demanding that the teacher prepare (with the help of the curriculum design) for a variety of situations. And the teacher must do this before and with an audience that must be more than entertained, an audience that must be taught so that it learns — as in the finest forms of play making. Like an actor or actress, the teacher must practice and perfect techniques, learn and identify with the role (instructional hypotheses), as well as understand and believe in the play (the curriculum). Like a Burton or a Bancroft, the teacher is a creative artist — at the performance, leaving (*qua* teacher) plot and script to the playwright (curriculum designer), direction to the director (curriculum supervisor) and production to the producer (school principal).[8]

Teacher performance, like acting performance, must be credible and consistently credible in order for the pupils, like an audience, to be willing and able to interpret the act of teaching for what it is: a learning opportunity. Willingness to make learning the interpretation of the teaching act ultimately depends on the credibility of the teacher's performance. Does the manner belie the words? Does the frown belie the smile? Does even the overjoyed surprise at a pupil's unexpected correct response belie the low esteem for this particular pupil? On the other hand, the ability of the pupils to make learning the interpretation of the teaching act ultimately depends on the consistency of the credibility of the teacher's performance. Does correction always provide individualized instruction — or does it sometimes express disappointment at the pupil for the mistake? Does the presentation of the lesson's objective always imply its importance and inherent interest — or are some lessons' objectives not really to be taken seriously as learning tasks? The recurrence of inconsistency increases the probability of error, the error of giving an interpretation other than learning to an act of teaching.

The seriousness of inconsistency is difficult to overestimate. As inconsistency repeats inconsistency in teaching, inconsistency begins to infect related areas like discipline, affection, esteem. . .and eventually inconsistency repeats inconsistency on all levels of communication between teacher and pupils. . .until finally mood and feeling alone dominate. The effect on the pupils? Anxiety.

Or, worse, as inconsistency repeats inconsistency, the importance of the teaching act, and its intended product — learning — becomes suspect: "What does teacher really want? Not learning. Not all the time anyway. Sometimes teacher just wants me to speak up loudly. Sometimes to make mistakes. . .when I get something right, teacher finds some other mistake I've made. . .I guess I'm stupid. Sometimes to behave. . .calling on me when I'm not paying attention. . .what I say is not important so long as I start paying attention again." Learning as the meaning of class activities loses importance and other meanings for the school experience gain importance. Eventually, the primacy of learning loses its hold on the students and the primacy of conformity to teacher's wishes takes over. Only the teacher's personality can hold the class now, and if that loses its attraction (as is likely with inconsistent personalities), the pupils' chances of maturing into self-learners are those of a poker addict playing against a crooked dealer. But, unlike the poker addict who can't quit playing poker, the learning addict (he is born an addict) may very well decide to quit the game of learning when he realizes the odds against inconsistent teachers. If he is blessed with wisdom, appreciating the high stakes involved, he only quits school, not learning.

On the other hand, a consistently credible teacher, especially one so confident in his techniques that he consistently expects learning as the appropriate interpretation of his teaching, emphasizes the importance of learning, underlining it with talent, effort, time, and sincerity. There is no better way to keep students hooked on learning.

III   DEFINITION: THE INTERPRETATION OF LEARNING

The title of this section is intentionally ambiguous. First, it suggests the activity of the learner in learning, as in the definition of *learning assumption* in the preceding section. Second, it suggests an understanding (mine) of the learning process: its bases, its stages, its uses. Together, the first as subject and the second as predicate, they form the proposition: "The learner learns." This is by way of saying that the purpose of this section is to provide an appreciation of the independence of the learner from teaching. (The dependence of the learner on teaching is the theme of another paper.)

Rather long quotes from the writings of Jean Piaget and Jerome Bruner will have to be made; as a pedagogue, I can only select and take the views (of psychologists) which I consider to be promising learning assumptions, promising in that they will provide me with a fertile source of effective and efficient instructional hypotheses.

The learner

The interesting thing about learning is that it occurs. It doesn't have to. Take learning as simply a changing. Changing occurs. Hit a glass bottle with a hammer, and the bottle shatters. The bottle is pieces of glass. But changing does not have to occur. Hit a brass bottle with a hammer, and the bottle does not shatter. It remains a bottle. Point out a bird a child has never seen, and the child learns about the bird in some visual way; but point out a bird a blind child has never seen, and this child does not learn about the bird in any sense visually. Learning does occur, but it doesn't have to.

For learning to occur, there must be an organism that can learn. For specific learning to occur, there must be a learner capable of such specific learning. If learning in a specific manner is to occur, say visually, then there must be a learner capable of learning visually. If learning about something specific is to occur, say a visual image of a bird, then there must be a learner capable of learning in such a manner that learning about the something specific is possible (visually about the bird).

For learning to occur, there must be an organism willing to learn. A rat is willing to press a lever to get food or avoid a passageway to prevent shock. For learning to occur in a specific manner, e.g., play the piano by reading notes (i.e., visually) rather than by ear (i.e., auditorily), there must be a learner willing to learn in just such a specific manner rather than the other. And if learning about something specific is to occur, then there must be a learner willing to learn about that specific something. The blind child is unable to see the bird; the child unwilling to see the bird is just as blind. (Bruner, 1968; chapters 6 & 7)

Able and willing — and both inherent in the organism. The rat is able to press a lever though it may not know enough yet to do so; and the rat is willing to press a lever though it may not know enough yet to want to nor hungry enough to do so. The pupil is able to read though it may not know enough yet to do so; and the pupil is willing to read though it may not know enough yet to want to nor interested enough to do so. These two classes of potential functions are not learned, not from the experimenter by the rat, not from the teacher by the pupil. To say inherent of these is to say innate: in the genes.[9]

What is the pupil able to do?

> . . . .all such behavior that has innate roots but becomes differentiated through functioning contains, we find, the same functional factors and structural elements. The functional factors are assimilation, the process whereby an action is actively reproduced and comes to incorporate new objects into itself (for example, thumb sucking as a case of sucking), and accommodation, the process whereby the schemes of assimilation themselves become modified in being applied to a diversity of objects. The structural elements are, essentially, certain order relations (the order of movements in a reflex act, in a habitual act, in the suiting of means to end), subordination schemes (the subordination of a relatively more simple schema like grasping to a relatively more complex one like pulling) and correspondences [recognition, invariance, causality as in getting at things by using a stick — RDW]. (Piaget, 1968; 63)

This is the way the pupil begins his life as an organism. He grows, develops, matures, i.e., "becomes differentiated through functioning," by means of these very same functions and structural elements; for example:

> As soon as the semiotic function (speech, symbolic play, images, and such) comes on the scene and with it the ability to evoke what is not actually perceived, that is, as soon as the child begins to represent and think, he uses reflective abstractions: certain connections are "drawn out" of the sensori-motor schemata and "projected upon" the new plane of thought; these are then elaborated by giving rise to distinct lines of behavior and conceptual structures. The order relations, for example, which on the sensori-motor plane were altogether immersed in the sensori-motor schema, now become dissociated and give rise to a specific activity of "ranking" or "ordering." Similarly, the subordination schemes which were originally only implicit now become separated out and lead to a distinct classificatory activity; and the setting up of correspondence soon becomes systematic: one/many; one/one; copy to original, and so on. (Piaget, 1968; 64)

What is the pupil willing to do? In other words, if the Piagetian view of the ability to generate structures and behavior is all that the organism begins with, what explains an organism's willingness to generate specific sorts of structures and behavior and not others, human language by humans, flying by birds, and neither by horses, for instance? As Piaget puts the question to himself: "Why does it look 'as if' the results were 'predetermined'? " (1968; 62)

> The behavior of the living subject depends upon quite explicit meanings; instinctual structures, for example, function in terms of all sorts of hereditary "clues" — the IRM's, "innate releasing mechanisms," of the ethologists. But meanings are implicit in all functioning, even the specifically biological distinction between normal and abnormal conditions depends on them; for example, when at birth there is danger of suffocation, the coagulation of the blood immediately gives rise to regulation through the nervous system. (Piaget, 1968; 48)

He is apparently unwilling to view as innate the underlying structure of behavior even while criticizing empiricism's view that all learning is dependent on the environment:

> . . .what is no less essential is that contemporary ethology tends to show that all learning and remembering depend upon antecedent structures (conceivably the DNA and RNA themselves). Thus, the contacts with experience and the fortuitous modifications due to the environment on which empiricism modeled all learning do not become

stabilized until and unless assimilated to structures; these structures need not be innate, nor are they necessarily immutable, but they must be more settled and coherent than the mere gropings with which empirical knowledge begins. (1968; 51)

What Piaget proposes is an innately guided (by the meanings, the clues, the IRM's) process of construction that of necessity generates species-specific structures of behavior. (Piaget, 1968; 67, 90) It is instructive to have Piaget elaborate on this:

> In the construction proposed. . .the function (in the biologist sense of the word) chiefly credited for the formation of structures was "assimilation". . .Biologically considered, assimilation is the process whereby the organism in each of its interactions with the bodies or energies of its environment fits these in some manner to the requirements of its own physico-chemical structures while at the same time accommodating itself to them. Psychologically (behaviorally) considered, assimilation is the process whereby a function, once exercised, presses toward repetition, and in "reproducing" its own activity produces a schema into which the objects propitious to its exercise, whether familiar ("recognitory assimilation") or new ("generalizing assimilation"), become incorporated. So assimilation, the process or activity common to all forms of life, is the source of the continual relating, setting up of correspondences, establishing of functional connections, and so on. . .(1968; 71)

Note in particular the phrases, "fits these in some manner to the requirements of its own physico-chemical structures" and "produces a schema into which the objects propitious to its exercise, whether familiar or new, become incorporated," for they lead to the next question.

What is the pupil willing to do that he is able to do? For example, which of the thousands of languages he is capable of learning will he learn? Or, what does the pupil become? Piaget's view is that the organism particularizes not by itself alone but by interaction with the environment while reaffirming again the influential role of the organism's responses, influential on itself and on succeeding generations. He remarks on C.H. Waddington's work (1957):

> Waddington has shown that environment and gene complex interact in the formation of the phenotype, that the phenotype is the gene complex's response to the environment's incitations, and that "selection" operates, not on the gene complex as such, but on these responses. By insisting on this point, Waddington has been able to develop a theory of "genetic assimilation," i.e., of the fixation of acquired characteristics. Roughly, Waddington views the relations between the organism and its environment as a cybernetic loop such that the organism selects its environment while being conditioned by it. (1968; 49-50)

> Waddington, by reestablishing the role of the environment as setting "problems" to which genotypical variations are a response, gives evolution the dialectical character without which it would be the mere setting out of an eternal predestined plan whose gaps and imperfections are utterly inexplicable. (1968; 50)

Piaget is insistent on taking the learner as the controlling agent of the learning process:

> Everyone grants that structures have laws of composition, which

amounts to saying that they are regulated. But by what or by whom? If the theoretician who has framed the structure is the one who governs it, it exists only on the level of a formal exercise. To be real, a structure must, in the literal sense be governed from within. So we come back to the necessity of some sort of functional activity; and, if the facts oblige us to attribute cognitive structures to a subject, it is for our purposes sufficient to define this subject as the center of functional activity. (1968; 69)

Piaget has been suggesting that the pupil brings with him all the processes and all the structural elements — the innate ability (as well as the innate willingness) — to learn species-specific behavior like language and thinking and sensory-motor skills, needing only contact with the environment, i.e., needing only experience, to particularize the language, groove the thinking, and sharpen the sensory-motor skills. Remember that Piaget's pupil brings with him only the structural elements (order, subordination, and correspondence), not structures themselves; structures (that is, particular structures, like a particular language) are constructed by means of the processes of assimilation and accommodation regulated by the pupil himself on the basis of his nature. In short, species-specific particularized structures and behavior are learned; they are not given, but they are inevitably learned. The learner learns.

The learning

The purpose of this subsection is rather ambitious: to provide a model of learning that takes Piaget's stages of intellectual development as the given rules of a race and Jerome Bruner's modes of representation as the tactics for running the race. It is not an explanatory model, for it does not provide data about behavior needing explanation. It is not a hypothetical model, for it does not provide hypotheses about behavior for testing. It is simply a heuristic model in that it has helped me to organize the learning assumptions that underlie the instructional hypotheses of the curriculum. And it is limited, providing only for the intellectual domain of the curriculum.

Piaget's work of the last thirty years has produced a description of the intellectual development of children that is consistent with the behavior of Swiss children and shows promise of being consistent with the behavior of children in other cultures, allowing for accelerations and delays. (Piaget, 1970; 37) It is only a promise, but it will do. I now quote Piaget, letting him describe his theory in his own words and in the least technical language I could find. (Each of the four stages will be named for later reference; they are not part of the quote.)

Sensorimotor

With perceptions and movements as its only tools, without yet being capable of either representation or thought, this entirely practical intelligence nevertheless provides evidence, during the first years of our existence, of an effort to comprehend situations. It does, in practice, achieve the construction of schemata of action that will serve as substructures for the operational and notional structures built up later on. At this level, for example, we can already observe the construction of a fundamental schema of conservation, which is that of the permanence of solid objects. . .Correlatively, we can also observe the formation of structures that are already almost reversible, such as the organization of the displacements and positions of forward and backward or circling movements (reversible mobility). We can watch the formation of causal relationships, linked first of all to the action proper alone, then progressively objectified and spatialized through connection with the construction of the object, of space, and of time.

Semiotic

The onset of this second period is marked by the formation of the symbolic or semiotic function. This enables us to represent objects or events that are not at the moment perceptible by evoking them through the agency of symbols or differentiated signs. Symbolic play is an example of this process, as are deferred imitation, mental images, drawing, etc., and, above all, language itself. The symbolic function thus enables the sensorimotor intelligence to extend itself by means of thought, but there exist, on the other hand, two circumstances that delay the formation of mental operations proper, so that during the whole of this second period intelligent thought remains preoperational. The first of these circumstances is the time it takes to interiorize actions as thought, since it is much more difficult to represent the unfolding of an action and its results to oneself in terms of thought than to limit oneself to a material execution of it: for example, to impose a rotation on a square in thought alone, while representing to oneself every ninety degrees the position of the variously colored sides, is quite different from turning the square physically and observing the effects.

In the second place, this reconstruction [to interiorize actions as thought — RDW] presupposes a continual decentering process that is much broader in scope than on the sensorimotor level. . .the child must not only situate himself in relation to the totality of things, but also in relation to the totality of people around him, which presupposes a decentering process that is simultaneously relational and also social, and therefore a transition from egocentrism to those two forms of coordination, the sources of operational reversibility (inversions and reciprocities).

Lacking mental operations, the child cannot succeed during this second period in constituting the most elementary notions of conservation, which are the conditions of logical deductibility. Thus he imagines that ten counters arranged in a row become greater in number when the spaces between them are increased. . .that a quantity of liquid in glass A increases when poured into the narrower glass B, etc.

Concrete operations

. . .there begins a third period in which these problems and many others are easily resolved because of the growing interiorization, coordinating, and decentering processes, which result in that general form of equilibrium constituted by operational reversibility (inversions and reciprocities). In other words, we are watching the formation of mental operations: linking and dissociation of classes, the sources of classification; the linking of relations A B C. . .the source of seriation; correspondences, the sources of double entry tables, etc; synthesis of inclusions in classes and serial order, which gives rise to numbers; spatial divisions and ordered displacements, leading to a synthesis of them, which is mensuration, etc.

But these many budding operations still cover no more than a doubly limited field. On the one hand they are still applied solely to objects, not to hypotheses set out verbally in the form of propositions (hence the uselessness of lecturing to the younger classes in primary schools and the necessity for concrete teaching methods). And, on the other hand, they still proceed only from one thing to the one next to it, as opposed to later combinative and proportional operations, which possess a much greater degree of mobility. These two limitations have a certain interest and show in what way these initial operations, which we term "concrete," are still close to the action from which they derive, since the linkages, seriations, correspondences, etc. carried out in the form of physical actions also effectively present these two types of characteristics.

Formal operations

. . .there begins a fourth and final period. . .characterized in general by the conquest of a new mode of reasoning, one that is no longer limited exclusively to dealing with objects or directly representable realities, but also employs "hypotheses," in other words, propositions from which it is possible to draw logical conclusions without it being necessary to make decisions about their truth or falsity before examining the results of their implications. We are thus seeing the formation of new operations, which we term "propositional," in addition to the earlier concrete operations: implications ("if. . .then"), disjunctions ("either. . .or"), incompatibilities, conjunctions, etc. And these operations present two new fundamental characteristics. In the first place, they entail a combinative process, which is not the case with the "groupings" of classes and relationships at the previous level, and this combinative process is applied from the very first to objects or physical factors as well as to ideas and propositions. In the second place, each proportional operation, corresponds to an inverse and to a reciprocal, so that these two forms of reversibility, dissociated until this point (inversion of classes only, reciprocity of relationships only) are from now on joined to form a total system in the form of a group of four transformations. (1970b; 30-33)

The four stages are not to be associated with actual age groups; Piaget only claims that they occur in the sequence given. (1970; 37) He provides approximate ages as guidelines, ages based on his observation of Swiss children. The sensorimotor stage begins at birth, the semiotic at about the age of two, the stage of concrete operations at about the age of seven or eight, and that of formal operations at about eleven or twelve, of which the plateau coincides with adolescence (1970; 30-33). The Navajo children participating in the curriculum at present are six and seven years old, and they will be ten when the planned five-year curriculum is completed. My (informal) observations permit me to cautiously estimate that they begin the curriculum when they are in the last mile of the semiotic stage and are well into the concrete operational stage by the end of the second year of the curriculum.

The heuristic model of learning takes Piaget's theory as constituting the rules of a race. There are just three rules. One, that there are always to be these four stages: perhaps more by a finer classification, but not less, i.e., no skipping. Two, that the four stages occur in the sequence given: sensorimotor first, semiotic second, concrete operational third, and formal operational fourth. Three, that the bottom rung of each stage is a *sine qua non* for beginning that stage: purely verbal hypotheses for the fourth stage, operational reversibility and internal representation of action (interiorization) for the third stage, language for the second, and perception and movement for the first. On the other hand, there are no rules against acceleration or deceleration, as Piaget himself has pointed out, (1970; 37) nor are there rules against using a preceding stage as basis for acceleration in the following stage, as implied by Piaget's view of each stage being a preparation for the next in his description and discussion above.

Bruner, too, has developed a view of intellectual development, which he calls instrumental conceptualism:

> . . .that is organized around two central tenets concerning the nature of knowing. The first is that our knowledge of the world is based on a constructed model of reality. . .that rests on what might be called an axiomatic base. . .That is, the physical requirements of adaptive action "force" us to conceive of the world in a particular way, a way that is constrained by the nature of our own neuromuscular system. So, too, are we constrained by the primitive properties of visual, auditory, and haptic space in our effort to represent our knowledge in terms of imagery. Finally, our representation of reality in terms of language or symbolism is similarly constrained by what again seems to be our native endowment for mastering particular symbolic systems, systems premised on rules of hierarchy, predication, causation, modification, and so forth.
>
> . . .the second is that our models develop as a function of the uses to which they have been put first by the culture and then by any of its members who must bend knowledge to their own uses. . .Our instrumentalism is inherent in this double emphasis on the role of use . . .one cannot separate (except analytically) cultural instrumentalism and individual instrumentalism. (Bruner, 1966; 319-320)

The parallel with Piaget and Waddington is evident: the innate necessity of choosing and performing species-specific behavior in a certain way, yet modifying that behavior in a particular way in interacting with the environment; for example, the innate necessity for humans to choose to communicate through (human) language and inventing — performing it in a certain universal manner yet modifying it so that it becomes the particular language needed for a particular environment.

What distinguishes Bruner's theory from Piaget's that is of interest to the heuristic model are the three techniques Bruner posits man has for constructing a model of reality: the enactive, the ikonic, and the symbolic. Briefly, and his words:

> . . .the means by which growing human beings represent their experience of the world; and how they organize for future use what they have encountered. There are striking changes in emphasis that occur with the development of representation. At first the child's world is known to him principally by the habitual actions he uses for coping with it. In time there is added a technique of representation through imagery that is relatively free of action. Gradually there is added a new

and powerful method of translating action and image into language, providing still a third system of representation. Each of the three modes of representation — enactive, ikonic, and symbolic — has its unique way of representing events. Each places a powerful impress on the mental life of human beings at different ages, and their interplay persists as one of the major features of adult intellectual life. (Bruner, 1966; 1)

To understand how these three techniques of representation serve as available tactics for running the race of learning according to Piaget's rules, one must understand representation as *act* (as Piaget would prefer) or as *medium* (as Bruner would have it) towards some *objective*. It is uninstructive to make an issue between act and medium; since Bruner infers medium from behavior (as he must, methodologically), one might agree to see the act/behavior as creating the medium/representation in the mind.[10] In explaining the three modes of representation, Bruner begins by viewing each as external:

With respect to a particular knot, we learn the act of tying it and, when we "know" the knot, we know it by the habitual pattern of action we have mastered.

Representation in imagery is just that: the picture of the knot in question, its final phase or some intermediate phase, or, indeed, even a motion picture of the knot being formed. It is obvious. . .that to have a picture before one (or in one's head) is not necessarily to be able to execute the act it represents, as those who have invested in books called "Skiing Illustrated" know all too well.

The representation of a knot in symbolic terms is not so readily stated, for it involves at the outset a choice of the code in which the knot is to be described. For symbolic representation, whether in natural or mathematical "language," requires the translation of what is to be represented into discrete terms that may then be formed into "utterances" or "strings" or "sentences," or whatever the medium used to combine the discrete elements by rule. . .it is also necessary to specify whether one is describing a process of tying the knot or the knot itself (at some stage of being tied). There is. . .a choice. . .whether to be highly concrete or to describe this knot as one of a general class of knots. (Bruner 1966; 6-7)

But it is as "internal" that the three techniques of representation must be understood if they are to serve some objective: they must be understood as *plans* (Miller *et al*, 1960) by which objectives may be reached, if the individual is willing. The characteristics of internal representation are only beginning to be understood; but they show promise of being in the right direction. It is only a promise, but it will do. So, in Bruner's words (the headings are not part of quote):

Enactive representation

When motor activity becomes "regularized" or "steady," is it converted from a "serial" to a "simultaneous" form? . . .In order for behavior to become more skillful, it must become increasingly freer of immediate or serial regulation by environmental stimuli operative while the behavior is going on. I believe that this "freedom" is achieved by a shift from response learning to place learning — in effect, the placing of the behavior in a spatial context or "layout" that makes possible detours and substitutions to meet changed conditions. . .For example, over time all hammering behavior becomes translatable into a common schema, even though the different hammering acts may each involve different muscle groups.

(Earlier in the same chapter, page 10, Bruner provides two examples of "substitution:")
What is at first a habitual pattern for using sensorimotor activity to achieve some end later becomes a program in the sense that various "substitutes" can be inserted without disrupting the over-all act. Even a chimpanzee who is unable to get a hand into an opening to extract a desired object can substitute a stick in place of reaching. Or in skilled tool-using by humans the carpenter who forgets his plane can substitute a chisel in the smoothing routine, a pocket knife, or the edge of a screwdriver, if need be.)
It is of some comfort to quote. . .Leeper (1963, pp. 404-405) on the relation of motor activity to underlying representational process. . ."Maybe the whole point can be summed up by saying that movements often are like symbols or actually are symbols. Their significance is determined by the relations of those movements to a larger context of the situation. A person blows on his hands to warm them, he blows on his soup to cool it." (Bruner, 1966; 18-21)
. . .— all suggest a system that, unlike the serial ordering of action and enactive representation, is labile (subject to change) and highly lacking in. . .economy. . .It is as if the young child, having achieved a perceptual world that is no longer directly linked to action, now deals with the surface of things that catch attention rather than with deeper structures based on invariant features. Or, to put it another way, it is as if the child has as its next principal task to find precisely a way of getting to the base structure of the world of appearance. In one experiment after another. . .we. . .see the younger child failing to solve problems by virtue of using surface cues while the older child succeeds by learning to respond to such "invisible" or "silent" features as relations, hierarchies, etc.
. . .the inferior conceptual performance of children with imagery preference is a result of their use of surface features in grouping.
Ostensive definition (e.g., pointing), as we shall see again and again in later chapters, is critical to the child's thinking in ikonic representation. It is only when he can go beyond this "match by direct correspondence" that he comes to deal with such "nonsensory" ideas as the relations between quantities, invariance across transformations, and substitutability within a conceptual category. (Bruner, 1966; 21-29)

Symbolic representation
. . .symbolic activity stems from some primitive or protosymbolic system that is species-specific to man. This system becomes specialized in expression in various domains of the life of a human being: in language, in tool-using, in various atemporally organized and skilled forms of serial behavior, and in the organization of experience itself. We have suggested some minimum properties of such a symbolic system: categoriality, hierarchy, predication, causation, and modification. We have suggested that any symbolic activity, and especially language, is logically and empirically unthinkable without these properties.
What is striking about language as one of the specialized expressions of symbolic activity is that in one of its aspects, the syntactic sphere, it reaches maturity very swiftly. The syntactical maturity of a five-year-old seems unconnected with his ability in other spheres. He can muster words and sentences with a swift and sure grasp of highly abstract rules, but he cannot, in a corresponding fashion, organize the

things words and sentences "stand for." This asymmetry is reflected in the child's activities, where his knowledge of the senses of words and the empirical implications of his sentence remain childish for many years, even after syntax has become fully developed.

One is thus led to believe that, in order for the child to use language as an instrument of thought, he must first bring the world of experience under the control of principles of organization that are in some degree isomorphic with the structural principles of syntax. Without special training in the symbolic representation of experience, the child grows to adulthood still depending in large measure on the enactive and ikonic modes of representing and organizing the world, no matter what language he speaks. (*mine* — RDW)

In view of the autonomy of the syntactic sphere from other modes of operating and of its partial disjunction with the syntactic sphere, one is strongly tempted to give credence to the insistence of various modern writers on linguistics that language is an innate pattern, based on innate "ideas" that are gradually differentiated into the rules of grammer. (Bruner, 1966; 47-48)

One of the striking observations Bruner makes regarding these instruments of intellect, these plans, these techniques of representation, is that — except perhaps for enactive representation — they could possibly not "occur." Ikonic representation would begin but could remain locked in by the strategy of attending only or mostly to surface features on grouping. Symbolic representation, too, would begin — language certainly — but could remain locked in by the strategy of attending only or mostly to the goals of communication and conformity that language makes possible, but not to the goal of thinking. It is this observation that makes Bruner's techniques of representation something like decision-making acts, strategies, tactics, for intellectual development. The wrong tactics can knock a pupil out of the race. The right ones help him win the race. If the rules are obeyed, Piaget will permit the runner to go faster:

The development of intelligence, as it emerges from the recent research just described, is dependent upon natural, or spontaneous, processes, in the sense that they may be utilized and accelerated by education at home or in school but that they are not derived from that education and, on the contrary, constitute the preliminary and necessary condition of efficacity in any form of instruction. (Piaget, 1970b; 36)

As plans, modes of representation are put to use to serve certain purposes, the most important of which, for the heuristic model, are the translation or transformation of one mode of representation to another. (Bruner, 1966; 11, 48-49) This is a two-step process. A mode of representation guides behavior: doing, sensing, and symbolizing. The behavior in turn, creates a representation. When a mode of representation guides behavior other than the behavior specific to it, then the new kind of behavior creates the representation specific to *it*. Suppose the teacher says, "Point to the ship" or "Point to the sheep," the student's looking is guided by language, and the looking creates an ikonic representation.

It should be evident that the transformation of one mode of representation to another is a combination of tactics that could just possibly accelerate the pace of a student in the race of learning. All possible transformational combinations are available to the child of school age, to the bilingual learner as well as to the monolingual. Indeed, the Navajo child has a potential advantage: he can combine the awareness of the structure of the second language (specifically, its syntax) that comes from his deliberate learning of it with an awareness of thought processes as isomorphic to that structure — if the curriculum provides him with "special training in the symbolic representation of experience."

From all this, from Piaget and Bruner (as I understand them), the pupil is to be taken as central: his is the ability and the willingness to initiate and incorporate learning; his are the acts that initiate and incorporate learning; his is the culture or cultures that measure his learning. Thus, that the *learner* learns is one of the assumptions. Also, that the learner *learns*.

But does the learner learn *enough*? Or, does the learner learn *well enough*? That is, on his own? In other words, can he construct a model of his experience with *all* three modes of representation? Put differently, can he reach his full intellectual potential as *homo sapiens* on his own?

> Then, if the child lives in an advanced society...he becomes "operational" (to use the Genevan term for thinking symbolically), and by age five, six, or seven, given cultural supports [*mine* — RDW] he is able to apply the fundamental rules of category, hierarchy, function, and so forth, to the world as well as his words. Let us be explicit, however, that if he is growing up in a native village of Senegal (Chapters 11 and 13), among native Eskimos (Chapter 13), or in a rural mestizo village in Mexico (Chapter 12), he may not achieve this "capacity." Instead, he may remain at a level of manipulation of the environment that is concretely ikonic and strikingly lacking in symbolic structures — though his language may be stunningly exquisite in these regards. (Bruner, 1966; 46)

(Whether one of the "cultural supports" needed, even in an "advanced" society, is teaching, and specifically teaching that provides "special training in the symbolic representation of experience," is the theme of another paper.)

IV   STIPULATION: THE CONDITIONS FOR LEARNING[11]

A learning assumption, one remembers from section II, postulates that an interpretation on the part of the learner will generate learning of some kind. The interpretation on the part of the learner is input in a learning assumption but output in an instructional hypothesis, which, one remembers, predicts the condition under which the learner's (appropriate) interpretation is likely to be secured. This section of the paper reviews those interpretations of the assumptions of the curriculum that are derivable from the learning theories discussed in the preceding section. How the interpretations from these learning assumptions are made manifest in the curriculum will be phrased as instructional hypotheses.

It will help at this point to observe that Bruner's term, "representation," and my term, "interpretation," are equivalent. Also, Piaget's view of the learner as the "center of functional activity," i.e., as the source of learning acts, constitutes a representation the learner has of himself; otherwise, it would not be within him to be willing to learn. In my terms, the learner interprets — sees, feels, intuits — himself as the agent of learning.

The first learning assumption, then, is that the learner who sees himself as a decision-making agent of learning is willing to learn. (His willingness to learn is actualized into learning when other conditions for learning are present, but these other conditions are not relevant here except as they appear below in the explanation of the instructional hypotheses.) Two of the instructional hypotheses that express this learning assumption in the curriculum are volunteering and breaks. Volunteering was explained in section II under the heading, "The tasks of formulation and reformulation." Breaks predicts that pupils who are given an opportunity to decide whatever they want to do or to choose among several activities will see themselves as decision-making agents of learning. The curriculum provides for break time after each and every lesson. The children's decisions fall into two classes: problem-finding, i.e., deciding whatever they want to do, and problem-solving, i.e., choosing among several activities much like those independent problem-solving tasks found in Montessori classrooms. The realia for the breaks fall into the same two classes. For example, in the problem-solving category, a jigsaw puzzle may be chosen instead of a pair of cubes with matching equivalent number sentences. If a child chooses the jigsaw puzzle, he obligates himself to put the pieces together and form the expected picture. On the other hand, if the jigsaw puzzle is in the problem-finding category, a child who chooses that may also put the pieces together to form the expected picture, or he might stack them up to see how high they will go (or for whatever reason he may have in mind), or he might deploy them on the floor, imagining them to be horsemen on a hunt, etc.

Another assumption stems from the learner's actions, a basic concept in Piaget's theory:

> . . .the essential fact. . .is that knowledge is derived from action, not in the sense of simple associative responses, but in the much deeper sense of the assimilation of reality into the necessary and general coordinations of action. To know an object is to act upon it and to transform it. . .To know is. . .to assimilate reality into structures of transformation, and these are the structures that intelligence constructs as a direct extension of our actions.
> The fact that intelligence derives from action. . .leads up to this fundamental consequence: even in its higher manifestations, when it can only make further progress by using the instruments of thought, intelligence still consists in executing and coordinating actions, though in an interiorized and reflexive form. . .intelligence, at all levels, is an assimilation of the datum into structures of transformations, from the structures of elementary actions to the higher operational structures, and that these structurations consist in an organization of reality, whether in act or thought, and not in simply making a copy of it.
> (Piaget, 1970b; 28-29)

What this implies is that a pupil need not actually participate in the condition-response situation of a lesson himself but that he participate in such wise that the "condition-response" fact is acted upon and transformed by him. This provides the curriculum with the learning assumption that the pupil who accurately interprets the response of another pupil as either correct or incorrect himself assimilates the response. The mental transformation consists in rendering the expected response in the form of an evaluation. Observe that this rendering need not occur overtly and needs only to be intended for some sort of transformation to take place and make the response a part of the evaluating pupil. The instructional hypothesis that expresses this learning assumption in the curriculum is evaluation. It predicts that pupils who have been taught to expect to be asked to evaluate the response of another will interpret the response of the other pupil as correct or incorrect. It should be noted that this instructional hypothesis effects the promise of the learning assumption only for those pupils who evaluate accurately. For those who do not, another instructional hypothesis (actually a subsystem of instructional hypotheses), correction, provides the desired learning. One of the teaching techniques for implementing evaluation is simply to call on another pupil, selecting on a random basis, to evaluate the response of the (overtly) participating pupil by saying, "Is that right? " Because this is done virtually all the time, day in and day out, the procedure becomes an accepted convention to the point of being taken for granted. Any use of the procedure to embarrass an erring child would not be due to the procedure as such but to the deliberate lack of charity of the abuser — if it ever happens. Notice, too, that such a convention gets all the pupils in the class to expect to evaluate at any time, making them participate vicariously as evaluators until one of them is chosen (randomly) to overtly evaluate: everyone learns.

Bruner's three modes of representation are classes of representations, taking their form in the curriculum in many different ways. The enactive mode is particularly useful in the pronunciation and rhetoric (in the first level, dramatics) strands. The ikonic mode is itself the objective of the visual strand. The symbolic mode is a major objective of the entire curriculum. To explore their systematization and implementation in the curriculum is too formidable a task at present. Suffice it to say that they constitute a major portion of the system of learning assumptions on which the curriculum is based.

However, one learning assumption from Bruner's theory is too interesting to ignore. And that is: the pupil who interprets language as an instrument of thought becomes a willing builder of symbolic representation. Bruner motivates this assumption as follows:

> Once language is applied, then it is possible, by using language as an instrument, to scale to higher levels. In essence, once we have coded

experience in language, we can (but not necessarily do) read surplus
meaning into the experience by pursuing the built-in implications of the
rules of language. (*mine* — RDW 1966; 51)

In other words, language is not necessarily applied as an instrument of
thought, that is, language is not necessarily used to read surplus meaning into
an experience. But, because the rewards are so great and inherent in the act
itself and because symbolic representation is a natural ability available to
homo sapiens, a realization of language as an instrument of thought should
succeed in persuading the student to use language to structure his world in
terms of symbolic representation.

One instructional hypothesis that grows out of this learning assumption
is the prediction that pupils who are constantly expected to verbalize their
school learning experience will interpret language as an instrument of
thought. Obviously, this does not prevent the children from interpreting
language as a means of communication or a form of conformity. The
deliberate implementation of this instructional hypothesis in a technical
society might not seem too useful to Bruner:

What has become much plainer to us in the course of our work is that
there are important institutions and pressures that develop within
societies of the technical type, which lead to the demand for
confirmation between the three modes of knowing. Whenever learning
occurs outside the context it will be used, outside the range of events
that are directly supportive in a perceptual way or indirectly available
for pointing, then language enters as a means of conveying the content
of experience and of action. Under these circumstances, there is more
often than not a requirement of developing correspondence between
what we do, what we see, and what we say. It is this correspondence
that is most strikingly involved in reading and writing, in "school
learning," and in other abstract pursuits. The confrontation may not
always work its way to correspondence, to be sure. (1966; 321-322)

Still, his last statement, the risk of not achieving the correspondence
between enactive or ikonic representation and language, is enough
motivation for the instructional hypothesis. The odds may be good, but the
stakes are high. An even more important motivation for the instructional
hypothesis, however, is to effect another related learning assumption as well:
the pupil who constantly interprets language as an instrument of thought
learns to prefer symbolic representation over the other two modes of
representation. (Other instructional hypotheses maintain a sense of
importance for the other two modes of representation: for the enactive
mode in strands requiring performance, e.g., music and rhetoric, and for the
ikonic mode in strands requiring visual structure, e.g., geometry, rhetoric
(stage layouts with make-believe props), and art activities.

The implementation of this instructional hypothesis in the curriculum
is thorough. Virtually every lesson presents its objective perceptually with
very carefully selected sentences to express it. The lessons that require action
also provide the necessary language. Many lessons need to set up situations
and the teachers use imperatives to direct the students in the set-up. Most of
the lessons expect the students to generate questions about actions or scenes

previously associated with language of their own so that transformation from imperatives or statements to questions are the order of the day. And most importantly, this instructional hypothesis is supported by another instructional hypothesis, correction, which gives priority to semantic errors over grammatical or phonological ones. In other words, the correction procedure is primarily aimed at structuring experience, and structuring it symbolically, I might add.

V   LIMITATION: THE SITUATIONS OF LEARNING

Situation is context. It is a limitation only in the sense that a general theory of instruction needs to be transformed to be effective and efficient in a particular situation. Changing a situation can be one of the objectives of a theory of instruction, for example, the design of a school building could be changed to better serve learning. Still, changing the situation is but a preliminary step if and when it can be done. Very soon, and in some cases at once, attempts to change the situation cease. At this point the situation is a given. And it is neutral. Wailing and complaining about the situation may be effective for the long run, but for the here and now it is inefficient.

Situation is not always a handicap. In the case of Navajo children in American schools, creating a bilingual and bicultural situation, the situation provides opportunities for the Navajo pupil that are not available to his monolingual-monocultural fellow American. The bilingual situation provides the Navajo pupil with the opportunity to better develop symbolic representation. The theory of instruction should take advantage of this opportunity by providing the already predisposed pupil with an ESL course of study that elicits a deliberate learning of the second language. And it should take the same advantage of the opportunity in the other areas of the curriculum, emphasizing even more the deliberate learning of the semantics of the new language. L.S. Vygotsky, in his impressive work, *Thought and Language*, remarks:

> Specifically, our experiments brought out the following inter-related facts: The psychological prerequisites for instruction in different school subjects are to a large extent the same; instruction in a given subject influences the development of the higher functions far beyond the confines of that particular subject; the main psychic functions involved in studying various subjects are interdependent — their common bases are consciousness and deliberate mastery, the principal contributors of the school years. (1962, 102)
>
> [Our] chief purpose was to test experimentally our working hypothesis of the development of scientific concepts compared with everyday concepts...Analysis of the data compared separately for each age group...showed that as long as the curriculum supplies the necessary material, the development of scientific concepts runs ahead of the development of spontaneous concepts. (1962, 106)
>
> ...though he can correctly answer questions about "slavery," "exploitation," or "civil war," these concepts are schematic and lack the rich content derived from personal experience. They are filled in

gradually, in the course of further schoolwork and reading. One might say that the development of the child's spontaneous concepts proceeds upward, and the development of his scientific concepts downward, to a more elementary and concrete level. This is a consequence of the different ways in which the two kinds of concepts emerge.

In working its slow way upward, an everyday concept clears a path for the scientific concept and its downward development. It creates a series of structures necessary for the evolution of a concept's more primitive, elementary aspects, which give it body and vitality. Scientific concepts in turn supply structures for the upward development of the child's spontaneous concepts toward consciousness and deliberate use. (1962, 108-109)

The influence of scientific concepts on the mental development of the child is analogous to the effect of learning a foreign language, a process which is conscious and deliberate from the start. (1962, 109)

The bicultural situation provides the Navajo pupil with an even more impressive opportunity. Consider what one culture does for an individual: "Insofar as man's powers are expressed and amplified through the instruments of culture, the limits to which he can attain excellence of intellect must surely be as wide as are the culture's combined capabilities." (Bruner, 1966, 326) Imagine what two cultures could do for the individual. Consider further the rare opportunity of perceiving not just the differences between the two cultures but the deep similarities as well. In so doing the Navajo child might wonder if the similarities aren't accidental, that perhaps, just perhaps, the similarities reflect genuine human values. And one day someone will make a chance remark like "We are all brothers under the skin," a cliché, nothing more: but the Navajo child, now a little grown, will read surplus meaning into it.

NOTES

[1] The original invitation by Allen Yazzie, former education officer of the Navajo Tribe, for me to participate in what is now known as the Rough Rock project eventually led to the decisions by Dr. William Benham of the Navajo Area Office of the Bureau of Indian Affairs for me to design and direct a thousand-participant workshop, two workshops for academic administrators, and the development and implementation of the bilingual-bicultural curriculum (one of the number of curricula available to his teachers) discussed in this paper.

CITE (Inc.), for Consultants In Total Education, was formed to facilitate the legal and financial processes required in undertakings such as this. Materials and services from CITE include the following: (1) Planned programs for 160 effective teaching days (approximately 1000 separate lessons) per school year for each grade level. These are produced in approximately 30 manuals. Each lesson is essentially a complete plan for the teacher and aide, including specifications of materials to be used, staging, and a brief explanation of the theory behind the instruction. Specific visuals (picture materials) and other realia are also furnished. (2) In-service training of teachers and aides. Planned in the context of specific objectives, this training provides the teacher/aide team with appropriate practice in the use of the curricula and supplies evaluation of post instruction behavior of the team as learners. Training takes the form of a summer workshop and a midyear workshop as well as clinical supervision by CITE staff and CITE-trained supervisors from the U.S. Bureau of Indian Affairs.

[2] "In the Rizal statistics there are strong implications that the degree of mastery of a language (be it Pilipino or English) that a pupil achieves depends much more on extensive use of the language than on direct language instruction. The evidence is particularly clear with regard to the mother tongue, which is, of course, almost the only language the average pupil uses outside of school hours. Conclusion 2 of the Rizal experiment states: 'The average level of literacy in Tagalog (Pilipino) *is not* closely related to the number of years in which it has been used as a medium of instruction.' In other words, the pupil learns his mother tongue largely by using it to satisfy his normal nonacademic needs for communication. With regard to the second language, Conclusion 1 states: 'Proficiency in English *is* directly related to the number of years in which it is used as the medium of classroom instruction.' A little reflection seems to resolve the apparent contradiction. It is in his subject-matter classes that the Filipino child gets his best opportunity to use English for communication purposes." (Prator, 1967; vi)

[3] Except for the limitations due to the level of funding; but this was adequate if not generous.

[4] The level of performance is also systemic, requiring a coordination of

skills and a recurring pattern of such coordination in order for the performance to be effective and consistently effective. This is implied in the section, "the task of improving performance." The reason for discussing performance separately from the other levels is that the others are more amenable to analytic systematization while performance is more amenable to synthetic systematization.

[5] Perhaps, if the children in group B through E are self-teaching rather than simply keeping out of the teacher's way with busy work, some amount of increased learning can be claimed; that is, if.

[6] No one instructional hypothesis can dominate all of the class time; otherwise, other useful hypotheses would have to be excluded. The effectiveness of an instructional hypothesis often depends on the presence of another instructional hypothesis (or more) in the same teaching situation. In this case, randomization is related to volunteering (to be discussed later).

[7] The notion of inference from sample to population (parameter) in experiments on human behavior is currently being debated; cf. Denton E. Morrison and Ramon E. Henkel (eds.), *The Significance Test Controversy*, (1970).

[8] A similar comment was made by Bernard Spolsky in "An Evaluation of Two Sets of Materials for Teaching English as a Second Language to Navajo Beginners," Final Report, U.S. Bureau of Indian Affairs Contract No. N00 C 1420 2415, June 13, 1969. The comment:

> To what extent does a precise curriculum free a teacher, and to what extent does it bind her? A difficult question to answer in the abstract, but in practice much simpler than it appears. An excellent teacher with unlimited preparation time will be more creative with less guidance, but the average teacher, with a full teaching day, performs best when she is called on to "perform" rather than "compose." The musical analogy is reasonable: one senses individual interpretative creativity in a performer of a piece of music rather than in an improviser. In practice, I felt more individual variation, more evidence of teacher personality, in those using the Wilson than in those with. . .materials.

[9] "Having solely a genetic basis. This is what I, and I believe most geneticists and psychologists, ordinarily understand by the term (innate). According to this definition, only the genes are innate." (Braine, 1971; 184)

[10] Though Piaget reportedly "doubts whether. . .enactive representation ought to be called representative at all." (Bruner, 1966; 10).

[11] The title of this section refers to the conditions stipulated in instructional hypotheses. It is intended to emphasize the importance of converting learning assumptions into instructional hypotheses, even in a paper on learning assumptions if the paper is intended as a paper in education. A remark by Bruner is appropriate here:

> One might ask why a theory of instruction is needed, since psychology already contains theories of learning and of development. But theories of learning and of development are descriptive rather than prescriptive. They tell us what happened after the fact; for example, that most children of six do not yet possess the notion of reversibility. A theory

of instruction, on the other hand, might attempt to set forth the best means of leading the child toward the notion of reversibility. A theory of instruction, in short, is concerned with how what one wishes to teach can best be learned, with improving rather than describing learning. (Bruner, 1968; 40)

Bibliography

de Bono, Edward. *Mechanism of Mind.* New York: Simon & Schuster, (1969).

Braine, Martin D.S. "On Two Types of Models of the Internalization of Grammars," In Dan I. Slobin, ed. *The Ontogenesis of Grammar. A Theoretical Symposium.* New York: Academic Press, (1971).

Bruner, Jerome S. *The Process of Education.* Cambridge: Harvard University Press, (1960).

Bruner, Jerome S., Rose R. Olver, and Patricia N. Greenfield, *et al. Studies in Cognitive Growth.* New York: John Wiley & Sons, (1966).

Bruner, Jerome S. *Toward a Theory of Instruction.* New York: W.W. Norton & Co., (1968).

———. *The Relevance of Education.* New York: W.W. Norton & Co., (1971).

Chomsky, Noam. *Language and Mind.* New York: Harcourt, Brace & World, (1968).

Lenneberg, Eric H. *Biological Foundations of Language.* New York: John Wiley & Sons, (1967).

Miller, George A., Eugene Glanter, and Karl H. Pribram. *Plans and Structure of Behavior.* New York: Henry Holt & Co., (1960).

Morrison, Denton E., and Ramon E. Henkel (eds).*The Significance Test Controversy.* Chicago: Aldine Publishing Co., (1970).

Piaget, Jean. *Structuralism.* New York: Basic Books, (1970).

———. *Science of Education and the Psychology of the Child.* New York: Orion Press, (1970).

Prator, Clifford H. "Development of a Manipulation Communication Scale," In R. Fox, ed., *1964 Conference Papers, NAFSA,* (1965).

———. Foreword to Frederick B. Davis. *Philippine Language-Teaching Experiments.* Quezon City, Phil: Phoenix Press, (1967).

Spolsky, Bernard. "An Evaluation of Two Sets of Materials for Teaching English as a Second Language to Navajo Beginners," Final Report, BIA Contract No. N00 C 1420 2415, June 13, (1969).

Vygotsky, L.S. *Thought and Language.* Boston and New York: M.I.T. Press and John Wiley & Sons, (1962).

Wilson, Robert, *et al. Guide for Teaching English as a Second Language to Elementary School Pupils.* ERIC Accession Numbers: ED 018 801 and ED 018 802 (1967).

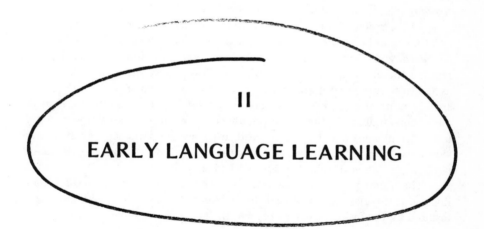

II

EARLY LANGUAGE LEARNING

5

First Language Acquisition of Swedish
Ragnhild Söderbergh

I.   READING IN EARLY CHILDHOOD

Introduction

This paper is a summary of my book *Reading in Early Childhood: A Linguistic Study of a Swedish Pre-school Child's Gradual Acquisition of Reading Ability* (Stockholm: Almqvist & Wiksell, 1971).

I have studied closely a child learning to read from the age of two years and four months by the method described by Glenn Doman in his book *How to Teach your Baby to Read* (New York: Random House, 1964). By this method the child learns whole words as entities. I have shown how the child, as it learns more and more words, gradually breaks down these words into smaller units: first morphemes, then graphemes. At last the child arrives at an understanding of the correspondence between sound (phoneme) and letter (grapheme) and is able to read any new word through analysis and synthesis. In my experiment this stage is reached after fourteen months of reading, i.e., when the child is three and a half years old.

The findings of this study have been viewed in the light of recent linguistic theories as presented by research workers in child language, inspired by Chomsky — such as Brown, Bellugi, and Lenneberg.

1.   Learning to read: Theories and methods confronted with different linguistic theories.

In this chapter a short summary is given of the debate on reading in the USA in the 1950's. The author's main source here has been Jeanne Chall, *Learning to Read: The Great Debate* (New York: McGraw-Hill, 1967).

According to Jeanne Chall there are, theoretically, two dominating methods in reading instruction, the phonics method and the reading-for-meaning method. In practice, however, there is often a mixture between the two.

The pure phonics method implies that the pupil is taught the letters of the alphabet and the corresponding sounds. Then he is taught to read by "sounding and blending," i.e., he sounds out the new words and then synthesizes the sounds so that the right word is produced.

The sponsors of the reading-for-meaning method oppose this, as they think, unnatural and boring way of reading and instead teach whole words and sentences from the very beginning, thus giving their pupils at once the experience of what are the ultimate goals of reading: comprehension, appreciation, and, finally, application.

In the pure phonics method the child is presented with the code and taught how to use it. In the extreme reading-for-meaning method the child is not taught the code.

Jeanne Chall has summarized the results of recent research in England and the USA on methods in beginning reading and arrives at the following conclusions: "Early stress on code learning. . .not only produces better word recognition and spelling, but also makes it easier for the child eventually to read with understanding" (Chall, p. 83).

Chall gains support for the view that an early acquisition of the code is necessary also from the theoretical considerations of linguists, particularly Leonard Bloomfield and Charles C. Fries. These linguists, however, both consider written language as secondary to and completely dependent on spoken language. Bloomfield is apt to disregard written language altogether, from a scientific, linguistic point of view: "Writing is not language but merely a way of recording language by means of visible marks" (*Language*, p. 21).

Bloomfield was the linguistic pioneer of his time, and his views dominate the opinions of many linguists during the 1940's and 1950's. Recently, however, the written language has been considered an object worthy of investigation independently of the corresponding spoken language. There has been a strong tendency among linguists towards stressing the differences between the two codes, differences not only on the phonemic-graphemic level but also as regards morphemics and syntax. Linguists have even claimed that written language should be considered as a more or less independent system. (See Sture Allén, W. Nelson Francis, H.A. Gleason, and H.J. Uldall.)

The current trend in linguistics represented by Chomsky and his school has more or less revolutionized the ideas about language learning and language acquisition. According to Chomsky, we have a biologically founded innate capacity for language. This means that when a child is exposed to language he does not just imitate but attacks the language he is being exposed to, observing it and constructing hypotheses about it. He builds his own model of the language, working out his own linguistic system consisting of sets of rules which are gross approximations of the correct system. As he is exposed to more and more linguistic material and as he is able to test his model by actual use of the rules when speaking, these rules are continually reconstructed and modified until, finally, the model becomes identical with the normal adult model. Chomsky's theories have been partly verified by many studies on child language presented during the 1960's, by Roger Brown, Ursula Bellugi, Colin Fraser, Paula Menyuk, and others. Belief in the biological foundations of language has been convincingly advocated also by Lenneberg in a book so titled which appeared in 1967. According to Lenneberg, it is indisputable that the onset of speech and of certain linguistic abilities such as babbling, speaking isolated words, producing two-word sentences, etc., are determined by maturational processes (Lenneberg, pp. 127 f.).

The maturational processes and the innate capacity that cause children to start learning to speak at a certain age (18-28 months) without any form of instruction — the only requirement being that they are exposed to language — should also explain why this highly complicated learning process is being completed so quickly; within a period of two years all basic syntactic constructions of the language are mastered by the child.

Now, if a child learns to talk at a certain age without formal instruction, solely by being exposed to language, and if written language is to be considered as an independent system, why cannot a child learn to read at the same age and in the same way as he is learning to talk, solely by being exposed to written language? He would then be supposed to attack the written material, forming hypotheses, building models, all by himself, discovering the code of the written language, of its morphematic, syntactic, and semantic systems, etc.

That this is possible we know from the fact that some children learn to read "all by themselves," i.e., just by observing a text while listening to other people reading it.

In a talk given at the annual meeting of American reading specialists in Boston, in April 1968, Professor Arthur I. Gates, one of the foremost reading specialists in the United States, said that a recently finished investigation in the USA has shown that 80 percent of the children beginning school in the USA can read a certain number of words. There are also facts revealed in this investigation that hint at the possibility that very soon children will learn to read exactly in the same way as they now learn to understand and express themselves in spoken language, i.e., by living a normally active and verbal life.

That children can learn to read at an early age without real instruction is well known, but how children succeed in doing so has not yet been systematically studied. The chief interest then, when the child is learning to read a language written with an alphabet, must be centered on the following question: How does the child on its own discover the relations between letters (graphemes) and sounds (phonemes)? Not until these correspondences are evident to the child can he be said to have achieved full reading ability, i.e., to be able to read any word irrespectively of whether he has seen that word earlier or not.

2. The aim of this treatise. Method used in the experiment

The author decided to teach a child to read from about the age of two in a way that resembles as much as possible the way in which spoken language is acquired, i.e., to present (written) words and sentences in such contexts as to make clear the meaning of these words and sentences. Then the author intended to study the process by which the child arrives at full reading ability, i.e., at the understanding of the correspondences between letters and sounds.

For me to be able to follow this process, however, the child must in some way communicate it to me. The most reasonable way of communication, then, seemed to be through speech; the child must read aloud, which meant that I had to present written language to the child through the medium of spoken language, by showing written words and telling what they said. But this had to be done with an absolute minimum of instruction. To this end I chose the Doman method.

For the benefit of the reader, I shall here give an account of Doman's method, trying to analyze it and to state in what respects it might accord with or violate our principle of "free exposure" without inflicting any instruction on the child.

Words are written on cards, one word on each card. To begin with the letters should be red and 12.5 cm.-high.[1] The cards are presented to the child at a maximum rate of one a day.

The first word is *mother*. When the child says "mother" as soon as you show that card, you go to the next card, which reads *father*. When you are sure that the child can discriminate the "mother" card from the "father" card, you proceed to nouns denoting parts of the body (*hand, nose, ear,* etc.). These words are written with 10 cm.-high, red letters. Then you go on to what Doman calls the vocabulary of the home: words denoting the child's toys and other personal belongings, words denoting well known things in the house, etc. The child should be able to see and touch the thing at the same time as the "teacher" pronounces the word and shows the card to him.[2]

The domestic vocabulary also includes some verbs denoting simple actions well known to the child. The teacher may, to begin with, illustrate a verb by performing the action at the same time as he pronounces the corresponding word and shows the card. The domestic vocabulary should be written down in red letters 7.5 cm.-high.

All the time the "teacher" should be careful not to go on presenting new words without making sure that the child recognizes the old ones.

Then a book is provided. It should be a very simple and short book, not containing more than 150 different words. The letters should be 3/4 cm.-high.

The "teacher" copies the book, rewriting it in black letters 2.5

cm.-high. Then each word is written on a card, in 5 cm.-high, *black* letters. These cards are presented to the child one by one in the same way as before.

When the child knows all the words, the words are put together to form the sentences of the book. The cards are put on the floor side by side, and the child now learns to read sentences, one sentence a day. When the child can read all the sentences of the book in this way, he is given the handwritten copy of the book and is taught to read the sentences from this copy, reading left to right, from the top of the page to the bottom of the page.

When the child is thoroughly familiar with this handwritten copy, the printed book is presented to him. And now he will be able to read this fluently, in spite of the fact that the letters are only 3/4 cm.-high.[3]

You go on with other books, and now it is not necessary to have an intermediate handwritten copy. All words new to the child are written down on cards and shown to him. When the child knows these words, he gets the new book.

After the child has read one or two books, you write down the alphabet, small letters and capitals, each letter on one card. You present the cards to the child, telling him the names of the letters like this: about *a* "This is a small /ei/," about *A* "This is a capital /ei/" etc.

It is to be observed that the child is not taught the sound values of the letters but is just given the conventional names — with the qualifier *small* and *capital* included in the name of the letter. This is obviously done to help the child to discern the letters within the word units.

By presenting the letters you no doubt draw the child's attention to the code. But as one avoids any kind of sounding and instead obscures what associations there might occur between letter and sound by adding the qualifier "small" and "capital" to the conventional name of the letter, this presentation cannot be said to help the child to discover the relation between letters and sounds. Nor, as the letters are presented in their alphabetical order without being grouped according to distinctive features, do you give any hint about the graphematic system; instead the child is left to make the discoveries totally on his own.

The real instruction given is purely technical and nonlinguistic. The child is taught to read from left to right and from the top of the page to the bottom. The child is taught to turn the pages right-left.

By using the Doman method you *leave it to the child* to find out the interrelation between the codes of the written language and of the spoken language all by himself.

The Doman method is, then, a way of presenting written material to a child *with a minimum of instruction and through the medium of the spoken language*.

Using the Doman method, it is therefore possible to make observations about how a child discovers the correspondence between letters and sounds, how he succeeds in interrelating the graphematic and the phonematic systems — in "breaking the code" — which is the necessary prerequisite if he is to attain full reading ability.

3. The experiment

The experiment started at the end of September 1965. A girl, two years and four months old, was taught to read. During the first six weeks she was shown 50 concrete nouns and verbs.

From the middle of November the vocabulary of the first book was shown to her, and the girl read this book on the 22nd of December 1965. The experiment was then continued with new books. All the time notes were taken about the girl's reactions and comments on reading cards and reading.

At the beginning of March 1966, the girl spontaneously tried to read some of the new cards I presented to her. These readings were noted down. At the beginning of April 1966 these spontaneous readings had become so frequent that I changed the method of showing new cards. Instead of taking a new card and saying "This reads X," I took the new card, showed it to her and asked "What does this read?" Often she suggested many different readings. Every attempt at reading was carefully noted down. In cases where the girl did not succeed in arriving at a correct reading, I finally read the cards aloud to her.

In August there was no reading because of my holidays. On September 1st the experiment was continued. At the beginning of November 1966 the child was able to read almost any new word presented to her on a card: the code had been broken.

From the beginning of December 1966 the child was given new books directly, without the intermediate stage of showing cards. The girl read the books aloud to me and I took notes. Some grapho-phonematic irregularities in Swedish (such as the spelling of /ç/) were not mastered by the girl until the autumn of 1967.

4. First period: From the first word to the first book

From the very first day the girl was enthusiastic about the reading cards. She treated the cards as if they actually were the persons or things written on them. The cards with *mormor* (grandmother) and *morfar* (grandfather) became favorites, and words with unpleasant associations were met with disgust ("Mother, I get so frightened when it says *frightful* on a reading card.").

When we started with the vocabulary of the first book, the girl was shown a few so-called functors (prepositions, conjunctions, pronouns, etc.). These turned out to be difficult to grasp. It is to be observed that children learning to talk acquire the often unstressed functors later than nouns, verbs, and adjectives, which normally have heavy stress (cf. Roger Brown and Ursula Bellugi, "Three Processes in the Child's Acquisition of Syntax"

[1964]).

Already at the end of the first reading month the girl observed similarities between different words: "Mother, *mage* (stomach) is like *öga* (eye)."

In the third month of reading the girl learnt the word *precis*. She then observed: *"precis* liknar *pappa" (precis* is like *pappa),* pointing at the *p* in *precis,* "men i *pappa* e de tre stycken" (but in *pappa* there are three of them).

This shows three things: (1) She was able to discern the letter *p* in *precis* and looked on it as an entity. (2) She was able to identify and sum up three samples of the same entity. (3) She had a visual image of the word *pappa* that was strong enough to enable her to pick out the three *p*'s in it.

The visual image of the word *pappa* must have been very clear. This does not imply, however, that all the other words the girl was able to recognize were necessarily as clear in her visual memory. *Pappa* belonged to the early words; it does contain only two different kinds of letters; it is symmetrically built up with the double *p* surrounded by *a's* on each side; and it appealed to the girl's emotions.

Nevertheless her observations on *precis* and *pappa* give us a cue to the process behind the acquisition of reading ability: words are learnt visually and stored. As soon as a new word is introduced, this word is not only "put into the bag" but it is analyzed and compared with the visual images of the words learnt before. By means of such comparisons structure is discovered.

Further evidence of this process is that the girl, when she was shown a new word that very much resembled an earlier learned one, often told me to show her this earlier word. On being shown the new word *det* she said *"det* is like *dem,* show *dem* to me and let us compare."

5.   Second period (Dec. 23rd 1965-March 31st 1966): The first attempts at spontaneous reading of new words

During this period functors still seemed to be a bit difficult, but the girl solved the problem by immediately putting them into a linguistic context. On getting *fram* (along) she said "Vi går fram" (We go along). Many other examples can be given.

From the beginning of March the girl made spontaneous efforts to read new words by herself.

The new words that the girl tried to read were all made up of material from words learnt earlier, i.e., they might be: (1) parts of already learnt words, (2) combinations of words and/or parts of words learnt before.

The method of putting all the words of the books on reading cards gave me a complete index to the child's reading vocabulary. This enabled me to find very easily the patterns for every attempted independent reading of a new word.

According to how the girl made use of already learned material when trying to read new words, the attempted readings could be divided into three groups, here called adjunctions, deletions, and substitutions.

Adjunctions

On the 1st of March the girl was shown the new word *bäcken* and read it correctly. Earlier she had learnt to read *bäck*. The rest of the word was also well known to her as she had already met *en* as an indefinite article eleven times in her first book. I assume the underlying process producing the correct reading *bäcken* to be as follows.

1. First *bäcken* is analyzed into two parts, *bäck* and *en*. The child is able to make this analysis because she is well acquainted with these parts as written entities.

2. The two parts are then read together, forming a spoken entity that is well known to the child and immediately associated with a meaning.

3. Thus the new graphic entity *bäcken* is tied to the corresponding spoken entity and is associated with the same meaning, all without the intervention of the teacher.

Putting the stress on the second step in the process, which is the adding up of already known entities, we call this reading adjunction.

In the examples given above two parts already learned as separate graphic entities are put together. A more complicated kind of adjunction was made for the first time at the end of March, when the new word *pengarna* was read correctly. Earlier the girl had learnt to read *pengar*. But the rest of the word, *-na*, does not occur as an isolated entity; it is a so-called bound morpheme, functioning as a definite article in the plural: *pojkarna, flickorna, ballongerna*, etc. The adjunction here implies putting together one entity already learnt as a "word image" with another entity that is only a part of word images learnt before.

To be able to read *pengarna* the child must thus be able to recognize *-na* from previously learnt written words with this ending, i.e., she must already have made a grapho-morphemic analysis of these words.

At the moment of the independent correct reading of *pengarna* the girl had already met the following words ending in *-na: tassarna, kattungarna, fjärilarna, fåglarna, grodorna, insekterna, blommorna*. The question is now: How did she succeed in distinguishing *-na* as an entity?

Above we have shown that as soon as the girl learnt a new word, she compared this word with similar ones learnt earlier and tried to find out the differences between them. In two of the books read by the girl before she made the correct reading *pengar-na* she had met the word *kattungar*, which word appeared twice before she met *kattungarna* (compare above!). In the word pair *kattungar - kattungarna* the only difference is *-na*, and as soon as the child had found this out she had in fact made the grapho-morphemic analysis necessary to look at *-na* as an entity within the higher units *tassarna, kattungarna, fjärilarna*, etc.

Theoretically she would now be able to read any previously learnt word + *na*.

Deletions

On the 2nd of March the girl read the new word *ugglan*. Earlier she had learnt *ugglans*. To make such a reading the girl must be able to analyze *ugglans* into *ugglan* + *-s*, an analysis made possible by pairs occurring earlier, such as *Anna - Annas*, *Astrid - Astrids*, *Mirran - Mirrans*, etc. I assume the underlying process to be as follows:

1. *ugglan* calls up the mental image of *ugglans*, learnt earlier;

2. *ugglan* is compared with *ugglans* and the difference is observed;

3. On the basis of pairs like *Anna - Annas*, etc. *-s* has already been identified as a meaningful unit. This helps the reader to analyze *ugglans* into *ugglan* + *-s* and to recognize the new word *ugglan* as *ugglan(s)*.

If we stress this last part of the process we might call the reading deletion.

Substitutions

On the 25th of March the girl was shown the word *hittade*. She read it as *hittde*. Although unsuccessful, this reading was the earliest example of a third type of spontaneous reading on the basis of material learnt earlier.

An already known word was *hittat*. The graphemic sequence *de* was well known as a separate word (she had not met it earlier as a bound morpheme in verbs because her books so far had been written in the present tense). The mental process is assumed to be as follows: When being shown *hittade* the girl remembers first *hittat* then *-de*. She realizes that *hittade* is *hittat* minus something at the end plus *-de*, and she then deletes *-at* and adds *-de*, that is substitutes *-de* for *-at* getting the (incorrect) form *hittde*. This reading might thus be called a substitution.

Adjunctions, deletions, and substitutions are the result of an analysis of the presented words; we therefore choose to call these readings analytical readings.

During this period the girl also made technical progress in reading aloud.

When reading her first book the girl had been taught to point at the words. This was to accustom her to the left-to-right convention and to make sure that she did not skip any words.

On the 4th of March I noticed the girl sitting in a corner reading a book that she had finished a fortnight earlier. She read it whispering and without pointing. About three weeks later (March 23rd) she had just finished the reading cards of another book and was going to read it aloud to me for the first time. She then read it without pointing. I did not make any comments to her about this, but I noticed that her reading now was much more like natural speech. When pointing she had been apt to make pauses between every word. After some minutes, however, she suddenly began to point, then interrupted herself: "No, it is much better not to point." "Much better" probably meant that she experienced reading without pointing as more meaningful. She was then able to take in bigger portions of the text at one time; her eyes could always be a good bit ahead of her voice and so the understanding of the text was better. Evidence of better understanding was the fact that her intonation, stress, and reading rhythm improved when she did not point.

6.   Third period: Misidentifications

From April 1966 the girl is asked to try to read all new words by herself. Generally she makes at least one try to read every word. These tries may be analytical readings — right or wrong. They may also be so-called misidentifications, which means that a new word is mistaken for an already learnt word, as when *mugg* (cup) is taken to be *mun* (mouth) or *sig* (himself) is read *sin* (his). When making misidentification the reader evidently is looking upon the new word as an entity.

It is significant that the proportion of misidentifications — where the new words are treated as entities — to analytical readings remains constant, during April, May, June, July, and September, the analytical readings being 3.5 to 5 times as common as the misidentifications, until the month of October, when the code is broken. Then the analytical readings become 18 times more numerous than the misidentifications.

The reason for this is that in October when the code is broken, i.e., when the girl suddenly understands completely the correspondence between grapheme and phoneme, she begins to use a quite new analytical technique when trying to read new words that cannot be read by means of adjunctions, etc., of previously learnt words or morphemes; she "sounds" the words letter by letter. Earlier, on being asked to read a word that resisted the operations of adjunction, etc., she had often just suggested a word learned previously that looked similar, i.e., made a "misidentification." At the time when, as soon as a difficult new word is attacked, the analytical-synthetical process of identifying graphemes, sounding them, and adding the sounds replaces the mere "looking," we may safely presume that full reading ability is being attained.

Thus the increase in the analytical readings as compared with the misidentifications indicates that in October the girl is reaching the stage of full reading ability.

From what has been said above it might be concluded that the misidentifications are the result of an inferior kind of reading in which a new word is carelessly observed, without any kind of analysis, and mistaken for one learned earlier. This is not true, however. Some of the misidentifications are the result of chance readings, but as a rule they are the outcome of most careful considerations.

An investigation of the misidentifications shows that certain rather constant relations, as to length, letters, and position of letters, exist between a new word given and the word it is wrongly supposed to be.

As to the *length* of a new word given compared with the word it is wrongly supposed to be, the following observations have been made:

1. Out of 121 misidentified words 40 percent (48) have been mistaken for words of exactly the same length and another 35 percent (42) have been mistaken for words that are just one letter shorter or longer. Nineteen percent (23) have been mistaken for words that are two letters shorter or longer and only 6 percent (8) for words that are three to five letters shorter or longer.

2. Words shorter than three letters are not misidentified.

3. A given word that is three letters long or more is never mistaken for a word that is shorter than three letters.

4. Apart from this the length of a word assumed does not seem to differ from the length of the corresponding word given by more than about half the number of the letters in the given word.

5. It is also evident that the shorter a word given, the more often it is mistaken for a word of exactly the same length.

As to the number of letters common to a new word given and the word it is wrongly supposed to be, I have observed that when a new word is mistaken for a previously learnt word, on average 65 percent of the letters in the new word are contained in the previously learnt word it is wrongly supposed to be.

In only 12 out of 121 cases of misidentification is the *order* between the common letters not the same in the new word as in the word it is assumed to be.

At last the author has tried to find a way to measure the degree of similarity (S) between a given word and the word it is assumed to be, a way which takes into account the following facts: length of words, letters in common, order of common letters, and position of common letters.

An investigation shows that this S is surprisingly constant. There is some tendency, however, towards a lesser degree of similarity when the given word becomes longer.

7. Third period: Analytical readings of morphemes

The growing reading skill, that is, the gradual development towards an insight into the grapho-phonematic correspondences, and a capacity for using this insight actively when reading new words, is reflected in the analytical readings. Both independent and dependent morphemes are involved in the processes. Analytical readings with only independent morphemes might be considered as comparatively easy, because these morphemes may occur as separate graphic entities. The handling of dependent morphemes is, however, a bit more complicated, as these only occur tied to other morphemes. The reader must thus be able to abstract the dependent morphemes from previously learnt words in order to cope with them in analytical readings of new words presented.

The dependent morphemes are only gradually mastered. In the table below we have a survey of the use of simple dependent morphemes in analytical readings during the different months. The first appearance of a morpheme is marked with an italicized *x*.

	March	April	May	June	July	Sept.	Oct.
-a	*x*	x	x	x	x	x	x
-an		*x*			x	x	x
-ande				*x*		x	
-ar	*x*	x	x	x	x	x	x
-are			*x*	x		x	x
-d				*x*		x	
-de	*x*	x	x	x	x	x	x
-e			*x*	x	x	x	x
-el							*x*
-en	*x*	x	x	x	x	x	x
-er		*x*	x	x	x	x	x
-et			*x*	x	x	x	x
-ig			*x*				
-ing			*x*				
-is					*x*		
-it					*x*		
-n				*x*	x	x	x
-na	*x*	x	x	x	x	x	x
-or		*x*	x	x	x	x	x
-r		*x*	x	x	x	x	x
-s	*x*		x	x	x	x	x
-t		*x*	x	x	x	x	x
-te				*x*		x	x

When we looked at the analytical readings *pengar* + *na* and *ugglan(s)* above, we found that there were patterns in the earlier reading material which made these readings possible. An investigation of the 23 morphemes in the table above shows that 18 of these have clear patterns in earlier reading material when they appear for the first time in an analytical reading. The five morphemes without immediate patterns (*-ande, -d, -ig, -ing,* and *-is*) might themselves be explained as the result of analytical readings: *-ing* for instance might be looked upon as a deletion *ing(en)*, where *en* (one) has been deleted from *ingen* (nobody).

Dependent morphemes are being used in analytical processes from March and on. As March is the very first month of analytical reading, it is quite evident that the processes themselves (adjunction, deletion, substitution) are very difficult to the reader.

Deletion, however, being a passive process, must be easier than adjunction. In the same way the first part of a substitution (which is in fact a deletion) must be easier than the second part (which is an adjunction). An investigation of the material shows that during March and April dependent morphemes are always introduced in passive processes. From May onward, however, not only morphemes previously introduced figure in the active processes; all "new" morphemes occur directly in adjunctions and in the active part of substitutions. That the reader has attained greater skill in May is also evident from the fact that in this month for the first time we find correct readings of new words containing dependent morphemes without immediate patterns in earlier reading material (compare above).

The reader's growing skill also manifests itself in an ability to cope with more and more complicated structures. In March only single dependent morphemes are used in the analytical readings. But from April strings of morphemes also appear, as when the new *bilarna* is read correctly because the reading material already known contains *bil* and pairs like *boll - bollar*, *klapp - klappar*, *ankor - ankorna*, *blommor - blommorna*, etc., from which the dependent morphemes *-ar* and *-na* might be drawn.

As time passes, more and more strings of dependent morphemes are introduced into the analytical readings. A table of these strings and their occurrence during the different months, with the first appearance of every string denoted by an italicized *x*, looks like this:

	April	May	June	July	Sept.	Oct.
-a-de	x		x	x	x	x
-a-de-s			x			
-an-de-s			x			
-ar-na	x	x		x	x	x
-are-n				x		
-de-s			x			
-en-s				x	x	
-er-na		x				x
-ing-ar				x		
-lig-a		x				
-lig-ast						x
-lig-en						x
-lig-t				x		
-na-de				x		
-na-r					x	
-na-s				x		
-ning-en				x	x	
-ning-s						x
-or-na		x	x			x
-r-na				x		
-st-e					x	

Now, what are the patterns for each one of these strings of dependent morphemes when they first appear in analytical readings?

Three cases occur:

1. There may be patterns for the whole string of morphemes, as when *somliga* (16.5) is read as an adjunction of *som* and *-liga*, where the combination *-lig-a* might by drawn from *vän - vänliga*, which words occur already in March. When there are patterns for the whole string, the analytical reading is mainly of the same kind as where a simple morpheme is involved.

2. The process is more complicated, however, when there are patterns for each one of the morphemes in the string, i.e., the reader must herself combine the parts. This is the case when *bilderna* (22.5) is read as an adjunction of the earlier learnt *bild*, *-er*, mastered in April, and *-na* mastered in March.

3. We have a slightly more complicated case when one or more parts in the string has no immediate patterns but must be produced by means of analytical readings. This happens when, in September, *jätteroligt* is read as an adjunction, where *-lig* must be formed on the basis of the already mastered *-liga* by deleting *-a*.

The material shows that the more complicated types 2 and 3 increase, whereas the easier type 1 decreases as time passes. Now what about the wrong analytical readings? The number is steadily decreasing, from 44 percent in April to 25 percent in October. It should also be noted that the mistakes very seldom occur with the dependent morphemes; in only 13 percent of the analytical readings containing dependent morphemes is there a mistake involved in the reading of a morpheme during April-July; in September the percentage is still lower, only 5. The mistakes instead occur with the bases of the words, as when *gröten* is read *grönen*, i.e., the base *gröt* (porridge) is supposed to be *grön* (green).

8.   Third period: Analytical readings of graphemes

We have observed that the analytical readings start in March with simple morphemes; strings of morphemes do not occur until April and are only gradually mastered. In April there are also instances of readings of "false" morphemes. The word *fönster-ruta* (windowpane) is read as *fönster + ut + a* (window + out + "a"), where the identification of the *a* is made possible by the fact that *-a* has previously been learnt as a dependent morpheme and that *-a* in *fönsterruta* takes the same position as the dependent morpheme *-a* in *grön-a*, *läs-a*, etc. It is a "false" morpheme.

With the "false" morphemes the reader is not supported by the semantic component. To make the reading *fönsterruta* she must depend solely on her knowledge of grapho-phonematic correspondences in certain positions: that, for instance, an *-a* corresponds to an /-a/.

From here it is a short step, however, to the realization that a certain grapheme may correspond to a certain phoneme in many positions, sometimes in any position. When this is realized, the reader has left the morphematic level and has entered the graphematic reading level. A still more advanced stage has been reached when the reader makes analytical readings, using graphemes which are not homographic with morphemes, such as *b, k, l, m.*

A reading is, however, very seldom solely graphematic. Often one or two dependent and/or independent morphemes are involved in the reading process together with one or many graphemes. A reading is, however, considered as graphematic when the child's way of reading or the child's own comments give clear evidence. A few examples should be given.

A misreading may often give us the clue to the reading process, as when *gråta* (weep) is read /grota/, with a short *å*-vowel, which shows that *-åta* has been mistaken for *åtta* (eight), part of the earlier reading material. Thus the reading process must be an adjunction of the grapheme string *gr-* and the independent morpheme (word) *åtta.*

Two or more successive readings might give us the clue. This is the case when *ägg* (egg) is read "lägg...ägg"; the earlier material contains *lägger* (puts) from which the morpheme *-er* is first deleted. Then the grapheme *l* is taken away. Other examples are *länge* read "*hängde...längde*" (*hängde* was part of the old reading material), *bur* read "*bu...bur*" and *brum* "*rum...brum*" (*bu* and *rum* being part of the previous reading material).

Another way of reading which reveals what parts are observed is sectioning. When *musikkår* (band) is read /mɯ:s-i-k-spɔ:r/ (the earlier material contains the words *mɯ:s* (mouse), *i* (in), and *spår* (track)), it is evident that *k* is added as a grapheme to the rest.

The sectioning is a most important criterion of graphematic reading. At the end of October *högre* is read /hø:-gr-e/ in spite of the fact that the earlier reading material contains both *höga* and *högar*, which would lead us to expect the morphematic substitution *hög/a, -re* or *hög/ar, -re.* In this case, however, /hø:gr-e/ is considered to be a graphematic reading on account of the sectioning, although there do exist patterns for a morphematic reading. It is to be observed that not until October do such instances occur.

Sometimes the girl herself reveals, by comments on the reading material, that the patterns she uses are graphematic. The earliest example is from the 16th of May. On being presented with the earlier unknown *parken* the girl reads it correctly. I ask her: "How can you read that?" She answers: "I have had *marken* before." The process must thus be substitution: *m-* in *marken* replaced by *p-.*

Following Sture Allén, the author makes a distinction between autographemes and syngraphemes. In Swedish the autographemes are *a, e, i, o, u, y, å, ä, ö;* the syngraphemes are *b, c, d, f, g, h, j, k, l, m, n, p, q, r, s, t, v, w, x,* and *z.* Then the grapho-phonematic relations in Swedish are discussed.

The author then treats the readings where the girl handles such syngraphemes as are not homographs of morphemes. (The autographemes are excluded for two reasons. First, some of them are homographs of independent or dependent morphemes. Second, all autographemes correspond to one long phoneme-variant which is used when the alphabet is recited.)

Eleven syngraphemes without corresponding homographic morphemes appear in graphematic readings during the period of April-October 1966. In the table below, first appearance has been italicized. If a grapheme only occurs in passive processes during one month — deleted or substituted — it has been put with parentheses.

April	May	June	July	Sept.	Oct.
	p	(p)	p	p	p
b	b	—	b	b	b
	m	—	m	m	m
			v	v	v
				f	f
	k	k	k	k	k
g			g	g	g
			j	j	j
		(h)	*h*	h	h
		l	l	l	l
					c

From the table above we see that more and more syngraphemes without homographic morphemes are used in graphematic readings; in April there are only b and g; then one or two further graphemes are added every month, until in October all 11 syngraphemes are used. It is to be observed that the syngraphemes with one or several phonematic correspondences are always read in the most "normal" way: k is read /k/, g /g/, j /j/, and c /s/.

When a graphematic reading is made, this means that the reader has realized the "sound value" of a grapheme or a sequence of graphemes, which is to say, the grapho-phonematic correspondence in question. Such correspondences must be drawn from the reading material learned earlier. By reading words beginning in ba. . ./ba:/, ba.../bɑ/, bu. . ./buɯ:/, bå. . ./bɔ/, etc., where the second element is an autographeme, the sound value of which is known from the reciting of the alphabet, the specific sound value of b is easily perceived. If we look at the first correct readings of syngraphemes (cf. the table above: b and g in April, p, m, and k in May, etc.) and examine earlier reading material, we will find that there are always clear patterns in this material.

If we look at all the graphematic readings during the April-October period, we shall find that very often there are strong patterns in earlier reading material for exactly the grapho-phonotactic structure of the surroundings of the grapheme thus read. This tendency seems, however, to be weaker in the readings of September and October, which should indicate a growing reading skill where the occurrence of direct patterns is no longer necessary for the reader to produce a correct graphematic reading.

Let us take a few examples. Thirteen graphematic readings of *k* from May to September all have immediate patterns for the grapho-phonotactic structure of the immediate environment of the *k*. We find *k* in the initial combinations *skr-*, *kr-*, *kl-*, *kv-*, *ka-*, *ko-*, in the final combinations *-ka*, *-kade*, *-kar*, *-ken*, and in the medial combinations *-ik-* and *-uk-*. In September, however, the reading /faskiti:sa/ — wrong for *faktiskt* — and in October the reading /k-i:-lade/ for *kilade* show a complete knowledge of the correspondence between *k* and /k/ without the support of surrounding graphemes. A *k* before an *i* being normally pronounced /ç/, there are no patterns for the correspondence *ki* /ki/. In the same way, the reading in October of *förarhytten* as /fø:rarhten/, where the *y* is overlooked, shows a sure knowledge of the correspondence *h* /h/.

The development towards analytical reading on the graphematic level is clearly illustrated by the fact that during the last three days of October the reader overlooks in many cases a more simple way of reading a word — through analysis into morphemes — and makes a more complicated graphematic reading.

As an example might be mentioned the reading of *bakåt*, where the easiest way would have been an adjunction of the well known parts *bak* and *åt*, but where the girl reads the word in three sections /ba: -k ɔ :t/, isolating the syngrapheme in the middle of the word.

The final evidence, however, that the code has been broken and the child attained full reading ability was given on the 31st of December. Some weeks earlier I had told her a story in which the Nordic goddess Freja plays an important part. It may be noted that she had never seen the name *Freja* printed. On the 31st of December the girl asked me "Who do you think I am today? It begins with an *f*. . .(spelling in a loud voice) *f*, *r*, *e*. . .(almost silently, to herself) *fre*. . ., *frej*. . .(spelling again in a loud voice) *j*, *a*."

This transforming of a word from the spoken language to the written, from phonemes to graphemes, which is the reversed process of graphematic reading, gives full evidence that the code has been broken by the child.

After a period of 14 months the child has, by observing, learning, storing, analyzing, and comparing written words, and through the processes of adjunction, deletion, and substitution — first of morphemes and graphemes homographic with morphemes, then of nonmorphematic graphemes — arrived at a knowledge of the grapho-phonematic correspondences that is a prerequisite for being able to decode any written message.

9. **Capital letters — Double syngraphemes — Grapho-phonematic irregularities**

New words written all in capitals are not mastered by the girl until November, i.e., when the code has been broken.

In Swedish double syngraphemes indicate a short vowel. Thus *hat* is pronounced /ha:t/, but *hatt* /hat/. This rule is not mastered by the girl until February — March 1967, and she still violates the rule now and then in April and May.

At the end of the chapter the grapho-phonematic irregularities of Swedish are discussed, and the girl's gradual mastering of the difficulties is described. All irregularities are mastered before November 1967. It is also evident that the rules are discovered gradually as the reading material affords patterns that might be imitated.

10. Conclusions: Intonation, meaningful reading, application, appreciation, writing, and spelling

In this chapter the result of the experiment is compared with the recommendations of Jeanne Chall, that the child should be taught the code. An important thing is that the children studied in the research work mentioned by Jeanne Chall are school children who start learning to read at the age of five and a half to seven. With Lenneberg, Chomsky, and others in mind, we may suggest that a child two to three years old, the age of extraordinary linguistic capacity, might profit more from a method which enables him to find out the system all by himself.

Finally, some additional remarks on intonation, etc., are made. The girl was not taught intonation when reading aloud, nor did she receive any instruction about punctuation marks. Also here she found out by herself. It seems that much of this discovering was done when she re-read the books. I sometimes noticed her sitting practicing different intonations and stress patterns when re-reading the books aloud to herself.

From the very beginning the girl intimately connected reading and reality. New words on reading cards were often, in the girl's comments, put in relation to known linguistic and nonlinguistic contexts. On reading the surname *Larsson* she interrupted herself saying: "The little baby's father living down there, he is called Larsson, and her grandfather (i.e., the baby's) is a bit bald."

Naturally, reading was experienced as more meaningful when the girl read about things that were well known to her from real life. But I have also witnessed that when she had first read about certain things and phenomena in her books, her later experience of the thing in real life became much more intense and rich than it would probably have been without the literary anticipation. Thus her first sunset, experienced in August 1967, was a sheer delight; and the first time she saw cows grazing she was in a rapture, stopped, and shouted in a voice full of joy: "Oh, this must be a *pasture*! " The sunsets and pastures of literature had finally come to life. The girl's books also inspired her nonverbal life in many other respects. She often introduced scenes from books into her games, building houses after having read *The New House*, constructing roads for her cars after having read *The New Road*.

Last but not least, she identified herself with all the heroes of the literature she read.

The problem of fiction and its relation to reality was very keen to her. When, at the age of three years and nine months, she was reading the Dutch author Ninke van Hichtum's book about Mother Afke's ten children, she asked: "Have these people really existed? " "Possibly," I said. "Yes," she replied, "for if so, we will meet them in Heaven and then they can teach us to speak Dutch."

It is also evident that a small child can appreciate literature. An example is given here:

A favorite book was *The Children's Bible* by Anne de Vries. I noticed that the girl often stopped her oral reading of the Bible after having finished a very dramatic passage, and then she went over this passage again, silently. On the 21st of October 1967, at the age of four and a half, the girl had read about the crucifixion. She went back and re-read the passage telling how Jesus asks St. John to take care of his mother Mary and be like a son to her ("When Jesus therefore saw his mother, and the disciple standing by, whom he loved, he saith unto his mother, Woman behold thy son! Then saith he to the disciple, Behold thy mother! And from that hour that disciple took her unto his own home.") She then said: *"Det här var en fin liten dikt. Mittemellan det hemska var det en fin liten dikt."* (This is a fine little poem. In the middle of all the frightful things there is a fine little poem.)

At about the age of three and a half the girl began trying to write letters herself. For some reason she concentrated on the capitals. By June of 1967 she could write all capitals except B, J, M, N, Q, U, V, and X; in July only X was still missing, and she then also failed to write G and Y. On the first of November 1967, I tested her again and found that she then could write the whole alphabet, capitals and small letters. By that time she had also begun to write little missives to invented persons.

When the girl was four and a half, her spelling had already become remarkably good. Now, at the age of seven and a half she simply knows how to spell and needs not devote any time to learning how. This skill, which is normally attained only after many years of hard school work, had come to her quite unconsciously as a byproduct of her early reading. Would it not be a good thing if all children had this experience: of learning to read as easily as they learn to talk and of learning to spell without knowing that they are learning how, of having attained full literacy at an age when children normally begin to learn the ABC's? During the first school years a lot of time and hard work are being devoted to acquiring the elementary skills of reading and spelling. With these skills already at the pupil's command there could be time for more meaningful and stimulating work and activities at school. Thus still more could be made of the wonderful, receptive, and harmonious years before puberty.

11. Suggestions for further investigation

Here it is stressed that, this preliminary study of one single child being finished, the experiment should be carried out on many children of the same age, let us say, 100-150. Such an extended study might be done by a team of linguists and psychologists.

These 100-150 children should be followed through the years, and the effect of early reading on their general and linguistic development investigated.

Similar studies might also be carried out on children speaking other languages than Swedish. Do different languages raise different problems? Is it easier to find out the code of written Finnish, which is almost completely phonematic?

Might early reading along these lines be of importance to retarded children? What about deaf children, if spoken language as a medium is replaced by pictures, gestures, and film?

There are numerous tasks involved in further investigation on this subject. As I see it, there is great hope that both normal and retarded children might benefit from this approach to attaining literacy, where learning to read is defined as learning a written language and where the learner is therefore exposed to suitable reading material at the age when spoken language is normally acquired — not acquired because the environment imposes language upon the child at that age, but because the child has then reached a biological stage where his preparedness for language is at its prime.

NOTES

[1] The letters should be red to attract the attention of the child, and they should be big enough to make even a small child able to perceive the word. Doman makes a great point of this. In his opinion the reason why small children do not learn to read all by themselves at a very early age is that the letters of printed matter are generally not big enough.

[2] In this way one makes sure not only that a strong association is established between the written and the spoken form but also that meaning is attached immediately to the written form.

[3] Note the successive adaptation to smaller and smaller letters.

II. SWEDISH CHILDREN'S ACQUISITION OF SYNTAX: Preliminary Report

This is a preliminary report on a project on child syntax being carried out at Stockholm University. Six children are being carefully studied from the age of 18 to the age of 42 months. Tape recordings are taken every two weeks in the children's homes.

The aim of this project is to examine the development of Swedish-speaking children's syntax from the appearance of the first two-word sentences until all the basic syntactical rules are mastered.

So far no systematic studies of Swedish-speaking children's syntax have been carried out. Realizing that every child learning his mother tongue has got his individual language which cannot be interpreted without a thorough knowledge of the child's environment, habits, and experience — his "cultural context" — we abandoned the idea of a statistical examination of a great many children in which every child is recorded for only a couple of hours. Instead we chose to make a deep study of a few children.

Following Bellugi, Brown, Gvozdev, Lenneberg, and others, who state that the first two-word sentences appear at age 1 1/2 to 2 and that the basic syntactical development is finished at age 3 to 4, we decided to start with children 1 1/2 to 2 years old and to follow their linguistic development during two years.

Finally we chose six children, four girls and two boys, all first born. The parents have university or college education and the children are all looked after at home.

The children are recorded in their homes for half an hour every second week. One of the parents or a nurse is present at the recordings, playing and talking with the child. There are normally three of us assisting at these recordings. One is helping the parents to provoke speech and is trying to guide the games in such a way that they give the child an opportunity to talk as much as possible. Another is keeping an eye on the recorders and the microphones, which have often to be moved from one end of the room to the other. The third person is a kind of reporter, commenting in a low voice on what the child is doing, what is happening in the room, etc. These comments are recorded on a stereo recorder (Tandberg), channel one. A synchronous recording of the conversation between child and adults is made on channel 2.

To record the conversation between child and adults, our chief aid, however, is a Nagra recorder with two microphones, one of which is reserved for the child.

To elicit as much speech as possible from the children we bring with us toys and pictures. To provoke the children to say full sentences we have tried to choose pictures where something is happening. Otherwise there is a danger that they resort to pointing at the things in the pictures all the time, talking in one-word sentences, either asking "what" or saying "there" or, possibly, the names of the things.

Another way to provoke speech has been to show new toys to the child and to play with these toys when the parents are not present. Then one of the parents is summoned and the child is asked to show mummy or daddy the toys and tell what we have just been doing.

Tests have also been tried, on a very modest scale, mostly to get an idea of the children's understanding of different syntactic structures (questions, commands, subject-predicate, subject-predicate-object, etc.). Finally we have a very useful and necessary collaboration with the parents, who not only act as interpreters but also supply us with information about the daily life of their children, what they say and do, etc.

The recordings are transcribed as soon as possible after the sessions. The transcriptions are morphematic, except when it is impossible to understand what a child says. Then a phonematic transcription is made of the incomprehensible word.

A transcription is written in two columns: in the left-hand column the conversation between child and adults is rendered, in the right-hand column the reporter's comment is given.[1]

A very short abstract (in English translation) is the following:

Child:	Boil.	he puts the coffee pot on a
	It is boiling.	saucer turned upside down
	Now it boiled.	
Adult:	You must lay the table.	
Child:	Mm.	
	I have got no paper.	looks towards his mother

Two assistants are transcribing the same recording; for greater correctness they are working independently of each other. Then the two versions are compared and every discrepancy between the two is marked. Finally, a third person, the editor, listens to the recordings a last time and on the basis of the two transcriptions makes the final version, trying to decide about the passages where the transcriptions differ. Often it is obvious that one of the transcriptions is the right one, sometimes the right version is a mixture of the two transcriptions. In very problematic cases the editor and the two assistants listen to the passage together and try to make a decision.

The project started on the first of September 1970. There are four of us engaged in it: two full-time assistants who are at the same time preparing their doctoral dissertations, a part-time secretary, and myself. Every week three recordings are taken, and to make one single transcription takes about 10 hours. Every recording, then, requires 30 hours' work totally before the manuscript can be handed over to the typist. Under these conditions there is not much time to analyze the material systematically. We will have to leave that until the two-year period is finished.

Nevertheless we have been able to make many useful observations which will be good starting points for our future analyses.

The first thing we observed was that the children are all extremely different from one another in spite of their rather homogeneous social background. Some are normally very gay and happy; others rather sulky. Some have a steady temper; others a more fluctuating one. Most children were willing to collaborate with us and to take part in the games and tests. But in one case we met with a stubborn resistance.

As regards speech, two are extremely talkative (one boy and one girl), three are moderately talkative, and one little girl is almost completely silent. This girl, however, had developed a whole system of gestures, which she used together with "yes" and "no" and a few nouns. Moreover, she turned out to be unusually sociable, extremely willing to collaborate, good-humored, and happy. To get something out of this girl we had to test her understanding of language, and therefore constructed questions to find out whether she knew the different types of clauses (declarative, interrogative, imperative), if she understood the subject-object relation, if she knew the meanings of certain prepositions, etc. Thanks to the girl's willingness to collaborate, we got rather good results, and we also used the tests with the other children to check if understanding precedes production. As regards the prepositions we made the following observations:

1. During a certain period the child only understands a few prepositions, such as *in, behind.*

2. Later the child *understands most prepositions* quite well but *uses them incorrectly.* Often one single preposition is used in a great many cases, preferably "in."

As an example the following experiment may serve. We hid several toys: one under a pillow, one behind a pillow, and one in a handbag. We gave the child instructions where to find the toys, and she succeeded very well, looking behind the pillow (not touching it) to find the toy, lifting the pillow to find the toy under it, etc. Immediately afterwards the mother took the toy which had been under the pillow, asking "Where did you find this? " The girl answered "In the pillow." Her mother tried to make the girl correct herself and said "No, you did not find it in the pillow, did you? You found it —" "In the sofa," the girl cried out happily.

Brown, Bellugi, and others have shown that the earliest sentences of children are "telegraphic," containing only the contentives of the clause, which are also the words with heavy stress. We have noticed the same thing. But we have also observed the development of the unstressed words, and we have also noticed that at certain moments there appear some mumbling sounds where there should be an article, a preposition, a pronoun, etc. Some weeks later these sounds are here and there replaced by something very much resembling the correct unstressed word, until finally the word is there. This might be compared with a much earlier stage in the linguistic development of the child, when it is practicing intonational patterns with nonsense words. Little by little these patterns are filled out with the first real words.

It also seems evident to us that children practice language. At an early stage our children were practicing single words. One of our girls was once trying to say the same word again and again while she was putting her doll to bed: /bɛ ba/ /baba/, etc. The word she tried to say was /bɛ da/, which means "make the bed."

Later in their linguistic development the children practice sentences. One and the same sentence can be uttered up to ten times with different word order and different intonation. One or two tries might give a correct result, but this is almost never the last try. The other tries usually give ungrammatical sentences.

It also seems evident that imitation plays a great part in the linguistic development of the child. Here the parent-child communication is most revealing. Our most advanced children have parents who talk a great deal with (not *to*) their children and who listen to them, trying to understand what they say. These parents often "translate" (not correct) and develop what their children say in order to check that they are on line with each other. The child might for instance say: "Dolly eat." Then the father says: "Shall Dolly eat? Yes. Here is a saucer and a spoon. Now we let Dolly eat." Such translations or "imitations with expansion"[2] made by the parent seem to be of great importance to strengthen the right structural patterns. As mentioned above, the child often practices semantically the same sentence again and again with different syntactic structures. When one or two of these tries are right, the child evidently knows how to produce a correct sentence. Then it is essential to have these potential patterns strengthened.

With the three best speaking children in our group there is mutual parent-child communication and understanding, and parents and child have a rich linguistic and nonlinguistic context in common to which they perpetually refer and we, as visitors, must constantly ask about. One reason for this unusually good parent-child communication is that in all three cases one of the parents — or both, alternatively — are together with their child most of the day.

With the children who do not speak so well this common context is lacking, and it is evident that parent and child do not talk so much together except for the sessions when the children are recorded. The children are cared for all day by young girls, 17-19 years old. In the case of the non-speaking, gesturing child, however, the mutual parent-child communication is quite good, but the child here is left all day with a nurse who is passive and silent.

We have also noticed that the children often try very hard to say what they want to say. Talking is hard work for them, especially when they try to produce sentences longer than two words, if they still belong to the two-word stage. Suttering seems to be a very common phenomenon. Very often the child breaks off a sentence two to three times and begins anew until he succeeds moderately well.

These are glimpses of such observations as we have been able to make during our first year of recording. Later we shall make a systematic description in terms of phrase structure, grammar, and transformational grammar. If time permits, we shall also try to check some of the results of the longitudinal deep study by making a statistical study of 100 children aged two to four. Such a study is necessary for us to be able to make statements about Swedish-speaking children's language in general, although it is not the right way to take if you want an all-round picture of the syntactical development of the child from two to four, where extreme attention must be paid to nonlinguistic factors, particularly the background and equipment of each child.

NOTES

[1] The idea of making synchronous comments on a tape recorder I got from Dr. Grace Shugar at the Conference on Child Language held in Brno, October, 1970.

[2] To use the term coined by Brown and Bellugi. See Roger Brown and Ursula Bellugi, "Three Processes in the Child's Acquisition of Syntax" *Harvard Educational Review*, XXXIV (1964), pp. 133-151.

Bibliography

Allén, Sture. *Grafematisk analys som grundval för textedering.* Göteborg: Almqvist & Wiksell, (1965).

——. "Förhållandet mellan skrift och tal." In *Språk, språkvård och kommunikation.* Stockholm: Prisma [Seelig], (1967). (Verdandi-orientering, Nr. 5.)

Bloomfield, Leonard. *Language.* New York: Holt, Rinehart & Winston, [1933, 1958].

——. "Linguistics and Reading." *Elementary English Review*, 19 (1942).

Brantberg-Frigyes, Birgitta. *Kan en treåring lära läsa.* Lund: Gleerups, (1969).

Brown, Robert, and Colin Fraser. "The Acquisition of Syntax." In C.N. Cofer and B.S. Musgrave, eds., *Verbal Behavior and Learning*, New York: McGraw-Hill, (1963).

Brown, Roger, and Ursula Bellugi. "Three Processes in the Child's Acquisition of Syntax." In Eric H. Lenneberg, ed., *New Directions in the Study of Language*, Cambridge, Mass.: M.I.T. Press, (1964).

Chall, Jeanne. *Learning to Read: The Great Debate.* New York: McGraw-Hill, (1967).

Chomsky, Noam. *Aspects of the Theory of Syntax.* Cambridge, Mass.: M.I.T. Press, (1965).

Dahlstedt, Karl Hampus. "Homonymi i nusvenskan," *Nysvenska Studier*, XLIV (1965).

Doman, Glenn. *How to Teach Your Baby to Read.* New York: Random House, (1964).

Elert, Claes-Christian. *Ljud och ord i svenskan.* Stockholm: Almqvist & Wiksell, (1970).

Erdmann, B., and R. Dodge. *Psychologische Untersuchungen über das Lesen.* Halle: S. M. Niemeyer, (1898).

Flesch, Rudolf. *Why Johnny Can't Read.* New York: Harper, (1955).

Francis, W. Nelson. "Graphemic Analysis of Late Middle English Manuscripts," *Speculum*, XXXVII (1962).

Fries, Chàrles C. *Linguistics and Reading.* New York: Holt, Rinehart & Winston, (1963).

Gates, Arthur I. *Strömninger i tiden.* Published by Landsföreningen af Laesepaedagoger on the occasion of The Second World Congress on Reading, Copenhagen, August (1968).

Gelb, I.J. *A Study of Writing.* Chicago: University of Chicago Press, (1963).

Gleason, H.A. *An Introduction to Descriptive Linguistics.* New York: Holt, Rinehart & Winston, (1966).

——. *Linguistics and English Grammar.* New York: Holt, Rinehart & Winston, (1965).

Hayakawa, S.I. *Language in Thought and Action.* London: Allen & Unwin, (1959).

Hockett, Charles F. *A Course in Modern Linguistics.* New York: Macmillan, (1958).

Huey, Edmund Burke. *The Psychology and Pedagogy of Reading.* Cambridge, Mass.: M.I.T. Press, (1968), First published 1908.

Kavanagh, James F. (ed.). Proceedings of the U.S. Department of Health, Education, and Welfare Conference on Communicating by Language: The Reading Process, New Orleans, Louisiana, February 11-13, (1968).

Lenneberg, Eric H. *Biological Foundations of Language.* New York: Wiley, (1967).

McCarthy, D. "Language Development in Children." In L. Carmichael, ed., *Manual of Child Psychology,* New York: Wiley, (1954).

Menyuk, Paula. *Sentences Children Use.* Cambridge, Mass.: M.I.T. Press, (1969).

Reading Research Quarterly. Published by the International Reading Association. Newark, Delaware, (1965) ff.

Rūke-Draviņa, Velta. *Zur Sprachentwicklung bei Kleinkindern.* Lund, (1963).

Sigurd, Bengt. *Phonotactic Structures in Swedish.* Lund: Uniskol, (1965).

———. *Språkstruktur.* Stockholm: Wahlström & Widstrand, (1967).

Smith, Frank, and George A. Miller (eds.). *The Genesis of Language.* Cambridge, Mass.: M.I.T. Press, (1966).

Söderbergh, Ragnhild. "Strukturer och normer i barnspråk," *Nordisk Tidskrift,* (1968).

Stauffer, R.G. *Teaching Reading as a Thinking Process.* New York: Harper & Row, (1969).

Uldall, H.J. "Speech and Writing," *Acta linguistica,* IV (1944), pp. 11 ff.

Wardhaugh, Ronald. *Reading: A Linguistic Perspective.* New York: Harcourt, Brace & World, (1969).

Wiegand, C.F. "Untersuchungen über die Bedeutung der Gestaltqualität für die Erkennung von Wörtern." In *Zeitzchrift für Psychologie und Physiologie der Sinnesorgane,* (1907).

Zeitler, J. "Tachistoskopische Untersuchungen über das Lesen." *Wundt's Philosophische Studien.* Leipzig, (1881-1903). Bd. XVI.

Printed Books Used as Reading Material in the Experiment: December 1965 to December 1966

Ainsworth, Ruth, och Ronald Ridout. *Den lilla geten.* Svensk Läraretidnings Förlag, (1965).

———. *En anka på äventyr.* Svensk Läraretidnings Förlag, (1965).

———. *Lek med mig.* Svensk Läraretidnings Förlag, (1965).

———. *Rullbandet.* Svensk Läraretidnings Förlag, (1965).

Baker, Marybob, och J.P. Miller *Det snälla lejonet.* FIB, (1965).

Beim, Jerrold, och Ylva Källström. *Bollen som kom bort.* Rabén och Sjögren, (1965).

Fujikawa, Gyo. *Djurens barn.* Illustrationsförlaget, (1964).

Heilbroner, Joan, och Mary Chalmers. *Mamma fyller år.* Illustrationsförlaget, (1962).

Higgins, Don. *Jag är en flicka.* FIB, (1966).

——. *Jag är en pojke.* FIB, (1966).

Hughes, Shirley. *Lisas och Toms dag.* Berghs, (1965).

Janus Hertz, Grete, och Veronica Loe-Hongell. *När Lisa och Lena hade röde hund.* Rabén och Sjögren, (1965).

Meeks, Esther K., och Mel Pekarsky. *Kossan Kajsa.* Illustrationsförlaget, (1960).

Peterson, Hans, och Ylva Källström. *Den nya vägen.* Rabén och Sjögren, (1965).

——. *Det nya huset.* Rabén och Sjögren, (1966).

——. *Gubben och kanariefågeln.* Rabén och Sjögren, (1960).

Pfloog, Jan. *Kattboken.* FIB, (1965).

Prysen, Alf, och Nils Stödberg. *Byn som glömde att det var jul.* Rabén och Sjögren, (1962).

Risom, Ole. *Kajsa Skogsmus.* FIB, (1965).

——. *Kalle Kanin.* FIB, (1965).

Selsam, Millicent E., och Arnold Lobel. *Fias Fjärilar.* Illustrationsförlaget, (1862).

Sigsgaard, Jens, och Arne Ungermann. *Katinka och dockvagnen.* Rabén och Sjögren, (1865).

6

Minority Language Skills before Age Three
Chester C. Christian Jr.

Bilingual objectives of emphasis on minority language

A large segment of the population of the United States has bilingual abilities in some degree;[1] but where a language other than English is learned by the pre-school child at home, the only abilities in that language which usually are developed are understanding and speaking. Since these abilities later are rarely utilized by the school as a basis for teaching reading and writing, mental and emotional development for the child in terms of his home language and related cultural values is severely limited.

In view of the fact that for such children limited abilities in English upon entering school are associated with a limited spectrum of intellectual and social experiences, forming a weak foundation for reading and writing in that language, the result of the combination of home and school experience often is lifetime mediocrity in two languages and cultures.

To avoid this, initial teaching of reading and writing in the home language has been proposed and, in a limited number of instances, effected.[2] It has been generally assumed, however, that the teaching of reading and writing should be delayed until the child reaches school age; by this time inevitable conflicts seem to arise between the desirability of teaching in the home language and the necessity of teaching the majority language.

This conflict might be avoided by teaching the child to read and write his home language before entering school. There is increasing evidence that children — even those with brain damage — have a natural interest in and potential ability to read even before the age of two,[3] and the evidence of the present study supports this view decisively. It seems particularly significant in relation to children who speak a minority language at home.

One of the traditional objections to teaching reading in the school language at home is that the child later is bored in school, and creates special problems for the teacher. On the other hand, the child who speaks a minority language at home creates another type of special problem for the teacher. With respect to the child with nonstandard home experience, both

94

problems might be minimized for the teacher without sacrificing the potential of the child. On the contrary, the child might be provided a foundation for full development of bilingual abilities and for an unusually rich intellectual, emotional, and social life experience.

The parents of Raquel, the child under consideration in the present study, wish to provide their children the most favorable conditions possible for the learning, retention, and continuing lifetime development of a full range of abilities in at least two languages, Spanish and English. This involves, they believe, building the strongest possible foundation in the minority language before the children reach school age, including the teaching of reading and writing.

Methods and rationale for skill development

To accomplish this objective, Raquel's parents decided to speak only Spanish to their children at home, although it is the second language of her father and the family lives in an English-speaking neighborhood.[4] The children were expected to learn English as a second language largely from playmates. There is no television set in the home. With respect to written language, they decided to teach reading and writing in Spanish early, so that before entering school the children would be literate in Spanish. It was assumed that by this time they would have learned to understand spoken English.

These language policies were chosen for practical, psychological, and sociocultural reasons, with the purpose of giving the children highly developed capabilities in at least two languages, motivation to use each of them as permanent vehicles of spoken and written expression, favorable attitudes toward those who speak each of them, and a deep understanding of the sociocultural value systems associated with each, with preference given to Spanish as a vehicle of personal experience and relationships, and to English for the manipulation of cognitive structures. These purposes are considered desirable by Raquel's parents for most children living in bilingual communities in the United States whose home language is Spanish.

These purposes are similar to those of many bilingual school programs, but implementation is difficult in school because of the pressure to build a structure in English without an adequate foundation in the home language.

Conditions for effective minority language development

In terms of general implications, this study attempts to state tentatively the most favorable conditions for the learning, retention, and continuing development of abilities in a minority home language throughout the lifetime of the person. It is assumed that, although children are capable of becoming skilled in the use of two or more languages before the age of six, practical ability to use a minority language may be lost rapidly after that age unless certain conditions are met.[5] Some of these conditions are thought to be the following: 1) continuing exclusive or almost exclusive use of the minority language by a person of the child's household in speaking with the child; the greater the prestige of this person in the view of the child, the more favorable the prognosis for continuing use and development of the language; 2) development of literacy in the minority language; the earlier the development of literacy, and the more completely abilities are developed before learning the majority language, the more favorable the prognosis; 3) absence of television or highly restricted viewing of shows in the majority language; the less time spent in viewing television presented in the majority language, the greater the possibility of preserving and developing the minority language in teaching the child academic subjects other than language; the higher the prestige of the teacher and the more academic the subject, the greater the possibility of continuing development of the minority language.[6]

The prestige component of minority language development

The key concept in these statements is regarded as "prestige," and the degree of success or failure of bilingual education in the home or in the school is considered proportionate to the degree to which prestige is associated with each language being learned. In this respect, the following generalizations may be subsumed under the hypotheses stated above: 1a) the person of least prestige in most households is the family servant, and the father the person of greatest prestige (even though — or perhaps because — emotional ties to the mother are usually strongest); 2a) the prestige of a language is in proportion to the degree to which one is literate in that language and is acquainted with materials written in the language which are known to be admired by persons whose opinions are respected; 3a) the prestige of a language is proportionate to the degree to which the family responds to the mass media, especially television programs, presented in that language; and 4a) in the United States, the most prestigious subjects in school are those associated with cognitive development, and the least prestigious those associated with artistic or emotive sensitivity.

At the age of thirty-six months, Raquel appears just now to be becoming conscious of the prestige component of language, but her foundation in Spanish seems to be strong enough to withstand the subtle and not-so-subtle attack which will come from the English-speaking world at least until she speaks English well enough to conceal the "foreignness" of her home language and background.

In the neighborhood park where Raquel plays, for example, older children sometimes accuse playmates of knowing how to speak Spanish, or of having been born on the Mexican side of the border, with inevitable denials from the accused.

An example of the more subtle form of criticism occurred when another family with a child about the age of Raquel visited her home. When the child started to talk to Raquel in English the mother remonstrated, "It's no use trying to talk to her; she only speaks Spanish." Raquel's father remarked, "Let her talk — we would like for Raquel to learn English." Up to the present, however, Raquel has succeeded in influencing most neighborhood children to use with her what little Spanish they may have learned from maids, and they have seemed to feel at more of a disadvantage than she has. Nevertheless, she now shows evidence of feeling the necessity for more English.

Language Environment: Home and Travel

At the present writing, Raquel has spent eight of the twenty-four months she has been using words in South America (Peru and Colombia), including time periods during which she was fourteen to nineteen and twenty-eight to thirty-one months of age. Her response to English was developed almost entirely, therefore, between the ages of nineteen and twenty-eight, then thirty-two to thirty-six months. Between twenty-nine and thirty-one months, it diminished to understanding only a few words and use of no more than three or four.

At the age of thirty-one months, when she returned to the United States with her family, they were joined by Karen, a half-sister of Raquel, who began to learn Spanish at age five and used it until one year before leaving for India at age fourteen, where within two years her ability to understand it apparently diminished rapidly, and she lost the ability to speak it in normal conversation.[7]

Since Karen speaks English to her father and step-mother, Raquel quickly became more interested in the language and began to imitate sounds consistently, whether they represented new vocabulary items in English or in Spanish, and whether or not she understood their full meaning. She began to ask the English name of almost everything new to her, repeating it carefully.

A month later, the family was also joined by Norma, a cousin from Lima of Raquel's mother, who speaks Spanish to Raquel's parents and English to Karen. Also, Norma speaks French fluently and Karen is studying French at a nearby university; Raquel has been interested in learning French words from Karen, clearly differentiating French from Spanish and English.[8]

Raquel has a brother, Aurelio, sixteen months younger than she, who has also begun to read words at the age of twenty months, and has thereby stimulated her interest to an even higher level. She is jealous of "her words" and at times does not allow him to read them. Aurelio is reading words earlier than Raquel did, as a result, apparently, of beginning with words rather than with letters.

Thus the household is now composed of six persons: Raquel, her younger brother, her mother, her mother's 26-year-old consin, her father, and her father's 19-year-old daughter.

So far there seem to have been no serious psychological or interpersonal complications. The children seem as close to the relatives of the father who do not speak Spanish as to those of the mother, a very warm and highly positive relationship in both cases. There seems to be no "language barrier" whatsoever in the formation of friendships with either adults or children, nor the least evidence of anxiety at incomplete ability to communicate in English.[9]

Language abilities at 36 months

At the present writing, at the age of thirty-six months, Raquel can understand at least two thousand words in Spanish and fewer than fifty in English.[10] She uses regularly approximately twelve hundred words in Spanish and twenty in English.

She reads more than eighty words in Spanish and twelve (including proper names) in English. The maximum sentence length which she reads easily is four words. These are written on 3" x 7" cards in pairs so that many two-card combinations form sentences. The combination (article, noun/verb, adjective) is read more easily than (article, noun/verb, adverb).

She writes four words (*mamá, papá, ojo, rojo*) with consistent correctness (including the accents) on the typewriter, and others occasionally (such as Karen and K-Mart). She writes *ojo* by hand. In writing, she usually remembers the letters in words, but does not know how to write most of them in the correct order. She is presently more interested in writing numbers than words on the typewriter.

She enjoys many recordings in Spanish and two (*Peter and the Wolf* and *Sesame Street* selections) in English. One of her favorites at the present time is from her parents' collection, a record of Negroes from Lima, Peru singing and talking in a very rhythmic, audacious, and carefree manner — and with extreme rapidity. When she is listening she sometimes says, "Ese hombre me quiere" (That man loves me); she understands some of the most rapid and difficult phrases used on the record.

With respect to grammatical structures, Raquel has a much more marked tendency at the age of thirty-six months than previously to demand regularities which do not exist in the language, making all forms of the verb, for example, agree with the third person singular. She has always used *sabo* (I know) instead of *sé*, the standard form (*saber* is the infinitive), but used the standard form of other verbs. She now creates nonstandard forms where she previously used the standard form, as "Nos encierramos," (3rd person singular *encierra*, infinitive *encerrar*), or even "¿Quieres abiertarnos la puerta? " (Do you want to open the door for us?), basing the verb form on the past participle *abierto* instead of the infinitive *abrir*. It seems that the type of regularities demanded in the alphabet at the age of two are now being demanded in the structure of the language at the age of three.

Another form of nonstandard usage has been the possessive adjective, with the third person form almost invariably used rather than the first person; when talking about her mother, she says "tu mamá" (your mother), for example. Explanations have not yet changed this practice. She does make the reverse distinction, however: when another person refers to "mi hermano" (my brother), she says "tu hermano" (your brother) with reference to that person.[11]

When Raquel was two, her father administered a Spanish version of the Peabody Picture Vocabulary Test used in one of the bilingual elementary school programs, and she scored a mental age of two years and two months (raw score 7). Her score in English was zero. The test was administered again at the age of 36 months, and the resulting mental age measurement was 47 months (raw score 41), with the score in English still zero.

Development of Spanish and English vocabulary

From the age of nine to fourteen months, active vocabulary was limited to six words in Spanish: *mamá, papá, Raquel, gracias, no,* and *ya.* During the following five months, spent in Lima, Peru, approximately twenty words were added. Upon returning to the United States at the age of nineteen months, rapid vocabulary development began within three weeks, and during the twentieth month at least thirty-six new words were used, all in Spanish.

By the age of twenty-five months her active Spanish vocabulary was more than 300 words, but she had used only five words in English: *bye-bye, okay, Susy* (her next-door playmate), *water,* and *this.* In other words, during the time in the United States that she was adding approximately fifty words per month to her active Spanish vocabulary, she was adding only one per month to her English vocabulary, in spite of almost daily contact with neighborhood children who spoke only English. She insisted that they "understand" her Spanish rather than attempting to communicate with them in English.

During a second visit to Lima the following year, Raquel stopped responding to English almost entirely; following the visit, she would protest if her father used English with her, shaking her head and saying, "no, no, no, no, no."

Her only utterance in English during the week following the visit to Lima was in response to her father, when he told her, "You are a lovely girl." She replied, "Thank you. Please." After another month in Bogotá, Colombia, however, her response to this remark in English was: "No. Soy Raquelita." (No. I am Raquelita).

Upon returning to the United States from South America the second time, there was another period of intense learning; the return to the security of the home seems to have stimulated this in both cases. Interest in written language began to develop with special intensity, as is described in the following section.

Both vocabulary and complexity of expression in Spanish developed very rapidly, but growth in English was still minimal in spite of increased exposure to the language. More than one hundred words per month were being added to active Spanish vocabulary, and fewer than five in English.

Development of reading abilities[1][2]

Although it may be to a degree coincidental, rapid vocabulary development began with the gift of a Spanish alphabet book with large clear capital letters, no words, and rather abstract illustrations. Raquel was more interested in the letters than in the illustrations, and between the ages of twenty and twenty-four months she learned to recognize twenty-four letters, eleven written words (one-inch capital letters written with ballpoint pen on 3 x 5 cards), and attempted to write several letters, reproducing in recognizable form the written *a*, *e*, and *o* (manuscript form), and calling the letter by its Spanish name. A month later she was able to read ten more words upon sight only, and an additional six after hearing the letters pronounced.

One assumption related to the learning of written Spanish first was that it would be learned more rapidly than English might be, owing to the predictability and clarity of the sound system and the close correspondence between the sound and the writing systems.[1][3] This was partially verified by the fact that Raquel wanted to make the systems even more predictable and less ambiguous, with still closer correspondence between the speaking and writing systems.

For example, she insisted that the *W* was an inverted *M* and at first refused to pronounce the term *ve-doble*. She had learned the term *ve* or *be* (same pronunciation in Spanish) for the *B*, and refused to use the same term for the *V*. She did not regard it appropriate to use a sound for a double letter, such as *LL* or *CH*. Although she learned to make these distinctions, it was with much reluctance and continuing skepticism.

At the age of twenty-one months she was given a set of blocks in order to be able to learn to put letters together to form words, and of course several of the Spanish letters were not included. She apparently missed them, because several months later when she saw a written Ñ, she repeated the term for it again and again, with all the thrill of having seen an old friend.

In the meantime, she had been given a set of plastic lower-case letters with magnets to attach to a slate; she favored the letters similar to capitals and those which did not change name when reversed or inverted.

Shortly after receiving the blocks, she noticed the typewriter and tried to put her blocks on top of the keys, matching them to the typewriter letters. For almost a year she regarded the typewriter as a machine for producing letters rather than words; at the age of 33 months she began to write words with it, but still enjoys playing with it just as a letter-producing machine. When she learned to produce words with it, she wanted to know the pronunciation of any series of letters she would produce, and was delighted at the unpronounceability of her "words."

During the period from twenty to twenty-five months Raquel seemed to live in a world of letters, discovering them on signs, in newspapers, and throughout her environment — although largely in English sets, of course. For example, at twenty-two months she was so impressed by the huge letters spelling out SAFEWAY on a store that she cried to climb up and play with them. When she saw an advertisement for K-MART in the newspaper at twenty-four months, she pointed to the name and said "tienda" (store).

From the age of twenty-five to twenty-eight months, although play with words and letters continued on much the same basis as before, generally with Raquel's father, her interest in both letters and words declined steadily. She treated these sessions with ever less seriousness, laughing and often responding in nonsense syllables. One reason seemed to be an increasing interest in other forms of language play and graphic representation.

From twenty-five to twenty-eight months she was interested in drawing and would reject written symbols: *mamá* became a drawing of her mother, and she did not want the word to be written. She began to draw, first faces, then adding bodies, legs, and arms, and assigning names to her drawings. She was not much interested in attempting to write letters or words, but usually asked for materials by saying "Quiero escribir" (I want to write) rather than "Quiero dibujar" (I want to draw), although she knew the latter expression. She apparently does not distinguish clearly between the two activities.

The first step in learning to read was in learning the Spanish alphabet; the second step (at twenty-three months) was to give the sound for any consonant-vowel combination, which included both words and nonsense syllables. She responded much more readily to combinations which produced words *(sí, no, se, su, te, tu, etc.)*. Combinations caused some confusion between, for example, the *s* and the *c;* the latter, in combination with the *i* or the *e,* is pronounced like *s.* The difficulty was compounded by the pronunciation of the names of the letters, *s* (ese) and *c* (ce) (pronounced like *se*). These relatively minor problems with the Spanish alphabet suggest the magnitude of comparable problems with the English alphabet for young children.

It had been assumed that learning the pronunciation of all possible consonant-vowel combinations in Spanish, then learning syllabication, would make it possible to produce the sound of any written word in Spanish at sight. Progress in this direction was made rapidly for only about three months, when the "negative" stage was reached. After interest in reading was renewed, it was on a distinctly new basis, in terms of words rather than letters and sounds. There was still little interest in sentences and stories, however, either in terms of reading them or of having them read. At the age of thirty-six months, Raquel is still primarily interested in reading words, and secondarily in reading short sentences, of four words or fewer.

At the age of twenty-eight months, Raquel went for a visit with her mother to her grandparents' home in Lima, Peru, remaining seven weeks.

During this period of time, she forgot almost all the English she had learned, and lost interest in reading and also in responding to words spelled orally. Her response to the latter was by repeating the letters very rapidly rather than saying the word.

In Bogotá, during her thirtieth month, her interest in reading was revived when her brother, sixteen months younger, began to receive books. At the age of fourteen months, he would respond with Spanish vowel sounds upon seeing a book, writing instrument, or paper. She would then "correct" him, as well as take his book away from him.

Upon returning from South America, at the age of thirty-one months, Raquel re-discovered the blocks, plastic letters, records, typewriter, etc. that she had left three months before, and her interest in written language was quickly renewed. By the age of thirty-two months, she was developing language skills more rapidly than at any other time since her twenty-sixth month.

The major change during this month insofar as written language is concerned was from a focus on capital letters to lower-case letters, encouraged by her father. This was partly a result of acquaintance with Glenn Doman's work in teaching young children to read,[14] which takes the view that it is better to teach whole words written in lower-case letters.

Although she could read pica type, the size of letters was and is important. During her 32nd month a new store (K-MART) was being built near her home, and on a trip by bicycle with her father she discovered piled on the sidewalk the huge letters which were to be put up on the store. She insisted on returning six times in the first hour after her discovery, and every day thereafter for weeks until all the letters were installed on the store. Still, four months later, almost every time the family leaves the home she says "Vamos a ver las letras" (Let's go see the letters).

She noticed spontaneously that FOODWAY had two *o*'s and was like WOOLWORTH'S and also like SAFEWAY (the two latter stores also visible from K-MART and FOODWAY). She could not pronounce *Foodway* correctly, and for two weeks after being corrected refused to try again, until suddenly she was saying it correctly.

As previously stated, ambiguities in letters were not easily accepted at first. However, at the age of thirty-one months, Raquel became intrigued rather than dismayed at the ambiguities of lower-case letters, and with the possibilities of inverting them to change the name: *b* became *q*, *d* became *p*, etc. On her own initiative, she also "changed" letters which were not identical to others when inverted; for example, *h* to *y*, and *m* to *w*. She said that the inverted *m* was "un tipo de *w*" (a type of *w*).

In view of this interest, her father re-wrote some of the words she had previously learned, this time in lower-case letters (upper-case initial letters where appropriate) with a blue felt-tip pen in one-inch letters on 3 x 5 cards. During her thirty-second month she learned quickly and easily to recognize these words, which included family names: Chester, Nancy, Raquelita, Aurelio, Karen, and Norma.

A distinct and notable change occurred during this period in her reading technique: she changed spontaneously from phonetic reading to sight reading. She wanted, and learned, to recognize words instantly, without looking at the separate letters. Evidence of this was in her frequent initial response to the name of a family member with the word for the relationship, or vice versa. After taking a second look, she would always correct herself. In this fashion, she would also respond to *dedo* (finger) with *mano* (hand), or vice versa, and so with other related words. Responses were always instantaneous.

Another evidence of sight reading was the tendency at times to give a longer word which included the word or letters of the word used as a stimulus. For example, *pelo* for *el, pollo* for *calle, hermano* for *mano*, etc. Her tendency seemed to be to look at the middle or end of words for the stimulus, rather than at the beginning. However, when she saw the word *garden* in English, she said that it looked like *gato.*

Since she could invert letters to make others, she wanted to invert words and change them, and seemed to think that this should be a possibility. The word *dedo* was one which, inverted, still looked like a word, but she finally gave up trying to make sense of it. She found *oso* somewhat satisfying, although it remained the same word. It should have become another.

During her thirty-third month, her father prepared larger (3 x 7) cards with pairs of words so that two cards put together made a sentence. Different parts of speech were written in different colors — blue for nouns, red for adjectives, green for verbs, etc. Her favorite sentence was *mi papá/me asusta* (my daddy/scares me), which she thought very amusing. She likes best sentences which are most agreeable to her: *mi mamá/es bonita* (my mommy/is pretty), *el avión/es grande* (the airplane/is large), etc. She does not like sentences with which she does not agree, or negative sentences in general, and resists reading them: *mi hermanito/no me gusta* (I don't like my little brother); "Pero mi hermanito *sí* me gusta" ("But I *do* like my little brother"), she exclaims. She does not like the word *feo* (ugly) and often refuses to say it, using *mono* (monkey) instead. This is an ambiguous term in Spanish, also meaning "cute"; she likes monkeys (and pictures of them), but seems to think they are ugly.

An important motivational factor in learning to read for Raquel has been the interest in the process shown by her younger brother, and a degree of rivalry with him. The reading sessions usually have been at lunch, and Aurelio frequently reaches for the words as soon as dessert is served, exclaiming *¡u, a, o!* At first he would hold up cards and say indiscriminately, *papá, mamá,* and other familiar words. He first learned to recognize one card on which was written *Norma* (the name of his aunt), but since he was not able to say her name he would say *tía* (aunt). Later he learned to say *Norma*, and learned to recognize *mamá, papá, Karen, Susy,* and *carro* by the age of twenty months. His reading vocabulary seems to be increasing more rapidly at present than did Raquel's at the same age.

He and Raquel are strong rivals for the use of the typewriter; he hits keys individually, and calls out the names of letters indiscriminately. She is so fond of the typewriter that once when her father took it with him on a three-day trip her first remark upon seeing him and being greeted effusively upon his return was, "¿Dónde está la máquina de escribir? " (Where is the typewriter?).

At the present time Raquel has little sense of left-to-right order either in reading or in writing. Except for the few words she has memorized, she starts with any letter in a word when trying to write it on the typewriter. In writing *ojo* by hand, she usually starts with the *j* and then writes an *o* on either side.

In reading sentences written on the cards, she at times reads the second card first; for example, *el payaso/come mucho* (the clown/eats a lot) as *come mucho/el payaso* (eats a lot/the clown), which is acceptable form in Spanish. At the age of twenty months, her brother Aurelio also puts the cards together and tries to read them.

Anticipated language development

It seems reasonable at the present writing to predict that between the ages of three and five years Raquel will learn to read books in Spanish and to speak English fluently. This prediction is based upon the expectation of relatively greater strength of family rather than school and community influences, however, with the crucial factors being the continuing use of the minority language by both parents and the development of literacy in it through home instruction before literacy in the majority language is imposed by formal public education.

The two forces later most capable of destroying the full capabilities of the child in the home language, the parents believe, are television and the public schools. Their community, through its proximity to Mexico, offers public and private education as well as television in Spanish, but neither commands the resources — or the prestige — that television and public education command in the United States.

The purpose of the parents is not to make the minority language the only or even principal language of their children, but to create a balance between the languages in a situation where almost all social and psychological factors are weighted in favor of the majority language.

In this process, bilingual education in the public schools is seen as a possible ally, but at the same time there is reason to suspect that it may, through association of more prestigious persons and language activities with English, sabotage the structures it attempts to build. The parents, therefore, consider it their duty to put all their weight — all their prestige in the view of their children — on the side of minority language, and to encourage the fullest possible development of skills in it both before and after their children reach school age.

Summary

This study of a child whose home language is Spanish but who has alternately lived in English- and Spanish-speaking environments (the United States, Peru, and Colombia) attempts to state the optimum conditions for continuing lifetime development of a full range of abilities in a minority language. These are thought to include the provision of materials for and instruction in reading and writing the minority language at the earliest age at which interest on the part of the child may be expected; the age of eighteen months to two years is considered typical. In the case described, there is a transition from phonetic to sight reading of Spanish words between the ages of two and three years. Reading is considered to be one of the prestige components of language use; this and other prestige components are considered essential for the continuing development of full bilingual abilities after school age is reached. Since the school rarely provides these components, it seems necessary for the family to maximize early the prestige of and skills in the minority language if for the child it is expected to be an educational benefit rather than a detriment.

NOTES

[1] Approximately one person in every ten in the United States speaks natively a language other than English. See Manuel T. Pacheco, "Approaches to Bilingualism: Recognition of a Multilingual Society." In Dale L. Lange, ed., *Britannica Review of Foreign Language Education*, Vol. 3. Chicago: Encyclopaedia Britannica, Inc., 1971, p. 97. Pacheco quotes Muriel R. Saville and Rudolph C. Troike, *A Handbook of Bilingual Education.* Washington, D.C.: Center for Applied Linguistics, (1970).

[2] Some of the most significant work in this area has been done by the Summer Institute of Linguistics, Inc. This is described in another paper in this volume by Sarah C. Gudschinsky, "Mother Tongue Literacy and Second Language Learning." These programs demonstrate that it is not necessary to teach reading and writing in the home language before school age in order for children later to become competitive with others who speak the majority or official language at home. However, school systems in the United States usually combine a sense of urgency with respect to learning the majority language with an increasing intolerance of the minority language in formal communication, making the process described by Dr. Gudschinsky a practical impossibility in most U.S. schools.

[3] Evidence for this is presented briefly and convincingly in the book by Glenn Doman, *How to Teach Your Baby to Read* (New York, 1964). This book was recommended to the writer by Theodore Andersson after the latter had heard of Raquel's interest in reading. It will be clear that some of the errors of technique in teaching her could have been avoided by consulting the book at the beginning. For example, there should have been more emphasis on words written in lower-case letters, rather than the recognition of capital letters. Most of the techniques Doman recommands are being used with Raquel's younger brother Aurelio, who is learning to read words with the same facility and at the same age (20 months) that Raquel learned to read letters. However, neither size nor color of letters seems to be of the importance one might expect. *Mamá* and *papá* were written in thick two-inch letters for Aurelio, but the first word he learned to read, *Norma,* was written in 1/2-inch letters on a 3 x 5 card for his sister. Raquel favors large, bright-colored letters, but easily reads pica type.

[4] Raquel was born in El Paso, Texas on January 14, 1969. Her mother is Peruvian, but began to study English at the age of six years in a U.S.-sponsored school, continuing for eleven years and becoming a bilingual secretary after graduation. Her father began to study Spanish as an adult, and has taught Mexican-American and foreign students in Spanish for a total of eight years, beginning in 1959, and developing a progressively stronger interest in and association with bilingual education since that time.

[5] A "forgotten" language may be re-learned rapidly later, however, and with more accurate pronunciation than would otherwise be possible. But the

writer has observed children whose parents were born and reared in Latin America speak Spanish with much hesitation and with an English accent, although they had earlier learned to speak it rapidly and with a standard accent. In these cases, prestige may be associated, albeit unconsciously, with hesitating, accented speech in the minority language.

[6] The two greatest weaknesses of most bilingual programs where Spanish is used seem to be the lesser prestige of the language as compared with English, which results in its functioning as a crutch to be used only in case of emergency, and the discontinuance of its use as soon as the most severe and obvious stage in the emergency is past. With this attitude prevailing, it is hardly surprising that pupils in general would continue to regard it as a weak secondary means of communication in school, or that use of it as an officially tolerated jargon should do little to improve the self-image of those pupils who use it as a home language.

[7] This also happened with a younger brother and sister, who had learned Spanish from a maid simultaneously with English. However, an older sister who learned Spanish later (after age seven), but who became highly literate in the language, seems to have retained almost her full abilities after four years in India out of contact with it.

[8] One day, for example, Karen was looking for chalk to write with Raquel on the blackboard. She could not remember the Spanish word for "chalk" and so could not tell Raquel what she wanted. Finally Raquel understood, and said *tiza.* Karen responded, "Bueno, los franceses dicen *craie*" (Well, the French call it *craie*). Raquel's reply: "¿Y por qué dicen los franceses *craie?* " (And why do the French say *craie?*) in a tone of indulgent amusement. Later, Karen mentioned another French word without specifying the language and Raquel exclaimed, " ¡francés! " At times Karen tries to use English with Raquel in order to help her learn it, but finds it easier to use Spanish, in which she is quickly regaining her fluency.

[9] English, however, seems to be regarded as a "strange" language, especially in terms of its phonetic characteristics. There seems to be the same sort of initial discomfiture in pronouncing English words that one sees in adult foreign language classes. For example, a pre-school English lesson developed by Dr. Edmund Coleman of The University of Texas at El Paso has been used. Raquel recognizes the written words *cat, can,* and *stop* from this lesson, but will not attempt to say the latter two. She subvocalizes them, but refuses to pronounce them aloud. She has learned to pronounce "cat" from the record *Peter and the Wolf,* but says it as if she were conscious of the fact that she is not producing the standard English sound. However, her parents do not attempt to correct her pronunciation of English words, nor in any way to make her conscious of it.

[10] These estimates are based on a dictionary count, marking the words which she uses and those which she shows evidence of understanding but does not use. A pocket dictionary was used, and some words were added

which were not listed in it. Reading ability seems to be limited to those words she has been taught, especially since she no longer pays attention to the phonetic representation. It is assumed that this form of attention will develop again, and that it will lead rapidly to the ability to read any word in Spanish she uses or understands. There are some recent indications of it in response to listening to poems.

[11] This generalization on one occasion was carried too far. When her father was recording her speech she pointed to the microphone and asked, "¿Qué es eso? " (What is that?). He answered, "Micrófono." She responded, "Es tu crófono." (It is your crophone). He corrected her, "No, es mi micrófono." (No, it is *my* microphone), and she replied, "Sí, es tu tucrófono." (Yes, it is your yourcrophone)!

[12] There are many parallels in this section with the data presented in another paper in this volume, the section on "Reading in Early Childhood" by Ragnhild Söderbergh. The latter is much more detailed and exact than the present account, and serves as a better introduction to the reading process in general at an early age. The present account focuses particularly upon the special characteristics of Spanish as a written language which, at least theoretically, should be much easier to learn to read than most other languages. However, this supposition is not borne out by comparison with teaching reading in Swedish as described by Söderbergh, nor with data offered by Doman in the aforementioned book, nor in his paper also presented in this volume. Nevertheless, it still would seem that at later stages Spanish reading should proceed much more rapidly than in languages with much less regular correspondence between sounds and symbols. This is indicated by differences in the level of materials used in Spanish-speaking countries at given grade levels. The writer is familiar with a number of cases (including his secretary) whose initial reading material in first grade was the Spanish-language newspaper, a marked contrast with "Dick and Jane." Textbooks in Spanish for third or fourth grade seem comparable in reading level to English for fifth or sixth grade. Materials at the "Dick and Jane" level are almost nonexistent.

[13] The transition described by Carol Chomsky as necessary in English is not necessary in Spanish, and this should allow much more rapid development in Spanish reading. See "Reading, Writing, and Phonology," *Harvard Educational Review*, XL, No. 2 (1970), p. 297. "It is highly likely that the child, however, in the beginning stages of reading, does assume that the orthography is in some sense regular with respect to pronunciation. In order to progress to more complex stages of reading, the child must abandon this early hypothesis, and come eventually to interpret written symbols as corresponding to more abstract lexical spellings. Normally he is able to make this transition unaided as he matures and gains experience both with the sound structure of his language and with reading."

[14] Doman, Glenn *How to Teach your Baby to Read*. New York: Random House, (1964).

7

Indian Child Bilingualism

Jane M. Christian

I. STYLE AND DIALECT SELECTION IN
    HINDI-BHOJPURI-LEARNING CHILDREN

Necessarily, in order to work at all on discovery procedures in child
language acquisition and in bilingualism and to integrate our findings into a
more comprehensive field of enquiry, we utilize and adapt systematic
assumptions from the general discipline of linguistic research with adults and
monolinguals and the resultant theory, both structural and generative. This
being a much larger, better-worked and established field than the
subdisciplines concentrating on language learning or bilingual processes, it is
only reasonable that we should expect to bring to bear its current concepts
and methods when working with bilinguals and with children, to ask
questions related to current general questions of theory and method, and
then to relate these matters to the field at large. However, this has its
drawbacks as well as its advantages. Some methods and terminology, by the
very fact of this extension of the field of research, may well need to be
reconsidered and their meanings reshaped and broadened to fit the larger
context. Basic orientation may also require adaptation to different language
and culture systems, as their defining features and the domains based on
these may segment and structure 'reality' in ways unexpected by the
researcher. This again may serve to indicate needs to broaden theory; and
this is, after all, the history and process of any growing discipline. However,
though we are coming to expect this broad kind of adaptability in bilinguals
and in young children, we as system-oriented scholars may sometimes be less
ready or able to adapt our own thought and research behavior sufficiently to
other systems.

In the case of children and bilinguals, and more especially in the
combined case of bilingualism in young children, we are probably witnessing
an extreme of adaptability. If an understanding of the range and parameters
of possible communication strategies and behaviors is central to the study of
linguistics, then the description and creation of explanatory models for

bilingualism in young children is important indeed for the development of linguistic theory. Here we may observe linguistic manipulation and creativity concentrated, and here models of competence may well be made and tested. In fact, any powerful and general model of linguistic competence must be able to take into account the varieties of bilingualism and developing language use in children, and of these combined, as perhaps a sort of ultimate test. Bending our energies towards fuller understanding of these phenomena may be difficult indeed, a task with so many dimensions as to be a trap for the unwary, but one with the ultimate possibility of high rewards.

In the present case of style-dialect selection, by Hindi-Bhojpuri-speaking children in and near the ancient holy city of Banaras in North India, there are complexities which beggar the terminology which this writer had previously learned to use with regard to dialects, styles, and related phenomena, and their analysis — as well as the whole question of what we may define as bilingualism in the adult scheme and especially in the schemes of child learners. To reap some degree of understanding out of much initial confusion required two things: considerable time spent thoroughly immersed in the situation, with close attention to what adults and children actually were saying and doing in a wide variety of contexts; and a casting aside of numerous inadequate preconceptions. The object specifically, then, was (1) to define the operative distinctive features for adults and for children in styles or dialects and in the contexts for which these were selected; (2) to note what and where were the markers of communicative behavior, and where their parameters; and, most difficult, (3) to come to decisions as to their basic meanings or psychological reality;[1] and (4) to group and categorize these behaviors at a higher level of broad cultural meanings and social functions.

The need to view developing child language as process rather than state seems clear enough. In North India this view of language is further underlined by the factor of rapid linguistic change, change which for centuries has added in complex ways — at any time — to an already complex situation. Speech differences traditionally tend to demarcate the enormous variety of crosscut social and religious groupings and emphasize other distinctions made among them. There is ritual power and bargaining power in language choices. On the one hand language is conceived as having a divine nature and power, some types having more *mana* than others; on the other hand individuals and groups define and can raise their social status in specific ways by making stylistic changes in their communicative behavior, provided, of course, this is done by small increments and discreetly.

Kali C. Bahl of the University of Chicago makes some pertinent comments along these sociolinguistic lines in a review of M. Jordan-Horstman's "Sadani: A Bhojpuri Dialect Spoken in Chotanagar" (1969).[2] It is noted by Bahl that the author fails to mention anywhere that wholesale language-switching has been going on in this area [the Ranchi District of Bihar] for quite some time. . .Several Sadani speaking

communities are in the process of switching over to modern Hindi.
[Further,] language-switching...from Sadani to modern Hindi...
serves to signify socio-cultural progress in this area where a particular
language or dialect identifies the social status of an individual or a
group in relation to other individuals or groups.

The important comment is made that

The problems of correlation between language and dialect grouping
along the lines of social stratification can be fruitfully studied in
North India.

The additional comment might be made that definitions of languages
and dialects in North India are presently, and understandably, in a somewhat chaotic state.

In this land of overwhelming linguistic diversity and fourteen official
state languages an enormous amount of writing and verbal exposition
continues to deal with the subject Hindi, but it must be said that few
issues have been settled. Throughout, there is little agreement about how
many speakers of Hindi there are, who actually speaks "true" Hindi, how
well and to whom, how much and what sorts of bilingualism and multilingualism exist, what dialects are dominant in what ways, just what the
Hindi or Hindustani language consists of, and whether or not scores of
dialects and subdialects are part of the Hindi language. Out of this of
course rises the question as to just what is a dialect and how it is to be
operationally defined. It would appear that to some extent each has been
empirically and separately defined on the basis of varying criteria by
people with varying qualifications to evaluate them. Especially has
controversy continued as to the relative status of Hindi and Urdu, for
political, communal, religious, and regional reasons more than narrowly
linguistic ones.

Extreme separatists in Banaras and elsewhere argue Hindi and Urdu
are two distinct languages and point for conclusive proof to their different
scripts — *devnagri* for Hindi stemming very closely from Sanskrit and
Persian for Urdu. Ordinary Muslims of course speak Urdu in Banaras; their
Hindu neighbors speak Hindi or Bhojpuri, they say; aside from a few
differences in formal greetings and prayer formulae, a linguist would be
hard put indeed to detect any difference at all when they converse with
each other or among themselves, in terms of phonology and grammar. It is
true that there are some small differences in kinesic and paralinguistic
features and differences in dress, etc., some of which can be consciously
exaggerated or pointed out if need be. There is of course some larger
difference in lifestyle; in other words the differences are primarily social
rather than strictly verbal, but it is not always easy to see where language
fades into other aspects of culture through the communicative devices of
such items as gesture and dress.

But it is interesting and informative to compare the Hindi-Urdu
stylistic differences given in a standard text with actual usage in everyday
speech in this holy city of the Hindus. By far the greatest number of

stylistic lexical alternates listed in the text as Urdu were those in ordinary use among both Muslims and Hindus. My informants, both Hindu adults and children over eight who were able to select and identify dialects or styles by name, contended these were by no means Urdu, but ordinary Hindi.[3] Many of the words listed as Hindi variants were rejected as either not known or considered bookish. Some were commonly contrasted with a lexeme from the Urdu list, but the difference given was that of respect-religious form versus ordinary. A few typical examples of the latter are:

grih	good house	ghar	ordinary house
pustak	religious book	kitāb	ordinary book
yātrā	pilgrimage	safar	trip
śuddh	pure ritually	sāf	clean
sāhāytā	divine aid	madad	ordinary help
sthān	sacred place	jagah	place
	(e.g., tīrth-kā sthān)		
snān	ritually purifying bath	nahān	bath
	(e.g., ganga snān)		

This question of what is Hindi or Urdu is matched and overlapped by the question of what is Hindi or Bhojpuri, according either to adults or children. Bhojpuri is what is spoken at home, say all informants old enough to be aware of named sorts of speech. Then they add Bhojpuri is the medium of ordinary bāzār contacts, contacts with consanguineal kin, with close friends, with women, and children. One also prays and sings for the gods in Bhojpuri, alone at one's pūjā or in company at a bhajan or ārthī. Bhojpuri can also be partly grammatically defined by children of eleven in that they can deliberately speak in Bhojpuri and contrast this with Hindi speech and can give paradigmatic structure of Bhojpuri verbal inflections, etc.

Hindi is said to be that which is spoken at school, in formal business contacts or government offices, in formal ceremonies either public or private, in some contacts with affinal kin; and Hindi is what is written. One uses Hindi if possible to indicate respect given to another, and one raises the respect to be accorded to himself by his proficiency in spoken and written Hindi. Religious books are written in śuddh Hindi, a designation given a more formal Sanskritized, and ritually pure form of the language; religious discourses, dramas, and some ceremonies are conducted in śuddh Hindi. Virtually every child over eight is aware of this style, and an increasing number of boys over this age become more or less proficient in its production as well as comprehension. Nearly every pandit, pūjārī (priest), or vyās (learned commentator on various scriptures) knows śuddh Hindi well and can expound sonorously and dramatically, quoting at times from Sanskrit for hours. He is unlikely to use śuddh Hindi in his ordinary speech. Very many serious-minded men, whether of *dviya* or twice born *varna* or not, know considerable *śuddh* Hindi.

This dimension or continuum with regard to respect or *ādar* in speech is commonly labeled in terms of high, ordinary, and low, or *nirādar*, though finer distinctions can be made if it is considered necessary in special situations. This is a measure of distinctions, both linguistic and social, which transcend and complicate very much of what we are accustomed to think of in terms of dialect or style throughout India. Here these categories are inadequate to describe or explain the interrelationships in a country where some languages may be ritually high and others low, where paradoxically *thetha* can mean both pure and unmixed and the unwritten language of common people. Hardly any aspect of Indian thought or life remains untouched by this continuum of the ritually pure and worthy of respect to the ritually defiled and unworthy — persons, groups, objects, ideas, and even languages or dialects not remaining constant but rather sliding along the scale according to a multiplicity of factors and a complex etiquette.

And all this points to the problem of how speech behavior is conceived and defined by the speakers. Factors such as attitudes, vested interests, and cognitive assumptions as to the nature of ritual, social, and linguistic context clearly can effect how utterances are produced, received, interpreted, and understood. On the basis of these factors plus kinesic and paralinguistic markers we can thus sometimes distinguish a "dialect" in India. Linguistic distance is generally measured according to social and ritual distance. For example, a child of eight or more, or an adult, would quickly and positively state what dialect or style another person was using or would use, even on the basis of photographs or the mention of certain categories of persons, where both verbal and paralinguistic-kinesic features were largely ruled out. It was a matter of who ought to be speaking what to whom, a matter of established expectations. An informant's more considered decision would be based not necessarily on listening but on further knowledge of such factors as age, sex, dress, residence, *jātī*, education, occupation, plus the speaker's relationship to the person spoken to, his current ritual status, and where the speech act took place: home, neighborhood, *bāzār*, *mandir* (temple), school, office, etc. Even where listening was clearly possible, as in overhearing street conversations, listening for grammatical constructions or lexical items proved secondary to the social-ritual considerations, for which largely visual evidence or non-verbal information stimulated cognitive classification.

This is not to say that either children or adults were unable readily to specify styles through listening alone. They classified easily on the basis of hearing taped samples of speech of individuals unknown to them, though here I could find no way to separate cues derived from the semantic content of the taped speech from purely dialectal or stylistic differences. Before the age of three years children could easily recognize their own taped speech and that of family members, could recognize speech directed to babies by its style, and usually could pick out the *śuddh* Hindi style by labeling the speaker *bābūjī*, a cover term for any sort of holy man, often used by children as well as adults. Between three and five they became proficient in picking out Bhojpuri neighbor-*bāzār* type conversations, in which they were already participating daily, and could differentiate by respect style markers speech of children and adults to individuals of high status, outside or within the family. Also they could recognize the simplified style of an adult speaking to a young child in simple short sentences with a restricted set of lexical items and lack of respect forms. Generally they were familiar too with curt or even abusive language style, recognizing it as low, bad *gālī*, or *burā-bōlī*. They identified standard Hindi with the radio broadcasts generally, as most of these Bhojpuri-learning children had little or no contact with standard Hindi speakers before going to school. School-attending children of six or so identified standard Hindi with school and textbooks, though their teachers admitted rather unwillingly that most instruction for the first two years was in Bhojpuri dialect, the teachers speaking Bhojpuri among themselves and at home as well. Some called the speech of the children *khārībōlī* or uncultivated speech, literally bitter. By eight years school-attending children were developing some proficiency within this restricted environment in standard Hindi, though they exhibited a wide range of interest and ability in this. Only a little *śuddh* Hindi learning takes place in the schools, and boys from this age generally learn more or less formally within the context of religious instruction from an elder family or outside preceptor, or, failing this, may pick up some informally by attendance at religious festivals or other functions where it may be heard and seen. Within one neighborhood of artisans of several *jātī*-s, boys from about ten to twelve varied widely from little or no ability to produce *śuddh* Hindi to proficiency at nearly adult level. The variable most closely associated with this seemed to be religious and ritual interests of a traditional sort and an interest in myth and narrative in general, in other words, a semantic context. In many families it is considered improper for a girl to speak anything but Bhojpuri or to attend school, at least beyond the age of nine or ten. Standard Hindi[4] and *śuddh* Hindi are considered the province of males, especially elders, but this does not prevent girls from being able to recognize, identify, and understand these styles and to respond to them appropriately. Within Bhojpuri it is possible for them to produce all of the main patterns along the respect continuum, and they learn much as the boys do from religious functions. At the same age as boys, girls develop the characteristic narrative style of Hindi,[5] beginning with simple conjoined sentences with narrative intonation patterns at five years and increasing the length and imbeddedness of the sentences and overall length and semantic complexity and cohesiveness of narrative to early adolescence, when they have mastered production of the adult style. A difference between speech styles of boys and girls is discernible by the age of seven or eight; each recognizes that of the other and will not use it. Here again the differences are largely paralinguistic and kinesic, with a general feature we may call emphasis[6] predominating more in the boys' style with more variability in intonation patterns and a wider scope for the same general postures, gestures, etc., plus a greater overall amount of talking allowable. Boys may with impunity use some forms like slang and nicknames which most families will not allow their girls to use. Most families, again, are quite particular that their children in general conform to the standards of good, clean Bhojpuri and not use abusive language. When asked what they most liked to hear, children varied considerably in their answers; in answer to what they dislike most to hear, most replied abusive language. Some few families, it must be said, diverge from this norm.[7]

There is an important difference, currently receiving considerable attention, between linguistic competence and performance. This underlies much of relevance in bilingualism and language acquisition, of course, and as a concept possesses the virtue of testability with both bilinguals and children. Children's recognition, understanding, and classification of dialect-stylistic differences, as well as their appropriate responses to them within this Hindi-Bhojpuri system can, it is clear, be mapped out in process of development. Working out the best model to explain the children's changing distinctive feature systems and analytic strategies is more difficult, but can be approached through study of their behavioral and linguistic performance, both spontaneous and tested in various ways.

It is generally agreed among Bhojpuri speakers that Bhojpuri seems most natural and comfortable, some parts of the traditional *śuddh* Hindi next so, the standard Hindi of necessary use third, and last of all the more formal Hindi of upper castes. It is useful perhaps to note that this is the same order in which these are acquired by Bhojpuri-speaking children. Children also absorb early a basic set of important knowledge of their culture and how to behave in it; in fact, it is instructive for a researcher seeking important patterns to observe what it is that young children are learning, what they may be imitating and mastering, and in what ways they express creativity within their language and culture. In studying children themselves it is also often useful to pinpoint "mistakes" as defined by their elders' system, in that this can be a guide to developing cognitive patterns and strategies of thought, or competence within the larger system.

Bypassing the earliest stages of vocal production in cooing and babbling, and even that of global, one-"word" utterances, we note that the Bhojpuri-learning child at approximately eighteen months develops pivotal utterances of two component "words," has already mastered most intonation patterns of Bhojpuri, and has a rudimentary stock of gestures indicating negation, affirmation, and respect to gods and some elders, among other things. He also has some of the emphasis markers in his repertoire, has a stock of verb root imperatives, and generally an impressive list of kinship terms. He has learned some of the important features of family and temple *pūjā*. From one to about three we may say he speaks as he is spoken to in the family generally, in a style devoid of formality or respect markers, except that he is early taught to say *namaste* as well as perform the gesture, and will definitely add the *-jī* honorific particle appropriately to his speech, as in the early morning greeting often extended to me by one two-year-old, *namatēē, behenjī* (greeting + emphasis, sister + respect). Also he may early indulge in a bit of abuse as *rośanlāl* at 2.6, threatening his mother's sister's small daughter: *mārā, bāī* (beating, brother?) apparently recognizing that *behen* cannot be used in such a context but *bhāī*, brother, can be used in a slang as well as ordinary context. Before three, children will be well in command of a stock of minor expletives, such as *hath, (h)ē, arē*, and others, used appropriately, for example, to warn off a dog or even another child. By three they have the particle *-vālā*, which may be roughly translated doer, and is neutral referring to things or persons of artisan occupations, but disrespectful for anyone else; and they use it appropriately. In general they will have the system whereby a child or adult addresses non-kin persons respectfully by kinship terms referring to elders of the appropriate generation and sex, often with the *-jī* particle added. By three and earlier they know to address kin who are older by kinship terms only, since it is disrespectful to call anyone older by his name. Somewhat later they learn the use of kin terms is elastic also in that one can use a term belonging to the next higher generation from the person addressed in order to convey still more respect in some cases; for example, *dādā*, literally father's father, for father's elder brother; or *cācā*, literally father's younger brother, for one's own elder brother.

In Hindi and Bhojpuri respect patterns are not equivalent to politeness formulae: there is no "please" as such, nor are words for thanks used under any but very exceptional circumstances; and expressions such as "excuse me" are rarely used. Children usually do not learn these at an early age. They do learn to supply all relevant inflectional markers as a sign of respectful speech by the age of four, and that long, involved sentences rather than abbreviated ones are a sign of respect. A few children by three, but nearly all by four, appropriately use polite *-iyē* verbal request forms, such as *baithiyē* (please sit), *caliyē* (let's go), and *khaiyē* (please eat); and use *mat*, the negative before polite request forms.

But even though isolated and increasing incidents of utterances appropriate to a definite style occur in the speech of children as young as two and three, we have little reason to suppose that they have as yet any abstract concept of two separate stylistic systems. It would be more faithful to the data and to children's capacities to judge novel contexts to suppose they have internalized bits and pieces as yet too scanty to form any coherent broad pattern on an adult style. Furthermore they combine elements of different styles in the same utterance often up to the age of about eight and often interestingly reduce the respect forms in sentences they choose spontaneously to imitate from older children or adults. For example, Sītā, 6.2, returned to me rather unwillingly my pen, with the -õ particle related to the sacred syllable ōm and thereby respectful but signifying half consent: *kalamõ lẽ lā, behenjī*; then later followed with *rūlõ lẽ lāta ha.* (The ruler, all right, is being brought.) which her four-year-old brother echoed without the -õ as *rūl le lāta ha.* Or Hunamān, 6.5, included the standard Hindi -*thah* marker after his numbers, while his four-year-old brother immediately afterwards failed to do so. Hunamān: *hamār pãc thah fōtō hõ.* (I have five photos.), and Bhāgavandās: *nahi, ēk kar lẽ.* (No, one bring.) Bindesvarī at five was well in command of such respectful utterances as, *caliyē, behenjī-kō, dikhaiyē* and *dēkhaiyē.* (Please look.), but sometimes dispensed with them, as when it began to rain and her mother respectfully said, *andar āp-lōg baithi ē.* (You people please be seated inside.), Bindesvarī hurriedly insisted, *ghar-mẽ calõ.* (Come in the house!)

By about six it appears a rudimentary sort of systematization of styles is taking place, perhaps catalyzed by school and other experiences outside the home, but still children of this age can rarely sustain production in the less familiar dialect or style for over a very few utterances at a time. Here their recognition greatly outstrips their ability to reproduce. Some children at this age can imitate teachers and even holy men in production of standard Hindi and of *śuddh* Hindi, but generally exhibit shyness over doing so in the presence of adults — a different situation from their bold imitation of street vendors at three. By six they could produce a haughty style of formality for semantic effect, as Hanumān's *ah apnē-kō bahut calākh ha.* (To the conceited one himself he is very clever.) They continue with their peers to indulge in abusive speech at times, as Pannalāl, 4.8, to Gita, 4: *aur mattī khavēgē, nāk capatarā.* (And you will eat dirt, flattened nose.)

Systematic instruction, of course, could produce a clear demarcation of styles or, even more clearly, languages by this age. At six, the son of the *mahārāja* of Banaras could publicly recite from a vast store of memorized Sanskrit *sloka*-s, and knew *śuddh* Hindi. At ten, an apprentice to his *dādā*, a *pūjārī*, could recite Sanskrit and use *śuddh* Hindi easily, while the eleven-year-old son of a clerk and particularly pious man followed his father in conducting his own daily home *pūjā* in Sanskrit and *śuddh* Hindi, separating these clearly from the Bhojpuri he spoke at home ordinarily, and the standard Hindi he spoke at school. Another not unusual eleven-year-old boy could easily recite myths with almost a full command of *śuddh* Hindi style in all features, keep his school Hindi separate from this for the most part, and keep his home Bhojpuri entirely separate.

It would appear that, by ten or eleven certainly, these children exposed to different styles in different contexts have almost entirely separated them according to different sets of distinctive features into integral patterns, and that they are thus able to do what many adults within their same social groups have not completed. There seems to be considerable elasticity in the system itself, which allows many to overlap their styles yet encourages some to separate them more fully. And the closeness of these styles on a respect-level continuum makes their study interesting, and their development in children revealing, as it shows the types of confusions and the kinds of separations made during the process of learning as well as sometimes indicating criteria and strategies used for developing systematizations.

Summary

In researching child language and especially child bilingualism some of the problems met with in linguistic study of adults are both redoubled and made more obvious and inescapable. We are forced for one thing away from the comfortable notion of language as state and to a view of language as process in developing child. We thus may incline towards the explanatory power of mentalistic models in current psycholinguistics, towards criteria of testability and psychological reality, and towards more emphasis on semantic analysis. Another problem of studying such bilingualism is that of definition terms. Are we justified in simply transferring concepts inhering in and surrounding terms such as dialect or style from the adult Western or European framework (a) to children or (b) to a very different social and linguistic complex as India presents? Should we perhaps re-define the semantic distinctive features for these terms to increase their discriminatory and explanatory powers in accordance with what we find in the field? And can we safely ignore the importance of paralinguistic, kinesic, and other contextual features in the study of child language acquisition, particularly bilingual? These questions are here illustrated in the context of dialect-style learning by children of Banaras in North India.

NOTES

[1] The question always remains open and theoretically unprovable as to whether psychological reality has really been captured, and is further vexed by the question of whose reality and when, and how many psychological realities may coexist in a social group sharing a culture and language, and how much these need to and do overlap. One can be surer by observing and checking carefully with informants what solutions do *not* represent psychological reality, or the semantic set, and at least markedly narrow the possibilities.

[2] See *American Anthropologist*, 73, No. 4 (1971), pp. 909-910.

[3] It should be noted that *esteśan, motar, pensil, pen, rūl, kāpī* (copybook), *saykil, rediyō, leyt,* and *taym,* connected with the new mechanization and literacy in North India, were regarded and inflected as Hindi too.

[4] Within the last thirty years more girls of educated families are using the standard language of literacy.

[5] This is virtually the same for Bhojpuri as a style, allowing for the grammatical and lexical differences.

[6] Semantic emphasis is signaled by several different means in Hindi and Bhojpuri, often conjointly used. These include:

(a) vowel lengthening beyond the phonemic $V \sim \bar{V}$ contrast,

(b) use of the emphatic particle *-i* or *hī* which is employed in many ways and places, such as negative *na + hī → nahī* emphatic negative,

(c) reduplication of lexemes, phrases, clauses, or whole sentences,

(d) use of a rhymed doublet of the word requiring emphasis,

(e) increasing the voice volume,

(f) exaggerating the intonation patterns, and employing other paralinguistic devices, and

(g) exaggerating kinesic features such as posture, expression, and gesture.

Children firmly possess all these features by age three. Communication of emphasis is closely related to that of respect levels: all its forms enter to some degree in both plus and minus respect communication, the greater use being correlated with greater divergence from neutral or ordinary respect. Further, the particle *jī* expressly denotes respect, as in *ganga-jī, bau-jī* (father), *ha-jī* (yes, sir), and *jī-nahi* (no, sir); and pluralization is used to some extent in Hindi and more often than not in Bhojpuri to indicate respect rather than literal plurality.

[7] Also abuse language is compulsory under certain circumstances; for example, at marriages old women must come to sing insulting songs.

APPENDIX

CONFIGURATION OF STYLE-DIALECTS IN BANARAS, INDIA: A Continuum Based on Respect Forms

Bhojpuri	standard Hindi	*śuddh* Hindi
[3]ordinary Bhojpuri with sets of neutral markers & set of respect markers	[5]formal polite style, highly inflected, Sanskritized, a formal literature written, highest respect markers	[6]extreme respect for religious exposition, public speeches, highly Sanskritized and inflected, the highest style of writing, three highest sets of respect markers
[2]rude style or without respect markers		
[1]abuse style or *gālī*, *burābōlī*, defined as with its own para-linguistic and kinesic features, and lexicon additions	[4]ordinary style written, three sets of respect markers as in Bhojpuri, but more inflection	

Sample respect forms in imperative-requests, for the above styles:

[1]verb root only *jā* (go!) disrespectful

[2]verb root only *jā* (go!) disrespectful, also simplified for babies

[3]verb root plus -*ō* (go!) lacking respect

verb root plus -*nā* (go!) neutral

verb root plus -*iyē* (please go!) respectful

[4]same as 3

[5]also same as 3, and

verb root plus -*iyēgā* (please have the pleasure of going) extreme respect

[6]verb root plus *nā* (go!) neutral

verb root plus -*iyēgā* (please have the pleasure of going) extreme respect

Bhojpuri arose as a dialect indigenous to southeastern Uttar Pradesh and southwestern Bihar, centered along the Ganga or Ganges River, as an unwritten Indo-Aryan dialect, presumably from the medieval Prakrits. It exhibits considerable variation from west to east and, on its edges, blends in with other dialects.

Standard Hindi was created artificially in part from dialects closer to Delhi in Mogul and British times as a useful *lingua franca* across broad stretches of North India and has always been identified with the government and with literate speakers. It has tended also to be identified with outsiders; though this aspect is diminishing, as Hindi served for a unifying force in India's struggle for freedom and as such was consciously developed. A Hindi literature has appeared in this century, and Hindi is definitely spreading through North India at several levels: as the main film medium, as the government radio medium over large areas, as medium of instruction in schools, as government medium in several states, as *bāzār* and commercial *lingua franca*, and in other ways. Furthermore it has become a prestige language associated with literacy and important posts, and its use is a mark of upward mobility. It is gaining as a second language or dialect for many speakers.

Śuddh Hindi is a purely literary and formal expository style used traditionally in religious contests and increasingly in political expository style in some parties where the dress of religious sanction is useful and even necessary. Characterized by the incorporation of many words and roots from Sanskrit, it was developed especially in and around Banaras as a self-conscious elite style in this holy city of *pandits* and publishers. In *śuddh* Hindi, and indeed in other speech to some extent, the verbal symbols have something of the quality of signs as well. The sanctified syllables and words are directly associated with sanctified being and action; the sacred syllable *ōm* is more than an invocation in the Western sense; it is an automatic evocation of transcendence. The idea is strong that form implies meaning as part of the same basic unity, so Sanskritic scholars would not agree with the assumption in Western linguistics of a necessary dichotomy between sound and meaning in human speech. It is no accident, therefore, that people under this influence tend to treat language as an important thing itself to be treated respectfully, whether they are speakers of *śuddh* Hindi, standard Hindi, or Bhojpuri.

Notes on Some Outstanding Features of Comparative *śuddh* Hindi, Standard Hindi, and Bhojpuri Structure

1. There are some phonemic differences between *śuddh* Hindi, standard Hindi, and Bhojpuri; the most noteworthy for mention here perhaps is the general and progressive tendency to simplify consonant clusters from $C_1C_2(C_3) \rightarrow C_1(C_{2,3}) \rightarrow C_1 \rightarrow C_2$, etc. Also some phoneme sets such as spirants and nasals have a tendency to collapse somewhat, from three to two, and five to three to two respectively, while the vowel system follows a simpler pattern in Bhojpuri as well. We find this same tendency towards simplification of these items redoubled in young children, not only in this area, but in all the languages thus far studied for acquisition patterns. Caution and further research should, of course, precede any interpretation of this.

2. A few outstanding grammatical divergences along this same scale are:

(a) Increasing use of pluralization from *śuddh* Hindi to Bhojpuri for a respect marker over literal enumeration — plurality becoming more of a semantic marker in Bhojpuri, where it rarely is used to denote pluralization;

e.g., Bhāgavandās, age 4.1, offering a sweet to an old neighbor woman: *lē*, dādiyā, lē. "Take, father's mother + plural marker, take." It should be noted that this tendency is present even in *śuddh* Hindi, for example, in the substitution of plural for singular pronouns and verbal inflections to indicate respect. All similar tendencies of *śuddh* Hindi are present and increased in standard Hindi; this process continues with Bhojpuri.

(b) *Śuddh* Hindi most closely parallels the enormous inflectional complexity of Sanskrit, for example, in large multidimensional paradigms for nouns, verbs, and adjectives along such axes as number, "gender," direct-oblique constructions, and several specifically on verbs with regard to person, time, causality, transitivity, aspect, etc. In standard spoken Hindi we find very similar verb patterns, but less complexity and less regularity in such items as direct-oblique, singular-plural, masculine-feminine distinctions. In Bhojpuri a few verb constructions are absent and others changed in their phonological realization; not only number markers but gender sometimes shows more affiliation with respect.

(c) Correspondingly, *śuddh* Hindi depends less upon word order than inflectional markers and agreements, is characterized by intricately imbedded sentences dependent upon this inflection and by parallel grammatical constructions of phrases, clauses, etc. Standard spoken Hindi possesses a more closely defined word order and less range of variability in imbedding and other features of syntax. Again in Bhojpuri this process is carried somewhat further, though the parallel structures continue in profusion.

(d) Some intonation patterns of *śuddh* Hindi appear to be derived from ritual Sanskrit chanting, or at least to be related to it; narrative intonation patterns conform to the intricate syntactic structure. In standard Hindi and in Bhojpuri these are correspondingly modified to fit the syntax, but features of rising and falling pitch, length, juncture, etc., are very similar in narrative patterns.

3. Paralinguistic and kinesic features are, in this system at least, of far greater overall importance than they are usually accorded in narrowly defined linguistic terms, in conveying often the bulk of the semantic context of a communication, and being certainly capable of definition, study, and analysis. One speaking *śuddh* Hindi sits erect or stands, head back and eyes directed somewhat down to listeners; arm and hand gestures are broad and relatively slow; he does not smile, but his expressions are intended to convey power and dignity; he gazes down on listeners with brow drawn down, chin and mouth somewhat forward. He speaks relatively loudly, and he is the one to initiate speech or conversation if different styles are being used in one group. His intonation patterns are exaggerated beyond ordinary Hindi. If *śuddh* Hindi is used in private reading or *pūjā* these features are less marked. In standard Hindi use they are again less marked, though gestures tend to be more rapid, along with speech. With standard Hindi and Bhojpuri there is considerable variation in paralinguistic, kinesic, and proxemic features, depending upon the respect

relationship between the participants in communication. To give respect one makes *namaste* or, more respectful, *namaskār*, in a slight bow from the waist with palms together before the chest or face, depending upon the degree of respect to be given. A high degree of respect is conveyed by *pranām*, prostration on knees and face. Both may be given the gods, to certain kin, and to certain others in a complex system. In giving respect one also keeps silence, or speaks when spoken to, maintaining an erect posture, a solemn countenance, and correct distance, and speaks clearly but not loud. To a guest one shows respect by offering water and ritually pure foods or *pān* (betel). In neutral respect contexts speech tends to be somewhat louder, and a complex array of facial expressions and gestures, postures, etc., comes into play, formalized as *bhāva* and *mudra* in the dance systems of India. No learner can speak the language without learning and using these; children are masters of nearly all patterns before the age of three years. There are also several features of these sorts which indicate disrespect: posture, gesture, facial expression all exaggerated, and speech loud and rapid, without the customary pauses for replies found throughout polite styles. This may also be learned very early, but in nearly all cases is soon eliminated in the presence of any elders. These features of language and style structure are, of course, only a minute selection from what could well occupy volumes, and are intended only to be a hopefully representative enough sampling to convey some appreciation of what dialectal and stylistic items and differences children within the system must learn; and learn they do, mastering their home dialect-style before five, and learning more or less all which are pertinent within the lifestyle of their group by about the age of eleven.

This study of style-dialect learning was part of a larger thirty-one months project researching the acquisition of linguistic, cognitive, and behavioral patterns in young children from two widely separated regions of India. Those contributing to this paper live in and near Banaras (or Varanasi), Uttar Pradesh; the others being Telugu learners of southern Andhra Pradesh. Most are children of handloom silk weavers of fairly low but clean caste, and are members of agnatic joint families. Formal education of mothers and other elder female kin ranged from zero to two years; that of fathers and elder male kin from zero to five years. Most families today try to send their children to local government schools for more years of formal education than they had themselves, though this is often difficult. Pressures are strong for the children to work at home by nine or ten, for several reasons. Children are exposed to various linguistic styles and even languages beyond those of the family in the larger neighborhood, school, temples, and religious functions, and occasionally by being taken to another community to visit kin or a holy place.

II   DEVELOPING BILINGUALISM IN A TWO-YEAR-OLD GUJARATI-ENGLISH-LEARNING CHILD

In this short preliminary report on English acquisition by a 2.6-year-old Gujarati-speaking child we perforce will deal only partially with overall language development, concentrating upon two aspects that at present stand out in her bilingual development. There are (a) phonological accommodation of English and Gujarati in a changing and increasing system, and (b) concentration of English lexemes in specific semantic domains within a basically Gujarati-oriented grammar.

The only child of a university professor, she came with both parents from India to the United States at the age of twenty-one months, at which time she had the beginnings of a "telegraphic" syntax in Gujarati with remnants of a pivotal stage still in operation. In Gujarati she had been exposed both to standard literate Gujarati and to an unwritten northern dialect similar to Sindhi, the Kacchi spoken in the home of relatives. According to these informants Kacchi and standard Gujarati are mutually unintelligible; this child did not acquire the ability to speak Kacchi but came to understand some few requests or commands, and perhaps the names of some objects and people during her short contact with Kacchi. Both parents from the beginning of her language development have spoken to this child almost entirely in Gujarati, their aim being to protect her against confusion in her basic development of language skills while slowly introducing a few items in English. However, though Gujarati is spoken almost entirely among family members, English is spoken over the telephone, with frequent guests and colleagues, and by the dozen or so children with whom this child plays in and around the high-rise apartment building in which she lives. Furthermore she hears English daily on television in the home, in both children's and adults' programs. For several months during the earlier part of her stay in this country she was in frequent contact with a Panjabi-speaking boy of the same age, whose family often visited with her own, and whose speech development was roughly comparable to her own. From him she acquired a few words in Panjabi, but was evidently uninfluenced in either phonological or grammatical development, simply setting these Panjabi words in a Gujarati context. Very recently the child and her mother have been attending two mornings per week a nursery school in which English is the principal medium, though speakers of several languages participate. In all contacts with English-speaking children of various ages this child for the most part speaks with them in Gujarati, increasingly fitting in English words and phrases which she has learned, and appears to feel little or no inhibition from the language differences in this interaction. One reason undoubtedly for this is the great reliance placed upon proxemic and kinesic aspects of total communication in children around this age range; touch, close eye contact, facial expressions, gestures, and direct imitation of active play behavior are all important, and can often substitute for speech, or provide, as it were, an interpretation of verbal interaction through other sensory information. Furthermore this child is virtually always accompanied by one or both parents, to whom she can turn for verbal interpretation and even some translation services.

It is clear that the child's comprehension of English is greater than either her grammatical competence (which should not be confused with comprehension, the latter requiring considerably less complete grasp of details and even of structural principles) or her ability to produce novel utterances. Though to a considerably lesser degree, the same sort of statement can be made about her comprehension and use of Gujarati, the difference here being less marked. She reproduces, for example, in reduced, grammatically simpler sentences, the somewhat more complex embedded or conjoined parallel structures of sentences formed for her by the parents in Gujarati stories, and in other contexts. It should be noted here that neither parent speaks to the child in such long or complex utterances as are reserved for adult use, in either Gujarati or English, but in turn reduces these and the lexical range considerably, to fall just a short distance beyond the child's present competence. The same may be said with reference to the speech in English directed to the child by English-speaking children, though overheard English from the telephone or other adult conversations, television, etc. is, of course, not reduced in this way. It is interesting that the child is able increasingly to separate and sort out systematically items from the English, as well as Gujarati, which is intended for adult consumption, and then use them productively in her own speech. She shows the ability to pick out word classes in English to some extent, which implies a rudimentary grasp of English syntactical patterns, often quite different from those of Gujarati, and also, presumably, an understanding of English intonation patterns and paralinguistic features. Otherwise, how would it be possible for her to isolate and label, and then appropriately use English lexical items and even phrases from the barrage of English noise heard from adults or on television? Creation of an adequate explanatory model for this sort of linguistic behavior in the bilingual child is surely one of the most crucial tasks facing the field of developmental linguistics.

In Gujarati grammar this child is beginning to acquire several inflectional patterns, proceeding, it would appear, from a semantic base, and is fully capable of appropriately constructing several types of Gujarati sentences of NP, VP, adjectives, postpositional phrases and adverbials of a locative sort, question markers, emphasis and respect markers, and so on. She can use a few verb tenses such as present continuative and past continuative appropriately and fully, but lacks aspect, transitivity markers, etc. She is beginning to use gender and pronouns appropriately, but not yet pluralization (though, interestingly, she can count by rote in English nearly to ten, and associates this with enumeration). Possession is syntactically indicated by position, but morpheme markers are as yet absent. She is in command of some, though not all, imperative and request patterns, and negation. She inserts English lexemes of appropriate word classes into appropriate positions within her Gujarati grammar, but does not add Gujarati inflections to English words.

Gujarati and English being very distantly related as Indo-European languages, it is not too surprising that their phonological systems have many points of similarity. These and the differences will be apparent in much simplified form from the summary below, of Gujarati phonemes:

p ph	t th	ṭ ṭh	k kh
b bh	d dh	ḍ ḍh	g gh
	c ch		
	j jh		
m	n		
f ś	s	ṣ	
v	z		
	r		
	l	y	h

A most obvious difference from English is the aspiration of stops and affricates throughout, contrasting with nonaspirated ones, and the differentiation between dental and retroflex stops, plus differentiation among types of sibilants. Sanskritized written Gujarati would include other nasals, which, however, are homogenically determined by environment and thus more properly allophones of /n/.

The child under consideration has nearly completed acquisition of the full Gujarati set, though her system excludes the retroflex consonants, the /r/, which she coalesces with /l/, the voiced sibilant /z/, and the relatively rarely heard /jh/. She collapses all sibilants to /s/, the central one. Of English phonemes not occurring in Gujarati as such, she has developed a distinct /w/ which contrasts with her Gujarati /v/, the latter possessing an allophone [w]. An example of this is her clearly bilabial /w/ for the English grapheme y as /wai/, contrasting with Gujarati vāvā, frock. For English words she uses unaspirated consonants, ignoring the nondistinctive feature of English, whereby C- is slightly aspirated, in the case of stops. In both Gujarati and English her /s-/ and /c/ are realized as [ts], and /j/ as [ds], very slightly voiced. Thus sari becomes tsālī; train or cucu becomes tsūtsū. English /-z/ is realized as [-t], as in nose becoming nōt.

Gujarati has a distinction between long and short vowels in all cases:

i, ī		u, ū
e, ē		o, ō
	a, ā	

This child firmly possesses this contrast and all vowels, to which she has added the /æ/ of English, as in her kæt or dædi, which she consistently lengthens. Short vowels /ɛ/ and /ə/ she consistently realizes as short in English. Her short /i/ conforms in English to the Gujarati realization rather than to English /i/. She consistently lengthens final vowels in English, according to the Gujarati pattern. In Gujarati, consonants as well as vowels may often be geminated, a pattern which this child has mastered, but has no need for in English.

Gujarati consonant clusters of C_1C_2 which she uses include nasal plus stop, and stop plus continuant, such as /l/ or /y/. Stop plus /r/ becomes coalesced with stop plus /l/. These are transferred to English as *tłək* (truck), *tlī* (tree), *glīn* (green), *glēps* (grapes), *plīs* (please), and, for the former case, *tænka* (thank you), *elifənt* (elephant).

A generative morphophonemic analysis of this bilingual development over the span of perhaps a year would be most instructive, though beyond the scope of this paper, in which only a brief structural comparison and description of current features is possible.

With regard to semantic domains in which English lexemes are concentrated, it was possible as yet to find few, if any, true taxonomic structures labeled. In most cases it would be unjustifiable at this stage of development to argue more than configuration of items which somehow "go together" in sets, or perhaps even in lists. The process is certainly of systematization of more and more complex data; as it is received, it is oriented within the current system. Insofar as this proves impossible, the system is broadened to account for new items. It would seem that listing of items possessing a feature or collection of features in common, or perhaps only spatial or temporal contiguity, would be as simple a technique for early categorization as a child might find. In any case, some evidence for such a view appears in the English acquisition by this child, evidence eked out by the nonverbal context of speech.

For example, she can, either on command or spontaneously, draw a person, whom she variously identifies as herself, *dædī, məmmī, āntī,* or others in a group of known people for whom kinship terms are used. We may suspect that it is a factor of contiguity or some such which supplies the set, however, rather than literal kinship at this point. We may, however, be quite sure of defining it as a set, both by the continuity or production of the drawings, and by the fact that only the artist can identify whose is each portrait, their features looking very similar to an outsider. The features drawn and labeled verbally, mainly in English, can also be pointed out and labeled on herself or others thus, perhaps as a sort of distinctive feature system by which people are identified. The items duly drawn and labeled in English in each case include: *māt* (mouth), *nōt* (nose), *aibō* (eyebrow), *næk* (neck), *īah* (ear), *hɛh* (hair), and *āī* (eye). A circular face drawn goes unlabeled, though she appropriately applies the terms *hɛd* (head), and *fēs* (face) to herself and others; moreover, she thus labels *tīt* (teeth), *tɔn* (tongue), *fingə* (finger — for toes too, as in Gujarati), *tutums* (two thumbs), *bæk* (back) in English, and in Gujarati *pĕt* (belly), *nāk* (nose), *kān* (eye), *bagal* (armpit), and others. *Ūttū* is any hurt place. Dress may be another semantic set, though, if so, may be just emerging, in that production verbally of one item does not often stimulate a spontaneous retrieval of other items. There are several English lexemes in this category, if such it can be labeled: *pænt* (pant), *būt* (boot or shoe), *sāks* (socks), *bəpin* (button), etc., balanced by Gujarati *bangalī* (bangles), *vāvā* (frock), *tsālī* (sari), *tsappal* (sandal), etc.

Other Gujarati kin terms are used for non-kin frequent visitors who are Indian: for example, *māmā* (mother's brother) for older men, and *kākā* father's younger brother) for younger men, though, as her father has pointed out, the child has been instructed to address each person so, and we thus are unable to tell at this point whether or not the distinction is truly her own as well. We would need to present her with new examples and record her decisions on nomenclature. For American men *ənkā* (uncle) is spontaneously used, and for women *āntī* (aunty). Any boy may be called *bhaī* (brother) and any girl *behen* (sister), though in pictures and increasingly in flesh they are labeled *boi* (boy) and *gəl* (girl) respectively. Though she never confuses *bhai* and *behen*, she occasionally confuses pictured boys and girls. She clearly labels any picture or portrait *pits*, however, in English. For relatives she has in India she can tell the kinship terms, but, without photographs or some such, it is quite unclear just what she has in mind in this case — the term set itself or the actual family members.

Animals she groups and names as in her children's books, often in English: *ēlifənt* (elephant), *mənkī* (monkey), *hās* (horse), etc. For *kāu* (cow) she also has Gujarati *gulā*; for *pīkāk* (peacock) also *mōr* and a baby term *dakkuka*; for *dāg* (dog) also *kukkū*; for *kæt* also Gujarati baby term *miāu*; all used interchangeably. She has *patsī* for *paksī* (bird) and English *bəd*. In all cases she is bilingual with the animals' names in cases of more or recent contacts.

In the domain of foods, which seems clearly established, we find a clear demarcation into (a) all those found in the Gujarati-speaking world and (b) a much smaller set of American-type foods in English. She uses the Gujarati baby term *məmməm* for food in general. There is no indication that she divides the domain by languages in her use of it; and only rarely does she have two terms for the same food. In one case, she understands milk but uses *dūdh* or the baby term *dūdū*; in another she uses both banana and *kēlū*. Some English terms include *kok* (coke), *ɛg* (egg), *āmələt* (omelet), *glēps* (grapes), *bətəmilk* (buttermilk), *kukī* and *biskit* (cookie), *kantsip* (corn chip), *pətetətsip* (potato chip), and *kɛndī* (candy). On her father's suggestion that she say, "Mummy, please give me some candy," she repeated *məmmī, plīs gi mī kəndȳ*, ran off to the kitchen to reiterate her request, and returned with candy. Motivation can be a strong force in second-language learning. It will also be noticed that she has reduced the English model offered by her father by omitting the functor "some," in a way at least significantly similar to that of children reducing their native English at a telegraphic stage of development, and similar to her earlier treatment of Gujarati.

Another established domain is that of possessions: toys, clothing, ornaments, books, etc. *Buk* (book) is also *jāpalī*. She brings out and shows, naming spontaneously such items as *būt*, *dāl* (doll), *saikil* (bicycle), *piano* (piānō), *dləm* (drum) *bāl* (ball). She also points out and labels such sound and language-producing family equipment as *ēdivō* (radio), *tep* (tape recorder), and *tīvī* (television), with which she seems especially impressed. Most furniture so far goes unlabeled, though she knows her *kutsī (kursī)*, also called *tsε* (chair), and *bεd*, plus a few others in Gujarati. *Sisos* (scissors), *pen*, *pensil* in English are matched with *kāgəl* (paper), etc. Outside the home she has learned mostly words for motor vehicles such as *kā* (car), *tlək* (truck), *bəs* (bus), *tlēn* or *tsūtsū* (train), and *plēn* (airplane), plus a few others such as *tlī* (tree).

Beyond domains of palpable objects, however these may be defined, she has begun to use various qualifiers of a more abstract nature. Best established of these appear to be locatives, including question words such as *kanqī* (where?), *ancē* (there), *dūr* (far), *bājū* (near), *anda*(r) *bā*(r) (inside), *uppa*(r) (above or on), *nitsē* for *nicē* (under or·beneath) in Gujarati, as well as comprehension but not yet production of English right hand and left hand — extended to right foot, eye, etc. — well within her grasp. Her time sense has so far strayed little from the present *ab* (now), but shows signs of doing so as her verb tenses indicate on emerging. There appear to be no English temporals so far. *Atlā* (thus, in such a way) she uses both as affirmative and question; she possesses *āsuntsē* (What is this?) and *kān* (Gujarati *kaun*, who). She has no forms for causality in either language. With some coaching she has learned English *bæk* (black) *lεd* (red), and, sometimes, *glīn* (green), though at times she confuses the two former, and has no Gujarati color terms. This very confusion, however, points toward the establishment of a color set with these members. She says *sa(r)astsē* (It is good) and *khalāb* (*kharāb*, bad), as well as *tsītsī* (*cīcī*, dirty). Recently she has not only made such comments as *moṭi moṭi bəs* (big, big bus) — combining Gujarati and English — but *big big tlək bəd* fully in English, important indeed as emerging diadic constructions, for English grammar.

Also in English she says *vεlī gəd*, more as an interjection than like her *sā(r)astsē*. She also has *plīs* (please), *tænku* (thank you), and *ēkəm* (you're welcome), and *ōkē?* (okay?), none of which have any everyday correspondences in Gujarati. *Ēlō* (hello) and *bāibāi* (byebye) are appropriately used also in English contexts; and she has English *ləm* (come!) and *gō* (go!) — the former with a gesture half Gujarati and half English, and the latter with a Gujarati gesture. Though she uses *yεs* in English, she has no corresponding word in Gujarati; *natī* and *nō* seem of higher frequency, the affirmative appearing to be a sort of unmarked category for the most part.

Though she uses very few English verbs as yet, she responds appropriately to a considerable number in questions, imperatives, and requests: for example, "what/who is this? ," "go there (first)," "come here," "throw/kick/give to daddy/mummy/aunty" — but not "throw to me," "let's go," "give/get daddy/mummy/ (etc.) the ball/book/ (etc)," "bring/take the ball/book to daddy/mummy/ (etc)." Most of these are followed in the absence of visual cues, though some necessarily incorporate them. When asked a question in English she sometimes replies in Gujarati, but increasingly answers in English. When a question is put in Gujarati, she usually responds in Gujarati, but again the English replies are increasing, especially as they refer to her growing stock of terms for American items. If she gives the Gujarati term for any object and is asked for the English, she will often supply it; the reverse is so far not true; Gujarati, like the affirmative, may be an unmarked category!

Her response to the telephone is interesting, and seems to indicate she sees English as the appropriate language for telephone use. She speaks only a very little Gujarati on the telephone, plus a few recognizable English phrases such as *(h)ēlō hmm?* , *bāibāi*, and *və dəs ī sē?* (what does he say?). The bulk of her output is — to adults — a meaningless outpouring of syllables from her Gujarati store of possibilities, complete with Gujarati and one or two English intonation patterns for sentences, including questions, for which intonation is similar in Gujarati and English. It would be instructive to follow further this telephone speech in its development as she learns more English. Though at present it has a few similarities to babbling, this is evidently a different phenomenon, in that she appears to be carrying on a two-way conversation, and accompanies it occasionally with gestures. The gestures she uses are often bilingual, if the term can be extended thus far, or perhaps more exactly, bicultural. Those for come and go have been mentioned; for affirmation she has both English and Gujarati nods of the head, for negation both Gujarati and English shakes of the head plus the Gujarati hand gesture. these were all learned quite early, along with intonation patterns, and paralinguistic features. It is interesting that she sometimes uses the English head nod of affirmation in Gujarati conversation.

There are then, it would seem, some parallels between first-and second-language learning in this young child. Where she has altogether abandoned babbling in Gujarati some time ago, a similar phenomenon appears on the telephone. Where she has long since passed the stage of one-word utterances in Gujarati, these appear in her developing English. The first stage for verbs in Gujarati is something like uninflected imperatives: the only English verb usage so far is imperatives with no inflection. Terms for objects seem to develop early in most language systems so far studied; this is by far her largest system in English. Kin terms and names again came early in Gujarati, and in English are developing rapidly. The same may be said for contact formulas such as *namaste, ēlō, bāibāi,* and the others mentioned above. Again, it is interesting that in some areas now opening up in Gujarati, such as qualifiers of various sorts, the English is almost keeping pace. This is not true, however, in such areas as verb and other inflection. Perhaps Gujarati grammar must be well established under the circumstances of her particular kind of bilingualism before English grammar will be learned, though a few English dyadic constructions are recently appearing.

The process seems to be one of almost unquenchable systematization, incorporating more and more complex data until the current system can no longer handle it, then a modification of the system, and so on. These systems may or may not coincide with those of adults, other monolingual or even bilingual children, or with the same child's systems at earlier or later stages. Two strong complementary forces in her learning would seem to be the urge to collect more and more data, or perhaps the nearly complete receptivity to incoming information, along with the increasing need to simplify handling it by means of systematization.

Summary

Starting with the sociolinguistic background and some major adult contrasts in the phonemic, morphological, syntactic, and semantic systems of Gujarati and English, this paper considers the child's handling of these problems in the light of her currently different stages of development in each language. Note is made of her simple additive process in joining English phonemes to a basic Gujarati set, and to inclusion of English lexemes in a basically Gujarati syntax. The child is well into a telegraphic stage of Gujarati production and beginning to use inflection. Her English development parallels earlier Gujarati stages and presently includes a few English dyads, pointing towards English grammar development. Her handling of semantic domains contrasts in the two languages, for example, people, animals, possessions, food, kinship, etc. This is in no way a comprehensive accounting but serves to indicate some of the strategies she seems to employ: (1) a listing process in sets, and (2) incipient taxonomic categorization within sets to handle large numbers of items.

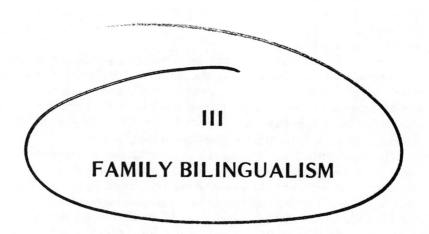

III

FAMILY BILINGUALISM

8

Language Strategies of the Bilingual Family
Ilonka Schmidt-Mackey

Introduction

Every year there are thousands of bilingual marriages between persons speaking different languages. Although statistics are not usually kept of such marriages, there are indications that they may be on the increase.[1] For example, Yugoslavia, one of the few countries which maintains such interlingual statistics, noted an increase of about 30% in such marriages within the decade 1950-1960.[2]

Unlike the unilingual, or common variety, multilingual marriages contain an additional dimension in the patterns of interpersonal relations which such unions involve; this is seen in the choice of medium of communication, not only by the couple, but also by their children and, in the case of the enlarged family, of relatives as well — in other words, in the choice of the working language or languages of the group.

To begin with, there is a choice of three different possibilities. Either everyone in the group uses the language of the husband, everyone uses the language of the wife, or both languages are used according to some overt or implicit pattern. The implementation of the pattern may be unconscious or conscious, unintentional or intentional. If it is unconscious and unintentional — a policy of *laissez-faire*, as it were — the dominant language is likely to prevail in the end, and assure the unilingualism of the succeeding generations.

On the other hand, if the way the languages are used is based on a firm decision to maintain the different languages — a policy of planned repartition — the successful creation of bilingual families, and bilingual communities, will depend on the wisdom and feasibility of the policy.

A policy of planned repartition is composed of one or a number of language strategies. For purposes of analysis, these can be divided into two categories — strategies of dichotomy or fixed alternatives, and strategies of alternation involving the practice of spontaneous switching from one language to the other.

1. Dichotomy

Strategies of dichotomy can be divided into those of person, place, time, topic and activity. Let us consider each of these in turn and see how they can be and have been applied in the practice of a number of bilingual families, including my own.

1.1 Strategies of Person

We are all familiar with the Grammont Formula: *une personne; une langue* (one person; one language), which began to appear in the literature on bilingualism at the turn of the century.[3] Grammont theorized that the separation of the two languages from infancy would help the child learn two languages without either additional effort or confusion. It is the formula used in most reported experiments on family bilingualism. One of the first such experiments was that of Ronjat which began in 1909. The Ronjats made it clear to their son Louis, born the previous year in Vienna, that if he wanted his spoon, he said *cuillère* to his father or *Löffel* to his German-speaking mother or her relatives. Ronjat thought he could thus place both languages on an equal footing. His report of the first five years, however, shows that this is not exactly what happened in practice.[4]

During the first few months, German predominated, and after two years Louis used German words in French sentences. After the second speech year, however, French began to dominate, and by the fourth year, French words appeared in German sentences. Following this there were periodic switches in language dominance, apparently caused by changes in the environment.[4]

Although most of Ronjat's details are on the first three years, there are some data on the fourth and fifth years as well. A decade after the publication of his monograph, Ronjat wrote to Michael West, who was about to embark on a study of school bilingualism in Bengal. Ronjat reported that his son had done well in the French primary and secondary schools which he attended, resulting in a dominant French academic and technical vocabulary but a preference for German in literature.[5] Ronjat summarizes his results as follows: 1. Continual use of two languages from infancy. 2. Parallel acquisition of two phonological systems. 3. Acquisition of two languages comparable in sequence of mastery and achievement to that of the average monolingual.

We had to wait almost another quarter century, however, before getting a comparable record of results of the application of the Grammont Formula. This one, however, was much more detailed and extensively informative. I refer, of course, to the four-volume study of Werner Leopold.[6] Born in London of German parentage, Leopold received most of his education in Germany, where his parents had settled when he was three years of age. In his twenties, he went abroad and after a period in Latin America, settled in the United States, where he married a third-generation German American.

After the birth of their first daughter Hildegard, in Milwaukee in 1930, Leopold decided to speak only German to her, while his wife limited herself to English. But more important, he also decided to keep a detailed record of the results, starting with the end of the second month of life, recording all utterances in phonetic notation.

The results show a striking similarity with those achieved by the Ronjats. Although the child achieved mastery of both languages, these were never equally strong. First the mother's language prevailed and later on the father's. There were periodic shifts in dominance as the language contexts changed, as for example during a trip to Germany when the child spoke only German. Returning to the United States, she spoke more and more English, until that language became stabilized as her dominant one. Like Louis Ronjat's, Hildegard's learning process was not adversely affected by her childhood bilingualism. The achievement test she took on entering the fifth grade revealed her English vocabulary as being at about the seventh-grade level.

My own personal childhood experience with a number of languages seems to confirm the findings of Ronjat and Leopold, as to the efficacy of Grammont's Formula. I should, however, add something on these elusive, emotive effects, which cannot easily be observed from the outside.

I shall first deal with the strategies of the family into which I was born and later with those of the family which I founded.

The strategies to which I was subjected in early childhood were as follows: three languages both inside and outside my home, one in the kindergarten and two in the neighborhood, functioning as two active and four passive languages, making a total of six.

As for the person-language relationship, it was a bit more complex than those of the Ronjats and Leopolds.

I remember that I always associated German with my grandfather since he usually spoke German — although he knew several other languages. My father was bilingual (Hungarian-German) but we always spoke German together. Yet — there was great difference between the German I spoke to my grandfather and that I spoke to my father: with my grandfather I felt at ease when speaking German; but not quite so with my father; perhaps because my father and mother spoke Hungarian among themselves and *that* language seemed infinitely more endearing to me than German. However, as a child, I reconciled myself to the fact that Hungarian was *their* language and that *I* was expected to speak German. In a way I felt like an outsider, and at times I was envious of my mother, who seemed to be getting a greater share of my father's love. Up to the age of four nobody in the family knew that I understood Hungarian, and even after it became known, I continued to speak German to my father until my university years. Only then did my father and I speak Hungarian with each other, and this brought us closer together, giving me a feeling of warmth and tenderness which was always lacking in our German relationship. He then reserved German for times when he scolded me or when we discussed an academic subject.

My mother spoke only German to me, up to the age of nine, when I changed from German schooling to Serbian; she then worked long hours with me to teach me Serbian. At the age of high school I alternated languages. I spoke mainly German to my mother except in all matters concerning school life, when I used Serbian. After high school I spoke to my mother almost exclusively in Serbian and she responded in either German or Serbian. As for my numerous uncles and aunts, they represented three language divisions: German, Hungarian, and Serbian. Most of them were one to one relationships, but I remember a multilingual uncle to whom I was never quite sure in what language to speak. We always had to wait for a situation before warming up and deciding upon which language we would choose.

1.2 Strategies of place

Another type of dichotomy is the strategy of allocating languages to places. This is a common practice, often imposed by necessity. It happens every year in the families of thousands of immigrants and migrant workers, which have always been present in American communities. Since World War II migrants have come to constitute one of the most important social phenomena in Northern Europe, with three million in France alone, and almost as many in Germany.

As a rule, a family moving to an area where another language is spoken will first continue to use its own language exclusively and gradually adopt the area language while maintaining the home language. The children develop a home language/community language dichotomy in their psycholinguistic associations. Quite often, however, the incursions of the community into the home, in the form of neighbors, visitors, school friends, and later, boyfriends, girlfriends and eventually in-laws, erode the status of the home language, especially after the children have abandoned it as a medium of communication among themselves — an area where the community language is bound to dominate.

Although the number of reports on the use of repartition by place is limited, this type of language strategy has been consciously used as a policy for the creation and maintenance of family bilingualism. One of the first studies was that of Pavlovitch.[7] The Serbian-speaking Pavlovitch family settled in Paris after the First World War and decided to maintain Serbian as the home language, while using French as their external or community language. Their son Dusan therefore learned his French outside the home. Since the Pavlovitch record covers only the first two years, it is not surprising that Dusan seems to know much more Serbian than he does French. Nevertheless Pavlovitch comes to some of the same conclusions as does Ronjat.

More than a decade later we have another report, this time from Geneva. In the 1930's, Elemér and Adèle Kenyeres arrived in Geneva with daughter Eva just turning seven. In Geneva they insisted on maintaining their native Hungarian as the home language, but sent their daughter to a local school where all the teaching was understandably done in French. The Kenyeres later published a study of what they observed.[8] After six months, French began to be used in some domains as the child's dominant language. There was little language mixture, and no confusion. The new language was acquired faster than had been the mother tongue, but in a somewhat different way, since it involved a certain amount of conscious effort.

A more recently recorded case is that of the Penfield family. The English-speaking Penfields decided to make German the language of the nursery and they hired a German governess for their two younger children (aged 6 months and 18 months). To the best of their ability they themselves used German when they entered the nursery, so that the children heard only German when there. As the children turned three and four, respectively, another dichotomy of place was imposed, when they were placed in a French nursery school. At school age they began and continued their studies in English without any harmful effects. A similar program was laid out for the two older children starting at the ages of eight and nine.[9]

Penfield concludes that there were no effects of retardation or confusion of languages. The language switch according to place became a conditioned reflex for the children entering the nursery or the school room. In retrospect Penfield believes that it would have been better to continue French until the age of seven, since the seven-year-old "hangs on" to things.

If a change of place can be instrumental in promoting the learning of another language, it can also be a factor in the forgetting of one. This is illustrated in a study made of the forgetting of her Spanish mother tongue and the learning of French by a six-year-old refugee from Madrid during the Spanish Civil War. The girl was adopted by a Belgian family living in Brussels; within about three months she had forgotten her first language (Spanish) and replaced it by her second (French). Two years later she started learning Spanish again, but this time more formally.[10]

It seems that if children learn languages quickly they can just as quickly forget them. Reasons for forgetting may vary, but by and large, changes of place seem to be among the most common causes. Children of diplomatic personnel, foreign business and military representatives and the like are exposed to different languages over sufficiently long periods to master them. In some cases, the children may be emotionally disturbed by having suddenly to abandon a language to which they had become accustomed. A friend of mine in the German diplomatic corps, has written that his ten-year-old son suffered a near depression as a result of having to switch suddenly from a German-medium to a French-medium school. Although he finally mastered the language, he did not like it. Two years later, when his father was posted to Ireland and he had to switch to an English-medium school, he developed a liking for French and a distaste for English. At the age of 13, speaking the three languages with almost equal ease, he preferred French to both his native German and his fluent English.

At an earlier age, however, children, even without conditioning, seem to associate the right place with the right language, with a stubbornness which often confounds their parents. The German father of a seven-year-old bilingual American whose mother is English-speaking, writes that his daughter refuses to speak a word of English when she lands in Germany for the summer vacation and just as consistently refuses to utter a word of German outside the family when she returns to the United States.

In my own case, the language-person dichotomy already described operated in a larger language-place repartition. Until the age of four I was exposed, as I have already mentioned, to the same three languages inside and outside the home, namely to German, Hungarian and Serbian. At the age of four and a half I was placed in a French kindergarten; and by the age of five, three more languages had been added to my repertoire, namely, French, Russian and Rumanian. Yet, before the age of four my only active language had been German. Hungarian was my secret language, that is, I had a complete comprehension of it, but never admitted it. Serbian too was a passive language which I understood fairly well, but did not speak until the age of nine. French was my kindergarten language and Russian became my post-kindergarten language, as a result of my association with the family of my kindergarten teacher, who was a native Russian, and Rumanian was spoken by a great number of my father's patients, whom I heard chatting in the waiting room. Of these additional three languages only French was active, while Russian remained latent until a later age; as for Rumanian, it never became active and I never had a desire to speak it.

1.3 Time, Topic and Activity

Times, topics and activities have also been allocated to the use of languages of a bilingual family, but with varying degrees of success.

In studying the strategies of time, a distinction has to be made between the sequences in which the different languages appear on the scene (staging), and the repartition of language uses among recurring time units.

The staging of languages in the life of the child may constitute the main strategy of the bilingual family. When parents want to make doubly sure that one of the family languages is well grounded, they may arrange for it to become the child's first language and maintain it to the point of fluency before the other language is brought in. This has been the practice of some educated immigrant families living in an area where the family language is not used. Some observers of the psychology of language learning have suggested that it may be a good idea to present both languages concurrently, or even learn a second language first.[11]

It is true that time divisions are the practice in certain bilingual schools, where the working languages may change regularly from morning to afternoon, from week to week, or month to month. In a federal military college in Quebec, for example, French and English have been used as working languages on alternate days. This approach has also been studied experimentally in schools in the Philippines.[1] [2]

In the bilingual family, however, such formalization into time units is difficult in practice. I have observed a number of families who have tried it, and should like to explain what happened. In one family, where the mother was French, the father English, and the common language as well as that of the school, French, the schedule for the two children aged seven and nine was the following: on weekdays the whole family would speak the language of the school (French), whereas over the weekend the family would switch to the father's language (English). The result of this strategy was that the weekend language inevitably got overshadowed by the workday language — possibly because of the artificial set-up of the situation, the habit-forming force of the five workdays, and also perhaps because of the domineering personality of the mother, who spoke the workday language.

Another family, where the mother was German, the father French, the common language, as well as the school language, French, operated on a daily alternation schedule, the result of which was the same as above, namely, that German was soon overshadowed by French, due again perhaps to the artificiality of the situation and the fact that the mother herself was not categorical enough to insist on the usage of German.

Why do time dichotomies seem to be unworkable as a strategy in so many bilingual families? It is perhaps because, unlike persons and places, the switch to another language must be inner-directed, as it were. In the case of time units, we do not have the same sort of conditioned reflex whose unconscious associations impose the appropriate language on the speaker. With time units, the speaker, with his eye on the clock, must make a conscious decision. Most families do not organize their time in such a way as to permit the use of time boundaries.

Another strategy of language repartition is by topic, whereby certain things must always be discussed in one language and other things in the other language. Sometimes, a family will use one of its languages only for giving orders, making formal pronouncements, or reproaches. As a matter of fact, I remember that it was when such topics came up — unpleasant topics involving reprimands — that my father would switch to German. Other families reserve one of their languages for such activities as praying, or learning, or singing, or telephoning, or for taking part in games and sports.

It is not very often, however, that activities or topics are chosen *a priori* as a basis of language strategies. The switching practice is more often conditioned by other factors such as the fact that a topic or activity has been associated with groups outside the home.

Of all these strategies of dichotomy it would seem that those of person are the most lasting and effective. And there is some experimental evidence — albeit with adults — that would seem to support the effectiveness of associating languages with persons.[13]

2. Alternation

In opposition to the division of language use within the bilingual family along the lines of person, place, time, topic and activity is the alternative use of both languages. This may be either conditioned or free.

Conditioned alternation results from the necessity of switching to the other language as a result of some compelling motive. It may have to do with the occupation of the husband, whereby his work and even his training was in the other language. So that he will continually be tempted to switch back and forth to this language when talking about his work. Or it may be emotional stress that would lead a grandmother to switch back and forth between her stronger and weaker language as the flow of thought rushes more and more quickly through her mind. Or it may be a heavily associated word or a homophone that would trigger a switch to the other language.[14]

Whatever the motive, the result for the bilingual child is that both his parents may use both languages indifferently when speaking to him. And the child may also use both languages indifferently when speaking to bilingual parents or relatives. It is sometimes claimed that unplanned switching may confuse the child and lead to language mixture and emotional disturbance.[15] It has even been suggested that exposure to two languages simultaneously may lead to mental blockage and stuttering.[15]

There is surely not enough experimental evidence or a sufficient accumulation of case studies to come to any hard and fast rule, since the conclusions drawn from the few cases studied may well be the result of *post hoc ergo propter hoc* reasoning. Anyone who has observed the language behavior of bilingual families and the language and emotional behavior of bilingual children must conclude that at least in some cases alternation of languages does not lead to disaster.

3. The use of multiple strategies

With all these possible strategies in mind, our own family had some difficult decisions to make when the time came to decide what languages we wanted our children to know. It may be of some interest if I were to recount how we used these strategies and what results we obtained.

Although it may seem ungracious to use my own family as an example, it is what I know best and at first hand. We started by reasoning that, living on a continent which is overwhelmingly dominated by English, the maintenance of this language would give no trouble. English, therefore, was given the lowest maintenance priority in our staging strategy. Secondly, living in a medium-sized city which is 98% French-speaking, there should be no lack of opportunity to maintain the use of the French language — especially if it were made the school and the neighborhood language. The third language, however, posed a problem. It first had to be chosen from such possible candidates as Russian, Serbian, Hungarian, Italian, and German. But its choice would depend on the strategy to be used for its maintenance. If it were a strategy of place, the choice was more limited than if it were to be a strategy of person, for the simple reason that one person might be sufficient, but in a place strategy several persons would be involved. Opting for the latter and taking into account the likelihood of eventual use, we elected German as the home language. And because of the great difficulty of maintaining the language outside the home in a completely non-German area, it was given top priority in time, place and person. The strategy was to make German the first and only language learned from infancy. At the age of four the inevitable home/street dichotomy would bring in another language, in this case French. This dichotomy was enlarged to include everything outside the home, once the children began attending French-language schools. Finally, the third language was introduced about the age of nine by using a person strategy, bringing in a father/mother dichotomy, thus introducing English into the home.

Under the headings of person, place and time, let me now take this opportunity to comment on how these different strategies worked in practice. At the beginning when German was the only language spoken in the family, there was no problem. It is only when we had decided that the time had come for the father to use his own language, namely Enlgish, to serve as a model and a stimulus that we ran into difficulties. Both children categorically refused to speak English to their father, with the logical objection "Why should we speak English to him, when he understands German? "

Seeing that there was no motivation and that the situation was ridiculously artificial, there was no hope for them to ever learn their father's language from their father. This problem was later solved by interlarding a new place dichotomy in the learning sequence. But let me first explain our earliest strategy of place.

Changes of place were significant enough to cause a noticeable difference in the children's command of German. Around the age of two, when she began to speak, to the age of five, the elder spent three consecutive summers in Northern Germany, by the Baltic. She has never returned; but at the age of fourteen, she still speaks German essentially with the accent of that area. The younger, who spent two summers in the area, one as an infant and the other at the age of three, did not preserve the accent of the area, and developed and preserved a pronunciation of German which is closer to that of her parents, but with slight overtones of French influence in rhythm and intonation. (e.g., *Ich 'hab das 'nicht ge'sagt.*) She became less attached to German than did her sister for whom it had strong emotional ties.

Other changes in place resulted in the strengthening of their English. These began with a term in Santa Monica, California in which the children spent most of the time absorbing the blandishments of ten television channels to a point where they would recite most of the oft-repeated commercials — including the singing ones. Being newcomers in a rather closed residential community and having not sufficient occasions to make friends, most of their English came from the air waves — and it turned out to be considerable. It stood them in good stead when four years later they spent a term in Florida and were able to continue their schooling in English with children their own age. Here they spoke only English to their friends, German to their family, and French among themselves, thus maintaining the three languages.

The term immediately preceding had been spent in Germany, where they were also able to follow classes with companions of their own age. This was a school in which about half the teaching was in English, thus serving as a preparation for the switch to the all-English medium in the United States.

As for the staging of the languages, German was used exclusively until kindergarten, when the children were exposed to French in preparation for their schooling, which the elder began at the age of four and a half — in retrospect I think unwisely — and the younger, at the normal age of six. The younger spent two years in a French kindergarten and always felt much more part of the milieu and more at home with her friends.

The resulting language distribution pattern in their verbal behavior, as they entered their teens is as follows: 1. German both ways to mother and grandmother. 2. French exclusively among themselves and outside the home. 3. English outside the borders of Quebec and increasingly as their father language. In pre-school years, as already noted, they used only German with their father, since that was the language of the home. In early school years (5-7) they interlarded their German with stretches of French only when speaking to their father, and in later school years (8-14), especially after having spent a term in an all-English school, they used more and more English with him. The strategy was to convert the father language to English, preserve German as the mother tongue, and French as the children's own language.

As in all reported cases from bilingual families, it was not surprising to find that one language was interfering with the other two. But because of the continual social control and feedback, it was ephemeral by nature, and never led to language mixture. In other words it had no effect on the codes, remaining as accidents of discourse. Interference began to appear about the time the children began attending French schools. It was first noticed in the interlarding of French school vocabulary, which soon became more available than the German counterpart. (e.g., *Ich weiss das schon par coeur.*) Then came the use of some French words in German, with added German morphology (e.g., *inventiert, exagériert, maîtrisieren*). Many amusing examples could be given if space permitted. At all events they were easily corrected and seldom appeared in their speech to unilinguals in German or English for the simple reason that the unilinguals would not understand. The greatest force in eliminating interference was that of conformity with the speech of their playmates.

How the children arrived at a systematization of their three languages is still something of a mystery, although a few theorists of the subject have suggested tantalizing explanations.[16] An even more difficult problem is to explain the processes of cognition; few explanations of the cognitive basis of language learning take the bilingual child into account.

In retrospect, I think that one can safely assume that the study of family bilingualization can also contribute to the psychology of language learning. Observation of the degrees of success or failure of different language strategies of bilingual families throws light upon the question of how man acquires the ability to speak. Is the learning of speech the building up of a skill step by step, as one would learn to play the piano, for example? Or is it like the blossoming of a plant which, in its own time and under the right conditions, brings forth the flower and the fruit? There seems to be growing evidence that the latter is the case, since man seems to be the only being with an inborn capacity to speak. The success of bilingual families argues that this general capacity can take a great variety of specific forms, and that, if there is an imprinted capacity to speak, it is not limited to one language. Everything that the infant needs in order to master any human language, or a number of them, seems to be already imbedded in his nervous system. This must include a capacity to generate an infinite number of different utterances from a finite — indeed a small number of units and patterns. It is also worth noting that the growth of language in the child goes hand in hand with the growth of its physical and mental skills. Like the plant, the child develops as a whole. And just as the growth of a plant can be guided in one or several directions, so can the innate abilities of the child be developed in a climate favorable to the learning of different skills including the mastery of more than one language. If the strategy is the right one and it is applied with concern for the feelings and interests of the child, it could enable the bilingual family to produce bilingual children.

Conclusion

From the above study of the language strategies used by us and other bilingual families to transmit our languages to our children, we might hazard the following very tentative conclusions:

1. If the situation is a natural one, it is likely to motivate the child to use the language of the situation.

2. If the parents do not interfere or force the child to speak a given language in a given situation, the overall linguistic development of the child is likely to be normal.

3. If the parents inconspicuously lead the child into natural contexts in which the probability of language switch is high, the full language learning potential of the situation will have its effects upon the children. It would seem unwise, except in later life, to let the child know that he is involved in a process of bilingualization.

NOTES

[1] Colette Carisse, *Orientations culturelles des conjoints dans les mariages bi-éthniques.* Montreal and Ottawa: Royal Commission on Bilingualism and Biculturalism, (1966).

[2] Dusan Breznik   and Milica Sentić, "Demography and Nationality in Yugoslavia." In *The Multinational Society*, W.F. Mackey and A. Verdoodt, eds., Rowley, Mass.: Newbury House, (1975).

[3] Maurice Grammont, "Observations sur le langage des enfants." *Mélanges Meillet*, Paris, (1902).

[4] Jules Ronjat, *Le développement du langage,. observé chez un enfant bilingue*, Paris: Champion, (1913).

[5] Michael West, *Bilingualism: with special reference to Bengal: Occasional Report 13*, Calcutta: Bureau of Education, (1926), p. 59.

[6] Werner F. Leopold, *Speech Development of a Bilingual Child: a Linguist's Record* (4 vols.), Evanston-Chicago: Northwestern University Press, (1939-1950).

[7] Milivoie Pavlovitch, *Le langage enfantin: acquisition du serbe et du français par un enfant serbe*, Champion, Paris: (1920).

[8] E. and A. Kenyeres, "Comment une petite Hongroise de sept ans apprend le français." *Archives de psychologie*, 26 (1938), pp. 321-366.

[9] Wilder Penfield and Lamar Roberts, *Speech and Brain Mechanisms*, Princeton University Press, (1959), pp. 254-255.

[10] Désiré Tits, *Le mécanisme de l'acquisition d'une langue se substituant à la langue maternelle chez une enfant espagnole âgée de six ans*, Brussels: Veldeman, (1948).

[11] V. Waterhouse, "Learning a Second Language First." *International Journal of American Linguistics, 15 (1949), pp. 106-109.*

[12] G.R. Tucker, F.T. Otanes, and B.P. Sibayan, "An Alternate Days Approach to Bilingual Education." *Monograph Series on Languages and Linguistics*, 23 (1970), Washington: Georgetown University Press., pp. 282-299.

[13] Lawrence Greenfield and Joshua A. Fishman, "Situational Measures of Normative Language Views in Relation to Person, Place and Topic among Puerto Rican Bilinguals." *Anthropos*, 65 (1970), pp. 602-618.

[14] G. Michael Clyne, *Transference and Triggering*, The Hague: Nijhoff, (1967).

[15] Kerstin Engström, *Ett gravt talskadat barn*,]Lizent.-Avhandling, Lund, (1964).

[16] Robert Maynard Jones, *System in Child Language*, Cardiff: University of Wales Press, (1970).

Bibliography

Braunshausen, N., "Le bilinguisme et la famille," In *Le bilinguisme et l'éducation*, Geneva: Bureau International de l'Education, (1928).

Cinquième congrès international des linguistes, *Résumé des communications* (J. Grauls, p. 36), Bruges: Sainte Catherine, (1939).

Dato, Daniel P. "Children's Second-Language Learning in a Natural Environment," *National Conference on Bilingual Education: Language Skills* (USOE Report), Washington: Educational Services Corporation, (1969).

Elwert, W.T. *Das zweisprachige Individuum, ein Selbstzeugnis*, Wiesbaden, (1960).

Emrich, L. "Beobachtungen zur Zweisprachigkeit in ihrem Anfangsstadium." *Deutschtum im Ausland*, 21 (1938), pp. 419-424.

Epstein, Izhac, *La pensée et la polyglossie*, Lausanne, (1915).

Geissler, Heinrich, *Zweisprachigkeit deutscher Kinder im Ausland*, Stuttgart, (1938).

Gerullis, Georg, "Muttersprache und Zweisprachigkeit in einem preussisch-litauischen Dorf." *Study Baltici*, 2 (1932), pp. 59-67.

Gordon, Susan B. *Ethnic and Socioeconomic Influences on the Home Language Experiences of Children*, Albuquerque, N.M.: Southwestern Cooperative Educational Laboratory, (1970).

Hanse, J. *Maîtrise de la langue maternelle et bilinguisme scolaire*, Liège, (1964).

Jakobson, R. *Kindersprache, Aphasie und allgemeine Lautgesetze* (Uppsala, 1941), Frankfurt/Main: Suhrkamp Ausgabe, (1969).

Lambert, Wallace E., and Grace Yenki-Komshian. *Concurrent and Consecutive Modes of Learning Two Vocabularies* (mimeo), Montreal: McGill University Department of Psychology, (1963).

Leopold, Werner F. "Das Deutsch der Flüchtlingskinder." *Zeitschrift für Mundartforschung*, 28 (1962), pp. 289-310.

Lowie, R.H. "A Case of Bilingualism." *Word*, 1 (1945), pp. 249-259.

Lozavan, E. "Expatriation et bilinguisme," *Orbis*, 4 (1955), pp. 56-60.

Luria, A.R. *Rec i intellekt gorodskogo, derevenskogo i bezprizornogo rebenka*, Moscow, (1930).

Luria, A.R., and F. Ja. Judivic, *Rec i razvitie psichiceskich processov u rebenka*, Moscow, (1958).

Macnamara, John, *The Cognitive Basis of Language Learning* (mimeo) Montreal: McGill University Department of Psychology, (1970).

Malmberg, Bertil, "Ett barn byter språk: Drag ur en fyraårig finsk flickas språkliga utveckling." *Nordisk Tidskrift för Vetenskap*, 21 (1945), pp. 170-181.

Murrell, N. "Language Acquisition in a Trilingual Environment," *Studia Linguistica*, 20 (1966), 9.

Nakazima, S. "A Comparative Study of the Speech Developments of Japanese and American English in Childhood." *Studia Phonologica*, 4 (1966), 38.

Oksaar, Els, "Zum Spracherwerb des Kindes in zweisprachiger Umgebung." *Folia Linguistica*, Acta Societatis Linguisticae Europaeae, Vol. IV, 3/4 (1971), pp. 330-338.

Österberg, Tore, *Bilingualism and the First School Language*, Umeå: Västerbotten, (1961).

Raffler, Walburga von, "Studies in Italian-English Bilingualism." *Dissertation Abstracts*, 14 (1954), 142 (Indiana University Diss.).

Rūķe-Draviņa, Velta, *Mehrsprachigkeit im Vorschulalter*, Lund: Gleerup, (1967).

———. *Zur Sprachentwicklung bei Kleinkindern*, Lund, (1963).

Schliebe, Georg, "Stand und Aufgaben der Zweisprachigkeitsforschung." *Auslandsdeutsche Volksforschung*, Stuttgart I, 2 (1937), pp. 182-187.

Smith, E. Madorah, "A Study of Five Bilingual Children from the Same Family." *Child Development*, 2 (1931), pp. 184-187.

———."Word Variety as a Measure of Bilingualism in Preschool Children." *The Journal of Genetic Psychology*, 90 (1957), pp. 143-150.

Stern, W. "Über Zweisprachigkeit in der frühen Kindheit," *Zeitschrift für angewandte Psychologie*, 30 (1928), pp. 168-172.

Valette, Rebecca M. "Some Reflections on Second-Language Learning in Young Children." *Language Learning*, 14 (1964), pp. 91-98.

Voskuil, J.J. *Het Nederlands van Hindoestaanse kinderen in Suriname*, Amsterdam, (1956).

Weisgerber, L. "Zweisprachigkeit." *Schaffen und Schauen*, 9 (1933).

Wiesn, G. "Russo-German Bilingualism: a Case Study." *The Modern Language Journal*, 36 (1952), pp. 392-395.

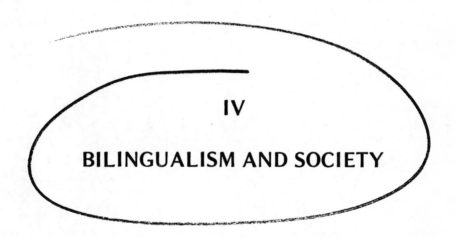

IV

BILINGUALISM AND SOCIETY

9

Child Bilingualism in an Immigrant Society
Aaron Bar-Adon

When the revival of Hebrew as a modern, living, spoken language began, a host of new terms, forms, and ways of expression were required in order to cope with the needs for a complete, normal daily vernacular, and for a modern literary language as well. Literary Hebrew, which was the basis of the revived language, was rich in the domains of religion, philosophy, poetical expression, and the like, but was very poor in the areas of prosaic daily life, in simple interpersonal communication. This lack had to be supplied fast and efficiently.

Most deprived of all were obviously the children and youth, who were lacking any Hebrew tradition of games and childhood folklore in the newly introduced Hebrew speech, and the adults were too busy or aloof to really provide them with their basic needs.

Some students of the revival of Hebrew have failed to realize what seems to be a general rule for a revived language, as for a creolized language, that even if the language of the adults around them is still hesitant, uncrystallized, the children who were born into this language in the new linguistic community accept it as a complete tool for communication, like any other native language.

For the bilingual (or multilingual) adults, Hebrew was not a native language. It was usually acquired as a second language, or additional language, either at the Hebrew school in their home country or after their arrival in Palestine, while the first language acquired by them was Yiddish, or Russian, or Polish, or Arabic, or Ladino, among others. And there is a difference between first-language acquisition and second-language acquisition, as there is between early childhood bilingualism and adult bilingualism. Moreover, in our case, the adults revived spoken Hebrew on the basis of the enormous literary heritage in Hebrew. Their acquaintance with the various sources and layers did not always make things easier. It often created problems of selection among competing synonyms, morphological patterns, syntactic structures, etc.; and it turned out that the richness of sources impeded, in a way, the crystallization of the general language. Besides, the adults had their home language at their disposal and could always resort to it whenever they wanted, which was not the case with the children.

The first native children were confronted with a different situation, the natural situation of first-language acquisition. Actually, they came to modern Hebrew equipped only with their innate capacity for language acquisition. As soon as they were exposed to some samples of it, they started deriving, as any first-language learner or early bilingual does, a theory about the language in question, a grammar of the language.

In the case of a less well-established speech, in a somewhat less crystallized linguistic environment, all processes are accelerated; young speakers are usually given more latitude, greater opportunity for original creations, neologisms, and innovations within the framework of the new children and youth cultures that they forge. As a rule, the less heeded children are while they speak and even the more independent and spoiled they are — and spoiled children are a common phenomenon in an immigrant, uncrystallized, melting-pot society — the more they create on their own and the longer they maintain their speech form in subsequent stages of their development, as individuals and as groups.

Obviously there was more in common among the different individually created speech habits of the adults than one would expect — although each of them may have relied on somewhat different written sources than his compatriots and created his idiosyncratic, eclectic continuity of Hebrew — since the fact is that the children all over Palestine came up with basically the same native language. Then through the special forms of interaction among the children — the density of children's "generations" (see below), child folklore, etc., — they succeeded in creating a more or less uniform, crystallized language, wherein processes of regularization prevail and exceptions are reduced to a minimum.

However, one important element was omitted from the previous description, namely, the role of older children, those children who were exposed to Hebrew and had to switch to it not in infancy but during their school years.

Hebrew speech was used and propagated in the context of the school. The parents, by and large, continued to use their native language at home; but the teachers tried their best to bring about the revival of spoken Hebrew by introducing it into the classroom and as much as possible also on the schoolground. Thus, the first zealous Hebrew teachers undoubtedly contributed the lion's share to the realization of the dream of the Hebrew revival.[1]

But those teachers were a mere handful. Perhaps the most significant aspect of the process of the revival was carried out by the children. They were the ones — and by definition could be the only ones — who turned

Hebrew into a native language. Theoretically, the nativization of Hebrew had to be done by the yet unborn children, but in reality it got off to a good start with the school-age children who constituted the link between generations. They carried it from the classroom into the schoolyard, and from the schoolyard to the playground where they continued their games, and from there into the street as well as into the home. And since the homes at the beginning were not Hebrew at all, the children were those who created the Hebrew environment there, demanding from their parents that they speak Hebrew with them and often teaching them too. So the children often became the teachers of their parents and of their younger siblings.

For the first school children, who were technically bilinguals — with the language of the home chronologically the first language and Hebrew the second — through constant use of the new language at school and outside it, Hebrew became a near-native language. This process started even before the turn of the century. It reached its peak during the first decade of this century, at which time Hebrew spread to the infant stage and started becoming a full-fledged native language. Perhaps the most important factor, certainly for quite a while during the initial period, was the example which those Hebrew-speaking school children set for their younger siblings, including the infants at home, and the younger friends on the block.

Let me now introduce an extension of the concept of "generation." Adults conceive of a generation as a 20, 25, or 30-year span. For children a generation boils down to a school year, more or less. The difference between, say, a second-grader and a first-grader, then between a first-grader and a kindergarten child, is comparable in the child's judgment to that of a "generation" among adults. An advantage of several years may give a child, especially a leader type, enormous authority and prestige among the younger ones; his power will be envied, his behavior will be followed, and his speech habits will be imitated. This impact is a very important factor in the creation of children's culture.

In this way, a special tradition of children's lore and language will be going on under the surface of the adult culture, handed down from one generation of children to the next, almost unheeded by the adults. The children determine the "seasons" for the different games, that is, when they start and when they end, and in what order they are played, etc., and this lore is transmitted from one generation of children to another in an admirable way. There are always some members in the children's community, e.g., the "leaders" on the block, who remember the time for the different games and who preserve the rules of the games, the nomenclature, and all the lore that goes with them, and thus maintain the continuity.

This is what took place in Palestine. While the adults were busy creating the new land and forging the new Hebrew society, the children were quite free to forge their own children's culture. This included the development of a new folklore, new games, and new speech habits which did not conform to the classical forms prescribed by the normativists. Children's speech was characterized by extensive regularization or simplification, for instance in the domain of the verb,[2] massive borrowings, especially from Arabic, in the language of games, and absorption of elements from other languages. We cannot here discuss all aspects of this subject, but I would like to elaborate on the contribution made by the early generations of the Hebrew-speaking children, those who nativized the language, to the development of the Hebrew language of games, especially through borrowing from Arabic.[3]

It would not be fair to say that adults showed no interest at all in children's games. Certain attempts at designing new Hebrew games for them were made by some well-intentioned teachers, but apparently they were not attractive to the children. Some of them were probably too artificial or too dull, and sounded "bookish" and too "adultish," like some of the first so-called "children's songs" which were devised for them.

Children don't go for such nonsense. They like a healthy, authentic children's game, not anemic substitutes. And above all, they were anxious to play, and were not willing to wait for "appropriate Hebrew games" to be devised for them, nor were they ready to wait for Hebrew terms to be invented for them later. They wanted them "now"!

As mentioned above, children's games are part of children's culture, which is basically an independent culture, transmitted mostly by older children to younger children, rather than from father to son. And in the matter of games children certainly appreciate more the authority of the older child, the leader on the block, than that of the parents and other adults. In a way, one may speak of children as a "class," mysteriously united against the tyranny of adults.

No wonder that as soon as the children of the first influxes arrived in Palestine they made contacts with the veteran children in the neighborhood who possessed a more or less well-established game culture. The fact that it involved in many cases direct contact with Arab children and the Arabic language evidently constituted no real problem. And before I go on to analyzing the children's sociolinguistic solutions to the problem of communication, let me say a few words about the sociopolitical aspects of the relations between Jews and Arabs in Palestine.

In spite of the instability in the relations between Jews and Arabs in Palestine, affected by the political fluctuations (friendly-indifferent-unfriendly-hostile), contacts of Hebrew-speaking citizens with Arabic did not diminish. There were Oriental bilingual Jews whose home language was Arabic, and there were others who acquired Arabic later as a second language.

Palestine was not divided into two cantons, one for Jews and one for Arabs, but it was inhabited by both peoples in either mixed or neighboring localities. There were several mixed, bi-communal cities wherein Jews and Arabs either lived in separate neighboring quarters or dwelled together in the same quarters, such as Jerusalem, Haifa, Jaffa (Tel-Aviv), Zefat, Tiberias, and, for some time also, Acre, Hebron, and other places. The same applied to numerous Jewish villages or settlements which had neighboring Arab villages, e.g., Petah-Tikvah, Zikhron-Ya'akov, Rosh-Pinnah, etc. All of these places provided ample opportunity for language contacts between speakers of Hebrew and Arabic. Insofar as children's games are concerned, naturally the mixed cities mentioned above and Hebrew villages which were adjacent to Arab villages played the crucial role.[4]

The contacts between the children of the two communities had great significance for the language of games and for childhood lore in general. It also affected various aspects of modern spoken informal Hebrew, and to some extent also formal, and even literary, Hebrew. I might add here that the boys were apparently more active than the girls in those contacts and borrowings. This would apply not only to the choice of games and to the lexical items used in each but also to derivative aspects (e.g., derivation of verbs from nouns), reinforcement of certain phonological trends which deviate from the normative, and, needless to say, slang, four-letter words, cursing, etc., which accompany any "healthy" game, an area in which traditional Hebrew was very poor.

The children of the first newcomers to Palestine, who were mostly from East Europe, borrowed not only from the Arab children but also from Jewish children of the veteran population who used Arabic and Judeo-Arabic dialects as their vernacular, as they may have done also with other veteran children who were originally speakers of Ladino or Yiddish.[5] At the same time, they turned to linguistic creation, involving independent derivations, extensions, and regularizations or simplifications of patterns (sometimes involving the so-called "false analogies"). In this way, hundreds of lexical terms were borrowed from Arabic dialects, as kinds of cultural items, in addition to idioms and other usages, through direct transfer or loan-translation.[6] In the same way Hebrew phonology and syntax were also affected.

Borrowing begins, of course, with the individual bilingual, as interference affects his idiolect. It will be multiplied by the number of bilinguals involved, and their collective impact on the general (recipient) language will be further reinforced when followed by other speakers, especially monolinguals unfamiliar with the contributing language.

It has been stated by Haugen that for any large-scale borrowing a considerable group of bilinguals has to be assumed,[7] which was the case in modern Hebrew. Interference which has a lasting effect on the borrowing system is carried out subsequently by the essentially monolingual and the fragmentary bilinguals who cannot keep the systems apart.

Since it is a case of an emerging language, some of the interferences persisted through the youth and even the adulthood of the speakers; and with the new groups of adults accustomed to those speech habits, they entered into general circulation.[8]

Let us sample the Arabic and Arabicized loans before moving on to drawing some general conclusions about the effects of this child bilingualism. We will start with the games.

The lexical list in this category is quite comprehensive. It is probably richest in the case of the game of marbles, involving their size, color, texture, roundness, and the like. Then, terms connected with playing with them, e.g., the ways of holding and throwing them, forms of hitting and missing; varieties of games with marbles which involve different ways of arranging the marbles on the ground; rules for conducting the various games, preparing the ground before the game, etc. Scores of those terms were borrowed from Arabic.

Although girls would sometimes play some mild games with marbles too, the real animated marbles game was the domain of boys. They would play it for hours, excited and tense, and it is hardly necessary to add that it was often accompanied by interjections, heated discussions, exchanges of "compliments," quarrels, and the like — and most of it was usually richly flavored with Arabic elements too.

In short, the game required an extensive vocabulary of precise terms for items involved (nouns) and for their description (adjectives), for their functioning (verbs), etc. It was also accompanied by special idioms and syntactic structures under the impact of Arabic.

Even the basic terms for designating the marble are illustrative of a variety of linguistic processes involved. The round marble may be made of marble (now a collector's item), clay, glass, even metal. Most common were the clay and glass ones.

There were basically three terms, *gul*, *ǧul* [džul], and *balóra*, the first two used to refer mostly to the clay marbles, and the last to the glass ones. In the meantime the clay marble has practically disappeared, and *gul/ǧul* became synonymous with *balóra*. The difference is now basically geographic rather than semantic (i.e., they are in complementary distribution from the geographical point of view): around Haifa and the North, *balóra*; in Jerusalem mostly *gul-gúla*, and in the Tel-Aviv area, mostly *ǧul*, or *ǧula*, but also *gúla*, and *bandora* (see below).

Let us start with *balóra*. In Arabic it is *ballo:ra*, *ballu:ra*, i.e., with gemination of the /1/ [balló:ra],[9] a form which was used in parts of Palestine and the adjacent Arab countries of Syria and Lebanon. In other places it was rather *bannu:ra* (see below).

Not only the Arab children would pronounce it [balló:ra], but also the Jewish Arabic-Hebrew bilinguals (i.e., the Jewish children of Middle-Eastern, Arabic-speaking ancestry). However, the predominant Ashkenazi, Hebrew-speaking children, i.e., those children of European ancestry with fragmentary or no knowledge of Arabic and without gemination in their own Hebrew phonology, adapted it to their system and pronounced it *balóra* (and mostly with a "uvular" /r/, rather than the alveolar in Arabic and in "radio

Hebrew"). But they left the Arabic penultimate stress, which accords with Arabic phonological rules but violates the formal modern Hebrew stress rules, where for instance words with the feminine ending -a have the ultimate stress (e.g., *baxurá* girl, young lady).[10]

The plural in Hebrew is *balórot*, i.e., with the regular *-ot* ending of the feminine plural, but without the ultimate stress which normally accompanies the *-ót* ending (as in [*baxurá-baxurót*] girl-girls). This is obviously influenced by the penultimate in the singular [balóra], and coincides with the trend in other borrowed nouns which contain an unstressed *-a* ending (e.g., [histórya-históryot] history-histories, [baláta-balátot] tile-tiles). The *-a* ending normally signals the feminine for the Hebrew except that in genuine Hebrew nouns it is also stressed, as mentioned above. Interestingly, children below the age of four or five may sometimes say [balorót] with ultimate stress, applying their regular morphophonemic rules.

As mentioned above, there was in addition to *ballo:ra/ballu:ra* another common form in Arabic, perhaps even more popular, i.e., *bannu:ra*[11] (and in plural *bana:ni:r*). This form would sometimes be used (switched to) by proficient Arabic-Hebrew bilinguals too (for instance, in the 1950's, in sections of Jerusalem populated by oriental Jews who knew Arabic well), but *never* by the nonproficient or fragmentary bilinguals.

On the other hand, there were two other variants used by the Hebrew children mainly around Tel-Aviv: *bandúra* and *bandóra*. It is obvious that the Hebrew *bandúra* is derived from the Arabic *bannu:ra*, involving a process of dissimilation which reduces excessive nazalization and dissolves gemination, since Israeli Hebrew disfavors gemination:

$$nn \rightarrow nd$$

This was already noted by Haim Blanc, too.[12] He states that *bandúra* displays a dissimilation of the geminate sound *nn*, both because of its absence in the Israeli Hebrew phonology and because of "contamination" with Arabic *bando:ra* tomatoes.[13] Blanc was evidently not aware that even the form *bandóra* itself was in use by quite a few children, especially in the Tel-Aviv area, and even in islands in Haifa, where the population was more mixed. I have firsthand evidence that many of those speakers actually perceived a semantic correlation between the red roundish tomato and the round colorful marble, hence the identification of names — *bandóra*.

Moreover, some of the speakers were convinced that *bandúra* was an incorrect form, and corrected it by relating it to the meaningful form *bandóra* = tomato. This is a kind of hypercorrection, with a semantic shift (*bandúra → bandóra* = tomato), superimposed on a borrowed form which had already undergone a process of adaptation (*bannu:ra → bandúra*), including vowel reduction (*u: → u*) and consonantal dissimilation (*nn → nd*).

Obviously, only a pseudobilingual, i.e., one with a clear deficiency in, or only a smattering of, Arabic could come up with such an identification and a hypercorrection. We will see later some interesting extensions of interlingual identification, e.g., *ná'al avíxa.*

I observed a similar process of dissimilation (*nn → nd*), in the form [lagánda] used, for instance, when a marble is thrown far away, as in *'af lagánda* "It flew to the *ganda*. . ." The form *lagánda* is evidently a metathesis of the Arabic form *li-gahannam* "to hell," which is used by Arabic-speaking children in the identical expression *ta:r ligahannam* "It flew to hell." The preposition *li* "to" is adapted to the morphophonemic rules of its Hebrew counterpart and becomes *la*; the /h/ is neutralized, since it is very rarely realized in native informal (non-Oriental), Israeli speech; and the final nasal is deleted. Thus, the form *lagánna* is obtained.[14] It then turns into *lagánda* after the application of the nasal dissimilation rule:

$$nn → nd$$

The proficient Hebrew-Arabic bilingual knows the word *gahannam* from other contexts too and may even combine it in a Hebrew context *'af ligahannam* "flew to hell." It is therefore very unlikely that he would metathesize *ligahannam* "to hell" to *laganda*. This could have been created only by speakers of Hebrew who heard it only in this context and did not know its exact meaning anyway. After having been in use for some time among such speakers, it would be transmitted to succeeding "generations" of children as an integral term of the Hebrew language of games. After being in circulation for some time, even native Arabic-Hebrew bilinguals could no longer recognize its origin, and they might start using it too. This is, then, one of the ways for thoroughly metathesized loanshifts to be fed back to proficient bilinguals and to become part of their usage in the borrowing language too (in this case, Hebrew).

All three forms, *balóra*, *bandúra*, and *bandóra*, have the feminine ending *-a*, as in Hebrew, although in Hebrew proper this final *-a* is stressed (ultimate), as mentioned above, while in the Arabic it is penultimate. As for the plural, the Hebrew speaker will not use the Arabic plural (*bana:ni:r*, etc.), but will rather use his Hebrew plural feminine ending *-ot*, though unstressed, which will yield *balórot*, *bandúrot*, *bandórot*. Retaining the Arabic penultimate stress, instead of the Hebrew ultimate, will be in violation of the formal Hebrew stress rules, but Hebrew child language is full of such penultimatizations in loanwords. As mentioned, even native Hebrew words, which normally have the stress on the ultimate syllable, may become penultimate, and even antepenultimate (which never occurs in formal Hebrew), in the language of games. A few examples should suffice: *rišon* "first" (masc.), normally *rišón; šéni* "second" (masc.), normally *sení; slísi* "third" (masc.), normally *šliší; reví'i/révi'i* "fourth" (masc.), for *revi'í*, etc.

And in the feminine: *rišóna/ríšona* "first" (fem.), normally *rišoná*, etc.

One may say that this counting is often connected with chanting, which may not favor ultimate stress as some people claim, but it also appears in words that are not chanted (e.g., *kláfim* "cards" and *prásim* "picture prizes" mentioned above). On the other hand, almost all the terms borrowed from Arabic are penultimate, including the corresponding ordinal numbers: *'áwwal* "first" (masc.), *tá:ni* "second," etc. This may be more than a mere coincidence. In other words, it is quite possible that the penultimatization of the Hebrew language of games is due, at least in part, to the impact of Arabic. In general, Yiddish plays the most significant role in various linguistic developments in modern Hebrew, but in this case, the role of Arabic was more important.

The other terms for "marble," *gul/ǧul, gula/gulá/ǧúla* (originally for clay ones) display other interesting processes of borrowing and interference. Which variant is conceived as genuine Arabic and which as Hebrew? Let us start with a vivid description by one of the foremost native Israeli novelists (born ca. 1920), Moshe Shamir, a delightful chapter (in Hebrew) about the children's game of marbles.[15] It reads as follows in the English translation: "Take between your fingers, for instance, that roundish slippery object which is (already) called nowadays *gula*, in the Hebrew language, but in those days we still used to call it plainly *ǧul*, in the Arabic language, if it was made of clay, and *bandura* (also in the Arabic language), if it was made of glass." Since the Hebrew text is not vocalized, the same symbol /w/ "waw" may stand for [u] as well as [o], that is, one may read it either as [bandúra] or as [bandóra]. Shamir probably meant the former.

His statements and criteria from the 1920's coincide with those of a ten-year-old girl thirty years later, i.e., that *ǧúla* is taken to be Arabic because of the sound [ǧ] which is not part of the standard phonemic inventory of modern Israeli Hebrew, whereas *gúla* is conceived as Hebrew, because it has [g] rather than [ǧ].

But the peculiar thing about *ǧul/ǧúla* is that it does not exist as such (nor as *ǧull/ǧulla* with proper gemination) in any major Arabic dialect, while, surprisingly enough, *gull/gulla (gulle)* is the standard pronunciation not only in Egyptian Arabic (where classical /ǧ/ → [g]) but in all other Arabic dialects which I have examined so far, expecially in those where /ǧ/ is realized as [j] (affricate [dž]; or by some as [ž]), not [g].[16]

One will naturally ask: If in all Arabic dialects the pronunciation is [g] rather than [ǧ], how did the [ǧ] creep into the speech of the young speakers of Hebrew, which does not itself have a [ǧ]? Evidently it was introduced by the pseudobilinguals, since the proficient bilinguals knew very well that in Arabic it is *gull/gulla/galle*,[17] not *ǧull*, etc.

This is then a hypercorrection: They wanted to make sure that this word, which they suspected was borrowed from Arabic, really sounded Arabic. In their innocent minds, the identification mark of Arabic is the [ǧ], not the [g]. They were afraid that their compatriots who had borrowed it directly from Arabic had already made the adaptation (ǧ →g) so they wanted to restore the "original" Arabic sound by changing it back to [ǧ] — thus ending up with ǧúla.

Through a different process of interlingual identification they identified gúla with the genuine Hebrew word gu(l)lá (which may also mean "ball," e.g., on top of a pillar), and therefore both of the above-mentioned witnesses and many others that I have interviewed maintained that gula was Hebrew.

I should like to return for a moment to Mr. Shamir's "historical" observations. According to him, earlier in the history it was called "plainly gul, in Arabic," and only later was the form gula introduced, which is Hebrew. Well, Mr. Shamir picked up history from his own childhood, i.e., in the 1920's and early 1930's. But if we go back to the children of the first influxes, around the turn of the century, who made the first direct contacts with the native speakers of Arabic, both Arabs and Oriental Jews, they undoubtedly started with gúl(l)a, and only those who obtained it from them second-hand changed it to ǧúla, as we have explained.

Children's borrowings, especially second-degree borrowings, direct or indirect borrowings by the nonproficient bilinguals, often bear a special flavor of innocence and naïveté, even when they are "slangy" forms, vulgar terms, or downright profanity. This can be easily concluded from their semantic extensions and shifts, as well as from their interlingual identifications. It goes without saying that processes of depluralization,[18] and degenderization,[19] which are commonly mentioned in the literature on bilingualism and interference between languages in contact,[20] were quite common in our case too, as were those of contamination or hybrid creation, of euphemism and semantic raising, and the like.

One representative example is ábu "the father of." It is usually in the construct state, except for connotation number 3 below, where it is in the absolute state. Following the Arabic, it is used (1) for denoting "the father of" in compound proper names, e.g., 'abu-bakr "Abu-Bakr" (lit., "the-father-of-Bakr"); (2) for designating "ownership, possession of...," e.g., 'abu-gull "the owner of a gained marble," i.e., one who has won a marble in the game (all in Arabic); or abu tne:n (Arabic) "the possessor of two," of one who has won two marbles (or two other items in a different game), and so on. Incidentally, it was quite customary to use Arabic numbers too, which means that all the "real" players of marbles, and a few other games, had to know how to count in Arabic, at least to ten, as part of the game requirements (which by itself did not imply bilingualism in any real sense). It is interesting, though, that one who had no "kills," "the father of nothing," was not transferred in full from Arabic ('abu sifr "the father of zero."), but resulted in a compound, "hybrid creation,"[21] using the Arabic abu- "father of" and the Hebrew éfes "zero," i.e., ábu éfes "the father of zero." If one wanted to know how many marbles were already won by his opponent during any individual game, he would ask him *ábu káma ata* "the father (owner) of how many [are] you? " where *abu* is the element borrowed from Arabic and the rest being Hebrew. This, again, corresponds to Arabic, word for word, and may be a translation thereof.

Now, what is interesting here is that in Hebrew the term *abu* was used not only for boys but also for girls, which is an instance of degenderization. Another development took place in the 1940's, when *abu-* combined also with Hebrew numbers, as *abu-šnáyim* "the father of two," for Arabic *abu tne:n.*

A third connotation involving a semantic shift in the use of *abu* by Hebrew speakers, not shared by Arabs, soon developed when the semantic range of *abu* was extended from the ownership of gains to the gains themselves, to the "winnings." Thus, if a winner is "hit" by another player, he will be told *ten li et ha-abu šelxa* "Give me the *abu* of yours," i.e., your winnings.

The use of *abu* + noun became quite productive, especially when the appended noun was in Hebrew rather than in Arabic. It started with constructions like *ábu-árba'* "the father of four [eyes]" (used as a derogatory nickname for one who wears glasses), which was adopted from Arabic *'abu 'arba^c*. Since "four" in Hebrew and Arabic sound alike, the Hebrew word "eyes" was soon added to that nickname *abu 'arba(^c) eynáyim* "The father of four eyes." By the way, it was used for girls too, which is another case of degenderization in a loanword.

Then, there was another nickname, *abu miškafáyim* "The father of spectacles" (*miškafáyim* "spectacles" in Hebrew). There is a parallel expression in Arabic *(abu naǧǧa:ra:t)*, and the question is whether it is a loan translation from Arabic initiated by proficient bilinguals or an extension of the productive construction *abu* + noun developed by the young Hebrew speakers, perhaps basically monolinguals.

A closer examination (and comparison with other examples) will reveal that, as a rule, translations of this kind are initiated by the proficient bilinguals, mostly when they have to communicate with those who are not acquainted with the other language (in this case Arabic). Conversely, pseudobilinguals in such situations would do their best to retain the borrowed expression, perhaps to show off a little. And it should be stated here that the tendency to show off with the knowledge of Arabic was quite strong among the Ashkenazi (European) descendants whose home language was not Arabic, which is quite understandable.

Naturally, once a loan translation of this kind is initiated by a proficient bilingual, it may enter into the general circulation and become part and parcel of a new language tradition, and as such be used by anyone, but, again, it must be started with a proficient bilingual. And there are other examples to support it.

As a productive construction *abu* + noun, where "noun" can be supplied by either Arabic or Hebrew, the form *abu miškafáyim* would have been produced by either kind. It is, therefore, quite possible that *abu miškafáyim* was produced as an instance of a secondary impact of Arabic, which provided Hebrew with a formula *abu* + noun, rather than the primary one of straight translation. Naturally, such a case has some significance for the general theory of bilingualism too.

An amazing development is represented in the related form *'avi-'arba'-'eynayim*, used by some children. Of special note is not so much the fact that *'abu* was *translated* into its Hebrew equivalent, and with a construct-state construction of *'av* "father" with *'arba'* "four" but that the formal construct-state of *'av* (i.e., *'avi*) was used at all, since the children like to use the (Aramaicized) form *'ába* for "father, dad," rather than Hebrew *'av*, and then obviate its construct-state form by using the periphrastic construction *aba šel.* . ."father of. . ." (as they avoid inflecting the noun with the possessive pronominal suffixes, again using the preposition *šel* "of," in a construction N + *šel* + N).

This has been the prevailing trend. And all of a sudden we hear not only *'aví 'arba' 'eynáyim* (not: *'ába šel 'arba' 'eynáyim*), but also *'éved avíxa aní? !* "Am I your father's slave? !" (when asked to do an objectionable service for someone), involving both a construct-state and an inflection (literally: "slave [of] your father [am] I? ") not *ha-'eved šel 'aba šelxa ani? !* "The slave of the father of yours [am] I? ! "; or in the curse *naal avíxa* "Your father's shoe! " (see below).

What is the rationale? Apparently all of it was influenced by Arabic: "Am I your father's slave" is a straight translation from a similar Arabic expression (*xadda:m* (or:*c̣abd*) *'abu:k 'ana*, "The servant (or slave) [of] your father [am] I? "), which has the same syntactic structure and the same word order,[22] and the etymology of two (or all three) of the components is very close. No wonder that *avíxa* is inflected too, like the Arabic *'abu:k*.

As for "Your father's shoe! " as a curse, this is borrowed from Arabic too, through a process of contamination and hybrid creation and disguise or euphemism, as often happens in slang, especially in a bilingual setting. The corresponding colloquial Arabic curse is *yinc̣al* or *'inc̣al abuk* (for classical *yalc̣an 'abaika*) [May he] curse your (masc. sing.) father (remember *abu-* "father"). As mentioned above, Hebrew had no living tradition of "cuss words." The adults could perhaps dig up some classical curses, or resort to their experience in Russian, Yiddish, etc. The first Hebrew-speaking children preferred to make extensive use of the rich Arabic cursing vocabulary. Many cuss words remained as **loanwords in Hebrew.** Some, like the one under consideration, merited also loan translations and other linguistic processes, as we shall see in this case.

'inc̣al abu:k was, **then,** borrowed from Arabic, alongside other cuss words, game terms, etc., and through assimilation in Hebrew phonology it sounded more like *in(')al abuk*. Soon some "blending" came in,[23] in the form of *'in(c̣)al avíxa*, i.e., translating the part of "your father" from Arabic

into Hebrew, and in the inflected (formal) form *avíxa* (not *ába šelxa*). It is obvious that it was done under the influence of the corresponding Arabic form *abu:k*. This also allowed the "proper" use for gender and number too, e.g., *'in(ᶜ)al avix* to feminine singular, *'inᶜal avíxem*, i.e., curse on your (masculine plural) father, etc. In this manner Arabic contributed to the use of the neglected possessive inflection of the noun in Hebrew.

A subsequent development was in the association of the Hebraized form *in(')al* (originally a verb) with the Hebrew noun *ná(')al* "shoe," and, as a matter of fact, in a complete interlingual identification which produced strange curses like the following (which cannot make sense without knowing their Arabic origin): *ná'al avíxa bezug na'aláyim* "your father's shoe for a pair of shoes," and *ná'al avíxa bezug na'aley iméxa* "your father's shoe for a pair of shoes of your mother," and the like. This identification must have been initiated by Hebrew speakers who did not know the exact meaning of *'inᶜal* in Arabic.

Even without going into further detail, we can see how Arabic influenced not only the domains of play words and cuss words but also some processes in Hebrew morphology and phonology, and how this may be useful for the study of processes of language interference in child bilingualism.

One can take it for granted that the children did not usually know the exact meaning of the cuss words they used in the heat of the game, following the pattern of their Arab neighbors. They needed something powerful, and the stranger sounding a word in this area is the more magic and power is attributed to it. Therefore such words and expressions are not usually translated as a whole. They may be metathesized, blended, substituted in part by a similarly sounding word in the borrowing language but not translated in full. If children do understand the exact meaning, then its use in the borrowed form serves as a disguise (euphemism) to some extent; if they don't know the exact meaning, then all the magic is in the strange sounds, which one would not like to change.

Before concluding let us have a quick look at some phonological, morphological (derivational and inflectional), and syntactic effects on Hebrew through children's bilingualism and their language of games.

We mentioned earlier the forms *ǧul* and *ǧúla*, which were hypercorrected by the Hebrew children, instead of the Arabic (unique) use with [g], because *ǧ* has become an identification mark for Arabic in the eyes of the innocent Hebrew speakers. They had in active use such words with *ǧ* as *ǧóra* "pit, a hole in the ground for the game of marbles," and terms in the game like *be-ǧáxes* vs. *bli ǧáxes*, *balóra xalánǧit* (for a brand new, beautiful marble), *min ǧoz* (see below), *fránǧi* (European), *abu ǧílde* (nickname), and many others.

The idiom *min ǧoz* "from the pair (between the two)," produced an interesting semantic shift. It was originally used as an announcement on the part of a player who was aiming at two adjacent marbles, i.e., that if he hits either one (or both) that it would be O.K. Now, if he missed both, his playmates would usually exclaim *lo ba-min ve-lo ba-ǧoz* "neither in the *min* nor in the *ǧoz*" i.e., he hit neither the one nor the other. Thus, these two words *min* "from" and *ǧoz* "pair" were taken to be referring individually to the marbles involved, as if one were called *min* and the other *ǧoz*.

In connection with *franǧi* we might mention forms like *fasfus* "tiny,"[24] *fistuk* "peanuts," *falafel* "faláfel, a spicy Oriental food with a lot of *filfil* 'pepper,'" *fálta* "slip" and the verb derived from it *hitfalet* "slipped," and any others. The reason for mentioning this group is that all of them violate the basic Hebrew phonological rules of the complementary distribution of plosive and fricative allophones in the group /b g d k p t/, especially of /b k p/ (i.e., b ~ v, k ~ x, p ~ f), which are generally preserved to date in more formal Hebrew. I will not discuss here the entire rule,[25] but mention only one aspect of it, i.e., that in initial position and after a consonant or a closed syllable only the plosive allophone may appear, whereas in final position, following a vowel, only the fricative allophone may be used. In our examples all initial and postconsonantal positions were occupied by [f], as in Arabic, rather than by [p], as required by Hebrew phonology. The same applies to euphemistic forms which were apparently created by the children through multiple contaminations between Arabic, Hebrew, and Yiddish,[26] e.g., *fisfes* "he missed, goofed, failed," *figšeš/fikšeš* "he missed," *fikfek* "he missed," and secondary and tertiary derivations and mock derivations, such as *fincleax* "he failed," and the like.

On the other hand, in forms like *xabub* "darling" (masc.), *ya xabíni* "oh, my darling" (masc.), *rizdeb*, *rizdub* (see below), *akrab* "scorpion" (*akrav* in formal Hebrew), we have the stop allophone instead of the fricative.

Penetration of so many violations of the basic Hebrew phonological rules do not just "remain in the lexicon," as some people say. In due course they affect the entire phonological system, which in my judgment was the case here, i.e., children will often do the same thing in indigenous Hebrew roots too, as I have described in other studies.

As for morphology, while the inflection of the noun was practically abandoned by the children, as mentioned above (by resorting to the construction noun + *šel-*, etc.), the children were very active in the inflection of the verb, but with very substantial changes which they introduced,[27] as they were active in the processes of derivation.

We will mention here only one aspect — the derivation of verbs from borrowed nouns, singling out a few instances which affect the Hebrew root system.

We just mentioned some effects on Hebrew phonology in forms like *hitfalet*, *fisfes*, *rizdeb*, *fikšeš*, which according to formal Hebrew phonology should have been *hitpalet*, *pispes*, *rizdev*, *pikšeš*, etc. Some of those examples illustrate another point, i.e., derivation of verbs from nouns, and from four-consonant rather than three-consonant roots.

We said that the inflection of the noun was almost completely abandoned by the children. This means, among other things, that borrowed nouns could remain unaffected by the formal Hebrew morphological patterns, even by the stress system, except for the suffixing of the gender and number morphemes. As mentioned above, the borrowed nouns usually retain the stress on the original syllable, and the singular feminine and the plural endings are appended without any significant morphophonemic changes. Thus, the Hebrew noun became an "open," indiscriminate, category, in the sense that not only nouns that conform to the patterns, but any noun of any form and stress pattern, may be admitted.

The verb, however, is dynamic. It maintains its conjugations and its inflected paradigms. It assimilates whatever it absorbs by means of its paradigms. In this way, the verb could not only **Hebraize** foreign roots but also conceal their foreign origin, except that the children "spoiled" it to some extent by leaving certain alien phonological features (see some examples above) and by their excessive derivation of four-consonant roots from borrowed words. It is true that historical Hebrew had some four-consonant roots too, but it was basically a three-consonant system. By deriving large numbers of four-consonant verbs, especially from borrowed words, the children contributed significantly to the change in the appearance of the Hebrew verbal system and the ratio between the three-consonant roots (which is a typical Semitic feature) and the four- (and five-) radical roots.

We have mentioned several examples. We might add *timbel* "to stupify," from *tembel* "stupid, a fool" (Arabic *tanbal* from Turkish *tembel*), and the most popular verb *xirbén* "to mess up, goof, fix," etc., which is derived from *xerbón* "excrement, a mess, a fix, defeat," etc., which in turn is derived through a contamination with the Arabic word *xara* "excrement." All of these forms, like many others, have later moved on to the language of youth and of adults.

There are scores of other interesting cases, but we will mention here only one more type of interference from Arabic, which concerns the syntax of the verb and verb phrase constructions: following the Arabic, the children will usually say *caxak al-* "laugh at (lit., laugh on)" instead of the preferred form *caxak lə* (lit., "laugh to"). Of special interest are, for instance, constructions with the verb *axal* "to eat," which are influenced by Arabic, e.g., *axal makot* "he ate blows (i.e., was hit, spanked)": *axal xerbon* "he ate a defeat, failure (got in a fix)"; *axal xazuk*, of the same meaning, *xazuk* being an Arabic word meaning here, like *xerbon*, "failure," which was one of the original uses borrowed directly from Arabic, then inspired the creation of Hebraic and genuine Hebrew constructions on this pattern.

Conclusion

We have seen how modern Hebrew came into being as a revived language, some aspects of the sociolinguistic background, certain factors in its development, and the role of the children in it.

In this context we have studied the processes of the nativization of the language by the children, how they created, mainly by themselves, a new language of games, how they borrowed terms and expressions from Arabic, and how they initiated various processes of Arabic interference in Hebrew, some of which spread beyond the confines of the children's language of games, into the general language, and affected Hebrew phonology, morphology (derivation and inflection), syntax, and semantics. We have also noted their contribution to Hebrew slang.

From the point of view of bilingualism we have seen that national bilingualism does not necessarily imply individual bilingualism. Palestine was politically a bilingual country, but not too many Jews were proficient Hebrew-Arabic bilinguals, and there were even fewer Arabs who knew Hebrew. However, given a special sociolinguistic setting, as in the case of a revived language, where children may feel a special deficiency in their areas of language and lore and fun, certain reasons for borrowing may arise, and certain patterns of interference evolve.

Contacts between languages really start with the contact between individuals, which in turn may be multiplied and reinforced by the number of people involved. However, as we have seen in this particular case, only some effects of borrowing and interference are due to the proficient bilinguals (e.g., loan translations), whereas other processes and effects (e.g., loan shifts, hybrid creations) are due to the activities of innocent fragmentary bilinguals. The actual impact of the latter on the borrowing language may be greater than that of the former, so that, from a certain point of view, there is an inverse correlation between proficiency and interference.

Children's bilingualism in an immigrant society has its own features, particularly in the case of a revived language. Here they are especially free to create in their own way, borrow in their own way, and nativize the language in their own way. While transmitting it to the succeeding "generations" of children, their innovations and borrowings go into greater circulation, and sooner or later they may affect the entire linguistic system (including the literary language in due course), whether the adults realize it or not, as seems to be true in this case.[28]

Summary

The revival of Hebrew as a modern living tongue started in the 1880's within the framework of the national revival of the Jews in Israel (formerly Palestine). Bilingual and multilingual adults initiated it, on the basis of written literary Hebrew of generations past, zealously trying to replace their native languages by Hebrew. But only the children could nativize it. Owing to special sociolinguistic circumstances, the children played an important role in the development and crystallization of Israeli Hebrew.

In the process of nativization the children affected various linguistic domains. One is the domain of games, in which they created their own language, in part through borrowing from Arabic, since there was no Hebrew tradition available to them in these areas.

We analyze here the sociolinguistic setting and some processes of nativization: the reasons for borrowing, the processes and results of interference, the rapid spread of the children's innovations into the general language, and their contribution to Hebrew slang on the one hand and to literary Hebrew on the other.

Some theoretical implications concern the distinction between national and individual bilingualism and the relationship between bilingual proficiency and interference. There seems to be an inverse correlation between the two.

NOTES

¹ See details in A. Bar-Adon, *The Rise and Decline of a Dialect: A Study in the Revival of Modern Hebrew.* The Hague: Mouton (in press).

² See details in my *Children's Hebrew in Israel* (2 vols.), Jerusalem, 1959 (in Hebrew, with English Summary); and "Analogy and Analogic Change as Reflected in Contemporary Hebrew," in H. Lunt, ed., *Proceedings of the Ninth International Congress of Linguists*, The Hague: Mouton, 1964, pp. 758-63.

³ For details on nativization see my "Processes of Nativization in Contemporary Hebrew" (in mimeograph form), in *The Revival of Modern Hebrew*, University of Texas Press (to appear).

⁴ We mention in Note 8 that there were more Hebrew-Arabic bilinguals than Arabic-Hebrew bilinguals. (Note 8 refers to a longer version of this paper.) In other words, Arabs made less effort in acquiring Hebrew than Jews in learning Arabic (this is not the place to analyze this sociolinguistic phenomenon). But there definitely were some Arabs who did learn Hebrew, e.g., the children of the Arab village of Ja'uni in Upper Galilee, which was adjacent to the Hebrew village of Rosh-Pinnah. Those children even learned Hebrew formally for some time at school from a Jewish teacher, in addition to playing with their Hebrew neighbors.

⁵ It should be noted that many Yiddish-speaking children of the veteran population (the "Old Yishuv") of the Holy Cities in Palestine knew Arabic. In fact, many Jews in the Old City of Jerusalem, in Zefat, and Tiberias, and perhaps elsewhere, were pretty fluent in all the three major vernaculars, i.e., Arabic, Ladino, and Yiddish. Then Hebrew was added to them, until it captured the hegemony.

⁶ Cf. U. Weinreich, *Languages in Contact.* New York: Linguistic Circle of New York, 1953, pp. 47 f.

⁷ "The Analysis of Linguistic Borrowing," *Language*, 26 (1950), pp. 210 f.; in revised form in *The Norwegian Language in America*, 1953, Vol. 2, 383 f.; cf. *Bilingualism in the Americas*, 1956, p. 14, and in subsequent studies. (Cf. his quotation from Hermann Paul's *Prinzipien*, 1886, Chapter 22.)

⁸ In the 1940's there was a special flourishing of a Hebrew style flavored with an excessive display of Arabic words and Arabicized structures, used especially by the young men of the "Palmeh," the underground commando. But we cannot elaborate here on this beyond stating that it was essentially an extension of the special Hebrew of games of the children, as described before. For details see my *Children's Hebrew in Israel* (1959).

⁹ *ballo:ra* is probably connected with classical Arabic *billawr* "beryl," and the /l/ may therefore be the original sound, not /n/, in *bannu:ra*.

¹⁰ But this coincides with a host of forms in the Hebrew language of games which were made penultimate by the children, e.g., *klafím* "cards"

(used by adults) vs. *kláfim* "cards" used by children; *prasím* "prizes" vs. *prásim* "pictures," and similar little "prizes," found in chocolate boxes, etc.

[11] Again, the form with /l/, not /n/, seems to be the basic one (cf. fn. 9).

[12] "On the Arabic Elements in Spoken Israeli Hebrew," *Leshonenu Laᶜam*, Vol. 6, 1, (1954/55), p. 6-14; 2, p. 27-32; 4, p. 20-26. In Hebrew.

[13] *Op. cit.*, No. 2-3, pp. 28-29.

[14] Arabic *ǧahánnam* may be derived from the Hebrew *geyhinnó:m* "the Valley of Hinnom; Hell," but the lay speakers may not be aware of such an etymology. And indeed we heard *laǧanna* too. Cf. A. Bar-Adon, "Studies in the Lexicon of the Israeli Children," *Leshonenu Laᶜam*, Vol. 18, 2 (1966/67), p. 64.

[15] In *Atidot*, A Quarterly for Youth, Summer 1956 and Fall 1957, pp. 5-10.

[16] Most importantly, similar evidence is found also in the aforementioned study by Haim Blanc, who is certainly one of the foremost authorities on Arabic dialects. He emphasizes that in all the Arabic dialects known to him, the actualization is [g], not [j]. See *Leshonenu Laᶜam*, Vol. 18, 2 (1966/67), p. 64.

[17] By the way, an etymological survey leads me to the assumption that this Arabic word was influenced by Turkish.

[18] A borrowed word in its original plural form may be conceived as a singular in the recipient language. When it has to be pluralized in the latter, its original plural marker will be disregarded, and a new plural marker will be superimposed on it; e.g., *"Eskimos"* in younger Hebrew are *eskimosim*, where the Hebrew plural marker *-im* was appended to *eskimos*, because the latter was conceived as a singular. The form *eskimo* is more often used for "icicles," probably as an extension of a brand name.

[19] That is, disregard for the original gender; cf. the uses of *abu-* below.

[20] Cf. Weinreich, 1953, Haugen (1950, 1953, 1956), mentioned above, and his new concise essay on "Bilingualism, Language Contact, and Immigrant Languages in the United States: A Research Report, 1956-1970," in T. A. Sebeok, ed., *Current Trends in Linguistics*, Vol. 10. The Hague: Mouton (1973). We could mention also Vildomec and others, but there is no need here to give a full bibliography.

[21] As Haugen calls it. See Haugen, 1956, etc.

[22] There is a similar expression in Yiddish too (*Ikh bin ništ dayn tate(n)s mešores* "I am not your father's servant"), but in a different structure and word order, which adds support to the original derivation from Arabic. Also, Yiddish uses the Hebrew word *mešóres* (pronounced in Israeli Hebrew *mešaret*) for "servant," while in the new Hebrew expressions we hear the synonym *'eved* which is again closer to at least one of the Arabic variants, *ᶜabd.* Yiddish perhaps provided reinforcement for some.

²³ In my opinion, it started here too with the proficient bilinguals, although the etymology of *abuk* could easily be found by any Hebrew speaker. I think that the form *'i(ᶜ)al avíxa* was also used more by Oriental Jewish children, as in the case of *abu miškafáyim.*

²⁴ Originally meaning "a flea, a wart." It is often used with the aforementioned Hebrew diminutive *-on*, i.e., *fasfuson*, and even with one or more of the diminutive and endearment morphemes borrowed from Yiddish, e.g., *fasfusončik.* . .

²⁵ Which I do to some extent in *The Rise and Decline of a Dialect.*

²⁶ Naturally, the interference of Yiddish is also part of this child bilingualism, but we are now concerned mainly with the effect of Arabic interference.

²⁷ See details in our *Children's Hebrew.* . .and "Analogy. . ." Also in "Developments in the Verbal System in Contemporary Hebrew (especially of Children and Youth)," to appear in a volume in honor of A. A. Hill.

²⁸ For details see my forthcoming monograph *Child Bilingualism in an Immigrant Society.*

10

Bilingualism in the Six-Year-Old Child[1]

Bernard Spolsky
and Wayne Holm

With growing strength in the last twenty years, English has established its place as a second language on the Navajo Reservation. Spreading partly through contacts that take place off the Reservation and even more significantly through the influence of the school, its position is now such that over two-thirds of Navajo six-year-olds come to school with some knowledge of it. But not enough to do first-grade work in it: fewer than a third are judged by their teachers to be ready for this.

In this paper, we report on studies of the present situation, discuss some of the factors that contribute to it, and make some tentative predictions. In addition to the shift from Navajo to English, we discuss details of English borrowings in the speech of six-year-old Navajo children.

Our studies have been intended as background to an investigation of the feasibility and effect of teaching Navajo children to read in their own language first. We carried out a first survey in 1969[2] and repeated it in 1970[3] including a greater number of schools. The general method adopted in each survey was to send a simple questionnaire to all teachers with Navajo six-year-olds in their class. Returns to the 1970 survey provide data on 79 percent of the Navajo children born in 1964, covering 84 percent of those actually in school.

The questionnaire asked teachers to rate the language capability of each of their six-year-old Navajo pupils at the time he or she started school in September using the following five-point scale:

N: When the child first came to school, he or she appeared to know only Navajo, and no English.

N-e: When the child first came to school, he or she appeared to know mainly Navajo; he or she knew a little English, but not enough to do first-grade work.

n-E: When the child came to school, he or she knew mainly English and also knew a bit of Navajo.

E: When the child came to school, he or she knew only English.

To check the reliability of the instrument, ten teachers were asked to fill out the questionnaire a second time some six months after the first: overall correlation of 187 early and late ratings was 0.78. The validity of the questionnaire was investigated by having 194 pupils at 18 schools rated by pairs of trained bilingual judges using a standardized interview: a comparison of teacher and judge ratings gave an overall correlation of 0.67. Similarly satisfactory results were gained in a validity check in a parallel use of the instrument by Southwestern Cooperative Educational Laboratory.

The results of the survey for 1969 and 1970 are similar. The 1970 data are summarized in Table I.

TABLE I

Language scores in 1970 — Summary

School	Number of six-year-olds	N	N-e	N-E	n-E	E
BUREAU OF INDIAN AFFAIRS						
Chinle	385	45	43	10	1	2
Eastern Navajo	383	39	48	10	1	1
Ft. Defiance	388	25	49	23	2	
Shiprock	324	39	46	14	1	3
Tuba City	382	62	33	4	.7	.3
Hopi	11	73	18	9		
Total	1873	42	44	12	1.3	.7
PUBLIC						
New Mexico	1046	13	32	37	10	8
Arizona	471	22	35	21	10	12
Colorado	27	11	67	7		15
Utah	86	13	52	23	5	7
Total	1630	16	35	31	9	9
MISSION						
Arizona	56	11	23	20	35	11
New Mexico	35		23	23	37	17
Total	91	7	23	21	36	13
INDEPENDENT						
Rough Rock Demonstration	59	58	29	8		5
Total	59	58	29	8	0	5
GRAND TOTAL — all schools	3653	29.8	39	20.7	5.7	4.8

From the table, it will be seen that 29.8 percent of the children were reported as knowing only Navajo, 39 percent as knowing a little English as well, 20.7 percent as more or less balanced, 5.7 percent as mainly English speakers, and 4.8 percent as speaking only English. The weight is clearly on the Navajo side: the child who speaks English is an exception. It is clear that most parents still speak Navajo to their children and that school is the first real contact with English for most children.

But there is evidence that the use of English is growing. In the case of a good number of schools, we have data for both 1969 and 1970. Comparison of these data for the same schools gives the following results:

1969 Mean Language Score 3.99 (S.D. 1.01)

1970 Mean Language Score 3.90 (S.D. 1.04)

The change of 0.09 is significant ($F = 8.97$, significant at the $p. < .01$ percent level).

Any prediction based on these data is speculative, but certain guesses can be hazarded. Assuming the data are accurate (or at least that the error each year is likely to be the same), there was in one year a change towards English of .09 on a scale ranging from 5.00 (Navajo only) to 1.00 (English only). A conservative guess would choose 1949 as the last year in which almost all Navajo six-year-olds would have come to school speaking only Navajo. In twenty years, then, there has been a shift from close to 5.00 to 3.99, which averages 0.05 a year. A language shift is not a simple progression, but tends to accelerate: the larger the proportion using the new language, the faster others are likely to learn it. The 0.09 for 1969-70 is probably not a doubling of the average rate but a point on a steady increase. Assuming this to be the case, it is not unreasonable to suspect that by the end of the present decade, the mean language score might be close to 3.00, which is bilingual on the scale.

But it would be a mistake to predict that all Navajo six-year-olds will be bilingual in 1980. The kind of situation that is more likely is one developing out of the currently observable difference between children in rural areas and those living in the newly developing semi-urban settlements. This becomes clearer if one notes the distinction between public schools and Bureau of Indian Affairs schools. About 50 percent of the 55,000 school-age Navajo children attend public schools which operate according to the state in which they exist: public school districts on and near the Reservation range in size from Gallup-McKinley with close to 10,000 pupils to Navajo Compressor Station No. 5 with 21. By agreement between the Bureau of Indian Affairs and the Navajo Tribal Council, public schools usually enroll children who live within a mile-and-a-half of the school or on an established public school bus route. The widely dispersed pattern of traditional Navajo rural settlements and the lack of paved roads on the Reservation means that public schools draw their pupils mainly from government compounds or from the developing towns where most of the public schools on the

Reservation are located. A comparison of the language situation in the two kinds of schools reveals a striking difference: for BIA schools, the average language score in 1970 is 4.26 and for public schools it is 3.39. Only 14 percent of the children in BIA schools were considered to know enough English for first-grade work, while 49 percent of the children in public schools reached this figure.

From this additional fact, then, it might be guessed that an overall mean score of 3.00 in 1980 would be likely to reflect a situation where Navajo urban children will come to public school speaking a variety of English and Navajo rural children will still be mainly speakers of Navajo.

A study of some of the factors contributing to this increase in the use of English throws more light on the kind of bilingualism that the Navajo child lives with. For Navajo, there have been two distinct classes of contact with English. The first class is made up of contacts that occur off the Reservation. Many Navajos live and work in a city far away: Los Angeles, the Bay area, Chicago, and Denver all have large Navajo populations. Many leave the Reservation for schooling, attend a boarding school or a bordertown dormitory or go away to college. And the shopping trip to a town on the edge of the Reservation is becoming a more common event.

The second class of contacts is on the Reservation itself. In this class, the major factor is school. Traders generally have learned some Navajo; missionaries either talk some Navajo or use interpreters; Public Health Service officials who do not themselves speak Navajo use Navajo interpreters. Radio stations broadcast in Navajo about 150 hours a week. But the school is still almost completely monolingual in English. There are exceptions: a few pilot bilingual education programs, Navajo-speaking teacher aides in pre-first-grade classes, Navajo-speaking employees serving as interpreters, but basically school is a place where English is spoken and where one must speak English to participate in the activities of the institution.

In looking at the increase of English, two main centers of diffusion might be expected: off-Reservation towns, and schools on the Reservation. To investigate the relative influence of these factors, we studied the relation between six-year-old language use and ease of access to these two places.[4]

For language use, we used the teacher rating described above. For ease of access to off-Reservation towns, we calculated an index which consisted of distance plus factors added to represent the state of roads (paved roads for instance were taken at face value, ungraded dirt roads multiplied by four). The correlation between a school's mean language score and its accessibility index was calculated: in 1969 the correlation was .517 and in 1970 it was .55. We can reasonably conclude that the closer a community is to the edge of the Reservation, the greater the likelihood of speaking English at home.

The second kind of accessibility we considered is ease of access from the child's home to school. This shows up first in the variation between kinds of schools that was discussed above. It is almost always the case that children attending public schools find the schools more accessible than do those who attend BIA schools: the much greater amount of English spoken by the former has already been pointed out. This difference shows up when we compare cases of BIA and public schools in the same locality (and therefore having the same index of accessibility to town): in twenty such pairs, the six-year-olds coming to public school know much more English.

To look at this further, we calculated the correlation between individual language scores and individual ease of access in the case of two schools, Rock Point and Lukuchukai. In Rock Point, with 48 six-year-olds, the average language score in 1970 is 4.26, the average index of accessibility from home to school, 12.7 (S.D. 12.9), and the correlation between the two 0.28. In the case of Lukuchukai, we compared accessibility of the off-Reservation town (Gallup), accessibility of the school, and language score. The two accessibility indices correlate negatively in this case (-0.39) because the closer a family lives to school, the further it lives from town. No correlation (-0.01) showed up between individual language scores and individual accessibility from home to town, showing that this is a factor affecting a whole community rather than individual members of it, but there is a correlation (0.12) between individual language scores and ease of access to school.

Further light on linguistic acculturation comes from a study of English loan words in young children's speech.[5] Earlier descriptions of Navajo agreed on the lack of receptivity to borrowing. Haile summed up the general view when he wrote: "Pueblo contact has not influenced Navajo to a noticeable degree, while Spanish elements in the language are comparatively few, and English elements practically none."[6] This supported notions that there was something about the structure of Athabaskan languages that makes them unwilling to borrow.[7] But as Dozier points out,[8] sociolinguistic factors are more influential in borrowing than linguistic ones. With the increased contact that took place during and after World War II, there was increasing pressure from English, resulting in considerably more borrowing.

In our study, we looked at English words that appeared in interviews we had recorded with over two hundred young Navajo children. Of the 5,756 different words that occurred in the text, over five hundred were English loan words. Generally, as would be expected, they were words for objects or concepts introduced through the English-speaking culture. A large number of words were school-related (bus, book, chalk, ball, pencil, puzzle, blocks, math); others were names of objects or concepts probably introduced through the school (camel, elephant, alligator, Christmas tree, record player, teeter-totter, swing). A good number were names of foodstuffs or household objects (beef, oatmeal, lettuce, ice cream, butter, grapes, cookies, chips, chair, table, toilet, mouse trap, cup, spoon, clock), tending to be articles not traditional in Navajo life. Numbers and colors were also common, and terms for occupations (babysitter, cowboy, clown, policeman, principal). Surprising were the kinship terms (father, grandma, little sister).

As a general rule, the words borrowed were nominal in character: 453 of the 508 were nouns in English; and with a few interesting exceptions, they were all used as nouns in Navajo. Appropriate prefixes (*shipant* "my pants") and suffixes (*schooldi* "at school", *record playeryée'* "the absent or nonfunctioning record player") were added. Often, a complete phrase (*hide and go see, window close*) occurred, sometimes as a free form and sometimes integrated into the Navajo sentence. In no case, however, did we find an English word treated as a verb stem and integrated into the complex verbal system.

We have no definite evidence on the status of the words in Navajo. On occasion, a child was willing or able to give a Navajo equivalent when the interviewer insisted.

Four bilingual college students were able to think up Navajo equivalents for most of the words, but agreed that they themselves would be likely to have used most of the loan words when speaking Navajo to someone they knew to be bilingual.

Writing less than thirty years ago, Reed reported the Navajo as a people with a "highly independent spirit" and "a definite disinclination to learn and speak the languages of other people.[9] Absolutely and proportionately, the Navajo people remain the largest group of non-English speaking Indians in the United States, but there are clear signs of a growing diglossia. The six-year-old Navajo child is far from being bilingual, but there is a growing chance that he will be acquainted with English before he comes to school.

Summary

Although they live in what is still a language island, many Navajo children have some exposure to English before they start school. Ease of access to school and to off-Reservation towns increases the probability of this exposure, which shows up both in knowledge of English and in the presence of English loan words. An account is given of a survey of the relative Navajo and English proficiency of a computer-assisted study of a sample of speech of six-year-old Navajos.

NOTES

[1] The work reported in this page was supported in part by the United States Department of the Interior (Bureau of Indian Affairs, Navajo Area Office, Contract No. N00 c 1420 3462), in part by a grant from the Ford Foundation, and in part by a gift from John Nuveen and Company.

[2] Bernard Spolsky and Wayne Holm. "Literacy in the Vernacular: The Case of Navajo." In *Studies in Language and Linguistics*, The University of Texas at El Paso, (1970-71).

[3] See Bernard Spolsky. "Navajo Language Maintenance: Six-Year-Olds in 1969," *Language Sciences*, No. 13, December, (1970), pp. 19-24; and Bernard Spolsky. "Navajo Language Maintenance II: Six-Year-Olds in 1970." Navajo Reading Study Progress Report No. 13, The University of New Mexico, August 1971.

[4] Bernard Spolsky. "Navajo Language Maintenance III: Accessibility of School and Town as a Factor in Language Shift." Navajo Reading Study Progress Report No. 14, The University of New Mexico, August 1971.

[5] Agnes Holm, Wayne Holm, and Bernard Spolsky. "English Loan Words in the Speech of Six-Year-Old Navajo Children." Navajo Reading Study Progress Report No. 16, The University of New Mexico, August 1971.

[6] Fr. Berard Haile, O.F.M. *Learning Navaho* Vol. I. St. Michaels Press, (1941), p. 10.

[7] Edward Sapir. *Language.* New York: Harcourt, Brace, (1921; 1958), p. 196.

[8] Edward P. Dozier. "Linguistic Acculturation Studies in the Southwest." Dell H. Hymes and William E. Bittle, eds. In *Studies in Southwestern Ethnolinguistics*, The Hague: Mouton & Co., (1967).

[9] Erik Reed. "Navajo Monolingualism." *American Anthropologist*, Vol. 46 (1944), pp. 147-149.

11

Semantic Categories of Bilingual Children[1]

Rodney W. Young

As children acquire language, they gain control over an immensely complicated set of systems; and in acquiring the meaning or semantic system of a language, children come to recognize the many subtle differences in meanings of words and word relationships. For example, a child gradually realizes that not all motor vehicles are cars; some are pickups and some are trucks. As he gains in his perceptual capacity, his language reflects this increasing ability to differentiate and categorize.[2] However, a meaning system of a language is considerably more complex than the labels of objects. The child must come to realize that *if* and *unless* are not the same in meaning,[3] and that *more than* and *less than* are also not synonymous.[4] He must also acquire the subtle difference between expressions that are synonymous in one context but not in another, such as *return* and *take back*. It is permissible to either return or take back a book to the library, but it is not permissible to either return or take back a friend to the zoo.[5] The child further must realize that expressions of equality will be affected differently by negation. *Equal to* and *as many as* are quite similar in meaning, but *not equal* and *not as many as* are obviously different.

Many of these subtleties of the meaning system of a language appear to be forbiddingly complex; nonetheless, almost all children eventually gain adequate control over the semantic level of their language. The current controversy over semantics in linguistic theory provides considerable motivation for investigation of this element, especially in a cross-language situation. Different languages exhibit their own particular semantic systems, and study of how the systems differ can throw light on what is universal to language and what is specific to a single language.

The interesting question and subject of this paper is whether children who learn a second language — English in this case — will develop the same semantic system as monolingual children or whether their semantic system will be different because of linguistic or cultural interference. A second, closely related question is whether the bilingual child develops separate meaning systems for his two languages or whether he operates by means of a single system.

This paper will present evidence from a study investigating these questions by comparing the relative difficulty of certain semantic constructions in comprehension tests for two groups of young bilingual children: Spanish-English bilinguals and Navajo-English bilinguals. A group of English monolingual children provide a basis for comparison. These two groups of bilingual children were chosen because Spanish and English are semantically similar languages, and Navajo and English are semantically dissimilar languages in the area being investigated.

In this study ten categories of numeric comparison (five positive and five negative) were used to express the three basic concepts: superiority of number, equality of number, and inferiority of number, plus their denials. Each of these categories included three syntactically different sentences, which were parallel in each category except that half the categories were negative. In this way syntax could be investigated as well as semantics. The sentences were translated into Spanish and Navajo when the categories were semantically equivalent, and each bilingual child was tested for comprehension of the thirty sentences in English and thirty sentences in his other language for accuracy and latency (response time). This methodology is an adaptation of the one developed by Kennedy.[6]

The following two tables illustrate the ten semantic categories in English used in this study and the three syntactic types established for each category.

TABLE I

Semantic categories of numeric comparisons

Semantic Category	Symbol	Linguistic Construction
1 Superiority	$>$	*more than*
2 Denial of Superiority	$\not>$	*not more than*
3 Inferiority	$<$	*less than*
4 Denial of Inferiority	$\not<$	*not less than*
5 Positive Equality	$=^+$	*as many as*
6 Denial of Positive Equality	$\neq^+$	*not as many as*
7 Negative Equality	$=^-$	*as few as*
8 Denial of Negative Equality	$\neq^-$	*not as few as*
9 Neutral Equality	$=^\circ$	*equal to*
10 Denial of Neutral Equality	$\neq^\circ$	*not equal to*

TABLE II

Syntactic types within semantic categories

1 There are (not) more X than Y.
2 There is (not) a larger number of X than Y.
3 The number of X is (not) larger than the number of Y.

The translations of the sentences into Spanish and Navajo were done by native speakers and were verified by back translations. The Spanish paralleled the English in meaning and syntactic types and reflected the language of northern New Mexico. Two informants were used for the Spanish and both agreed that the meaning system of the ten numeric comparisons was the same as it would be for English. For example, the denial of positive equality (*not as many as*) and the Spanish equivalent (*no tantos como*) both unambiguously mean numeric inferiority of the first noun mentioned in relation to the second. For the Navajo version three informants were used plus five back translations. The first difficulty was the absence of the desired syntactic variety. One informant provided different types but only through use on the English word *number;* two informants agreed fairly well on the single syntactic type that was used after certain exceptions had been resolved. The Navajo version was left with only one syntactic type rather than the three in English and Spanish. This is not to claim that the pattern used is the only one available; the claim is that the pattern was readily understood for the back translations and seemed compatible with Young and Morgan's explanation of the comparative construction in Navajo.[7]

The concern over syntactic variety led to a more basic problem — directness of meaning. The relationship of numeric superiority can be expressed directly in English through the sentence *There are more X than Y.* The relationship can also be indirectly expressed by saying *There are many X; there are few Y.* Navajo informants produced comparative sentences that could be literally translated to parallel the indirect English expression just mentioned. They also produced constructions parallel to the English direct comparison, lending some support to a parallelism between the languages in directness of meaning for this category. The real concern came with the English construction *There are as many X as Y.* The Navajo equivalent would be parallel to an English construction *The X and the Y are equal and they are many.* A similar situation exists for constructions of *as few as.* The absence in Navajo of direct comparatives for equality which are built from adjectives of superiority and inferiority suggest that these categories (positive and negative equality) do not "directly" exist in Navajo. The clue comes when these expressions are modified by negation and they do not produce a parallel meaning. In English *not as many as* is not simple denial and unambiguously means less than. Negating the Navajo counterpart results in something like *The X and Y are not equal and they are many.* Four categories then could not be "directly" translated into Navajo and maintain a meaning system parallel with English and were omitted from the Navajo version.

The subjects were first and fourth graders recognized as bilinguals by their teachers and freely admitting to be so. All subjects were screened for knowledge of the lexical items used in the testing and general knowledge of the types of constructions in both languages. Subjects were not used without successfully completing the screening. The thirty sentences in English and the thirty in the other language were randomized and presented in blocks of ten sentences alternating between languages by blocks. The subjects were randomly assigned as to which language and which block of sentences they would begin with. They listened to tapes of the sentences which were recorded by native speakers and selected one of two pictures (rear-projected on two small screens in front of the subject) as a correct illustration of the meaning. In addition to accuracy, a latency measure was obtained. Figure 1 presents the type of illustrations used with an accompanying sample sentence. The letters represent drawings of common objects selected for their cultural neutrality. The relative positions of the compared objects were controlled experimentally.

FIGURE 1

REPRESENTATIVE ILLUSTRATION FOR TESTING

"There are more Z than W."

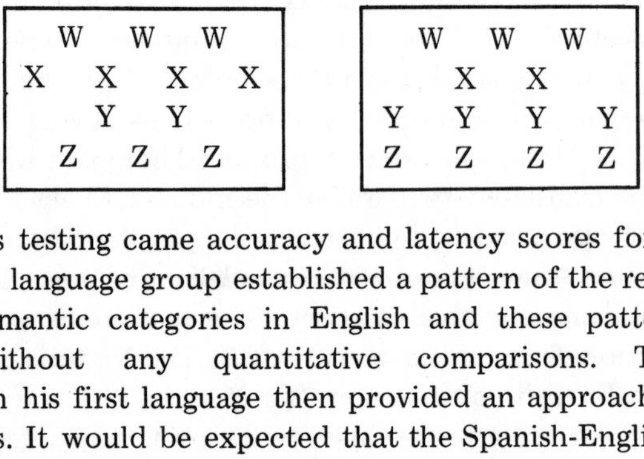

From this testing came accuracy and latency scores for each semantic category. Each language group established a pattern of the relative difficulty of the ten semantic categories in English and these patterns were then contrasted without any quantitative comparisons. The bilingual's performance in his first language then provided an approach for explaining any differences. It would be expected that the Spanish-English group would parallel the English monolinguals but that the Navajo-English group would deviate from the pattern because of language differences.

The idea of patterns of difficulty of the ten semantic categories presupposes meaningful differences among them. These ten categories express the three basic concepts of superiority, equality, and inferiority plus their denials in subtly different ways. The concept of superiority can be expressed by *more than* and it can also be expressed by *not as few as*. Similarly, inferiority can be expressed by *less than* and *not as many as*. Equality can be expressed by *equal to, as many as*, and *as few as*. Of these last three only *equal to* can be denied simply. The previous examples show that negation of *as many as* and *as few as* unambiguously represent expressions of inferiority and superiority respectively. Denial of *more than* and *less than* is simple and direct and means no more than just that. In other words, *not more than* can be factually illustrated by either equality or inferiority. *Not less than* offers the two possibilities of equality and superiority. When these categories refer to the same basic concept, the point is that there is also a difference in semantic structure and meaning. For example, *more than* and *not as few as* both refer to the same basic concept. The linguistic form is obviously different and the semantic construction is also different. The semantic information contained in *more than* is less complex than the semantic information in *not as few as*.

The semantic theory of Katz & Fodor,[8] Katz,[9] and Bierwisch[10] offers an approach to explaining this by means of semantic features, which are considered universal for languages (although any particular combination of features is not). By means of features, each of the semantic structures for the ten categories can be represented and these features can also provide a way to account for the hierarchy of difficulty of these categories. (The use of features and a theory of semantic markedness will be dealt with later.)

The method of study that is used for this paper determines the hierarchy of difficulty of the ten semantic categories in English for each language group and then compares the hierarchies. The first significant finding is that first-grade children do not sufficiently differentiate the categories to be able to establish a true hierarchy. There was little, if any, significant difference among the ten categories for first-grade children; scores were generally low, indicating that the younger children of all groups, regardless of language, were not comprehending the categories much beyond pure chance. However, the fourth graders sharply differentiated the categories on both accuracy and latency. This developmental finding strongly supports the notion that much of language acquisition is still going on after school age. With fourth-grade performance strongly suitable for the technique of comparing hierarchies, the first analysis permitted a comparison of English monolingual children from two widely divergent areas. Kennedy's[11] study was located in Los Angeles and the monolingual children for this study were in Albuquerque, New Mexico. The rank order correlation of the first eight categories (Kennedy's study did not include categories 9 and 10) was quite high in accuracy ($p = .958$) and also significant for latency ($p = .786$). This replication of Kennedy's study is in itself a significant finding. Two groups of monolinguals from distinctly separated areas found these semantic categories similarly difficult. This high degree of similarity suggests a certain degree of cognitive commonality in processing the information in the semantic categories. Certainly this finding supports the use of the English monolingual group as a base for comparing the two bilingual groups.

For the cross-language emphasis, the primary finding was that both groups of bilinguals established different difficulty patterns than the monolingual group. Figure 2 illustrates the relative pattern for all three groups in accuracy.

FIGURE 2

CATEGORY HIERARCHIES IN ENGLISH ACCURACY

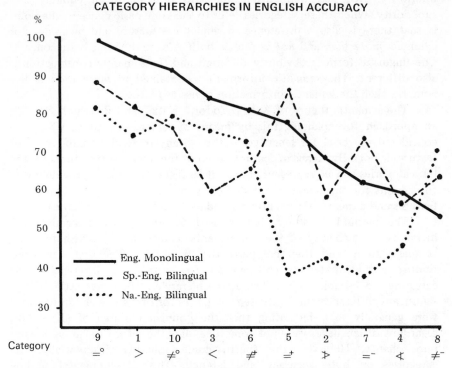

%

Category

It is noticeable from this comparison that much of the deviation comes from categories 5, 7, and 8. For the Spanish-English group, positive equality, negative equality, and denial of negative equality (categories 5, 7, and 8) are relatively easier than the other categories in comparison to the English monolinguals. If one supports the notion of identical semantic structures for English and Spanish, this relative preference for these three categories must be explained on the basis of familiarity and preference rather than inherent complexity. This indicates that it is not only necessary to investigate language performance linguistically, but it is also necessary to investigate purely psychological factors as well.

For the Navajo group it was expected that positive and negative equality would be relatively more difficult because of the absence of these categories in Navajo. This prediction is upheld by the data. The interesting point is how negating these categories removes the relative difficulty. Generally negating a difficult category would be expected to increase its difficulty. However, if the sentence *There are as many X as Y* is being erroneously comprehended as superiority of X over Y because *many* is connected to X alone, then denial of the many removes the source of error. The sentence is interpreted as *There are not many X in relation to the number of Y.* Interpreting denial of positive and negative equality in this manner is much the same as what the deep structure of the construction would be. Roughly the deep structure of negative equality would be *There are few X/ there are few Y.* Negating the structure produces *NEG + There are few X/ there are few Y.* The first structure uses *few* (or *many*) for equality while Navajo would express the equality and then add the number sense. The denial, however, is similar to the Navajo, which roughly translates *These X are not few/ these Y are few.* The Navajo child is used to a category that is expressed seemingly by both a positive and a negative. He puts the English sentences into this system and makes errors in comprehension. Navajo does not have positive equality that is built from *There are many X/ there are many Y.* This system is used only for meanings of superiority or inferiority. These data then would seem to suggest that the difference between the English and Navajo semantic systems is at the base of the Navajo-English bilingual's performance.

The latency measure (using right and wrong responses) generally supports the accuracy measure for the Spanish-English group as indicated by a significant rank order correlation ($p = .663$). However, the latency measure for the Navajo does not even differentiate the categories unless only the correct responses are used. Little difference exists for the Spanish-English group or the English group between latency of all responses and the latency of the correct-only responses. Time is not a significant variable for the Navajo unless he has some confidence in his understanding of the categories. The main finding from latency is that all three groups are quite similar in response time (correct-only responses for the Navajo) regardless of differences in accuracy. Latency seems to be a measure of confidence, which is quite similar for all groups.

Examination of the three syntactic types in English reveals no particular preference or ease in comprehension of one type over another for the Spanish-English group or the monolingual group. However, the second syntactic type (*There is a larger number of X than Y*) was significant for the Navajo children. This unexpected showing is best accounted for by noting that the order of the comparison device and of the nouns being compared is opposite to the order in the Navajo sentence, where the comparison is last.

To answer the question of whether the bilingual child is operating with one or two meaning systems for his two languages, the hierarchies of difficulty in the child's two languages can be compared. For the Spanish-English group all ten categories can be used while only the six mutual categories can be used for the Navajo-English group. The rank order correlations for accuracy ($p = .821$ for the Spanish-English group and $p = .943$ for the Navajo-English group) strongly support the presence of a single meaning system at this level of development. This suggests a certain universality of semantics and even of some of the semantic categories in language comprehension. The latency index is similar ($p = .810$) for the Spanish-English group, but no correlation is possible with the Navajo group because correct-only responses are contributing scores in English but total responses in Navajo.

It seems apparent from the data that, in comprehension, semantic categories are definitely significant factors for all groups. These categories are so powerful in determining comprehension that absence of them in one language greatly increases their difficulty in another. The semantic system of one language forces interpretation of another language accordingly. The bilingual is eventually confronted with the task of acquiring a new semantic system to express the same basic meanings. However, at this stage of development he definitely appears to be functioning with a single meaning system. Furthermore, presence of identical semantic categories in two languages does not guarantee the same hierarchy of difficulty as for the monolingual of the target language. Other factors are needed to explain these differences, such as preference and familiarity.

These results of analyzing comprehension by means of semantic categories can be formalized by extending a semantic theory based on features into a theory of semantic markedness on the same principle that Chomsky and Halle[1 2] use with phonological features. The simple presence or absence of a feature fails to reveal whether that feature is intrinsic or natural to the meaning, hence not adding to its complexity. Clark[1 3] establishes a principle of lexical marking to account for the extra difficulty of the negative half of a pair of polar adjectives. *More* is not as complex in meaning as is *less*. Clark uses features within a binary system to formalize this difference. Using Clark's basic principles but formalizing the use of features into markedness theory can account for this difference more realistically than can the binary system. Both *more* and *less* contain the feature of "polarity," indicating their existence as polar pairs; however, *more* is unmarked or natural as to "polarity" and *less* is marked. This captures the asymmetrical nature of polar adjectives and formalizes the fact that *less* exists in contrast to *more*, the basic member of the pair. For other examples, *equal to* can be differentiated from both *as many as* and *as few as* by being unmarked for a feature "equative" while both the positive and negative equality would be marked for "equative," indicating the unnaturalness of their use in expressions of equalty. *As many as* would further be differentiated from *as few as* by the previously mentioned feature "polarity," which is unmarked for *as many as* and marked for *as few as*. The principle determining complexity is that only unmarked features do not add to the complexity of meaning.

Each of the ten semantic categories can be represented with features according to markedness theory and a hierarchy of difficulty predicted on the basis of the number of marked features. The English monolingual's hierarchy highly correlates in accuracy with the one predicted by the theory ($p = .870$). Also important is the fact that this theoretical representation of semantic categories can be used to represent the categories from other languages. Positive and negative equality are marked for "equative" while neutral equality is unmarked for the same feature, as are the Navajo categories of equality.

Although this theoretical representation is sketchily presented here, it is not difficult to imagine its usefulness in semantic analysis. Semantics, like phonology, may well be representable in a universal set of features when formalized within a theory of markedness.

In review, this study has shown that bilingual children do not parallel monolingual children in patterns of difficulty of semantic categories. Categories not present in their first language are appreciably more difficult in relation to the other categories than for monolingual children. Even when categories are present in the child's first language, factors such as preference and familiarity are also significant. Semantic categories do appear to be important determiners of comprehension, especially when compared to syntax. A theory of semantic markedness can appropriately account for the relative difficulty of different categories and be quite suitable for use across language boundaries.

Summary

A basic question in cross-language research is whether the meaning system of a bilingual child is the same as that of a monolingual. When bilingual children were tested for comprehension of semantic categories, they showed patterns of difficulty that were different from those of English monolingual children but that were very similar for their two languages. The Navajo-English case seems to reflect Navajo semantic factors while the difficulty pattern for the Spanish-English group reflects non-linguistic factors. The findings are in agreement with a theory of semantic markedness.

NOTES

[1] This paper is based on the author's unpublished dissertation, "Semantics as a Determiner of Linguistic Comprehension Across Language and Cultural Boundaries," The University of New Mexico, (1971). Support for this dissertation came from the Ford Foundation in the form of an Ethnic Studies Dissertation Fellowship.

[2] Eric H. Lenneberg. *Biological Foundations of Language.* New York: John Wiley & Sons, (1967).

[3] Evelyn Hatch. "Four Experimental Studies in the Syntax of Young Children." Unpublished doctoral dissertation, UCLA, (1969).

[4] Margaret Donaldson and Roger J. Wales. "On the Acquisition of Some Relational Terms." In John R. Hayes, ed., *Cognition and the Development of Language.* New York: John Wiley & Sons, (1970), pp. 235-268.

[5] Dwight Bolinger. *Aspects of Language.* New York: Harcourt, Brace & World, (1968).

[6] Graeme D. Kennedy. "Children's Comprehension of English Sentences Comparing Quantities of Discrete Objects." Unpublished doctoral dissertation, UCLA, (1970).

[7] Robert W. Young & W. Morgan. *The Navaho Language.* Salt Lake City: Deseret Book Company (A Publication of the Education Division, United States Indian Service), (1958).

[8] Jerald J. Katz & Jerry A. Fodor. "The Structure of a Semantic Theory," *Language,* 39 (1963), pp. 170-210.

[9] Jerald J. Katz. "Recent Issues in Semantic Theory." *Foundations of Language,* 3 (1967), pp. 124-194.

[10] Manfred Bierwisch. "Some Semantic Universals of German Adjectivals." *Foundations of Language,* 3 (1967), pp. 1-36.

[11] Kennedy, (1970).

[12] Noam Chomsky and Morris Halle. *The Sound Patterns of English.* New York: Harper & Row, (1968).

[13] Herbert H. Clark. "Linguistic Processes in Deductive Reasoning." *Psychological Review,* 76 (1969), pp. 387-404.

12

Features of Child Black English

Mary Ritchie Key,
L. Fiege-Kollman
and E. Smith

This paper is a result of a linguistic seminar[1] and further individual study which focused attention on Child Black English. In becoming acquainted with the varieties of Black English (hereafter BE) we became increasingly aware that it is a language of power and vitality. Besides exemplifying the well-known abilities of rhyming and rhythm, it is a language rich in vocabulary, much of which is not known to the mainstream community; creative in metaphor; innovative in compounding; and replete with subtleties of irony and humor, which undoubtedly result from the exigencies of survival.

While reviewing the literature on Black English we collected a list of terms such as the following, which are used in some types of publications to describe BE or the speakers of this variety of language: pathological, disordered, lazy speech, disadvantaged, therapy, remedial, substandard, deviant, difficulties, corrective, handicapped, impoverished, inability, limited, deprived, deficient, nonverbal. None of these terms could be applied to the texts that we have transcribed and analyzed. Above all we found that these children have adequate language with a wide range of vocabulary and ability to express themselves in their own settings.[2] Recognizing the language differences and attempting to understand the children will, hopefully, strengthen the hands of the educators who have been stunned by the numbers of dropouts and failures in schools. From various studies across the nation, there is now enough information available so that language exercises and lessons can be constructed that will be productive in carrying the children over to a second dialect, which they will find useful in other realms of society. It should be emphasized that the language we speak of here is not the language of all Black children, i.e., those who learned mainstream English from infancy. Also it should be emphasized that there are many styles and varieties of BE, as in any other language. As one Black scholar has reminded us, BE has sometimes been unfortunately associated only with pool-room language, and this has added to the confusion and the difficulty of defining BE.

When we went over the tapes the second time, Smith listed examples of speech which the investigators misheard or misinterpreted or did not understand. Some of these were simply cases of not knowing the vocabulary, for example, "cause dat gran'father got jugged in his heart" (II, p. 11,[3] *jug* means to stab[4]). A more subtle kind of misunderstanding involves styles of speech and intricacies of Black grammar; for example, tense-aspect and referents. At the beginning of one taping session a cooperative child volunteered, "One haf to say it" (II, p. 1). It appeared that the investigators did not understand that the child was trying to establish the procedure, i.e., that only one person at a time could talk on the recorder. At another recording session, the investigators misheard *it* when the child said, "Whon' chu make it go fas', so i' kin go. . ." (I, p. 6) meaning "Why don't you make the recorder go faster, so our recording session will be more effective? " The investigators thought the children meant that they wanted to leave and launched out on a discussion of why the children should stay put!

A further example of misunderstanding occurred when the child used a play on words which is called "opposites."[5] The children were discussing their favorite records, and when Stevie Wonder's recording was mentioned, one of the children said, "He bad, hun" (IV, p. 24). The investigator said, "No, I think he's good." The child answered exasperated, "Oh, you know how I mean." A final example illustrates how the speaker of standard English has difficulty hearing the phonological arrangements of BE. The children were discussing the Jackson Five and used this name 23 times in the text. The preliminary transcription shows that the term never was heard correctly.

Throughout the studies on Black English there is reference to the distinct intonation patterns, the paralinguistic effects, and different rhythms. Nevertheless, there is not yet a very clear understanding of just how these patterns are different and what elements make up the rhythm. The following text (with an ersatz phonetic transcription) illustrates some observations which we believe are crucial in understanding the distinctive features of Black English.

We were góin' to the béach, dén when we gót dére, we was ón the rócks, den

I slípped dówn, we see. . .we séen a whóle búnch o' mússel-dúmp, whn I

trýin' t' gét one it wz óu' o' síght. . .uh túrnin' aróun'. Den I púlled it, den it
(?)

cáme off, den w' I wa' trýin' t' gét a lóok at it. . .I drópped it. Den. . .I séen
            when

dis cráb, hé was dís. . .dis bíg, den I tól' d' téacha t' cóme hére, but shé din'
                                        the

cóme, so dén whn I wén' on th' ótha' síde w' dese bíg ól' rócks, I séen
                                        were/with (?)

dis. . .uh. . .bédda. . .cáve, dén when I cálled th' téacha'. . .when I
better (?)

cálled. . .uh. . .m. . .uh sómebody mótha', den when néy came, ít had

sómethin' whíte up in nére, an' it wz móvín' thín' was góin' jús' like tha̧t.
(there was)

(conversation: teacher, children — sea flowers, crab)

Den, den. . .when I seen nát. . .Dat thín' was góin'. . .hé was góin'

fás'. . .n'. . .I wz rúnning. . .n' dis líddle cr'. . .Dis líddle thín'. . .déy was

hóppin' an' flýin' aróun'. . .n' wálkin' on th' rócks,. . .mos'ly éverybody got

scáred but cép. . .Wé din' rún awáy from 'em, dén. . .when I was góin' to gét

s'. . .when I wz góin' in th' wáter. . .(silent pulse-beat) lóok for mé some
to (?)

sán'crábs I wen' déeper, den we we(re) práyin', den whn I wz trýin' t' gít
playing

awáy from th' wáves, I wz trýna gó den I fáll dówn, n' the wáter was cómin'
trying to

I há' my hán' out jús' like dát n' I wz góin dís-a-wa̧y.
have

The canonical form (or shape) of the syllable in BE is strongly a consonant-vowel (CV) pattern. Previous studies have described the deletion of final consonants such as the stops and /1/ and /r/ and the reduction of final clusters such as /-st, -ft, -kt, -ld/ to a single consonant. When a syllable does end in a consonant there is a tendency for the consonant to carry over and begin the next syllable. For example, *get a look* is syllabically divided into /ge.ta.look/; *all the* /a.le/ /al.le/; *cause I* /kə.zai/; *down there* /dau.ner/; *than that* /den.nat/ or /de.nat/; *trying to* /trai.na/.[6] This strong tendency toward the CV structure influences sound change, as is heard in a phrase *was this, this big* (line 5, above text). The final *-s* of *was* makes the following /d/ of /dís/ *this* sound affricated and can be easily misheard as *was just dis big*.

While the rhythm of SE (Standard English) has been described as stress-timed, BE should be described as syllable-timed,[7] with a fairly even beat. Some stresses are stronger than others, and the strong ones have a tendency toward higher pitch in rhythmic cadences. Occasionally there occur two stresses contiguously, for example in line 2 *a whóle búnch;* line 6 *t' cóme hére;* and line 7 *dese bíg ól' rócks.*" It is possible that these occur under certain syntactic and semantic circumstances, such as emphasis, quotation, and description. They usually occur in the final position of a rhythmic group.

The pulsating beat is maintained by what goes in between these strong and less-strong stresses in measured rhythm. Function words usually occur in these spots, and these morphemes are articulated in various degrees. They may even be phonologically deleted and occur as silence but with the pulsating rhythm maintained. In the text above where the deletion seemed especially apparent, we have tried to indicate it by spelling. Thus, when morphemes such as *was, when, to, the, with* are phonologically diminished, we have spelled them, respectively: *wz* (line 3), *whn* (line 3) and *w'* (line 4), *t'* (line 3), *th'* (line 6), *w'* (line 7).   For the reconstruction of diminished or silent morphemes such as /w'/ *when* (line 4) or *with* (line 7), we have depended upon native speakers and phonetic cues surrounding the contiguous elements. When silence occurs, as in line 17, we have indicated it by ( ), and in this text have labeled it "silent pulse-beat."[8] Partial deletion of a phrase may occur as in *over to my house* /o' m' house/ (V, p. 5). Function words of more than one syllable are reduced in order to keep the beat rhythmical: *didn't* /din'/, *except* /sep/, *supposed* /pos/. Careful attention to this silent pulse-beat will show the difference between such items as the following, where tense is involved. *He'll stop it* and *He stopped it* sound very much alike because of the deletion of final consonant /l/ and reduction of the consonant cluster /-pt/ to /-p/. The pulse-beat indicates the difference: /he ( ) stop it/ and /he stop ( ) it/.

Other morphemes that occur in these rhythmic spots are: *will ('ll)* /ə/, *could* /ku/, *of* /ə/. These deleted entities might be called "silent morphemes," but they should be considered in the grammar as valid; this is not grammatical deletion but phonological deletion with remaining pulse-beat. This might explain the apparently aberrant behavior of some morphemes which have baffled grammarians. For example, Loflin speaks of the optionality of the infinitival *to.* Schotta gives examples of the absence of the article. Legum *et al.* discusses article and preposition deletion.

In analyzing pulsation features, one must distinguish between these and hesitation phenomena. In the case of the latter, the rhythm is broken, however soon recovered. An example of a hesitation pause which was not recognized in our first rough transcription gave us a peculiar grammatical form: *he got blowed his head off...* (II, p. 3). Listening carefully and checking with Smith revealed that there was a hesitation pause following the *got*, where the child changed his mind and started a new structure.

In a study of Black preaching style, Rosenberg (p. 76) maintains that the overriding influence in the style is not language but rhythm. One can postulate that in general, the language of BE carries a high priority in rhythm and that even in the selection of words, rhythm takes precedence. The consequences on syntax are inevitable.

We do not consider this to be a complete or final statement on the suprasegmentals of BE. However, enough of these observations are indisputable, and the implications, for example, for learning to read should be of interest to educators. During the course of our investigation, one of the parents wanted to discuss the problem of breathing, which he believed interfered with his children's learning to read. This was a naive but extremely insightful observation on the phenomenon which we have discussed here, even though tentatively.

Regarding other phonological features, the children used structures described elsewhere in BE studies in varying degrees, depending upon their grasp of SE, and with some articulations which could be acknowledged as developmental. Some of the consonant substitutions in BE are considered developmental in SE speakers; e.g., the /f/ and /v/ replacements of /Ө/ and /ð/: *mouth* /mouf/ and *breathe* /briv/. Some forms, however, are not described in BE studies, and these should probably be considered developmental even though most of these children are 9 to 12 years of age. For example, the difficulty with /r/: *ēlectricity* /elektwisite/, *rob* /wob/, *rather* /waðə/. We also recorded a fluctuation between /l/ and /r/: *Irene* /ailin/, *playing* /prejɛn/ (line 18 of above text). It should be noted here that /l/ and /r/ are a common source of interference from language where a phonological distinction is not made, as for example in West African Ewe.[9] Difficulty with some initial consonant clusters, not characteristic of BE, could be developmental: *throwed* /Өowd/, *brought* /bɔːt/, *swim* /frwim/ (but note that /r/ is involved in these also).

Some articulations could be considered Malapropisms, not related to phonological structure in a strict sense: *detective* /pətektif/ (IV, p. 12), *nodule* /novel/ (IV, p. 13).

Phonological features which affect morphology have been discussed in studies in BE, particularly with regard to forming plurals, possessives, and the tense system. Some analogical forms which are considered child language in SE are common in adult BE: *teeth* /tifs/, *children* /ʃildɚnz/, *funnier* /moðfʌni/, *the best car* / ðəgudəst kað/, *threw* /Өrowd/. Some verb forms which occur in BE are older forms from Early Modern English: *clamb* (climb), *holp* (help), and *whup* (whip). Some syntactical constructions might be remnants of earlier forms: e.g., the Biblical double subject, "Thy rod and thy staff, they comfort me." Note that this construction also occurs in West African Hausa, "The chief he came."[10]

Stewart discusses child language in relation to archaic forms among BE speakers and among children in the Appalachian region.[11] As he points out, this has only recently been recognized because child language had hardly been recorded. Neither is there much information about white child language in those earlier plantation days when the white and Black children played together and white children were entertained by the tales of Uncle Remus and the like.[12] It is consistent with linguistic principles to recognize the possibility of linguistic exchange during these encounters. Before leaving the topic of child language and BE, it might be appropriate to mention a suggested connection between baby talk and pidgin English, where the sailors might have talked down condescendingly to the "ignorant savages."

Grammatical analysis is complex and lengthy, and we were limited by time and data in our study. Therefore we have chosen to highlight noun phrases by showing the great variety and types which we found in the six tapes only. It is possible that other types could be found in a more extensive study; it is also possible that some of these could turn out to be unique forms or slips of the tongue.

Noun Phrases

Simple noun phrases

a solid hit

the newest routine

all the girls

all those rocks

all these white mens

some little fishes

a real little pig

a old drunk man

a steel natural comb

your little skinny head

that shrimped up chest

double teaming

Noun + noun

sea flower

blood brother

soul stuff

a vampire bite

my pellet gun

my little tent home

that big old clown head

black eye pea juice

Pronoun substitution

a little one

the biggest one in class

one little one and another big one

Appositive

a shotgun, a double-barrel

that girl, this pretty girl

we, all of us

Noun phrases with prepositional phrases

    a whole bunch of souls

    a little bit of beer

    kind of little beads

    tomorrow in the morning time

    that black girl from Africa

    that girl from blackest Africa

    the goodest car in the world

    ugly boys with marks on their face

    this casket knife with a mummy on it

    a trip you from (a trip away from you) (developmental)

    all of them

    the name of it

Possessive modifiers

    the world's greatest champion in the world

    his daughter birthday party

    that other monster's mouth

    all Clay and Frazier's money what they won

Relative clauses

    that man who got bit

    this lady we seen

    a mountain what you could run down and you can't even stop

    a what you call it

    my sister next to the biggest

    a ape coming from Tarzan

    that boy named Billy

    Link tied on the back

    the heart like worms

    only little kid about my size

Our final comment on linguistic structures has to do with clause and sentence complexity. We did not try to do analyses of these structures, but did a statistical survey to make some preliminary comparisons with the language of children in similar age groups.

In analyzing structural complexity in the writing of school children and adults, Hunt used as a measuring device the T-unit or minimal terminable unit. He defines it as one main clause plus any subordinate clause or nonclausal structure that is attached to or embedded in it.[13]

O'Donnell, Griffin, and Norris used the T-unit in their analysis of the syntax of kindergarten and elementary-school children. Their investigation deals with speech and writing.

The clauses of Tape II (first half) were analyzed using the Hunt method. The results were compared to the third-grade norms of the O'Donnell study:

	Words per T-unit	Sentence-combining transformations per T unit: Rate of occurrence per 100 T-units
	Range mean	Mean
O'Donnell 3rd, 7.4-10.8	8.73	1.01
Monte Vista 3rd grade	7.27	0.86

Considering that in the O'Donnell study the discussion topic was somewhat controlled since the children retold stories seen on film (with no sound track) and that in our study extemporaneous speech was recorded, the results seem to be similar. The mean figure of words per T-unit of utterances are well within the range of words per T-Unit given by O'Donnell *et al.* in their study. No individual ranges were measured in our study.

A difficulty in analyzing speech is the matter of code-switching. In the school setting where the tapes were made the children were perhaps more aware that their speech should be "proper." Nevertheless the recorded texts evidenced many of the features of oral narrative which scholars have discussed: for example, Rosenberg, in his study of the Black preaching style; Dorson, in Negro folktales; Abrahams, Kernan, Kochman, Labov *et al.*, concerning verbal art. Even at this young age, the children were experimenting, perhaps unwittingly, with various speech styles and forms.

One of the most significant things we noticed was the increase of paralinguistic effects when the children moved into casual style[14] and talked about things dear to their hearts, such as the Clay-Frazier fight, vampires, and girls (boy speakers). A trait often noticed about young white males is that when they tell a story their voices are dull and expressionless. On the contrary the Black males in this study opened up all the stops when they got interested in narrating and they produced a wide variety of voice quality, expressive pitch differences, and noises. Dorson has perhaps given the fullest description of paralinguistic and kinesic effects that can accompany Black narrative, and even he has not completed the description of the exceedingly rich repertoire of possibilities. His chapter on the art of Negro storytelling could easily be applied to the children's narrative in such stories as the Monsters, King Kong (Tape I), the vampire, the rabbit party (Tape II), the Clay-Frazier fight, the Mod Squad, soul (Tape IV), okra, a backyard tent-home (Tape V). The following paralinguistic effects are all recorded in these texts: alveolar trill, bilabial trill, gasp, sigh (communicative), humming, singing la de da, snapping fingers, long consonants for effect /ussssss/, vowel change for effect, additional syllable for effect *vampire* /vam.pai.ah/, chanting, laryngealization, falsetto, whispered, tremolo, emphatic stress, sudden extra-loud stress, extra-high pitch, extra-soft quality, gravelly voice, deep voice, breathy voice, quivering voice, spooky voice, mocking voice, bragging voice, threatening voice, speech mimicry (baby talk, character representation), various qualities of laughter, giggles, snickers, intonation substitute for words, *I don't know* /⌐⌐⌐/, and wide variety of noises, rhythmic sound effects. These features were particularly noted in quotation passages (Kernan calls this "marking," pp. 70, 137-143).

A description of a Black sermon would include the following (among other things): begins in normal prose style; builds up a crescendo of delivery, with marked intensity, higher pitch, and vocal effects such as tremolo; elicits significant audience response. The same description (among other things) could be given for the vampire story which the boys recorded on Tape II.

When the children were narrating, at times it was difficult to tell which child was talking when we played back the tapes. (For example, the Clay-Frazier discussion, IV, pp. 7-8.) We are calling this "conversation cooperation" when different speakers fill in with the consent of the first speaker. It is almost as though the speakers were forwarded in their narration by the interjection of the listeners — faintly reminiscent of the "call and response" which the preacher and audience participate in during the sermon. This filling in by others was perfectly acceptable to the speaker — almost expected. A different atmosphere in this give-and-take response can be noted in the agonistic exchange that occurs in Playing the Dozens.

Repetition of a clause connector is common throughout the texts. It usually takes the form of "Then. . ." or "And then. . ." This is not unusual in oral literature described elsewhere.[15]

One child used an introducer *Because* to begin her narrative: "'Cause when we was goin' on the rock. . ." (Field Trip, p. 4). As far as we know, this is not described in discussions on BE, but Smith reminded us that it is a common introducer among Black people who feel that every time they are stopped by the authority they have to explain.

Repetition occurs often in the texts. There are precedents in Black verbal art for this repetitive, adding style, for example, in the chanted sermon and in hymn singing, where the leader gives a line which the congregation then sings.[16]

Creative constructions and metaphors occur in the children's speech. On the beach trip a youngster saw piles of mussels and called it a mussel-dump (line 2 of above text). In discussing boxing, the boys described one unfortunate as "pregnant in his lips" (II, p. 18). They carry on the tradition of the Black "bold spirit for word usage" as Dorson expressed it (p. 23).

In the language project started last year at the Monte Vista school the teachers have introduced the terms "everyday talk" and "school talk."[17] The children have understood and accepted this concept remarkably well. One little girl, while working with various language forms, told a teacher, "I'm gonna dress up this sentence for you." At the beginning of one of the taping sessions, the investigator wanted to clarify which variety of language he wanted to record, "Do you think I'm looking for school talk or everyday talk? " The boys answered,". . .everydáy talk! " and then one little boy, with a twinkle in his eye, said, "I talk év'ry dáy! "

Summary

At least some of the difficulties in attempts at analyzing child Black English stem from the fact that we don't seem to have much information on the differences between developmental and other-dialect structures. This preliminary study focuses on such grammatical problems as the time-aspect situation, number and gender agreement, and pronominal systems in Black children's speech. A significant feature of the dialect which we have recorded in one of the schools of Orange County, California, is the constant code switching, which may be differentiated in part by paralanguage.

NOTES

¹ Six tapes were recorded and preliminary transcriptions were made by the students in a graduate seminar conducted at California State College at Fullerton: Fernando Canedo, Laila Fiege-Kollmann, Michael Kohne, Mary Sánchez, Ingeborg Stotz, Sandra Ward, Katherine Watson, and Rudolph Wilkins. The tapes were recorded in collaboration with the teachers of the Language Development Center at the Monte Vista Elementary School in Santa Ana, California. The children were in grades one to three, but most of the children recorded were 9 to 12 years old. After the seminar ended, **Fiege-Kollmann** continued with the analysis of the tapes, and Smith, doctoral candidate at the University of California at Irvine, who is conversant in Black English, corrected the transcriptions and interpreted the difficult passages.

² See also Houston's observations (1969), pp. 601-602.

³ The figures given in parenthesis refer to the transcriptions made of the tapes. The Roman numeral refers to the tape and the page number to the typescript.

⁴ *jug* — See *Oxford English Dictionary*, where references date from 1377 and 1393, as used in the tilt or tournament, to prick or to spur (horse). See also F.G. Cassidy and R.B. LePage, *Dictionary of Jamaican English*. Cambridge: Cambridge University Press, 1967: *juk* — to prick, pierce,. . .stab — usually done suddenly.

⁵ See Labov *et al.*, 1968, Vol. II, pp. 36, 44-45, 60, 131; Major, pp. 13-14; Abrahams, p. 262.

⁶ Cf. fast speech SE (Standard English) forms: gonna going to, and wanna want to. However, BE lends itself more to such syllable reduction to accommodate the rhythm pattern.

⁷ The English of Nigerian speakers is also described as syllable-timed, in John Spencer, *The English Language in West Africa* (London: Longman, 1971), pp. 42 and 109.

⁸ This term is suggested by Abercrombie's discussion on silence, stress, and rhythm. David Abercrombie, *Studies in Phonetics and Linguistics*, Oxford University Press, (1965).

⁹ Spencer, p. 158.

¹⁰ *Ibid.*, p. 132. And see Riley Smith for discussion of the double subject.

¹¹ Stewart, in *Language and Poverty*, pp. 365-366. Some time ago I recorded a preschool child from Tangier Island, off the coast of Virginia, who showed the same characteristics.

¹² The first picture of Harris' tales of Uncle Remus shows a little white child in the hut of the old Negro storyteller.

¹³ Hunt, p. 9.

¹⁴ Labov (1969) says, pp. 730-731, fn. 15, "The criteria for

determining the shift to casual style are contrastive changes in 'channel cues' — pitch, volume, tempo, and rate of breathing (which includes laughter)." See also Kernan with regard to paralinguistic and kinesic features which signal a change in meaning and/or otherwise communicate, pp. 70, 126, 132, 137-143.

[15] In a description of the Hausa language of West Africa, Abraham notes that in a narrative there is often a long sequence of "then" clauses: "they asked us and then we said we agreed: so they replied that. . .then they. . ." This was also a style common in Old English texts, for example, "and after two months fought Athered King and Alfred his brother against the army at Merton, and they were in two bands, and they both were put to flight, and far on in the day. . ." Robert A. Peters, *A Linguistic History of English* (1968), pp. 236-237. For other examples from African languages, see Taylor.

[16] Rosenberg, pp. 16, 252. He gives other examples from oral epics, pp. 112 ff. I remember recording a similar type of repetitive, adding style by a well-known storyteller in a South American Indian language

[17] The terms "everyday talk" and "school talk" are used in the curriculum, *Psycholinguistics Oral Language Program: A Bi-Dialectal Approach: Experimental Edition,* and *Teacher's Manual,* with 8 accompanying readers, Chicago Public Schools, 1968-1969.

Bibliography

Abraham, R.C. *The Language of the Hausa People*. London: University of London Press, (1959).

Abrahams, Roger D. *Deep Down in the Jungle*. Chicago: Aldine Publishing Company, (1970).

Anon. *Psychololinguistics Oral Language Program: A Bi-Dialectal Approach: Experimental Edition*, and *Teacher's Manual*, with 8 accompanying readers, Chicago Public Schools, (1968-1969).

Dorson, Richard M. *Negro Folktales in Michigan*. Cambridge: Harvard University Press, (1956), Chapter 2, "The Art of Negro Storytelling," pp. 19-30.

Harris, Joel Chandler. *The Complete Tales of Uncle Remus*. Boston: Houghton Mifflin Company, (1955).

Houston, Susan. "A Sociolinguistic Consideration of the Black English of Children in Northern Florida." *Language*, 45, (1969), pp. 599-607.

———. "Competence and Performance in Child Black English," *Language Sciences*, 12 (1970), pp. 9-14.

Hunt, Kellogg W. *Syntactic Maturity in Schoolchildren and Adults*. Monographs of the Society for Research in Child Development, Serial No. 134, Vol. 35.1 (1970).

Kernan, Claudia Mitchell. *Language Behavior in a Black Urban Community*. Monographs of the Language-Behavior Research Laboratory, No. 2, (February 1971).

Kochman, Thomas. "'Rapping' in the Black Ghetto," *Trans-Action* (February 1969), pp. 26-34.

———. "Toward an Ethnography of Black American Speech Behavior." In Norman E. Whitten, Jr. (comp.), *Afro-American Anthropology: Contemporary Perspectives*, N.E. Whitten, Jr. and John F. Szwed, eds., New York: Free Press, (1970), pp. 145-162.

Labov, William. "Contraction, Deletion, and Inherent Variability of the English Copula," *Language*, 45 (1969), pp. 715-762.

———. "The Logic of Nonstandard English." In James E. Alatis, ed., *Georgetown Monograph Series on Languages and Linguistics*, 22 (1969), pp. 1-43; *Florida FL Reporter*, 7.1 (spring/summer 1969), pp. 60 ff.; Frederick Williams, ed., *Language and Poverty*. Chicago: Markham Publishing Company, (1970), pp. 153-189.

Labov, William, *et al. A Study of the Non-Standard English of Negro and Puerto Rican Speakers in New York City*. 2 vols. Cooperative Research Project, No. 3288, USOE, (1968).

Legum, Stanley E., *et al. The Speech of Young Black Children in Los Angeles*. Report 33, Southwest Regional Laboratory, (1971).

Loflin, Marvin D. "On the Structure of the Verb in a Dialect of American Negro English," *Linguistics*, 59 (1970), pp. 14-28. Reprinted in Harold

B. Allen and Gary N. Underwood, eds., *Readings in American Dialectology*, (1971), pp. 428-443.

Loman, Bengt. *Conversations in a Negro American Dialect.* Washington: Center for Applied Linguistics, (1967).

O'Donnell, Roy C., William J. Griffin, and Raymond C. Norris. *Syntax of Kindergarten and Elementary School Children: A Transformational Analysis*, Research Report No. 8. Champaign, Ill. National Council of Teachers of English, (1967).

Rosenberg, Bruce A. *The Art of the American Folk Preacher.* New York: Oxford University Press, (1970).

Schotta, Sarita G. "Toward Standard English Through Writing: An Experiment in Prince Edward County, Virginia," *TESOL Quarterly*, 4.3 (September 1970), pp. 261-276.

Smith, Riley B. "Interrelatedness of Certain Deviant Grammatical Structures in Negro Nonstandard Dialects," *Journal of English Linguistics*, 3 (March 1969), pp. 82-88.

Spencer, John. *The English Language in West Africa.* London: Longman, (1971).

Stewart, William A. "Continuity and Change in American Negro Dialects," *The Florida Foreign Language Reporter*, (Spring 1968). Reprinted in Frederick Williams, ed., *Language and Poverty*, Chicago: Markham Publishing Company, (1970), pp. 362-379; Harold B. Allen and Gary M. Underwood, eds., *Readings in American Dialectology*, (1971), pp. 454-467.

Taylor, Orlando L. "Historical Development of Black English and Implications for American Education." Paper presented at Institute on Speech and Language of the Rural and Urban Poor, Ohio University, (July 1969), Center for Applied Linguistics.

13

Dual-Language Process in Young Children
Eleanor Thonis

The Child's First Language

In the natural course of his total development, the normal child acquires his first language, the system of sounds which accompanies his experience. As the child encounters his physical and psychological world, he takes in information. He perceives not only sounds but also sensory data, images, and symbols. He sorts out a vast number of undifferentiated stimuli and begins to attach meanings to them as he becomes increasingly aware of objects, people, and events in his environment. These are his personal realities, which he encodes in sounds imitative of those who surround him. He soon discovers the wonder and the power of words. He understands what others are saying to him and can act or choose not to act in response. Others understand him and can respond in return. There are now perceptual constants and conceptual certainties to be shared by means of a mutually understood symbol system. He perceives, listens, talks, smiles, feels good about himself and about others. His own world is a fairly steady, reliable place. The specific symbols used to describe and to explain it are reasonably dependable and unchanging. Real and symbolic boundaries expand consistently with enriched experiences and improved language. Mastery in first language learning is commensurate with the child's inner potential and the diverse conditions around him.

The Child's Second Language

The young child may begin his second language at the same moment as the first language. If parents, grandparents, household members, or others responsible for his infant care use a second language, then he learns to listen, to speak, and to attach meanings to the sound systems of more than one speech community. When both languages are available from the start, the child may become very proficient in one language or in both, competent in one but only partially competent in the second, or equally deficient in both. The variations are endless, and unique to the individual child. Should the child have a good start on his first language prior to exposure to his second language, he will bring to his new language task the conditioning of his previous learnings. He already has a background of experience, sensations, percepts, images, concepts, sounds, and symbols. He possesses a store-house of information about language, what it is made of and how it works. He has imitated and internalized the symbol system of his first language. The extent to which he has done this is dependent on the depth and breadth of his initial language acquisition. He now has to learn to add new sounds and sound combinations to the reservoir of knowledge he has already stored. He may also have to undergo new experiences, specific to the cultural environment in which the new speech community exists. It is necessary for him to listen to the second language; to understand which sounds stand for which reality he has already encountered; to meet new, unfamiliar realities; to remember the order of sound combinations; to imitate accurately the available speech models; and, finally, to speak fluently. The degree of success which he enjoys in the second language learning process is determined by the amount of interference by his first language, the number and kind of his experiences, the accompanying feelings and expectancies, and countless other forces which shape human speech. It is difficult to predict whether he is to be blessed with a second language accomplishment or burdened with a second language handicap. Like matrimony, it may be for better or for worse, for richer or for poorer.

Two Languages — Burden or Benefit?

The literature is replete with studies which report the negative effects of dual language learning on speech production, concept acquisition, vocabulary growth, intellectual power, social adjustment, and personality development. These unfortunate effects on speech are said to involve errors in articulation, voice distortion, faulty rhythm, and inappropriate stress. Inhibition of language maturity is seen in fewer words, shorter sentences, confused word order, grammatical errors, and poor idiomatic expression. Slowness in intellectual growth is often related to the imprecise use of two languages, inadequately developed to serve as instruments of thought. Educational retardation begins early when reading, spelling, and writing are insufficiently supported by a broad base of oral language abilities. Access to knowledge by way of the weaker language results in limited achievement. Personality disorders and character disturbances reportedly accrue from the tension and stresses attendant upon straddling two different cultures, seeing the world from two different points of view, and using two different symbol systems to express them. From these gloomy prophecies of the many deleterious consequences, the burden of dual language learning is seen as overwhelming.

However, dissenting voices have been raised by theorists who state emphatically that the problems attributed to dual language learning in early childhood have been grossly exaggerated. According to this more positive view, the failure to control significant research variables has led investigators to overstate speech difficulties, to describe inaccurately language developmental delays, to distort intellectual limitations, to emphasize unduly educational retardation, and to magnify without adequate documentation personality disintegration or character disorders. Many scholars even claim a positive advantage in dual language learning both for the individual and for the society in which he lives. Jensen has provided an excellent research summary of the effects, both good and bad, of childhood bilingualism.[1] Because increasing contact among different nations and diverse individuals is greater than ever before in Man's history, adequate communication skills have become prerequisites for survival. It is therefore imperative to examine all the possibilities and to draw conclusions based on more careful research.

Dual Language Learning and Thought

The relationship between a child's acquisition of language and his ability to think is not very clearly understood. Three major positions are to be found among the scholars. Language and thought are identified as the same entity; they are said to be separate entities; or they are considered as somewhat loosely related entities. It is very difficult to observe what happens when children are engaged in thinking, and it is almost impossible to arrive at a universally acceptable definition of thought. Among the several raw materials of thought, however, are symbols, both verbal and non-verbal. Thinking, then, may rely totally upon the quantity and quality of verbal symbols; may depend partially upon these language proficiencies; or may not require specific verbal abilities at all — depending upon the theory of language-thought relationships espoused.

If and when children use verbal symbols as an accompaniment of thought, this inner language[2] is usually the mother tongue. It is reasonable to assume that the more precise the language used, the clearer the thinking results, when other conditions remain the same. Language carries content — ideas, generalizations, and relationships concerning the child's reality. When the child's experiences and encounters with the environment are clarified, stored, and available for retrieval in precise terms, it would appear that he has an incisive instrument to use in reasoning, judging, remembering, and understanding.

When it comes to dual language learning and its effect on the cognitive processes, we need to explore further the language-thought relationship. Central to this question is a consideration of the role of the mother tongue when it is not the dominant language of the community. If there is found a valid need for inner language for purely personal purposes in reflecting, musing, and thinking, then the social purpose of using expressive language in communicating must not be the only emphasis in language learning.

The Best of Both Languages

Fishman has stated that more than half of the world today uses more than one language while engaging in the activities basic to human needs.[3] With rapid technological advances in transportation and communication, bilingualism is bound to increase. It is important to consider thoughtfully the education of those children who are presently living in dual language settings. The language variables must be arranged to create a maximum of benefits and a minimum of burdens. There are several conditions known to be conducive to promoting success and preventing failure for children engaged in the acquisition of two or more languages. For example, parents and teachers should, as much as possible, keep languages in separate contexts so that coordinate language systems may result. Coordinate systems appear less subject to interference and confusion.[4] It is vital to have the best language models available in both languages, as children will readily imitate errors in phonology, intonation, forms, and syntax. Since language grows out of experience, it is essential to provide children with a rich and varied background of environmental encounters so that sensory impressions, images, percepts, and concepts may be tested, verified, and encoded in language. The press for early school achievement in the weaker language should be avoided. Since the school world, even on the primary levels, demands proficiency in receptive and expressive use of verbal symbols, every effort must be exerted to insure that the child's language competency is commensurate with the school's expectations. When the language of the home is not that of the school or of the majority culture, extra care must be taken to engender feelings of acceptance and equality. A child's first language learning takes place in the warmth and intimacy of his family. Such learning carries with it emotions and memories which become a permanent part of himself. When his language is valued, he feels himself and all that is a part of him valued as well. Premature demands for control of the conventions of the writing system in either the native or the second language should not be made. Reading and writing skills require responses to a set of visual symbols superimposed upon auditory symbols. It is logical to expect that the normal child will read and write first the language which he controls well in its oral form. The importance of arranging a program of dual language learning which provides for an appropriate sequence of skill development is evident. Though many of the social, economic, and political variables affecting the outcomes of dual language learning are outside the sphere of influence of educators, such factors as acceptance of the child's uniqueness, respect for his native language, appreciation of his cultural heritage, and attention to his specific language requirements will contribute greatly to his successful acquisition of two or more languages. The world needs speakers of many languages to share new ideas, to exchange technological knowledge, to preserve history, and to talk together for peace in the universe. Wherever dual language talents of young children are found, they should be nurtured and preserved.

Two Languages in a Curriculum for Young Children

A curriculum which would yield the valuable benefits of dual language learning while at the same time avoiding its burdens is presently the subject of discussion in educational circles of the United States. With concern for the rights of minority ethnic groups and with increased resources available for the creation of special programs, a number of plans have been tried. Though diverse in ultimate goals, classroom organization, staffing patterns, and teaching strategies, these curricula share the common title of bilingual education. The description which follows gives the basic framework for one approach to the education of young children who are currently using or who are actively learning two languages. There are six major strands which support activities designed to remove the major stumbling blocks to successful learning. The six primary areas are: (1) expanded experiences with the environment; (2) improved oral language ability in the vernacular; (3) introductory literacy skills in the native language; (4) intensive oral language development in the second language; (5) readiness for literacy in the second language; (6) access to knowledge by way of the stronger language and through the best language modality.

In schools of the United States, the uniqueness of an early childhood curriculum in which two languages serve as media of instruction lies in the opportunity to develop truly bilingual pupils during the period of optimum language learning. For the child who is not native to English there is provision for expansion and refinement of the vernacular across all language bands of listening comprehension, speaking fluency, reading, and writing. For the child who is a native speaker of English, there is an introduction to a second language according to a carefully ordered plan which can lead him to full competence in these same bands of language.

Essential to any successful educational plan is awareness of the environment in which the pupil is living and growing. His understanding of his immediate world as well as of the larger society to which he contributes must come from broad experiences at all levels. Such experiences should be at first hand when feasible or may be offered vicariously through pictures, films, slides, records, tapes, television, and other media. Each experience should be accompanied by language which enables him to label, classify, and store the experience for later retrieval. It is reasonable to expect that the child's stronger language will serve as the mediator when new experiences are presented. It is important to distinguish between the learning of the new language label for a known concept, already understood, encoded, and stored in another language and the acquisition of a totally new concept derived from a never-before-encountered experience.

The defeating press for written material must be avoided by arranging each language activity according to the developmental stage and educational background of individual learners. Formal literacy programs in either the vernacular or in the second language must be structured and supported by a broad base of oral language. Print stands for speech; print is secondary to speech; and print must be transformed into the language system which the child controls in its oral form.[5] The dual language curriculum must also take into account the difference between language as a study in itself and language as a carrier of content in other fields of knowledge. It is unjust to anticipate that a child will master a new language — its phonology, structure, vocabulary, and semantics — in both oral and written form at the same time as he is acquiring the body of knowledge carried by that language.

Pupils should be introduced to basic understandings in mathematics, science, social science, health, and safety through the medium of the stronger language. Pre-literate and functionally illiterate pupils should be provided with pictures, demonstrations, films, and oral explanations which are comprehensible to them. Textbooks, workbooks, study sheets, and other written materials which cannot be read and understood should be avoided until literacy skills are well established. The curriculum plan must provide for differential language proficiencies not only in the two languages but also among the many dimensions of listening, speaking, reading, and writing. At each grade level in each subject area and for each learner the expected performances must be consistent with the reasonable expectancies of children learning two languages.

Pupils who enter the program at any point should be placed where they are socially most comfortable. Prior learnings must be assessed and appropriate skills must be introduced for reinforcement and mastery. An expectancy of excellence of performance does not need to be lowered. Children learning by way of two languages do not require a dilution of the curriculum or a different set of educational goals.

Summary

The outstanding intellectual achievement of any child is his acquisition of language. When a child acquires two languages and uses them effectively in controlling the world around him, his accomplishment impresses us grown-ups as a remarkable triumph in human learning. The young child who grows up in the midst of dual language opportunities may enjoy the benefit of unusual mental flexibility or may suffer the handicap of mental confusion. Whether his early exposure to languages other than his mother tongue becomes an asset or a liability depends on a number of variables. Among these are genetic endowment, parental education, economic status, cultural background, social class, and life opportunities. In addition to these influences there are other factors: the age at which second language learning begins, the degree of proficiency in the first language, the quality of language experiences, the relative political position of both languages, and the acceptance afforded the speaker in each cultural milieu.

Children who learn two languages as well as use them both in order to learn other subjects are engaged in a highly complex process, one which influences their cognitive power, their emotional development, and their personality structure. The challenge to educators of young children lies in the preparation of an educational plan which will guide them safely through the dual language process so that they are competent, knowledgeable, and comfortable in two environments and in two languages.[6]

They need the same quality of educational program as their monolingual peers in a single language curriculum. They do need time, proper sequence of subject matter, appropriate teaching strategies, and careful appraisal of progress as they grow toward a standard of excellence.

APPENDIX A

Bilingual education of children, ages three to eight years
curriculum framework and time line — for the non-English-speaking pupil

	Pre-School	Kindergarten	Grade 1	Grade 2	Grade 3
Experiences:	Encounters with the environment through first-hand and vicarious experiences mediated by vernacular		Mediated by vernacular and/or English		
Oral Language Development in the Vernacular	Sound system	— →			
	Structural complexities			— →	
	Vocabulary development				
	Semantics				
Written Language	Pre-Readiness	Readiness — →			
Development in Second Language Reading and Writing		Introductory Program	Basic Skills — → Developed		
Oral Language Development English	Sounds			— →	
	Structures				
	Vocabulary				
	Semantics				
Written Language	Readiness (Pre-)	Readiness	Introductory Program — →	Basic Skill Development — →	
Fields of Knowledge	Mediated by vernacular on oral basis				
Concepts Information Use of Content Problem Solving Making Judgments		Written vernacular	Mediated by English on oral basis		
Reasoning					

- - - Activities in these areas may have to be
adjusted for individual pupils

Thonis, Eleanor — Marysville,
California

APPENDIX B

Bilingual education of children, ages three to eight years
curriculum framework and time line — for the English-speaking pupil

	Pre-school	Kindergarten	Grade 1	Grade 2	Grade 3
Experiences	Encounters with the environment through first-hand and vicarious experiences mediated by vernacular ————————————▶				
				Mediated by vernacular and/or second language — — — —————————————▶	
Oral Language Development in the Vernacular English	Sound system ——————————▶				
	Structural complexities —————————————————— — — — —▶				
	Vocabulary development ——————————————————————————————▶				
	Semantics ——————————————————————————————————————▶				
Written Language	Pre-Readiness	Readiness — — —▶			
Development in English Reading and Writing		—————————————————▶			
			Introductory Program	Basic Skills Developed	
Oral Language Development Second Language	Sounds ——————————————————▶ — — —▶				
	Structures ——————————————————————————————▶				
	Vocabulary ——————————————————————————————————▶				
	Semantics ——————————————————————————————————————▶				
Written Language Second Language	Readiness (Pre) Readiness Introductory Program ——————————▶			Basic Skill Development ——————————▶	
Fields of Knowledge	Mediated by vernacular on oral basis				
Concepts Information Use of Content Problem Solving Making Judgments		——————————————————————▶			
		Written vernacular ——————————————————————————————▶			
			Mediated by second language on oral basis ——————————————————▶		
Reasoning					

Activities in these areas may have to be
adjusted for individual pupils

Thonis, Eleanor — Marysville,
California

NOTES

[1] J. Vernon Jensen, "The Effects of Childhood Bilingualism," *Elementary English, XXXIX, 2 (1962), pp. 132-143, 358-366.*

[2] L.S. Vygotsky, *Thought and Language.* Cambridge, Mass.: M.I.T. Press; New York: John Wiley & Sons, (1962).

[3] J.A. Fishman, "Bilingualism, Intelligence, and Language Learning," *The Modern Language Journal,* XLIV, 4 (1965), pp. 227-236.

[4] Jensen, *op. cit.,*

[5] E.W. Thonis, *Teaching Reading to Non-English Speakers.* New York: Collier-Macmillan International, (1970).

[6] The Marysville Reading-Learning Center provides the direction and support for three preschool and three primary classes of Spanish-speaking pupils between the approximate ages of three and eight years. A large percentage of these pupils do poorly on tests of general ability and/or on school readiness inventories even when they are administered in their native language. We have noted, however, that when we provide language development programs in both Spanish and English many of the children show dramatic improvement. By comparison, Spanish-speaking children for whom no native language development program has been offered do not show such gains even though they are immersed in a total **English-speaking** environment.

14

Bilingualism in Primary Schools of Friesland
Kr. Boelens

Friesland is one of the northern provinces of The Kingdom of the Netherlands. Its area is about 60 by 50 km. or 3,227 sq. km., which is nearly 10 percent of the state's surface. The first of January 1971 it had 526,749 inhabitants, which is 3.71 percent of the population of the Netherlands. All Frisians understand and speak, read and write Dutch. Of Frisians 12 years old and above some 97 percent understand the Frisian language. Frisian is the home language of 71 percent of this group, while 13 percent talk Dutch at home, and the rest use some other dialect as a home language.

The minute a Frisian leaves his home, Frisian diminishes and Dutch increases. Standing in the doorway, 68 percent of Frisians use Frisian in greeting or taking leave of someone. Entering a shop, 62 percent stick to Frisian; but only 42 percent venture to talk Frisian to a doctor, a clergyman, a director, or a manager. In these situations Dutch has increased from 13 percent to 22 percent to 29 percent and finally to 54 percent.[1]

Everybody reads Dutch; and as Dutch and Frisian are linguistically akin, reading Frisian is not too difficult. Sixty-nine percent of the group are able to read Frisian, but only 41 percent actually do read a Frisian book now and again. The Frisian language is more difficult to write than Dutch because it contains a number of diphthongs and even triphthongs which do not occur in Dutch. Moreover, Frisian is more common in oral use than it is in writing; so only 11 percent of the population is able to write it well, and an additional 20 percent declare they master the spelling only partially. Strangely enough, older people read more and buy more Frisian books, and younger ones master writing better.[2]

In Friesland there are 552 *gewone lagere scholen* (common lower schools), which is our term for primary or elementary schools and some 2,000 teachers. It is clear then that most of these schools are small, some very small. In fact, this part of the Netherlands has the highest percentage of schools with only one or two teachers. Most of these schools are completely Dutch; 240 of them, or 43.4 percent, have Frisian in the curriculum as a subject. Of these, 87 start with Frisian as a subject in the third class and carry it through the sixth, the highest class in our primary school. As a general rule, Frisian is limited to one language lesson and one lesson in reading a week in the fifth and sixth classes.

These schools with Frisian as a subject could be called bilingual; but in Friesland the term *twatalige skoalle* (bilingual school) is reserved for primary schools with Frisian as a medium of instruction in the first and second grades. These schools date from 1955. In them the three R's are learned in Frisian. At the same time some oral Dutch is occasionally introduced, but the child is freely allowed to express his feelings and thoughts in Frisian, his mother tongue. In the second grade, reading and writing in Dutch are introduced, and by the end of the third grade these children are on a level with their mates from the other schools, even in Dutch, and are of course ahead of their mates in their knowledge of Frisian. So at the end of six years the pupils from bilingual schools enter secondary education with a command of Dutch at least equal to that of other children and with greater ability to read and write their mother tongue.

In the country practically everybody speaks Frisian, but the situation is different in the villages and small towns. Up to now "de twatalige skoalle" is found only in villages and small towns. If children from Dutch-speaking homes attend these schools, they have learnt Frisian on the playground and in their daily contacts with their Frisian-speaking friends. So up to now Dutch-speaking children have little difficulty in following their Frisian lessons, as they are more or less bilingual before entering the primary school. If this is not the case, these children get an introduction to the three R's in Dutch, or at least partially in Dutch.

As the place of Dutch in Friesland becomes steadily more important owing especially to the influence of radio and television, almost totally in Dutch, this system of bilingual schooling comes more and more under discussion. Quite apart from the deeply felt desire by many Frisians to maintain their ancestral language and its culture, there is the important educational question whether the average Frisian-speaking child has a sufficient working knowledge of Dutch to get his primary-school education in this language. It is this point which needs research.

The Pedagogisch Instituut, Rijksuniversiteit, Utrecht, began a longitudinal investigation of this subject in 1970, but it will be some years before the results are available.[3] When the results of this research are in, we can expect to have the data needed to plan the best possible school program. In the meantime we already know that the children of the bilingual schools can compete successfully with the other children — in itself a remarkable piece of evidence which favours the *twatalige skoalle*.

In the educational system of the Netherlands up to now most schools have been rather curriculum-centered and less child-centered. Now some of the schools have made a start with modern ways of reading and with "world orientation," as we call it. Instead of talking and giving orders, the teacher now more and more favours discussing and exploring by the children. It stands to reason that the function of the child's language becomes far more important then. So if we want to give him more elbow-room, we must give him an opportunity to express himself optimally, that is, in his own language.

As a consequence of this change in educational philosophy, the question is now being discussed whether the law should make it possible to use Frisian as a medium of instruction in the higher grades of the primary school, which is now not legally possible. It is important to know the teachers' views on this subject. Consequently in January of 1971 all primary-school teachers from the third grade on received a questionnaire. They were asked, first, whether they would favour legal permission to use Frisian as a teaching medium in the higher elementary classes. Secondly, their views were sought about making Frisian an obligatory subject. In both questions the social position, perhaps even the very survival, of Frisian as a fully developed cultural medium is at stake.

The results of the questionnaire were as follows: 9.7 percent of the teachers had no opinion; 26.1 percent were in favour of a change; and 64.2 percent had objections. Obviously many teachers spoke from their own particular situation. In some schools Frisian is the language of the playground, in others it is mixed with Dutch, and in a third group no Frisian is heard. In the first group 34.8 percent of the teachers were in favour of Frisian, in the second group 25.1 percent were in favour, and in the third only 14.2 percent favoured the maintenance of Frisian. Consciously or unconsciously, people voted according to their own particular situation. This becomes still more evident if we consider the teachers' command of Frisian. Of the teachers who could understand, speak, read, and write Frisian, 41.4 percent were in favour; of those who possessed only one of the basic language skills only 9.2 percent were in favour of creating the possibility for Frisian as a medium of instruction in the higher grades. It is significant that this 9.2 percent, though themselves non-Frisians, should recognize that Frisian as a Western European cultural language is possible only if it is used for teaching all kinds of subjects, orally and in writing, in the family and out in society. If one keeps Frisian for use in the home only, if children cannot follow moon-travellers in Frisian, for example, then Frisian is doomed to become a patois and nothing more.

The second question, concerning Frisian as a required subject, is of course related. In recent years proponents of Frisian have proposed moving into secondary education as well as primary. However, the place of Frisian in secondary education, and even in the pedagogical academies, where teachers are educated, is weak. A change is taking place, following a new *wet op het voortgezet onderwijs* (a law providing for secondary education). It would of course be good if secondary education could be planned to include a continuation of Frisian after a good foundation is laid in a great many primary schools. The present legal provision is for one lesson a week, from the third grade on. This is considered a bare minimum for educational success. At the same time exemptions should be made freely, for instance, in schools where Frisian is not used, in Saxon districts like the Stellingwerven, or in towns with many non-Frisian inhabitants, and also in schools lacking teachers qualified to teach Frisian.

A surprising fact in the survey was that more teachers voted for the Frisian language requirement than for the use of Frisian as a teaching medium; still the supporters of a Frisian language requirement constituted only a 36.5 percent minority. In schools where Frisian is spoken on the school grounds the support for Frisian amounted to 50.6 percent. In schools where Frisian is used as a medium of instruction, support amounted to 28.8 percent. And in schools where Frisian is used as a secondary teaching medium or is not used at all, there was still 19.4 percent of support. Of the teachers who could understand, speak, read, and write Frisian 62.5 percent supported the language requirement, whereas of the teachers who possessed only one of the four language skills only 8 percent voted for support of the requirement.[4]

For lessons in Frisian there are children's books and a training course for teachers. The government finances the Pedagogysk Advysburo,[5] and this Institute has proved its worth over the last twelve years. It has prepared suggestions for the schools and numerous work sheets for the teachers and the children in all kinds of situations. Moreover, its representatives visit the schools and submit oral and written advice and reports to everybody concerned. As for teacher training the Dutch Government has legalized a special Frisian certificate (in Frisian: *de Fryske akte;* in Dutch: *akte Fries lager onderwijs*) and every year more persons pass the examination and are certified for teaching Frisian in the primary school. Some 12 percent of the teachers in service now possess this certificate. Even when it is considered that after World War II this percentage was only 6 percent, the 12 percent are inadequate for sufficient bilingual primary education in Friesland.

It is my opinion that only two or three years ago the number of teachers favourable to Frisian as a vehicle of instruction and as a compulsory subject in the curriculum of primary schools would have been very much smaller than it is now. In social situations outside the school there is the same kind of development.

A new educational law is being prepared for the primary school in the Netherlands. It is expected to supply new provisions for Friesland and its native tongue.

NOTES

[1] L. Pietersen, *De Friezen en hun taal* (Drachten: Laverman, (1969), with an English summary.

[2] L. Pietersen, *op. cit.*

[3] See J. Winjnstra's description of Project Friesland.

[4] Her Majesty's inspection for primary teaching sent an inquiry to all teachers of the third grade and higher of the primary schools in Friesland. The Ministry of Education and Science, Nieuwe Uitleg 2, Den Haag (The Hague), has given me permission to quote from the results.

[5] The Pedagogysk Advysburo of the Frisian Akademy, Doelestrijitte 8, Ljouwert-Leeuwarden, will supply information about bilingual schools in Friesland.

15

The Friesland Project: A Brief Description [1]
Johan M. Wijnstra

The language situation in Friesland

Friesland is a province with some 500,000 inhabitants, situated in the north of the Netherlands. About 70 percent of the inhabitants use the Frisian language for daily communication. The adult population has a fairly good command of Dutch as well, certainly in the decoding domain.

Frisian is rather different from Dutch, although the two languages are closely related. There are a few syntactic and morphological differences, e.g. in verb inflections and verb order, between the Frisian and Dutch, and there are differences in vocabulary too.

The Frisian population has a strong sense of identity and its own literature, both stimulated by a nationalistic movement. This movement is rather moderate and not to be compared for instance with the French nationalistic movement in Quebec. The main aim consists in acquiring greater rights for the Frisian language in public life and in formal education.

The Frisian-speaking population is concentrated in 25 subcounties. In most of these subcounties Frisian is the home language of more than 90 percent of the families. (See map 1) This situation has not undergone much change in the course of the last twenty years. In some places, with the growth of industrial plants, an increasing number of Dutch-speaking families have settled, but most of the homogeneous Frisian-speaking area has kept its rural character, with many people working on the land or in agricultural industry.

Although the number of Frisian-speaking families has not changed much, the Dutch language has, since after World War II, begun to exert more influence because of the mass media and better means of transport.

Every year some 6,000 children who speak Frisian at home start elementary education. More than 90 percent of these children have attended kindergarten for two years. Until 1950 all teaching in elementary school in the province of Friesland was done in Dutch, even in the homogeneous

Map 1. *The location of the homogeneous Frisian-speaking area*

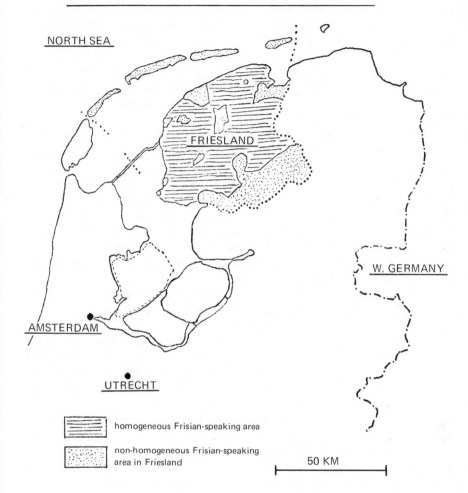

NORTH SEA

FRIESLAND

W. GERMANY

AMSTERDAM

UTRECHT

homogeneous Frisian-speaking area

non-homogeneous Frisian-speaking area in Friesland

50 KM

Frisian-speaking area. Most children understand Dutch rather well, but their spoken Dutch is in general poor. Their difficulties are partly overcome by the fact that more than 75 percent of the teachers are native speakers of Frisian, and in the first grades the children are sometimes allowed to use Frisian. Since 1950 about 70 schools (out of about 300) in the area have switched from a monolingual Dutch program to a bilingual program. In grades 1 and 2 of this program Frisian is used as a medium of instruction, with a preparatory course in Dutch in grade 2, while in grade 3 Dutch becomes the medium of instruction.

The discussion as to the advantages and disadvantages of the bilingual programs is still going on and is sometimes very emotional, as empirical data are lacking. Only very little research has been carried out since 1950. A recent investigation by this author clearly shows that children with Frisian language background do indeed have problems with language production in Dutch. Three subtests from the Utrecht Language Level Test were administered to 80 first-graders (ages 6-7), 40 children being from bilingual schools and 40 from monolingual schools. These subtests were:

1. A single-word comprehension test (point to the_____), comparable with the PMA vocabulary test.

2. A completion test of analogies and contrasts ("I'm sitting on a chair, and I'm lying in a _____"), comparable to the Auditory-Vocal Association Test from the ITPA.

3. A completion test concerning inflection of verbs and other types of morphological items ("Daddy buys a television set, and now he has_____(the television set)," while E is pointing at two pictures and expects the child to say "bought"). This test is comparable with the Auditory-Vocal Text from the ITPA.

On tests 2 and 3 the two Frisian groups scored about one standard deviation below the average score of the norm group from Utrecht City. (See Table 1) These two tests are completion tests, and some oral production is required. The vocabulary test only requires decoding behavior; the child is asked to point to one out of four pictures. On this test the Frisian groups do not differ significantly from the norm group.

Project Friesland

The aims of education in the province of Friesland are essentially the same as those in the rest of the Netherlands, except that "command of the Frisian language" may constitute an additional aim of education. In order to reach the goals of education with children from Frisian-speaking homes, we need adequate methods of teaching. These methods differ somewhat from those used with children from Dutch-speaking homes, because of differences in entering behavior between the two categories of children. The problem is serious because the Dutch language is a goal of education in itself and at the same time a medium for learning other school subjects.

The question is: Is a monolingual Dutch program for children with a Frisian language background — even if these children have attended a kindergarten where Dutch is spoken — the most adequate way to teach these children? If not, is it necessary to presume that the Frisian-speaking child's command of Dutch is so poor that Frisian should be the only medium of instruction for two years and that Dutch should not be presented as a subject until grade 2? The question to be answered in Project Friesland is this: To what extent and in what domains are children with a Frisian language background handicapped by this background if they go to a monolingual school and how can this handicap be overcome?

In the first phase of the project, four groups of Frisian-speaking children will be followed from the end of their last kindergarten year (spring 1972) up to and including grade 3 (1975), the control group being composed of a comparable group of children from a rural Dutch-speaking area near Utrecht City. The cluster of criterion variables is school success. Every year several achievement tests will be administered (readiness tests being used in the kindergarten year). The scores obtained on these tests will be analyzed in relation to general ability and language proficiency tests. If language handicaps can be located, the second phase will be an experimental one, in which different teaching strategies will be tried in order to overcome the problems identified in the first phase. A third phase would be the introduction of successful teaching methods in the Frisian schools.

The first investigation is longitudinal and therefore rather long range, lasting until 1975. It is unacceptable, however, to wait with the experimental phase until 1975. Consequently, in the summer of 1971, a cross-sectional study was undertaken in several third grades (Dutch and Frisian) to get some idea of the level reached by children with Frisian language background on some Dutch language proficiency tests as compared to rural Dutch-speaking children. A report on this cross-sectional investigation will be available within two or three months. After a one-year follow-up with the children in the first phase, the experimental phase will be prepared — if necessary — and carried out, starting in 1974.

Last December the sample for the first phase of the project was chosen from a population of 146 kindergartens in homogeneous Frisian-speaking places, the operational selection criterion being that the group of children in the last kindergarten year must consist of more than 70 percent from Frisian-speaking homes. The 146 kindergartens were divided into three groups: the Frisian-medium kindergartens, Dutch-medium kindergartens, and the mixed-language kindergartens. The information needed for this grouping was gathered by means of a questionnaire to 169 kindergarten teachers. The response was 100 percent, but 23 classes appeared to contain less than 70 percent of children with Frisian-language background.

In this questionnaire we also asked for the names and addresses of the elementary schools which these children are going to attend as of August

Table 1. Scores on three subtests from the Utrecht Language Level Test

	norm group n = 148		monolingual Dutch schools n = 40		bilingual schools n = 40		t-test norm gr. monol.	t-test norm gr. bil.	t-test monol. bil.
	X̄	s	X̄	s	X̄	s	t	t	t
1. vocabulary	27.4	3.87	26.8	3.37	26.6	3.11	0.88	1.19	0.27
2. analogies and contrasts	19.6	3.56	16.6	3.92	15.4	3.61	4.62	6.56	1.41
3. morphology	12.3	3.90	9.8	2.68	8.6	2.31	3.88	5.69	2.11

This table shows the average scores of the Dutch-speaking norm group and two groups of Frisian children of the same age (range 6.6 — 7.5). Differences between the scores of the Frisian groups and the norm group on the analogies and contrasts tests and the morphology test are very significant.

1972. Thus the following combinations of kindergartens and elementary schools could be planned:

1. Frisian-medium kindergarten followed by a bilingual elementary program in the first two grades.
2. Frisian-medium kindergarten followed by a monolingual Dutch elementary program.
3. Dutch-medium kindergarten followed by a monolingual Dutch elementary program.

The mixed-language kindergartens were not included in the sampling procedure.

From each list several combinations were planned: 12 combinations from the first category, with a sample of 80 children, subdivided into two groups according to the number of teachers in the elementary school (2 teachers or more than 2 teachers); 6 and 7 combinations from the second and third categories, respectively. From each of these two categories of 50 children will constitute the sample.

The control group will consist of at most 80 children from 5 or 6 combinations of kindergartens and elementary school programs. During the months of May and June several tests will be administered to these children:

1. *General ability tests:* Three subtests from the Wechsler Preschool and Primary Scale of Intelligence (WPPSI) and the Raven's Coloured Progressive Matrices. These tests will be administered in the child's mother tongue.

2. *Readiness tests:* Reading and arithmetic. These tests will be administered in Frisian if the child is going to follow a bilingual program (Frisian as a medium of instruction in the first two grades) and in Dutch if the program is monolingual, i.e., in Dutch right from the beginning.

3. *Language proficiency tests:*

a. *Non-verbal response to verbal stimulus (in Dutch):* Four single-word comprehension tests and one phrase-comprehension test. One of the single-word tests is based on contrastive features between Frisian and Dutch. The items in this test have been selected from first-grade reading materials and their lexical roots are very different from the Frisian equivalents.

b. *Verbal response to verbal stimulus (in Dutch):* One imitation test, two verb-form tests, one completion test based on analogies and contrasts, one test in which the child is required to answer questions, as in the WPPSI information subtest. The first three tests mentioned in this section are based on contrastive features. The critical structures in the imitation test are syntactic patterns. Two-form tests were constructed because of rather substantial differences between the Frisian and the Dutch verb inflection. The items for one of the form tests were selected from primary readers. In the course of the summer of 1971 the newly constructed tests and some others were pretested, and they are now being revised.

   c. *Verbal response to non-verbal stimuli:* Three vocabulary tests (labeling of pictures in Dutch).

   At first we intended to elicit a sample of free speech production in Frisian and in Dutch. This procedure was pretested last summer, series of 4 or 6 pictures being used as stimuli. Each child was asked to invent a story. This way of gathering speech samples did not come up to our expectations. It turned out to be very difficult to keep the situation uniform for every child; differences in inventiveness interfered with language-production skills, and the analysis of the taped speech samples was very time-consuming.

   According to us, oral language production tests on the level of discourse should be included in the battery. Instead of the procedure mentioned above, a procedure developed by Marion Blank and Sheldon M. Frank[2] will be adopted, with minor modifications. This procedure creates a well-structured situation, and scoring is much easier than the analysis of free samples. The child is told a story twice. Every sentence contains one or more critical structures. The first time the child is asked to reproduce every sentence after it has been read to him. This reproduction task can be used as an imitation test. The second time the story is told without interruption. The child is then asked to retell the story. In our adaptation three pictures will be used to guide the child in this task. The occurrence of critical structures in the story as retold by the child is tabulated. Some other scores are possible as well. This scoring can be done from the tape. The third task consists of answering some questions about the content of the story. In the Project Friesland two such stories consisting of ten sentences each will be used. Every Frisian child gets one story in Frisian and one in Dutch. The control group gets both stories in Dutch, of course.

   4. By means of an interview schedule, information about the home situation of the child will be gathered. The questions will center around the following topics: socio-economic status and education of the parents, contacts with Dutch-speaking people, attitudes towards Dutch and Frisian, educational-cultural provisions in the home, and activities involving the child.

   5. The kindergarten teacher will be requested to fill out a personality rating scale for each child.

   During the follow-up period (grades 1 through 3) scholastic achievement and language proficiency in Dutch will be tested every year. The follow-up period has not yet been planned in detail, however. Perhaps regular observation in the classrooms will be included.

NOTES

[1] The project is supported by grants from the Stichting voor Onderzoek van het Onderwijs (Foundation for Educational Research, established by the Dutch Government, 1965), The Hague. The first draft of this paper was critically read by Drs. J. Sixma and A.K. de Vries, general project directors, Mr. K. Boelens, and was corrected by Miss Nelly Stienstra.

[2] "Story Recall in Kindergarten Children: Effect of Method of Presentation on Psycholinguistic Performance." *Child Development*, XLII (1971), pp. 299-312.

V

PLANNING PRESCHOOL
LANGUAGE LEARNING

16

Home-Oriented Preschool Education
Roy W. Alford Jr.

The well-being and wholesome development of the individual during infancy and early childhood years is recognized by an increasing number of psychologists and educators as crucial. The importance of training in the formative years is predicated on the assumption that there is a high positive correlation between formalized preschool training and later performance in school and in society. The widespread acceptance of this hypothesis is clearly demonstrated by the nation's investment in Head Start. Additional evidence is contained in the many proposals, from Montessori (Hechinger, 1966) to Bloom (Crow et al., 1966), for early educational intervention into the lives of culturally disadvantaged children.

The traditional way for meeting this need in the past has been to establish public kindergartens. These have generally been limited to urban and suburban areas, however, and no state or section in the United States has provided an adequate program of preschool education to rural children. Neither has any of them begun preschool education for children under age five, although it is known that educational nurture should begin at an earlier age.

Two conclusions that may be drawn are that conventional kindergartens are not providing adequate preschool education for all of the children of America who need early formal training to enhance their chances for success in life and that an alternative program for providing preschool education at an earlier age and to rural children needs to be developed.

Such an alternative program is needed especially in Appalachia, where the population is largely rural and where publicly supported kindergartens are not available for the most part. Poverty and cultural deprivation strike deep in Appalachia, and many children caught in its pockets of social poverty have been doomed to lifelong separation from opportunities the outside world of America increasingly values as the inherent right of every child. The adults in the life of the average Appalachian child cannot provide sufficient means of escape because they themselves are victims of the same incapsulation.

West Virginia, the only state lying wholly within Appalachia, has taken a step which may lead to its becoming the first state to actually make preschool education available to all eligible children, rural as well as urban. On March 13, 1971, both houses of the West Virginia Legislature passed Senate Bill Number 343 (Mr. McKown, original sponsor), which specifically provides for an alternative to the usual classroom-oriented kindergarten.

The bill first provides for the West Virginia Department of Education to develop criteria and guidelines for certification of both professional and paraprofessional personnel and for the establishment and operation of both public and nonpublic early childhood education programs. It then states:

> Pursuant to such guidelines and criteria, and only pursuant to such guidelines and criteria, the county boards may establish programs taking early childhood education to the homes of the children involved, using educational television, paraprofessional personnel in addition to and to supplement regularly certified teachers, mobile or permanent classrooms and other means developed to best carry early childhood education to the child in its home and enlist the aid and involvement of its parent or parents in presenting the program to the child; or may develop programs of a more formal kindergarten type, in existing school buildings, or both, as such county board may determine, taking into consideration the cost, the terrain, the existing available facilities, the distances each child may be required to travel, the time each child may be required to be away from home, the child's health, the involvement of parents and such other factors as each county board may find pertinent. (*U.S. Senate Bill* 343, lines 38-56)

The language of Bill 343 can be recognized as having direct reference to the early childhood education program of the Appalachia Educational Laboratory. Two factors cited above — the persistent cultural deprivation of Appalachia and the importance of early years to later development — first prompted selection of early childhood education as a priority endeavor of the Laboratory. It was evident that separation of Appalachian children from the opportunities afforded by a preschool education was an obstacle to their wholesome development and well-being and had an accumulative debilitating effect on performance in school.

The strategy for the achievement of the objectives of the Appalachia Preschool Education Program has been the development of a child-centered, home-oriented program to be delivered by means of television broadcasts, home visitations, mobile classrooms, and other media. It has involved building a curriculum based on behavioral objectives and preparing materials and methods particularly appropriate for children of three, four, and five years of age living in rural Appalachia.

The physical constraints of Appalachia were factors which influenced selection of the strategy. Isolated schools (532 one-room schools in the region in 1967) in remote sections of a sparsely populated and mountainous region and a primitive road system precluded establishment of conventional classroom-oriented kindergartens common in urban areas. Further, funds are not available for this approach; and even if they were, prepared teachers are not available (67 certified preschool teachers in West Virginia in 1969). The establishment of such kindergartens would require a ten percent increase in classroom space, equipment, and auxiliary services. More importantly, however, the traditional design does not include instruction of three- and four-year-old children and thus does not provide sufficiently the readiness training required for first-graders entering school.

Another factor influencing the selection of the strategy was the presence of a television set in over 90 percent of the homes in Appalachia. Most preschool children in these homes watch television several hours a day, with 80 percent watching two hours or more (Hooper and Marshall, 1968). It was assumed they could be guided into viewing and participating in instructional broadcasts.

Parents, even those with low aspirational levels, usually want their children to have better opportunities than they have experienced. On the basis of their participation in Head Start, it was assumed that these parents would maintain schedules and participate in learning activities beneficial to their children if stimulated in the effort by home visitors.

Since the research community had shown renewed interest in early childhood education in recent years, it was possible for the Laboratory to find information useful in its developmental effort. This included work completed and in progress on Head Start; activities of research and development centers such as the University of Georgia's Center for the Stimulation of Early Learning; the resources of the National Laboratory for Early Childhood Education and its affiliates, such as the Demonstration and Research Center for Early Education at George Peabody College for Teachers; and the research done by Deutsch, Bloom, Segal, Piaget, Bereiter, and others.

The Laboratory program would provide preschool training without the constraints imposed by the traditional approach. In both the traditional approach and the one proposed, the objective is to facilitate development in language, cognition, psychomotor, and orienting and attending skills. The unique difference of the Appalachia Preschool Education Program is the method of linking teacher and learner. It would serve essentially the same number of preschoolers with the same number of personnel but would alter the roles and responsibilities of personnel by delivering the program via television, mobile facilities, and paraprofessionals.

A survey of the literature disclosed that much attention had been given to inner-city disadvantaged preschoolers and to urban or suburban middle-class kindergarten pupils, but very little was known about the rural child. One source of information about the Appalachian child was a paper by Stewart (1967) describing the dialect of the Appalachian Region. In it he states that older children, some even into early teens, retain a nonstandard speech akin to "baby talk." This is ascribed to peer-group imitation and a lack of adult correction as influence on language. The mountaineer child does little imitation of adult speech until he is ready to become an adult himself. This is a linguistic phenomenon which presents problems for the Appalachian schools.

In order to conduct a study of the characteristics of the rural preschool child in Appalachia, a sample of 160 children in Monongalia and Upshur Counties of West Virginia was selected. One group was rural farm and the other rural nonfarm as defined by the United States Census Bureau. The findings of this survey provided the following information: The family in rural Appalachia is basically stable and intact. Ninety percent of the homes had both the father and mother present. Negroes amounted to about eight percent of the total population, which is near the West Virginia average. About 45 percent of the parents fell in the 11th and 12th grades as the highest grade completed. About 60 percent owned their own homes. The income of approximately 68 percent of the families was below $4,000 per year. The aspiration of the parent for the child in school was higher than their own accomplishment. Sixty-five percent want their child to finish college, but this is not attainable in West Virginia at the present time. Currently less than 30 percent are completing college. One portion of the survey asked how often the child was read to by others. If the child was a first child he was read to by almost 85 percent of the parents. The incidence of reading for the second child dropped to about 40 percent, and the third child was read to in only 12 percent of the cases responding.

A second portion of the survey was an intellectual assessment. The instruments used in this assessment were the Peabody Picture Vocabulary Test, the Stanford-Binet Intelligence Test, Kagan's Matching From Familiar Figures Cognitive Tasks, Kagan's Draw a Line Motor Inhibition Tests, the Illinois Test of Psycho-Linguistic Ability, the Frostig Developmental Test of Visual Perception, and, for the five and one-half and six and one-half year-old children only, a series of Piagetian Tasks. The summary statement is as follows: "This initial assessment reveals a picture of cultural diversity rather than uniform cognitive intellectual deficits. These deficits tend to center upon verbal tasks or those problem settings which demand symbolic representation."

On the Peabody Picture Vocabulary Test, the IQ scores were below the national average at every age level, particularly for the females in the sample. On the Stanford-Binet, the IQ of all age groups was in the normal range. In every comparison the child was more likely to pass performance-type items than verbal items. On the Frostig, performance on figure, ground, and form constancy was notably weak. Dr. Frostig considers these tasks particularly relevant to reading readiness. On the Illinois Test of Psycho-Linguistic Ability there are nine theoretically distinct subtests. In the auditory vocal sequential subtest, the auditory decoding, and the visual decoding subtests, performance was considered adequate. On two association tasks there appeared to be intermediate difficulty. The coding tasks, visual motor sequential tasks, and auditory vocal automatic tasks revealed the greatest deficits and also showed increased decrement with age. On the Piagetian tasks, performance was quite adequate for the age range, which was five and one-half to six and one-half years. Males were superior to females on all conservation tasks, at both age levels.

Finally, a basic curriculum expressed in terms of behavioral objectives was written for the guidance of the people who would be implementing the program. These objectives were divided into cognitive skills, language skills, psychomotor skills, and orienting and attending skills. It was understood that list would be subject to revision, addition, and deletion as the project continued.

Concurrent with the above work, the staff of AEL was engaged in finding the people, the place, and the facilities required to implement the program.

The place sought for the field test was one which would (1) be typical of rural Appalachia, geographically, economically, and in population pattern; (2) have local school people interested in seeing an innovative preschool program in their area; and (3) be served by a local television station willing to cooperate on the necessary broadcasts. Such an area was found in southern West Virginia in the counties of Raleigh, Fayette, Summers, and Mercer.

A survey of five television facilities was made in the search for suitable production capabilities. A contract was signed with WSAZ-TV of Huntington, West Virginia, to use its Charleston studio. This contract provided for office space, studio space, videotape recording equipment, and technical personnel to operate the equipment. Technical equipment and personnel were available two hours per day on a set schedule.

A specially designed mobile classroom was ordered from a manufacturer in early July, 1968. Owing to procurement difficulties, this unit did not begin operation until early February, 1969.

It had been decided that a high degree of correlation between components would be required to make the program most effective, and the way to achieve this correlation would be to have all curriculum planning and materials designed and produced by one group of people. A five-member Curriculum Materials Team was assembled to begin work on July 1, 1968.

The field test began in September, 1968.

The Curriculum Materials Team set up natural groupings of objectives and from them constructed units of work and an allocation of the time to be devoted to the unit. It then decided on a theme to use as a vehicle for presenting and teaching those objectives. Each person on the Team had his or her own responsibility for one element; however, the group worked closely together to maintain correlation. For example, the person writing the home visitation materials knew what had occurred on the television program for any given day. A poem used on television might be printed and sent to the home or to the mobile classroom. The Curriculum Materials Team produced all of the curriculum materials — tapes, children's worksheets, parent guides, mobile classroom guides, etc.

At first the Curriculum Materials Team was guided by the information provided about Appalachian preschoolers in the initial research study. This helped to determine level of concepts to be presented, emphasis to be placed on various skills, and so on. However, a feedback loop had been built into the design so that after only a very short period of time it was possible to incorporate actual observations of children into the planning process.

"Around the Bend," the television element, was a 30-minute broadcast which was on the air at 9:30 a.m. five days a week from the end of September until the middle of May. This period of time was selected to conform to a school year, since it is anticipated that eventually local school systems will be administering the program.

The on-camera teacher is not presented as a teacher, per se. Instead, she is a friend who invites the young children into her home, where she talks to them about things of interest to them.

Film shot on location allows teacher and children to explore other places together, such as an airport or a library. The broadcasts are not "teachy" but are designed so that the child has fun as he explores new ideas and new things.

This is not to say that preschool activities are overlooked. Some of the concepts explored include large and small, same and different, classification, seriation, numbers and numerals, and letters. There are also rhythmic activities, body movement, sounds, textures, and weather.

Participation by the children is encouraged, both physical and mental, and feedback from the homes indicates that participation is enthusiastic on the part of most of them. Questions are asked and children respond. Activities are demonstrated and then the teacher and the children perform them together.

The home visitors were recruited from the area in which they were to work. The requirements specified that the applicants were to be 20 years of age or older, hold a driver's license, have a car available to them, and be a high-school graduate or equivalent. The eight home visitors employed ranged in age from 20 to 60, in education from General Educational Development Diploma to two years of college, and in previous work experience from house-wife to substitute teacher and Head Start aide.

The home visitors were given three weeks of intensive training before beginning their duties. The first two weeks were provided by a consultant from the National College of Education who had had previous experience in training Head Start aides and similar paraprofessionals. Time was spent on child development, particularly for the ages relevant to this project and to teaching techniques and materials for preschool children. The third week was devoted to sensitivity training, particularly interview techniques and acceptance of conditions as they are found. The sensitivity training was provided by Psycho-Dynamics, Inc.

The first thing that paraprofessionals had to do was to recruit the sample. In order to do this, each was assigned a certain territory to survey for preschool children. Thus, the initial contact with the home was made by the paraprofessional and was maintained through her. Parents with preschool children were asked if they would like to have their children participate. Less than five percent declined. From those who were agreeable, a sample was selected and the program got under way with the home visitor making a weekly visit of approximately one-half hour each. Her effort was directed toward helping the parent help the child. In order to do so she pursued three activities.

The first related directly to the television broadcast. During her weekly visit she explained the theme of the coming week's episodes and told the mother of items which the child would need in order to participate. These might be household items, such as buttons or acorns for counting, or the home visitor might deliver an item not usually found at home, such as finger paint, and remind the mother to spread out lots of newspapers. There might also be a sheet prepared by the Curriculum Materials Team which pictured the three bears which mother needed to cut out so the child could have samples of large and small as the teacher talked about the concept.

Secondly, the home visitor provided a set of suggestions for games or activities which complemented the TV episodes but were not dependent on them. These were aimed at the same set of objectives but were intended for use at any time during the week. These were also produced by the Curriculum Materials Team.

As a third facet to the job, the home visitor was an adult interested in children. As such, she provided a strong motivation for the mother to maintain her interest in the child and to follow through on activities. She also provided a broadened horizon for the child. In many instances, she was the only adult other than family members to visit the home during the week.

In addition, the home visitor was the prime source for feedback for the team. Each day she watched the TV broadcast with a child in order to make a direct observation. During the remainder of her visits, she talked with the mother and child about their reactions to the program and reported these to the Curriculum Materials Team. Each home visitor saw approximately 30 mothers per week.

Designing the mobile classroom was a four-stage process. A consultant with experience in designing mobile facilities of many types, a professor from Pennsylvania State University, was employed by AEL. He drew up the basic design and specifications. His design was then submitted to a panel of early childhood people who made several suggestions which were incorporated into a second version. The Curriculum Materials Team suggested certain items to be included in order to implement program ideas which were felt to be important. Last, the chief designer for a firm engaged in the manufacture of such equipment drew a final design which incorporated features required by sound engineering practices. Construction followed this final design.

The facility is an 8 feet x 22 feet box on a truck; overall length is 28 feet. Inside it is fully carpeted, electrically heated, air conditioned, contains its own water supply, and has a chemical toilet. All the furniture is child sized — low tables, small chairs, low sink — in other words, a unit custom designed for children. It is colorfully decorated so that it is a pleasant place to be.

The mobile classroom was staffed by a professional preschool teacher and an aide. They had at their disposal a complete audio visual unit, a cooking area, chalk board and bulletin board, cabinet space, bookshelves, a sound-activated colored light display, and books, toys, and games galore.

Into this setting was introduced a group of 10 to 14 children for one and one-half hours per week. There were individual activities, group activities, a snack time, and each activity was aimed toward the same group of objectives that the other two elements of the program had for that week. The Curriculum Materials Team prepared the list of objectives and some suggested activities and the mobile classroom teacher working within this framework drew upon her own professional skills to provide a group experience which was educational, interesting, and fun for the children.

Ten locations were visited each week by the mobile classroom. It was driven by the teacher or her aide and was attached by them to a power supply at a centrally located spot — a church lot, school yard, or community center. The parents brought the children and picked them up later. Many walked, some came in pickup trucks, and some in a Cadillac.

The summative evaluation of the AEL Early Childhood Education Program was based on program effort, program performance, and program pervasiveness. Program effort is defined as materials and personnel requirements, and program performance includes achievement gain by the children and attitudes toward the program by both children and their parents. Program pervasiveness is the extent to which a population is expected to use the program or, otherwise stated, the program market. Therefore, the three basic questions to be answered by summative evaluation of the ECE Program were (1) What is required? , (2) Does it work? , and (3) Who will use it?

It was hypothesized that there would be differences in the behaviors of children receiving the home-oriented preschool program as compared to the behaviors of children not receiving such a program. The combination of the three elements was expected to be more effective than the combination of television and home visits, and either combination was expected to be more effective than television alone. Further, it was predicted that there would be evidence that a home-oriented program would be an effective approach to providing a preschool program to rural children.

To test these hypotheses, a research design of four treatments was prepared. The treatments were:

Treatment I (T_1) — Intervention through a daily television broadcast, a weekly visit by a paraprofessional, and a weekly visit to a traveling classroom.

Treatment II (T_2) — Intervention through a daily television broadcast and a weekly visit by a paraprofessional.

Treatment III (T_3) — Intervention through a daily television broadcast.

Treatment IV (T_4) — No intervention.

The variables of age and sex were controlled so that there would be nearly equal numbers of boys and girls and nearly equal numbers of three-, four-, and five-year-old children during each year of the three-year field study. Ages were computed as of the birthday preceding November 1 of each year. There were approximately 150 children in T_1, T_2, and T_3 each year of the field study. The size of T_4 ranged from 26 during 1969-70 to 120 during the final field-test year.

Program performance was defined theoretically as learning which occurred in the target population — three-, four-, and five-year-old children — as a result of the AEL Early Childhood Education Program. Learning was classified according to language, cognition, psychomotor, social skills, and affective categories.

Language was defined operationally as responses to the *Illinois Test of Psycho-Linguistic Abilities* (ITPA). Cognition was defined operationally as responses to the *Peabody Picture Vocabulary Test* (PPVT), and responses to the *Appalachian Preschool Test of Cognitive Skills*, a criterion referenced picture test similar in format to the PPVT and ITPA. Psychomotor development was indicated by scores on the *Marianne Frostig Test of Perceptual Development*, and the social skills achievement by children was measured by a specially designed interaction analysis technique. Interest was defined operationally as responses to attitude checklists developed by AEL staff and responses reflected in anecdotal records systematically collected during the year.

The first year of the field study was September, 1968, to June, 1969, and an evaluation report was prepared based on data collected during that year (Evaluation Report, 1970). The children who received pre- and post-tests included a rather small sample of 34 in T_1, 29 in T_2, 32 in T_3, and 26 in T_4. The results from the first year indicated gains for the mobile classroom/television/home visitor group (T_1) and the television/home visitor group (T_2) on areas of the ITPA most related to program objectives such as verbal fluency and the ability to make coherent descriptive statements about physical objects. Also, the T_1 group exhibited gains on certain subtests of the Frostig which indicated increased figure-ground and embedded figure discrimination, both of which skills are thought to be highly related to reading readiness. However, no consistent pattern of gain for T_1 and/or T_2 was observed as a result of the first year's field test.

A separate study of child language was conducted on the same three treatment groups toward the end of the first year. Two films were shown to the children in small groups. Although these were sound films, the sound was turned off during the showing. Each child was then asked to describe what he had seen and his reply was recorded. The language on these audio tapes was then analyzed. A similar technique had been used with a group of kindergarten children in Tennessee, so some comparisons were possible. It was concluded that there was a lack of fluency with language, indicating a need for more encouragement to talk freely about experiences and their meanings. The older (kindergarten age) subjects generally exploited the syntactic resources of the language as proficiently as the Tennessee kindergarten children under similar conditions. Treatment effect was most noticeable in the youngest age group. (Griffin, 1969)

Much of the second year's summative evaluation (1969-70) was based on post-test scores of 40 children in T_1, 31 in T_2, 44 in T_3, and 45 in T_4 (Evaluation Report, 1971). The sample included approximately the same number of children in each sex and of ages three and four as of October, 1969. One of the analyses completed on the test data was a 4 x 2 x 2 analysis of variance (four treatments, two sexes, and two age groups). The means and significance levels of differences among the means for the different subtests of the ITPA, APT, PPVT, and Frostig are presented in Table I for each of the treatment groups.

The pattern of differences among the treatment group means for the ITPA indicates a definite trend toward increased language development for children in the treatment groups which received the ECE intervention. The significant treatment effect for the measure of transformational grammar (Subtest 7) was considered particularly important since disadvantaged children of the Appalachian Region have been previously shown to have large deficits in this area of language ability.

The differences in scores on the criterion referenced test of cognitive objectives (APT) favored the two groups which had received the mobile classroom and/or home visitors over the group which received only the television program. The two treatment groups which received visits from the paraprofessional (T_1 and T_2) also scored significantly higher on the PPVT, which was essentially a measure of vocabulary level.

In the psychomotor area which was measured by the Frostig, the treatment groups with the ECE intervention were definitely superior to the nonintervention group in eye motor coordination and visual perception. Significant differences in favor of the program groups were found in four of

TABLE I

Mean Scores of Each Treatment Group on each
Subtest of the ECE Testing Battery and
Significance of Differences

Instrument	Description	Treatment Groups				Sig.
		T_1	T_2	T_3	T_4	(Treatment)
Language						
ITPA 1	Vocabulary and hearing level	21.5	19.5	19.0	17.4	—
2	Ability to match from a sample	14.3	12.6	12.6	11.8	—
3	Vocabulary auditory association	16.6	15.5	14.1	13.3	—
4	Association and stimuli goal	15.8	15.1	13.0	12.4	—
5	Ability to describe objects verbally	9.7	9.4	8.0	11.4	<.025
6	Vocabulary and ability to communicate gestures	23.0	17.5	17.9	17.2	<.025
7	Ability to make grammatical transformations	11.3	12.2	9.4	10.9	<.05
8	Figure ground discrimination	12.9	11.9	12.8	13.8	—
9	Auditory recall	18.5	18.8	18.5	17.1	—
10	Visual recall	8.9	11.7	9.0	9.6	<.025
ITPA TOTAL		151.2	144.9	133.8	132.0	—
Cognition						
APT 2	Test of cognitive objectives	29.8	30.7	23.7	27.5	<.0005
PPVT Raw Score	Peabody Picture Vocabulary Test	46.4	45.0	39.8	42.8	<.05
PPVT IQ	IQ	98.2	98.1	90.3	92.5	<.10
Psychomotor						
Frostig 1	Hand-eye coordination in line drawing	11.9	13.6	11.3	6.6	<.0005
2	Figure ground discrimination	8.5	9.2	7.2	7.6	<.05
3	Recognition of geometric shapes	3.8	5.6	5.0	3.6	<.05
4	Discrimination of figural rotation	3.7	3.9	3.7	2.6	<.0005
5	Analysis and reproduction of simple patterns	2.1	2.0	1.6	1.8	—
FROSTIG TOTAL		26.9	31.0	23.3	20.1	<.001

$T_1 =$
$T_2 =$
$T_3 =$
$T_4 =$ No intervention

Definition: ITPA is Illinois Test of Psycholinguistic Abilities; APT is Appalachia Preschool Test (a Laboratory developed criterion referenced test); PPVT is the Peabody Picture Vocabulary Test (a measure of IQ); Frostig is the Marianne Frostig Test of Perceptual Development.

the five measures of perceptual ability. These differences were attributed to the emphasis on artistic and graphic activities which occurred throughout the ECE program.

It was hypothesized that exposure to the mobile classroom would result in the development of social skills important to learning. A sample of 54 children from T_1 and 51 children from T_2 were videotaped as they placed model furniture in a model house in groups of three or four. There were approximately equal numbers of each sex and of three-, four-, and five-year-old children. Their behavior was coded according to predetermined categories and then analyzed through interaction analysis techniques. The children who participated in the mobile classroom gave indication of having developed more constructive social skills than children who had received only the home visitor and the television program. The age group which benefited most from the mobile classroom experience was the three-year-old, and many social skills which would normally show in four or five-year-old children were already developed among the three-year-olds who had the mobile classroom experience. The children who did not receive the mobile classroom intervention were observed to be more withdrawn and tended to leave the task more often than children who had received the intervention.

Interest inventories completed each week by the home visitors indicated that the television programs produced during the second year (1969-1970) were more effective in eliciting responses from children, maintaining a positive attitude among the children, and generating enthusiasm from children than were programs produced during the first field-test year. This measure of attitude toward the ECE program indicated that both parents and children have favorable attitudes, but the attitudes of both tended to be less positive in late October, early January, and late February.

A survey of the audience appeal of three children's instructional television programs was completed through West Virginia University so as to control for bias due to association with AEL. On a measure of general appeal by T_1, T_2, and T_3, the number of first place ratings for "Captain Kangaroo" was 39 percent, for "Romper Room" 12 percent, and for AEL's black-and-white "Around the Bend" 51 percent. Practically all (89 percent) of the T_1 group parents reported that they watched the ECE television programs regularly with their children.

According to field-study results, eight professionals and three support staff would be required for production of curriculum materials including television lessons regardless of the number of children to be served. In addition, one certified teacher and one aide would be required for each 150 children, and one paraprofessional home visitor for each 37.5 children is required.

Based on ECE 1969-70 field-test costs, the program can be delivered to

25,000 children for an operational cost of $250.33 per child. An additional capital outlay cost of $21.98 per child (if amortized over five years) would be required.

These costs are approximately one-half of the cost of a standard kindergarten program in the state of West Virginia according to statistics provided by the West Virginia Department of Education. The per-pupil cost of operation for a kindergarten program was $496 during 1969-70, and the capital outlay costs were found to be more than 7.5 times greater than that for the ECE program.

The ECE evaluation has indicated that children who experienced the program have increased language development and cognitive learning, greater psychomotor and social skills development, and that the parents have a favorable attitude toward the ECE intervention. The cost of the program was found to be approximately one-half that for the standard kindergarten program.

Specific results from the third and final year of field testing were not available at the time this paper was prepared. Interested persons may write to the author at the Appalachia Educational Laboratory and request the final report.

The Appalachia Educational Laboratory Early Childhood Education Program was developed for the rural child. It can, however, be used in many areas of the United States where children are not presently being reached by existing preschool programs. Multi-ethnic groups have been identified as possible recipients, as have isolated American Indians, bilingual children, Chicanos, migrants, rural southern blacks, and mountain children. All of these might be characterized as children who seldom are encouraged to develop a healthy self-concept and pride in their cultural heritage.

Summary

Home-Oriented Pre-school Education (HOPE) as developed by the Appalachia Educational Laboratory consists of three elements   (1) television lessons, one-half hour per day, five days a week, for 34 weeks each year; (2) weekly home visits by trained paraprofessionals for the purpose of strengthening the educational role of the parent; and (3) small group sessions (10 to 15 children) with a teacher and an aide in a traveling classroom, where social interaction and development are stressed. All three elements are carefully correlated to teach and reinforce the same basic objective simultaneously.

The curriculum is built around a set of behavioral objectives consisting of language skills, cognitive skills, psychomotor skills, and such affective areas as self-concept and exploring the environment.

Part of the preliminary planning consisted of a research study to determine the characteristics of the rural Appalachian preschool child. This study shows a picture of cultural diversity rather than over-all deficit. Lack of command of language appeared to be a seriously handicapping attribute.

HOPE was subjected to a three-year field test in a rural area of West Virginia. Although third-year results were not available at the time this paper was written, results from the first two years were very encouraging. Significant differences in favor of the treatment group were shown on a criterion-referenced test of cognitive objectives, a vocabulary test (Peabody Picture Vocabulary Test), a standardized test of developmental perception (Frostig), and on three out of ten subtests of a test correlated with reading readiness skills and language (Illinois Test of Psycho- Linguistic Ability).

Bibliography

Appalachia Educational Laboratory, Inc. *Evaluation Report: Early Childhood Education Program, 1968-1969 Field Test.* Charleston, West Virginia: The Laboratory, (1970).

——. Evaluation Report: *Early Childhood Education Program, 1969-1970 Field Test.* Charleston, West Virginia: The Laboratory, February, (1971).

Crow, Lester D.*, et al. Educating the Culturally Disadvantaged Child.* New York: David McKay, (1966), pp. 118-119.

Griffin, William J. "Final Report of an Analysis of Children's Language Behavior." *Evaluation Report: Early Childhood Education Program, 1968-1969 Field Test.* Charleston, West Virginia: Appalachia Educational Laboratory, Inc., (1970).

Hechinger, Fred M. (ed.), *Pre-School Education Today.* New York: Doubleday, (1966), pp. 58-60.

Hooper, Frank H., and William H. Marshall. *The Initial Phase of a Preschool Curriculum Development Project, Final Report.* Morgantown, West Virginia: West Virginia University, (1968), pp. Q-27, Q-29.

Looff, David H. *Appalachia's Children.* Lexington, Kentucky: University of Kentucky Press, (1971).

National Center for Educational Communication. "Model Programs — Childhood Education: Appalachia Preschool Education Program, Charleston, West Virginia." Washington, D.C.: U.S. Government Printing Office, (1970).

Rentel, Victor M. "An Evaluation of an Oral Language Instructional Program and Its Effects on Speech and Reading Ability, Part I (Anderson County, Tennessee) and Part II (Raleigh and Fayette Counties, West Virginia." Knoxville, Tennessee: University of Tennessee.

Stewart, William A. "Language and Communication Problems in Southern Appalachia." Washington, D.C.: Center for Applied Linguistics, (1967).

Weller, Jack. *Yesterday's People.* Lexington, Kentucky: University of Kentucky Press, (1965).

17

Bilingual Learning for Preschool Children

Shari Nedler
and Judith Lindfors

Although numerous early childhood projects have focused on the development of educational programs for disadvantaged children, relatively little specific attention has been given to those children in our society who enter school speaking a language different from that of the wider community. For example, approximately 40 percent of the more than five million persons in the United States of Mexican origin or ancestry live in Texas. Most of these persons are native Spanish speakers living and working in an English-speaking society. The 1960 census in Texas reported that the median school years completed by the Anglo population over twenty-five years of age was 11.5 years, but only 6.1 years for the comparable Spanish surname population. Typically, the Mexican American child — urban and migrant — with a home language of Spanish, reaches school age with little knowledge of English. His proficiency in Spanish is often limited as well. One result is that a large percentage of Mexican American children in Texas fail the first grade. They fail because they are so involved in learning English they cannot master first-grade content.

According to Bruce Gaarder of the United States Office of Education, bilingualism can be either a great asset or a great liability. In our schools millions of children have been cheated or damaged, or both, by well intentioned but ill informed educational policies, which have made of their bilingualism an ugly disadvantage in their lives. Children entering school with less competence in English than monolingual English-speaking children will probably become retarded in their school work to the extent of their deficiency in English, if English is the sole medium of instruction. On the other hand, the bilingual child's conceptual development and acquisition of other experience and information could proceed at a normal rate if the mother tongue were used as an alternate medium of instruction.

Research on bilingualism indicates that whether or not bilingualism constitutes a handicap, as well as the extent of such a handicap, depends upon the way in which the two languages have been learned. The result of a study conducted in Montreal by Lambert indicated that if the bilingualism was balanced, that is, if there had been equal, normal literacy developed in the two languages, bilingual ten-year-olds in Montreal were markedly superior to monolinguals on verbal and nonverbal tests of intelligence. They appeared to have greater mental flexibility, a superior knowledge of content, and a more diversified set of mental abilities.

Proficiency in two languages is not, however, a sufficient goal for bilingual education. In the United States, increasing emphasis has been placed on the need for educational interventions which will provide the non-English speaker with the concepts necessary for success within the public school system. Initially, designers of such interventions focused on linguistic problems relevant to learning a second language. As these approaches began to be applied in experimental learning contexts, it became evident that the learner progressed more rapidly on both concept and language acquisition when he did not have to learn the concept through the new language, but rather was permitted to use his own language for concept acquisition. The subtle implication of this is that concept acquisition is facilitated by use of one's first language, not only because the language is familiar and presents no interference to the assimiliation of content, but also because the new concept can be readily tied to existing concepts within the learner's ideational system. Further, the integration of a new concept with familiar concepts is facilitated when the referents of the new concept grow out of the same culture as the referents of the familiar concepts.

This suggests that the concepts which the non-English-speaking child in the United States brings to school with him are far more sophisticated than his faltering use of the English language and lack of familiarity with the Anglo middle-class culture of the public school give him the opportunity to demonstrate. It also raises questions about the most appropriate way to teach English to non-English speakers in the United States and the most appropriate way to tie concepts based on the Anglo culture to the existing culture-derived concepts of the learner.

One institution for which this question is of primary concern is the Southwest Educational Development Laboratory located in Austin, Texas, one of eleven surviving regional laboratories created by the federal government to improve the quality of education within the United States. Children who are economically disadvantaged or culturally different compose SEDL's target population. The majority of the children within the target population speak little or no English when they enter school.

In determining the philosophy and approach for the creation of the Bilingual Early Childhood Education Program, the Laboratory drew upon research literature in the fields of bilingual education, early childhood education, and educational psychology; the empirical research conducted by the Laboratory's Migrant Educational Development Program on the educational needs of Mexican Americans; and the basic development goals of the Laboratory.

Staff members with varied background — educational psychologists, developmental psychologists, early childhood specialists, learning disability specialists, linguists, research and evaluation specialists, bilingual teachers, paraprofessionals, and parents — helped to identify strategies for the instructional program. Their knowledge contributed to the design of instructional sequences that matched the developmental needs of the children. Their interaction during the design stage minimized the possible conflicts that could arise between the curriculum of the school and the culture of the home.

Specific assumptions regarding the target population support the instructional program. These assumptions are based on extensive observations both in the home and the school, as well as objective test data, and represent the strengths developed during the child's early years.

1. The Mexican American child at age three comes to school with a language. He can communicate effectively in Spanish with both adults and peers.

2. For the most part, his basic perceptual abilities are intact and there is no evidence of the existence of unusual or extensive learning disabilities.

3. Owing to the existence of a strong family system the majority of the children have developed many of the inter-personal skills that usually do not emerge until later years.

4. The child has had many meaningful experiences within his home environment and brings to school an experiential knowledge base.

Goals for the instructional program build upon the strengths identified in the target population. All instruction begins with the child's home language. Acceptance and use of the child's language is critical to the development of a healthy self-concept. The objective of the program is to build up competence in the child's first language by expanding his basic fund of information, and only after a child has demonstrated mastery is the concept introduced in the second language.

Building upon intact basic perceptual abilities, experiences have been designed which require that the child use all sensory channels available for encoding and decoding information. These activities systematically focus on a sequential presentation of sensory motor experiences to which language can be attached through the use of concrete objects that are perceptually meaningful.

Typically, the three-year-old Mexican American child has internalized the values of cooperation, sharing, and independent responsibility for many of his basic needs. Extension of these strengths in terms of program goals involve the development of individually assigned tasks which enable the child to work toward an increased attention span, persistence in task completion,

Content of instructional units is carefully selected to relate meaningfully to the child's experience background. Instruction during the first weeks of school systematically focuses on the child's new environment. People in the room are identified, rules of behavior are specified, and instructional materials are located and labeled. This initial introduction to school is followed by materials on self-awareness. This enables each child to become more aware of himself as he relates to others, which he must do before he can meaningfully perceive his new environment. Stereotyped concepts are avoided, both for the child's culture and the dominant Anglo culture.

Unit organization integrates and reinforces the skills learned in the different types of lessons. Whenever possible, lessons in all areas have been planned to correlate with concepts introduced in the unit. Since many of the new concepts are unfamiliar to the child, he cannot be expected to fully master them in just one lesson. The unit approach allows opportunities for him to become familiar with these concepts in several types of lessons and to apply them in other contexts.

In all its aspects, the program moves sequentially from what the child knows to what he does not know. Concepts appear first in Spanish, then in English; content begins with concrete objects, moves to pictures and two-dimensional representations, and concludes with only the use of words. Within each skill level the child builds gradually in small steps, adding new elements to his skill or learning new applications for skills acquired in other contexts. Because of the unit construction, new knowledge and skills from one type of lesson can be reinforced, in either language, in different types of lessons. All of these features integrate the program and insure that the child's learning is firmly grounded, meaningful to him, and useful for thinking and problem solving.

The English language component of the preschool and bilingual kindergarten programs, has been strongly influenced by the Navajo Bilingual Academic Curriculum, prepared under the direction of Robert D. Wilson. This influence is particularly evident (1) in the underlying assumptions of the component (drawn from linguistic, learning, and pedagogical theory), (2) in the broad objectives of the component, (3) in the selection and sequencing of the material presented, and (4) in the basic teaching procedures used.

The English language component is firmly rooted in the notion that language is, basically, an internalized, self-contained system of rules according to which sentences are created, spoken, or understood. To "know a language" is to have internalized the system of rules according to which native speakers of that language utter and understand sentences. The goal of the teaching of English, then, is for the learner to internalize the set of rules according to which (1) he can create and utter sentences that an English speaker will readily understand, and (2) he can readily understand the

English sentences spoken by others, sentences which he may never have uttered or heard before. It is the learner's ability to speak and understand sentences beyond those used in the teaching that must be the final test of an English language program for non-native speakers of English. If at the end of a language program the learner is able to speak and comprehend only those sentences included in the language program, then he has learned the language program, but he has not learned the language. The language program described in the following pages is designed (1) to reveal to the learner, through carefully selected and sequenced English language samples, the system which underlies the particular sentences used, and (2) to involve him actively in the use of the language structures so revealed. The particular sentences used in the program do not have tremendous significance in and of themselves. They do not convey weighty meanings, but rather are clear manifestations of parts of the underlying language system according to which the child will ultimately comprehend and produce many other English sentences.

Each element of the basic definition of language (above) has been crucial in shaping the Basic English Language Structures Program. Let us look at those elements one by one to see how the key concepts in this notion of language (rules, internalized, system, self-contained, spoken or understood, created) have shaped the writing of this component.

Rules

Far less time is available for teaching our students their second language (English) than was available for "teaching" them their first language. Since we can provide our students with only a very limited amount of "second language data," we will have to control, to structure, the language data if we want our students to evolve — in a short period of time — a system of rules such as the native speaker possesses.

This English language program controls the language data presented to the child in three ways:

1. Selection: The items (rules) taught are those which are most general and basic, those which constitute the skeletal framework of English, those according to which native English speakers form, utter, and understand sentences. No nursery rhymes are included; no "pleasantry language" is introduced (e.g., "How are you? I'm fine. What's your name? John. Where do you live? " etc.); and very little vocabulary is taught. This component often uses the vocabulary taught in the other components. In short, the goal of revealing the system of rules of English has governed the selection of items for the lessons.

2. Sequence: The selected items are arranged so that the step the child takes from one rule to the next is small (e.g., "John is hopping," then, "John is hopping to Mary"); so that the new rules are constantly integrated with those previously learned (enabling the child to build a system of interrelationships). Rules and relationships learned earlier in a simple, basic

form are reinforced at increasingly complex levels. This involved spiral learning, not unlearning relearning.

3. Amount: In each lesson the number of new rules or relationships taught is strictly limited. The aim is for the child to completely control a basic framework according to which he can organize and interpret language he encounters subsequently. However, the activities for which the language is used, the games in which the children are involved, are deliberately varied. It is the language patterns presented — not the children's active participation — that are limited in each lesson.

Besides controlling the selection, sequencing, and amount of language data presented, the program employs a basic teaching method which increases the probability that the learner will internalize the rules. In each lesson there is a period of initial listening for the child, approximately three minutes long. During this period, clear, sharply focused examples of the rule(s) for that lesson are presented, from which the child can induce the rule(s). Traditionally, experts in the teaching of English as a second language have told us "Listening first, then speaking." But few programs have taken this advice to heart; the "Wilson program" is a notable exception. This program does take the "listening first" advice to heart; in each lesson the child is to listen first and induce the rule, and then speak, applying the rule. Notice that the listening is prior to the speaking; it does not replace it.

There seems to be some confusion among second-language teachers about what "listening" and "speaking" are. Some have regarded listening as passive. But "listening" is used here to refer to a very active and demanding process, one in which the brain relates, organizes, structures, and interprets the sounds it perceives. Development of this kind of listening ability can be one of the child's greatest intellectual assets throughout his school career, and beyond.

Some have regarded "speaking" in the second language as little more than making oral noises, using some vocabulary items from the second language, but to utter sentences in a language is to engage in rule-governed behavior. Far too much of our verbalization in the second-language classroom has required children to utter strings of sounds which they have not yet processed mentally through active listening. By having the children listen first and then speak, this program aims to substitute rule-governed English verbal behavior (i.e., speaking English) for the all-too-typical uttering of sounds learned by rote.

This procedure is sound scientific procedure as well as sound second-language learning. The scientist observes particular cases and makes a hypothesis based on his observations; the second-language learner listens to particular English language samples and induces the rule underlying the samples he has heard. The scientist tests his hypothesis in a controlled situation and either confirms or disconfirms it; the second-language learner speaks sentences according to the rule he has induced, and receives feedback from the teacher as to the correctness of his induction. The scientist makes his steps very explicit; the five-year-old Spanish speaker learning English does not. But the process this language program employs is composed of a comparable set of steps to discover and confirm language rules from a given set of data, just as the scientist attempts to discover and confirm physical laws or principles from his data. In using this learning procedure, the child is developing a powerful tool for all his learning, not just for language learning.

Internalized

At no point in the English language program is the child explicitly told a rule. Rather he is shown, through carefully selected and sequenced representative samples of English sentences, what does occur in English, what kinds of basic elements and combinations the language does include. Further, at no point in the program is the child asked to explain or justify why he selects and combines certain elements in one way rather than another. He is simply expected to induce rules from the samples provided and then to speak and understand according to them. We know that very few native speakers of a language are able to specify accurately to "externalize" — the set of rules governing their speech and understanding. We do not ask this of second-language speakers, any more than we ask it of native speakers. And we know further that ability to specify the rules does not cause a native speaker of English to be a better speaker of English. The group of native English speakers who are linguists by profession and are able to specify the rules of their language do not necessarily speak English better than the group of native English speakers who are physicists by profession and who may be unable to specify the rules of their language. So, the child in this program will not listen to or state language rules; rather, he will listen and speak according to language rules which he will internalize from the data provided.

System

An effort is made throughout the program to teach each part of the system in its entirety. For example, the entire set of subject pronouns is presented, then the entire set of object pronouns. The whole set of articles, of basic verb types, of basic adverb types, of basic question types, etc. — the total set of significant structures within some area of English syntax is taught, rather than just those specific items which are used most frequently in conversation. Further, the structures taught are deliberately presented in various combinations and relationships. Within each lesson related question and answer structures are paired (as is done in the "Wilson program"). New structures are regularly integrated with those previously learned. Many lessons are included which do not present new structures but serve only to use previously learned structures in new ways. And so the program gradually reveals the system: by presenting the total set of significant elements and relationships for each major syntactic area, by constantly combining and re-combining familiar structures, by incorporating new structures with those already learned.

Self-Contained

Contrastive studies of Spanish and English and the past experience of those who have taught English to native speakers of Spanish have been helpful in suggesting which parts of the English language system may be troublesome for the native Spanish speaker to learn, at which points the learner may encounter strong interference from Spanish. This information has helped us decide how much time to devote to the teaching of the various parts of the program. But the information from contrastive analysis and teachers' experience has not guided our selection of what to teach. Only the English language system itself — without reference to Spanish or any other language system — can determine what must be taught. And what must be taught is precisely the set of rules basic of English. This English language program is not a patchwork, a bits-and-pieces approach designed to prevent particular predicted errors. The child is not told "In Spanish you say X; in English you say Y." He is not encouraged to think of Spanish and English as sets of equivalences or near-equivalences. He is encouraged to learn English wholly within the system of English, to "think in English."

Spoken or Understood

This program provides for both of these basic language behaviors by utilizing listening activities followed by speaking activities in each lesson. The child's typical participation in a lesson is from listening only (approximately three minutes), to listening and overtly responding (e.g., following commands, nodding or shaking his head in answer to a "yes-no" question), to answering questions (responding to conversation initiated by someone else), finally to asking questions and giving commands — i.e., taking over the full responsibility for initiating and propelling conversation. Of course the later activities in a lesson require active listening as well as speaking, for the child is responding to meanings in his speech; he is not unthinkingly parroting a teacher's question or answer in a group.

Created

How does the program move the child toward the creative use of English, toward that capacity which the native speaker possesses to say sentences he has not previously encountered? Obviously, by presenting him with, and having him practice using, the basic system according to which such sentences can be formed. But also, by having the child select and ask questions in virtually every lesson (and not simply give rote answers), and by accepting — indeed, encouraging — a variety of verbal responses, the program conveys to the child the notion of flexibility, the idea that this language allows for infinite variety within the rule system. This notion is crucial to his eventual creative use of English. There is progressive movement from close control of language structures toward more flexible use of the language, both within individual lessons and within each level — each year's sequence of lessons.

Basic Tenets

The following principles apply throughout the Basic English Language Structures component:

1. *Realistic situations.* The situations which provide the context in which the language structures of a lesson are used are as appropriate and natural as possible. For example, the child who is going to ask a question about an action which was performed does not hear the teacher give the command for that action and does not see the action performed. If he heard the teacher's command ("Jump, John") or saw the action performed, he would have no reason to ask the question "What did John do? " — he already knows, so his question would just be carrying out drill practice in asking questions; it would not be practice in using language in a purposeful way. Every effort is made to keep the classroom situation from becoming "drill-like." We try to keep them "lifelike," for it is in life, not in drill, that we want the children to use English.

2. *Meaningful responses.* There is no mindless parroting of teachers' utterances written into this program. There are no instances like the following:

> Teacher: What's he doing? (Say it.)
> Children: What's he doing?
> Teacher: He's running.
> Children: He's running.
> Teacher: What's she doing?
> Children: What's she doing?
> Teacher: She is walking.
> Children: She is walking.

The reason for the exclusion of such parroting is simple: such parroting is verbalization, but it is not language, and language is what we are teaching. Language involves meaning, and therefore we teach the child to create, utter, and respond to sentences which convey meaning. This involves the mindfulness of inducing and applying language rules, not the mindlessness of repeating strings of sounds. Also, language involves a variety of responses, but parroting allows only prescribed responses.

3. *Individual response.* The children do not speak in chorus in this program because that is simply not the way people speak a language. It is language, not choral speaking, that we are teaching. Further, speaking in

chorus invariably distorts the natural rhythms of the language, so that the children end up practicing chanting, but not practicing speaking a language. And finally, the individual errors that the teacher needs to hear and correct are hidden when the children speak as a group.

4. *Acceptance of all appropriate responses.* Every correct and appropriate response (question, answer, nonverbal response, or whatever) is accepted, even if it is not the response the teacher expected. This is much harder than it sounds. But the teachers using the program are trained and regularly reminded to keep in mind always that the greater the variety of acceptable responses the children give the more we know that they are moving toward that ultimate goal — the creative use of English.

5. *Emphasis on questioning.* If a child does not know how to question, his speaking power is severely limited. The children ask questions in every lesson. The program teaches the children (a) to ask questions (in lesson after lesson, questioning is the fundamental activity), (b) how to ask questions (how to formulate each basic type of question syntactically), and (c) to select appropriate, relevant, spontaneous questions in various situations.

6. *Use of complete forms followed by shorter forms.* When a new structure is introduced, it is given in its complete form, even though the full form might seem somewhat unnatural in conversation. This procedure is dictated by our concern that the children induce the language rules. For example, the relations between *He is running* and *He is not running* or *He is running* and *Is he running?* are more immediately apparent and more unambiguous than the relations between *He's running* and *He isn't running* or *He's running* and *Is he running?* With the full forms, the addition of the negative element (*not*) to the basic sentence, and the rearrangement of the *He is* to *Is he* in the question are obvious; with the shortened forms, this addition and rearrangement are less obvious.

Just as it is important to present the full forms initially so it is important to move to the more conversational shorter forms once the children "have" the rules. Moving from the full to the shorter forms is not only important because the shorter forms are the more natural forms for native speakers to use, but also because they demonstrate the operation of another important process in English (and in every language), that of deletion.

7. *Initial emphasis on syntax, not vocabulary.* Lessons in this program include the teaching of vocabulary. However, vocabulary teaching is not the main purpose of the lessons. For the first part of the program, particularly, only enough vocabulary is taught to enable the children to use the structures with some flexibility. Later, with a shift in emphasis to content teaching, after some degree of syntactic control is assured, vocabulary teaching becomes more important.

The points discussed so far all concern the structural aspects of the

English language program: learning to use the processes for understanding and speaking English, learning how to manipulate the sounds, words, sentences of English, learning how to select elements and combine them in ways that convey intended meanings. What does the program do about the functional aspects of English? What about English as a tool for learning, for conceptual development? What role can learning English play in self-concept development?

There is a definite shift of focus in Level III of the three-level preschool program and in the latter part of the one-year kindergarten program, from learning to manipulate the syntactic structures of English, to utilizing those structures in conceptual learning. The syntax of English is the goal in the first part of the program; it is the means for achieving the goal of cognitive development in the latter part of the program. This arrangement assures that the child will, at any one time, be focusing either on gaining control of the syntax of the language or on gaining control of the content (the basic concepts and "world view" of the native speakers of the language), but he will not be required to cope with the two difficult areas simultaneously.

Notice that the two parts of the programs are not unrelated. Several learning processes which are basic to the expression-focus part of each program are also basic to the content-focus part of each program. Throughout the first part of each program there is a major emphasis on questioning. He is systematically taught to use the various types of question structures; he is submerged in the notion that questioning is a good thing. This same emphasis on questioning continues throughout the latter portion of the English program. Also, the basic procedure of first inducing the rule through listening and observation and then applying the rule in progressively freer, less controlled situations is constant throughout the program. In short, in the first part of the program the child is learning English, but he is also learning how to learn. These procedures for learning are utilized throughout the program and lend continuity to it.

Finally, we should ask "Does the Basic English Language Structures component serve in any significant way to enhance the child's good feelings about himself as a worthwhile human being? " There is little empirical data about what "self-concept" is and how it is positively developed; mostly we play our best hunches. However, we feel certain that building success upon success in the child's school experience can only serve to increase his feelings of personal worth. The English lessons try to assure the students' success by:

(1) carefully controlling the amount of structure being focused on within each lesson, so that the child knows that he will be responsible for a limited goal that is within his reach;

(2) informing the child clearly at the outset of each lesson what it is that he is responsible for in that lesson;

(3) providing ample practice of new structures and relationships in

each lesson;

(4) steadily sequencing and regularly integrating the syntactic structures;

(5) providing immediate, unambiguous feedback about the child's response;

(6) evaluating, at the end of each lesson, the child's ability to use the new structure or the new relation of structures which was presented at the outset of the lesson and practiced throughout, so that the child leaves each lesson with the definite and concrete knowledge that he has — once again — mastered the objective.

Summary

Components of a comprehensive bilingual learning system designed for Spanish-speaking disadvantaged children are described. Instructional activities, teacher training materials, and parental activities have been systematically designed, evaluated, and revised in an effort to develop an instructional program that could be individualized to meet the needs of each child. Evaluation results indicate that children enrolled in the program show significant gains in both Spanish and English when compared with other groups receiving a more traditional intervention approach.

Bibliography

Bruner, Jerome S., *et al. Studies in Cognitive Growth.* New York: John Wiley and Sons, (1966).

Chomsky, Noam. *Aspects of the Theory of Syntax.* Cambridge, Mass.: M.I.T. Press, (1965).

Gaarder, A. Bruce. "Teaching the Bilingual Child: Research, Development, and Policy." *The Modern Language Journal,* XLIX, 3 (1965), 165-175.

Grotberg, Edith H. *Review of Research: 1965 to 1969.* Washington, D.C.: Project Head Start, Office of Economic Opportunity, (1969).

Peal, Elizabeth, and Wallace E. Lambert. "The Relation of Bilingualism to Intelligence." *Psychological Monographs: General and Applied,* LXXVI, 27, Whole 546 (1962), 1-23.

Plumer, D. "Language Problems of Disadvantaged Children. A Review of the Literature and Some Recommendations." Monograph No. 6, *Harvard Research and Development Center of Educational Differences.* Cambridge, Mass., (1968).

Southwest Educational Development Laboratory. *Annual Evaluation Report 1968-1969, San Antonio Urban Education Learning System.* Austin, (1969).

Wilson, Robert D., *et al. Bilingual Academic Curriculum for Navajo Beginners.* Los Angeles, California: Consultants in Total Education, (1969).

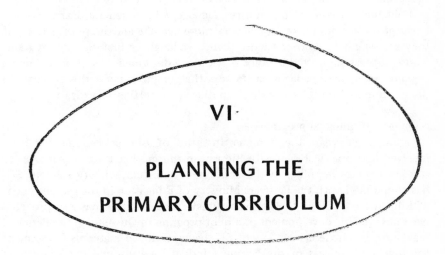

VI

**PLANNING THE
PRIMARY CURRICULUM**

18

Mother-tongue Literacy and Second Language Learning
Sarah Gudschinsky

No discussion of child language is complete without a consideration of the special case of a second language acquired as a medium of instruction in the primary school. It is the thesis of this paper that children who are monolingual speakers of a minority language will, in general, learn a second language as a medium of instruction more readily and more effectively if they are taught to read and write their own language first. Several programs whose success support this point of view are described in section 1. Social, psychological, and pedagogical factors that might explain this success are discussed in section 2, as working hypotheses for further investigation.

Summary of bilingual programs

For some years the Summer Institute of Linguistics, Inc. has been involved in a practical way with literacy in the mother tongue as a tool for second-language learning, in the context of bilingual primary schools. SIL has cooperated with the Peruvian Ministry of Education in the establishment of Bilingual Schools in the Peruvian Jungle. The Institute has also provided personnel for the development of a pilot program in Quechua in the Peruvian highlands. In Mexico, members of SIL have produced materials for some of the bilingual projects of the National Indian Institute and the Ministry of Education and have had some share in the training of instructors ('promotores'). In South Vietnam, SIL is under contract with the South Vietnamese Government and USAID to produce materials and train teachers for the Highlander Education Project. Elsewhere in the world, the Institute is participating in a number of other similar programs that are not yet far enough along for formal report.

The Peruvian Jungle program (Ratto 1955, Wise 1969)

Prior to 1953 there were few schools available to Indians in the Peruvian jungle, and those few had very poor results. It was difficult to staff such schools, isolated as they were from 'civilization.' The Spanish-speaking teachers had difficulty communicating with their Indian pupils. And the pupils seldom learned more than a mechanical ability to sound out Spanish syllables and to write from dictation. They did not learn to speak Spanish nor to read it with understanding.

In 1953, a bilingual education program was established for the jungle Indians. Teachers for the program were recruited from among the Indians themselves. In summer courses at Yarinacocha they were taught to read and write their own language, to speak Spanish, and the Spanish primary curriculum to Grade 2. When they reached Grade 2 standard, they were given further training in Spanish and pedagogy that prepared them to begin teaching. Over a period of six years they taught in their own villages during the school term and attended further training sessions during the long summer vacation. In this fashion they completed their own primary education while in service.

In the village schools, the pupil spends his first two years becoming fluent in reading and writing his own language and in learning to speak Spanish. In his third year he completes the requirements of the Spanish school 'transition' year, which involves reading and writing Spanish. In his fourth year he enters the Peruvian Grade 1. In Grades 1 and 2 he follows the regular Peruvian curriculum but with diglot textbooks (with a vernacular translation of the Spanish material on each page). In Grades 3-6 the jungle pupils follow the regular curriculum in Spanish only.

By 1969, 240 Indians of 20 different language groups who had come through the bilingual program were employed by the Ministry of Public Education as teachers in the jungle schools. Many Indian children from monolingual communities not only finished the Spanish primary school but have gone on to secondary school and in a few cases to university. Others have received vocational training that has fed back into economic improvements in their home villages.

A point of major interest is the success of the program in teaching Spanish. The children in this program enter Grade 3 (the first grade in which Spanish is the only medium of instruction) competitive with Spanish children at this level. It is of great significance that in most cases this competence in Spanish is gained in a non-Spanish-speaking community, where the source of Spanish is the school teacher. (Now, of course, bilingualism is increasing in the local communities. In many places the present generation of school children are the younger brothers and sisters, or the sons and daughters, of previous pupils who are bilingual through the school program.)

The Peruvian Quechua Program (D. Burns 1968, N. Burns 1970)

In the highlands of Peru, where the Quechua Indians are located, there were many more government schools than in the lowlands. However, no more than 30 percent of the Quechua children of school age were normally enrolled in school. And the academic record of those who did attend was very poor. The monolingual Quechua children as a rule learned little Spanish. They tended to repeat the transition year two or three times and then to drop out in discouragement. The government, in 1965, provided for the development of a five-year pilot project for the Quechua, similar to the bilingual program that had proved so successful in the jungle. In 1971 it was decided to expand this project to the remaining Quechua communities.

The Quechua program is shorter than the program in the jungle. Perhaps this is possible because the Quechua are more sophisticated and have more contact with the Spanish-speaking population. The pupils have two years of 'transition.' In the first year they learn to read and write Quechua and begin oral Spanish. In the second transition year they become independent and fluent readers of Quechua and learn to read and write Spanish, completing the regular requirements of the transition curriculum. In the first grade, all materials are diglot, Spanish and Quechua, but considerable attention is paid to the Spanish so that the child is ready for an all-Spanish curriculum in Grade 2.

The success of this program can be seen in the reduction of dropouts and in the fact that the children coming through the bilingual program are all doing work above the average of those in the Spanish schools who did not have bilingual education. The program has not been going long enough to follow any pupil beyond the end of primary school.

Mexican programs (Vásquez-Barrera 1953, Castro de la Fuente 1961, Modiano 1968)

In Mexico, government schools taught in Spanish have been available to most of the Indian population for many years. These schools, however, have not effectively taught either spoken Spanish or literacy in Spanish to monolingual Indians. In most Indian communities only a very small percentage of the school-age children are actually enrolled in school. The usual pattern for those who do enroll is to repeat the preparatory grade for two or three years and then drop out without having learned to read more than isolated syllables and without having learned to speak Spanish. It has been my observation, although I have no statistical studies to prove it, that success in school usually depended on having learned Spanish outside of school — as a house servant in a Spanish home, for example.

The first bilingual program was established in the Tarascan group in 1939 under President Cárdenas. It is reported to have been highly successful, but it was some time before a bilingual policy was spread to other Indian groups. At the present time there are bilingual schools being operated by both the National Indian Institute and the Ministry of Education. Both types of schools use bilingual Indians as the instructores or 'promotores.' The program is less extensive than its Peruvian counterpart. It consists of a single pre-year in which the Indian children learn to speak some Spanish and to read and write their own language before going on to the regular Spanish schools.

Nancy Modiano (1968) reports on the success of the Indian Institute schools in the Tzotzil and Tzeltal languages in Chiapas, Mexico. She notes that a significantly greater proportion of students in the Bilingual Institute Schools read with significantly greater comprehension in the national language than pupils in the all-Spanish schools.

The Vietnam Highlander Education Program

The Highlander Education Program in South Vietnam has not yet been reported in the literature, and the following summary is based on private communications from my colleagues who work in the program.

In 1967, USAID and the South Vietnamese Government contracted with the Summer Institute of Linguistics, Inc. to provide materials and teacher training in some of the Highland languages, in fulfillment of the government's agreement that the Highlanders were to have three years of education in their own languages. Previous to this project, the schools available to the Highlanders were taught in Vietnamese. Teachers who spoke the Highland languages were often assigned outside their home area so that only rarely did a monolingual child have a teacher who spoke his language. The performance of the monolingual Highland children followed the typical pattern, with low enrollment — especially of girls — repetition of the same grade, and early dropouts with little success in either literacy or oral language learning.

The Highlander Education Program provides for a pre-year for all Highland children, in which they learn to read and write their own language, to speak some Vietnamese, and to control in their own language some of the content material in arithmetic, hygiene, etc. When they enter first grade, they learn to read and write Vietnamese, they study the content subjects of the regular Vietnamese curriculum from textbooks in their own language, and they review some of the content material in oral Vietnamese lessons. In the second grade all textbooks are diglot, and education is bilingual. In the third grade the pupils move into a monolingual Vietnamese curriculum, except for continued classes in their own language and culture as subjects.

This program is still very new, and war conditions have prevented the careful evaluation of each classroom that would have been desirable. However, favorable results are already evident in increased enrollment, especially of girls, and in lowered repetition rates. Most of the children who enter complete the pre-year in a single year. There are scattered reports that children entering first grade from the pre-year already know more Vietnamese than is usual for children finishing first grade with Vietnamese as the medium of instruction. There are also by-products in community enthusiasm for the program, and a more favorable attitude toward the schools on the part of the monolingual parents.

Factors in the success of the bilingual programs

It cannot be assumed, of course, that the high degree of success of the bilingual programs outlined here means that such a program is a panacea for every multilingual school situation. It should be possible, however, to make hypotheses as to the factors that explain that success and to use these hypotheses for further observation and research. I would suggest the following as a first approximation of such a list. Social and psychological advantages of the bilingual programs include: (1) community understanding and support; (2) the minimization of culture shock for the child entering school; (3) augmentation of the child's sense of personal worth and identity; and (4) development of the child's habit of academic success. Pedagogical and linguistic advantages of literacy in both the mother tongue and the second language, before the second language is used as a medium of instruction, include: (5) full utilization of the child's fluency in his own language in learning the skills of reading and writing; (6) the contribution to second-language learning of focus on the mother tongue (a by-product of literacy); (7) the development of basic concepts for the content subjects, in the mother tongue; and (8) the use of reading as a tool in second-language learning.

Community understanding and support

An outstanding characteristic of the bilingual programs described in this paper is community support for them. There may be several reasons for this. Since beginning instruction is in the language of the monolingual pupils and their monolingual parents, the parents know what the children are learning and can understand what is going on in school. At the same time, oral instruction in the second language pleases the parents that are anxious for their children to learn the prestige language. Furthermore, the instructors are drawn from the local community. In every case, the ideal bilingual teacher is considered to be one who speaks the vernacular as his own mother tongue. It is true that he must also know the second language, but often his bilingualism is via instruction in the second language as part of his teacher training. These people are at home in the community and its culture and are able to reassure the parents and the community leaders as to the plans and purposes of the school.

Minimization of culture shock for the child entering school

One factor in the success of individual children is the minimization of culture shock at school entry. It is probable that most children experience some shock in the transition from the relatively free pre-school environment to the more rigid, formal, structured environment of the school. This shock is especially traumatic to children who are faced with a foreign language and foreign cultural values as well as the strangeness of the school environment. In the bilingual schools described here, the shock is limited to the transition to the school environment. The first classes are taught in the child's own language by teachers who share his cultural values and customs. His introduction to a new language and to a new set of values is gradual and is mediated constantly by a teacher who understands his struggle and is sympathetic.

Augmentation of the child's sense of personal worth and identity

This point is closely related to the previous one but is not identical with it. One important element in the failure of children of the ethnic minorities in the schools of the dominant culture is undoubtedly their loss of a sense of personal worth. A child who is punished for spitting on the floor or throwing stones may feel that he is being unjustly treated and rebel, or may learn to conform. But a child who is punished for speaking the only language he knows can only believe that he is inherently bad or inferior, for his language is an essential part of what he is. The teacher who does not speak the child's language has no choice but to insist that he use the dominant language — and so in some measure punishes him for using his own. This subtle alienation of the children does not happen in the bilingual programs which are built on a respect for the child's language and culture. The assurance of his own worth and identity provides a firm base from which he makes the transition into a new language and participation in a new culture.

Development of the child's habit of academic success

School failures and dropouts are often blamed on a long history of failure which has led to an expectation of continued failure. The child who fails completely in his early school work is unlikely to become a great success later. Such early failure is nearly inevitable for a large percentage of children who enter a school taught in a language they do not know. In the bilingual schools, however, the child is conditioned to success, not failure. Learning to read and write in his own language is relatively easy for him, and this early success leads him to expect — and to obtain — success in the more difficult transition to another language.

Full utilization of the child's fluency in his own language in learning the skills of reading and writing

A person becomes literate only once in his lifetime. Learning to read additional languages and scripts after the first one is a matter of enlarging his inventory of symbols and using his literacy skills in the context of a new language structure. He can become literate, however, only in a language that he speaks, as seen in my definition of literacy: that person is literate who, in a language he speaks, can read and understand anything he would have understood if it had been spoken to him; and can write, so that it can be read, anything he can say (Gudschinsky 1970).

Goodman (1968) has described the reading process in a way that emphasizes the role of the learner's oral language in reading. In his model, the beginning reader is seen as (1) taking an input of letter shapes, group of letters, and word shapes, and (2) recoding them as phonemes, groups of phonemes, or word names, (3) mixing this with an aural input — his knowledge of the language and its patterns — to (4) further recode it as oral speech, which he then (5) decodes for meaning.

The child who learns to read first in his mother tongue can make full use of his competence in the language. He recodes letters and word shapes to the phonemes and words that he already knows and uses; his aural input comes from a native speaker's control of the patterns of the language; and his decoding process is in terms of familiar vocabulary and discourse structure. To extend this basic literacy to a second language is a relatively small task compared with the overwhelming difficulty of learning to read for the first time in an unknown language.

The contribution to second language learning of focus on the mother tongue

Learning to read involves some conscious focus on the structure of the language to be read. Minimally, the child learns to focus on the phonemes represented by letters or letter patterns, and on the units represented by orthographic words. In the reading method that I have been developing, the reader is taught to recognize the phonemes of his speech, and the orthographic patterns of the written language, as contrastive substitutions within a pronounceable matrix (syllable or couplet). He uses this recognition for recoding (or decoding) content words. He is taught to recognize the functors (affixes, clitics, function words) at sight in the context of grammatical structures at word or phrase level. This means that the child develops considerable conscious control of the phonological and grammatical structures of his own language. It is my conviction that this conscious control of his own language is of value in learning a second language in the formal school setting.

Admittedly, this kind of control of a first language is not a prerequisite for learning a second language by free and friendly association with speakers of that second language. In the schools outlined here, however, there were no such moral contacts, and the second language was learned largely from the school teacher in formal classes. Where the teaching depended on conscious focus on features of the second language, practice in similar focus on the mother tongue facilitated the learning.

Development in the mother tongue of basic concepts for content subjects

Unfortunately, in the unnatural situation of the school, most learning is not by doing and experiencing, but by rote memory and verbalization. It is possible for an individual to do a great deal of verbal learning which is only a manipulating of word tokens without meaning. This is especially true in a language which the pupil does not know well. He may learn to parrot the appropriate collocations of words and yet have no real notion of what is meant.

In the bilingual schools, the child is introduced to a wide range of new ideas in his own language, for which he has adequate real-world referents. In most of the programs, he makes the transition to using the second language slowly, with diglot texts and instruction in both languages. By the time he is working monolingually in the second language, he has a fair understanding of what is being talked about and a habit of expecting to understand the words he is manipulating.

The use of reading as a tool in second-language learning

When it is necessary to learn a second language from a single teacher, there is a serious limit on how much the language can be heard and practiced in normal speech contexts. The use of written material can substantially increase the child's exposure to the language, and enhances his chances of learning it. In the bilingual programs, literacy in the mother tongue is followed immediately by learning to read and write in the second language. Thereafter the child has diglot materials (except in the Mexican programs) which help him in learning the second language — reinforcing and expanding what he learns orally.

Conclusion

This paper, with its observational reporting and its preliminary hypotheses, can only be taken as a starting point for more rigorous research. There is a need for more studies like Modiano's (1968) to quantify and confirm the nature and degree of the success of the bilingual programs.

It has been said that nobody has ever taught a language to a small child. There is need, therefore, for a careful study of what happens in the bilingual schools — how do the children learn the second language? In this connection, there is need of specific studies of the role in language learning of conscious control of the structure of the mother tongue and of the usefulness of reading. There is also need for research that compares the processes of learning language in terms of well-known concepts, and of learning language and new concepts simultaneously.

It is hypothesized here that literacy in the mother tongue minimizes culture shock and augments the child's sense of worth and his expectation of success. There is need for research into the relative usefulness of mother-tongue literacy for this purpose, versus other less costly strategies.

Summary

It is the thesis of this paper that children who are monolingual speakers of a minority language will, in general, learn a second language as a medium of instruction more readily and more effectively if they are first taught to read and write their own language. Suggested factors are social, psychological, and pedagogical, as well as linguistic.

Bibliography

Burns, Donald H. "Bilingual Education in the Andes of Peru." In J.A. Fishman, C.A. Ferguson, and J. Das Gupta, eds., *Language Problems of Developing Nations.* New York: John Wiley and Sons, (1968).

Burns, Nadine. "Materials for the Bilingual Schools of Ayacucho." *Notes on Literacy*, Vol. 9 (1970), pp. 15-19.

Castro de la Fuente, Angélica. "La alfabetización en lenguas indígenas y los promotores culturales." *A William Cameron Townsend.* México D.F.: Instituto Lingüístico de Verano, (1961).

Goodman, Kenneth S. "The Psycholinguistic Nature of the Reading Process." In Kenneth S. Goodman, ed., *The Psycholinguistic Nature of the Reading Process.* Detroit: Wayne State University Press, (1968).

Gudschinsky, Sarah C. "Psycholinguistics and Reading: Diagnostic Observation." In William K. Durr, ed., *Reading Difficulties: Diagnosis, Correction, and Remediation.* Newark, Delaware: International Reading Association, (1970).

———. "Linguistics and Literacy." In Thomas Sebeck, ed., *Current Trends in Linguistics*, Vol. XII (1963).

Modiano, Nancy. "Bilingual Education for Children of Linguistic Minorities." *América Indígena*, Vol. 28 (1968), p. 2.

Ratto, César Bravo. "Rural Education Campaign Among the Tribes of the Peruvian Jungle." *Fundamental and Adult Education*, Vol. 7, No. 2 (1955), pp. 55-57.

Vásquez-Barrera, A. "The Tarascan Project in Mexico." *The Use of the Vernacular Languages in Education.* UNESCO Monographs on Fundamental Education VIII, (1953).

Wise, Mary Ruth. "Utilizing Languages of Minority Groups in a Bilingual Experiment in the Amazonian Jungle of Peru." *Community Development Journal*, Vol. 4, No. 3 (1969), pp. 117-122.

19

Initial Reading in Spanish for Bilinguals

Charles H. Herbert Jr.

For the most part, Title VII programs funded through the Bilingual Education Programs Branch (BEPB) of the U.S. Office of Education focus on development of oral language in children who are served by these programs. Oral language development is also the aim of many other programs for foreign-language-speaking or non-standard English-speaking children. There are, of course, programs that undertake to teach children to read as well as to develop their oral facility with language. In many cases these programs involve the teaching of reading in English. A number of programs are also in the process of developing reading programs in Spanish.

In an informal series of discussions regarding the teaching of reading in Spanish, it was found that relatively little was known about the teaching of reading in Spanish to the Spanish-speaking child or about the process of transferring reading skills from Spanish to English. As a result of these discussions, and with the encouragement of the BEPB of the U.S. Office of Education, the project "Initial Reading in Spanish" came into being. The main emphasis of the project was to produce a detailed, descriptive analysis of procedures used to teach Spanish-speaking children to read in their native tongue.

Preliminary investigations into reading programs in the United States revealed that Spanish-speaking children were being taught to read English as well as Spanish utilizing the same procedures that are employed to teach monolingual English speakers to read their native tongue. Many methods in the teaching of literacy in English include ingenious and complex devices to show the underlying system in a written language that is intricate and oftentimes irregular. The Spanish writing system, on the other hand, has a relatively uncomplicated phonemegrapheme correspondence with few irregularities. It seems then that many of the methodologies employed to teach literacy in English do not apply to the teaching of that skill in Spanish.

Where does one go to learn about methodologies and materials used in effective teaching of literacy in Spanish? What better place than a Spanish-speaking country itself. Mexico, being geographically near and having an education system which responded to initial inquiries enthusiastically, was selected as the site for preliminary field study of the reading process in Spanish as taught to Spanish-speaking natives. Through the Ministry of Education in Mexico City, arrangements were made to visit a number of schools in which initial reading was being taught to Spanish speakers. A number of classrooms were visited in order to give a generous sampling of procedures used by different teachers. Videotapes were made in each of the selected classes so that a permanent record would be available for reference and study.

The teaching of reading in Mexico

Examination of the videotapes revealed the following generalities about the process used by most Mexican teachers observed.

1. A phonic method was used in which children were taught to sound out individual letters in order to decipher words from the printed page. In some cases letter names were used to identify the letters of the alphabet. Some teachers preferred to refer to the letters of the alphabet by their "sound names." The letter "s" was referred to with a sibilant, hissing sound, the letter "d" with the sound [də] and so forth.

2. Since almost all of the teachers used the textbooks provided by the federal government, the sequence of presentation of vowels and consonants differed very little. Vowels were introduced initially starting with "o," continuing to "a," "e," "i," and "u." In order that these vowels might be presented in whole words, the consonants "s," "d," "l," and "t" were introduced in the first few lessons. Two or three lessons were spent teaching single words, but the teachers rapidly moved to the presentation of short phrases or sentences in order to teach new letters. In effect, then, children were reading short stories made up of four or five three-word phrases within a week or two from the beginning of reading instruction.

3. Vowel and consonant presentation is initially limited to one vowel or one consonant per lesson. In later class sessions several consonants are presented in the same lesson. Apparently, teachers and textbook writers feel that the alphabetic principle has been established in earlier lessons and that children are ready to learn more than one letter at a time.

4. Vowel-consonant clusters are presented in later lessons after all letters of the alphabet have been introduced. The consonant clusters "cr," "gl" and so forth, are normally introduced in

combination with the five vowels. A reading is then given in which these clusters appear in combination with the vowels to afford students practice in reading them.

5. An important phase of the instruction is the practice of writing and printing the letters that have been learned in the reading lesson. The reading books used in the Mexican schools incorporate this procedure. Facing the reading page, a page is provided on which the students can practice writing and printing the letters that have been introduced on the previous page. A good deal of time is devoted to writing practice. Work both on the board and at individual desks provides opportunities for students to practice their writing and printing skills. It should be pointed out that Mexican students learn cursive and manuscript writing concurrently. Children in the observed classes learned to print and write both upper and lower case letters in the same lesson.

6. In all classrooms the instruction was carried on using the entire group of 40 to 50 children. There were no instances observed of individual reading instruction or of small group reading classes.

7. Student responses were given mostly in choral repetition in the large group. Children often read together as a total class, wrote from dictation given by the teacher and responded en masse to the teacher's questions. In some instances, teachers called children to the front of the room or had them stand at their desks to read aloud to the rest of the class.

   Although the large group instruction sounds formal, there appeared to be an interesting and warm interaction between the teachers and students in Mexican schools. The noise level in such classes was high, but it appeared to be a happy noise or at least one that was generated by work and interested interaction. Teachers readily accepted comments and questions from pupils, although the questions may have been irrelevant or at least an aside from the work at hand. Often, when a single child was called upon to read or perform at the blackboard, the rest of the class was busy performing the same work at their desks or coaching aloud the student at the board.

8. Because of the emphasis on writing in the reading classes, students accumulate a large number of worksheets and papers. The Mexican schools put these papers to an interesting use. At the end of the year, the worksheets and papers that students have accumulated are bound into a large book which then becomes the property of the student. According to the teachers who were interviewed, the book serves as a review reader for the student, and in several cases, serves to teach others in the same family to read at home.

The aforementioned description of the reading process employed in Mexican schools is a generalized one. There were, of course, variations from this generalization. For example, a school in Mexico City identified as an experimental school was using Gategno's words in color to teach reading. Another class in the same school was studying a variation of a structural grammar. In other schools, a type of language-experience program was being utilized to teach reading. One set of videotapes recorded in Mexico City presents an entire method, with demonstrations by several teachers, of a syllable based phonic reading program. In all of the reading programs mentioned above, much attention is paid to the traditional phonic reading program. This is the way that reading has been taught traditionally in Mexico and any new methods seem to refer back to the phonic method. Unlike English, the sound-symbol correspondence of Spanish is consistent; thus the phonic method lends itself well to the teaching of reading.

Initial reading in Spanish for bilingual children

There was one variable that could not be considered in the investigation of initial reading in Spanish in Mexico; that variable was the student's language. In Mexico, all of the students were monolingual Spanish-speaking children. For our purposes and for the application of the reading techniques that we had discovered in Mexico, it was necessary to consider the language and abilities of children who were bilingual, English-Spanish speakers.

For this reason the initial reading in Spanish for the bilingual program was conceived. The idea behind the program was to teach bilingual English-Spanish speaking children to read in Spanish, utilizing the same methods, materials, and other devices that were used by teachers in Mexico. The project was designed so that it could accumulate information regarding the teaching of initial reading in Spanish in a systematic fashion. The information was to be taken from observation reports, teachers' lesson plans, anecdotal records, and analyses of the teaching practices used by the native Spanish-speaking, Mexico-trained teachers of initial reading in Spanish. The project was sponsored by a grant from the United States Office of Education under funds from the Title VII administered by BEPB. Four field sites were selected at which the project teachers would carry out their instruction. The children to be included in the classes were to be fluent speakers of Spanish who were entering public school as first-grade students. The project was hosted by the Houston Independent School District with the first of the sites located in that city in a predominantly Mexican-American neighborhood. The other sites were in the cities of San Antonio, Alice, and Abernathy, Texas. Some of the children in the study were to be regular members of a bilingual education program while others would receive no extraordinary instruction other than initial reading in Spanish.

Standardizing procedures for data collection

Since collecting information was a primary goal of the project, several forms were developed to standardize the procedures for data collection. The first of these, observation form, was used by the observer-recorder, who sat daily in the classroom as the initial reading in Spanish instruction was carried out. The observer-recorder's observations were guided by the categories contained on the observation form. These categories included: (1) "object naming," in which the recorder would write any nouns that were given special emphasis or explanation in the classroom; (2) "question words," in which interrogatives were recorded; (3) "person and number influence on verbs," in which verb endings were recorded; (4) "object description," in which adjectives were listed; (5) "words that indicate position or direction," a category in which function words were recorded. From these categories a vocabulary list was composed at the end of the project. The list is basically one that contains all of the words that were given special emphasis in the classes and an indication of their frequency on a scale from one to five.

In addition to these categories, the observation form contained sections where information regarding the types of exercises or activities could be recorded. The additional categories of words with multiple meanings and idiomatic speech allowed the observer-recorder to preserve the occurrence of such language usage. The observation forms were filled out daily in each of the classes. The final report of the project contains lists of each of these categories taken from the observation forms from each of the sites. An interesting portion of the final report is that of the pupil-teacher dialectal differences. A list of the conflicts between the language used by the teachers in the classroom and that of the students was recorded. These dialectal differences include slang, local substitute words or synonyms for standard items.

The remaining dialectal differences that were reported can be classified into the following four groups: (1) "archaic forms," words carried down from old Spanish which because of the isolation of Mexican-Americans from other Spanish-speaking people have remained in use; (2) "Anglicisms," words taken from English and adapted to Spanish wherever there was a need for the word; (3) "interchanged letters," words in which certain letters have been used in the wrong order or position and (4) "pronunciation errors," made because of the substitution for the letters "f," "h," and "j."

Dialectal differences also are accumulated in the final report in the form of a word list that separates the differences according to frequency, and identifies them as to the site or sites at which the forms were used.

Another form was used to record pupil pronunciation errors. In this case, the error was one produced when a child attempted to read a word from the text or materials supplied by the teacher. In general, the kinds of pronunciation errors that were observed reflected some of the dialectal differences that were reported previously. The final report presents these pronunciation errors in a list that is coded according to frequency and geographic location of occurrence.

Materials used in the project

A complete description of the materials that were used in the project is also contained in the final report. The basic texts are listed and described in terms of their use in the classroom. The Mexican reading teachers were permitted complete freedom in the selection of textbooks. At the initial meeting with the teachers at the beginning of the year, the teachers as a group agreed that they would like to use the same textbooks furnished them by the federal government in Mexico. Because of the fact that these texts are not readily available in the United States through import, an alternate set of texts was selected. These textbooks were very similar in format to those published by the federal government in Mexico. The three basic books used by all four teachers were: *Mi Libro Mágico*, a basic reader with provision for writing and printing practice; *Mis Primeras Letras*, a supplementary practice book and reader; and *Felicidad*, a reader and book of activities. Some supplementary books also were selected, as well as a small library of readers or "read to" books. A detailed list of these books as well as their sources is listed in the final report of the project.

Care was taken to preserve all of the games, rhymes, songs, stories, and other devices used by the teachers in their classes. In the case of games, the name of the game and the rules for playing are given in the final report. Rhymes and their use also are given in the report and listed in an index. Songs, for the most part, are referred to by name, with the verse occasionally given if the song is not generally known.

Each teacher was requested to submit lesson plans weekly, samples and summaries of which are reproduced in the final report of the project. Some evaluations of materials and description of specially made materials also are included in the teachers' reports. The teachers employed a large number of specially prepared forms and charts. A description of these and their texts are supplied in the teachers' reports.

One appendix of the final report summarizes the sequence of presentation of letters of the alphabet. The reports of the observer-recorders contain anecdotal records of the presentation of the letters by the teachers at the different sites. When a teacher employed specific and unique methods to teach the formation of vowels or consonants, it was reported in detail in the observer-recorder reports. The final report contains the rhymes, special instructions, or games used in the teaching of the letter shapes.

Because the use of children's writing was so extensive, samples of children's handwriting are also included in the final report. Observers of the videotapes and samples often are impressed by the quality of the children's handwriting, particularly the examples of cursive writing, since children in the United States normally are not taught cursive forms until the third grade. The samples of the children's writing taken from the Texas classrooms compares favorably with the samples shown on the videotapes recorded in Mexico City.

Summary analysis of teaching

Classes began in most of the sites in September of 1970. The general pattern for class organization and teaching sequences was similar at each of the sites. This was to be expected, since all four of the teachers had been trained in Mexico in similar teacher-training institutions. At each site, an initial period varying from a few days to two weeks was used to accomplish some pre-reading practice. Teachers used songs, games, and other instructional materials during this period.

Extensive videotaping also was done in the four classrooms in Texas. This technique permitted re-examination of a class session and has also allowed us to preserve examples of the teachers' work. This footage has been assembled into eight videotapes of approximately 15 to 30 minutes each in length. Each of the tapes shows examples of a specific technique or techniques employed by teachers in the Texas project. One tape, for instance, presents several different class sessions in which the teachers are using writing as a reinforcement for reading practice. Another shows teachers using reading charts to teach children to read sentences in sequence to form a logical paragraph. Duplicates of these tapes are available to interested educational agencies.

The following summary is a compilation of the largest section of the report, in which the teaching methodologies used in the Texas classrooms are described.

1. When actual reading instruction began, all teachers taught vowels first. The teachers all used a phonic method to introduce the vowels. Rhymes were used as mnemonic devices to help children associate the sound of the letter with its graphic symbol. Like the teachers in the Mexico City classrooms, the Texas teachers referred to the letter of the alphabet by their sounds.

2. Consonants were then taught until the entire alphabet had been presented, using the sound of each letter to identify it, rather than a letter name. This practice was common to all the teachers. Needless to say, vowels and consonants were not introduced in the same order at each site. There was, however, a general consensus among the teachers for sequence of individual letter presentation which reflected the teachers' preference for the State textbooks in Mexico. The pattern consisted of presenting the vowel sounds as quickly as possible, followed by presentation of some consonant

sounds and letters to make up simple sentences that the children could read. The teachers paid careful attention so that each child produced the sound of each letter as it was introduced. The reading "lesson" consisted of presenting a word like *oso* and teaching the children the identification of the new letter in the context of letters already learned. Other words were introduced which contained the new letter in the initial position.

3. The teachers generally focused on the practice of sounding out words letter by letter. When children hesitated or stumbled in reading, the teacher would help them sound out each letter of the word, and then blend those letters into the pronunciation of the word in question. One of the teachers used the practice of multiple repetitions of a word so that children could memorize its pronunciation. This amounted to rote learning. The practice, however, was limited to one classroom of the four and did not seem to be a general practice used by Mexican teachers. Drill on individual words or letters usually was accomplished through games, songs, and repetition. Whole class participation, however, was the most commonly used mode of classroom instruction.

4. Much of the work in these games, songs, and repetitive drills was done using the entire class in a choral repetition. Individual children were called upon to point out letters as the class sounded out the words. Children often were called to the front of the room to point to a letter or a sentence on a chart.

5. The use of writing as a reinforcement of reading instruction was one of the most singularly outstanding practices in the program. Pre-reading instruction included practice in the basic movements needed for handwriting. This involved large motor movement practice usually accomplished at individual desks. The students were asked to write letters in the air or on their desk tops, using their finger tips. Some of the other practices included writing at the board, usually by one child, while the rest of the class practiced the movements in the air or on their desk tops.

    Group handwriting practice began with the first letters and words that were introduced for reading. The children were provided practice sheets on which to copy words and letters from the board or from their reading lessons. From the beginning, both manuscript and cursive forms of upper and lower case letters were presented simultaneously and then practiced by the students. The children progressed from writing single letters to words, phrases, and sentences as the reading material in the lessons became more complex. The teachers used dictation frequently to vary the handwriting skill. Dictation most often was based on familiar sentences that had been previously presented in the reading lessons.

6. The sequence of vowel presentation and consonant presentation differed from classroom to classroom. The general procedure, however, was much the same; the teachers introduced vowels early in the reading instruction, then proceeded to present one new consonant per reading lesson. All the teachers proceeded from single letter introduction to syllables and then to reading words and eventually whole phrases or sentences.

Reading and instructional materials

The reading and instructional materials used were selected by the teachers themselves. Their only limitation was the availability of materials. For this reason, the materials used at the four sites were not duplicates of the materials used in the first grade in Mexico. The Mexican federal texts are not available for importation to the United States. All of the teachers had brought materials with them that they had previously used in Mexico. These materials, particularly the teachers' guides, helped them to establish the sequence of presentation of reading material. The books that they did use were rearranged somewhat so that the order of the lessons coincided fairly closely with the order as seen in the Mexican federal textbooks. The final report includes several indices and charts showing the order in which vowels, consonants, phrases, and whole sentences were presented by the teachers.

The teachers made extensive use of printed materials for display. Some had brought with them large charts which duplicated whole pages in an enlarged form for presentation to the whole class. All of the teachers prepared supplementary ditto sheets for practice in reading and writing. Sometimes these were pages taken from other texts; at other times they were teacher-made lessons. The chalkboard was used extensively to present written stories for choral reading and for children to practice writing words and sentences that appeared in the reading lessons. Chart and flannel board pictures frequently were used by the teachers for both reading practice and language or concept development. The teachers indicated that the lack of Spanish language development in their American students was one of the basic differences between their classes in Mexico and those that they taught in the United States. The teachers all felt that the bilingual youngsters in their classes had, in general, limited Spanish-speaking ability. For this reason, the teachers moved at a slower pace, spending more time on developing oral language than they would have with monolingual Spanish-speaking children. The oral language practice was, for the most part, concept or vocabulary development.

Classroom interaction

An interesting phenomenon observed in the classes was that of the interaction between the students and teachers. In general, the classes seemed noisier than one would expect an American schoolroom to be. Although the class was conducted as a total group learning together rather than in small groups, the teachers seemed, for the most part, permissive in their control of movement about the room and particularly of talking by the students. They readily accepted correct, incorrect, and sometimes irrelevant questions or responses from students. The children appeared free to ask questions or make comments during any part of the reading lesson. In some of the classes, students moved freely from their seats to the teacher, who was standing at the front of the room addressing the class, and after asking a question or making a comment or showing a paper to the teacher, would move back to their seats again and the lesson would continue.

Reading progress and achievement

Aside from the extensive descriptive analysis resulting from the Initial Reading Program in Spanish, an evaluation was made of the students' progress in learning to read both Spanish and English. The teaching of English reading was generally delayed, except in cases where parents or school personnel objected. The evaluation and comparison of reading progress by students in and between the sites was difficult because of differences in socioeconomic status as well as the distances between the project sites. The sample differences between the various classrooms and the variations in the population densities of the four sites presented further difficulties. Because of these difficulties of across-site evaluation, the general feeling of the evaluator was that the within-site evaluations offer the best probability for interpretation of success of the students in reading. A test was developed to evaluate the Spanish reading progress of the students at all the sites. The results show that the children did indeed learn to read Spanish at a level that was somewhat above average. The conclusion was that their progress in Spanish reading was slightly better than normal, with one site showing extremely good progress.

Achievement in reading English was also shown. Only three sites reported on this phase. In one, the children in the Initial Spanish Reading Project learned to read English as well as the control group. In addition, they learned to read Spanish. At the other two sites, however, the English achievement of the students was somewhat below that of their control-group counterparts. The results also established that learning to read in Spanish was related significantly to the ability to learn to read English.

Statistical summary

The final report contains the statistical data from various tests and evaluations that were administered in the program. In summary, the results are basically these:

1. The children who scored significantly higher on the Spanish reading test were students participating in both a bilingual education program and the Spanish reading program. Apparently the combination of the two programs resulted in the highest degree of Spanish reading ability. There are many variables to consider in a study, such as ability, socioeconomic status, and educational opportunity. The fact that the other three sites were statistically alike, however, leads to an assumption that the children's success can be attributed to the combination of the bilingual program and the Spanish reading program.

2. In two of the three sites, the control groups had significantly higher English reading ability than did the Spanish reading students. This would seem to indicate that reading ability at this level is a function of the time spent in practice. The control groups did spend more time learning to read English than did the Spanish reading program children. At one site there was no statistical difference, which would lead to support of the theory that children experiencing early success in their reading will make a significant transfer of those skills to reading in another language.

3. There were significant differences in the English scores from one site to another. The statistics indicate that the one group showing the lower scores was perhaps of slightly lower ability. It also should be pointed out that the teacher at that particular site was the least secure of the four, and relied heavily on rote learning to teach reading.

4. An attempt was made to get an overview of all the reading groups on both English and Spanish tests. The overview indicated there was little difference in the various performances on both tests. This would seem to support the position that the children in the project did learn both English and Spanish reading. A final analysis was made of the relationship between the Spanish reading test scores and the English reading scores. There were strong relationships found which would indicate once again that there are individual differences among children, and those who scored high on the Spanish tests also scored high on the English test.

The evaluation contained in the final project report goes into detail concerning the relationships and results reported above. Interpretation of the results, of course, must be cautious. In a program such as the one that I have described, it is extremely difficult to control the many variables. The interpretations given here and in the report are presented, not as truths, but as stimuli for further investigation.

Enough was found, of both a descriptive and an inferential nature, to bring about greater insights into the teaching and learning process as it relates to Spanish-speaking bilingual children. It is hoped that the knowledge and information gained through the Initial Spanish Reading Project and contained in the final report and the videotapes will stimulate further investigation into what is most certainly an essential area of instruction for bilingual children.

Summary

A one-year project investigated the teaching of initial reading in Spanish to bilingual **Spanish/English-speaking** children of 6 to 7 years of age. Four reading teachers, trained and experienced in teaching initial reading in Mexico, taught bilingual children to read in Spanish during a one-year program. Detailed accounts were kept by observers and by the teachers themselves in order to report the process and the results of the research project. These accounts yielded a descriptive analysis of the children, teachers, methods and materials, and the settings in which the teaching took place. The resultant description is a detailed observation of the reading method that is widely used in Mexican schools in the first grade.

Bibliography

Arnold, Richard D. *1965-1966 (Year Two) Findings*, San Antonio Language Research Project. Austin: University of Texas, (1968).

Bernard, W. "Psychological Principles of Language Learning and the Bilingual Reading Method." *The Modern Language Journal*, 35 (1951), pp. 87-96.

Grieve, D.W. and A. Taylor. "Media of Instruction: A Preliminary Study of the Relative Merits of English and An African Vernacular as Teaching Media." *Gold Coast Education*, 1 (1952), pp. 36-52.

Gumperz, John. "On the Linguistic Markers of Bilingual Communication." *Journal of Social Issues*, Vol. 23, 2, p. 56. New York: Yeshiva University, April, (1967).

Modiano, Nancy. "National or Mother Tongue Language in Beginning Reading: A Comparative Study." *Research in the Teaching of English*, Vol. 2, 1, pp. 32-43, April, (1968).

Orata, Pedro T. "The Iloilo Community School Experiment: The Vernacular as Medium of Instruction." *Fundamental and Adult Education*, Vol. 8 (1956), pp. 173-178.

Patterson, W.R. and Eugenia Joyce. "Teaching Reading to the Bilingual Child." *National Elementary Principal*, Thirty-Fourth Yearbook, 35 (1955), pp. 103-106.

Spolsky, Bernard and Wayne Holm. "Literacy in the Vernacular: The Case of the Navajo." *Progress Report*, No. 8, Navajo Reading Study, University of New Mexico, March, (1971).

Strickland, Ruth G. "The Interrelationship Between Language and Reading." *Volta Review*, 60 (1958), pp. 334-336.

UNESCO. "The Use of Vernacular Languages in Education." *Monographs on Fundamental Education*, No. 8, Paris: UNESCO, (1953), pp. 17-44.

Walker, Willard. "Notes on Native Writing Systems and the Designs of Native Literacy Programs." *Anthropological Linguistics*, Vol. 11, 5 (1968), pp. 148-166.

20

Question-Generalization by First-Graders
Virginia H. Streiff

The objective of my paper is to describe some aspects of a classroom program for learners of English as a second language (ESL). The program called Listening was designed to provide primary-grade Navajo- and Spanish-speaking children a transition from learning English as a second language to learning in English. In fostering this transition, it is intended to provide the children some tools for learning how to learn in the second language.

The transition from learning the second language to learning in the second language is characterized, in part, by a shift in the children's responses to cues, from cues primarily of a syntactic focus to cues primarily of a semantic focus, as illustrated in these examples. The first represents an ESL lesson dialogue:

Teacher: Joe, ask Mary what she has.

Joe: Mary, what do you have?

Mary: A pencil.

The second example represents a listening lesson:

Teacher: I'm going to read you a story about some children who wanted a wagon.

Who has a question?

Joe: Who wanted a wagon?

Mary: Why did they want a wagon?

Susie: Did they get one?

In the ESL lesson, Joe knows that he's expected to perform transformations based on the teacher's indirect question cue, although the situation is also made meaningful in the sense that Mary is holding a paper bag with something in it, which turns out to be a pencil when she investigates in response to Joe's question.

In the Listening lesson, Joe and his classmates know they are expected to originate questions appropriate to the teacher's introductory statement, drawing on their own curiosity triggered by the information the statement contains.

The transition to learning in the second language is additionally characterized by a change in thinking tasks relative to the verbal material presented, from the recognition and recall of information required in the ESL lesson to the higher level thinking tasks described by Benjamin S. Bloom as comprehension skills. (Bloom, et al., 1956) These skills include paraphrasing, interpreting, and extrapolating, and the subcategories of each.

This means, in the Listening lesson, that (i) the teacher's introductory statement about a story will trigger a partially predictable set of questions by the children, and (ii) the story the children then listen to will contain information such that the children are required to paraphrase it, interpret it, or extrapolate from it in some fashion in order to be able to answer the questions they asked. The obvious question here is "What happens to the unpredictable questions children ask? " These unpredictable questions are referred back to their respective authors, with the teacher asking, "What do you think? " The children respond as they think appropriate, opting for "I don't know" if they think there wasn't enough information in the story to allow any other response.

The transition from learning the second language to learning in the second language is also defined as the child's comprehension of relatively longer, increasingly complex and abstract units of verbal material than used in the structurally-controlled sequences of the ESL program.

With respect to the learning-how-to-learn tools, this program is predicated on the notions that (i) a prime objective of curriculum should be the fostering of thinking skills and (ii) that inquiry can lead children into all kinds of thinking, as Norris Sanders proposes in *Classroom Questions: What Kinds?* (Sanders, 1966)

The value of having the children ask the questions, and ask them in advance of listening to a story, as a heuristic tool, is perhaps best underscored by two references. The first is to Postman and Weingartners' recent reiteration of the value of inquiry as a learning-how-to-learn tool, "the most important intellectual activity man has yet developed. . ." (Postman and Weingartner, 1969) The second reference is to Bruner's discussion of "The Psychobiology of Pedagogy" in *The Relevance of Education.* (Bruner, 1971) In discussing constraints on the nervous system for processing the amounts and complexities of data received, he reiterates his hypothesis theory of perception, "the central premise of which is that it is the processing of data that yields significance, not its receipt." He points out that, to foster economy in this processing, the implication for pedagogy is "that instruction must encourage the formulation and testing of hypotheses." A related finding in research on listening comprehension reveals that a listener's anticipatory set, that is, his ability to form and reform hypotheses as he listens, is a significant aid to his comprehension. (Keller, 1966) Fostering this skill is the intent in the first-grade Listening program of having the children ask questions in advance of a story. During the second half of the first-grade program, the hypothesis-forming-and-revising skill is extended. During this later stage, the children ask questions first on the basis of an introductory statement, and thereafter on the basis of information given in the paragraph just preceding the question-asking period. This kind of participation also has the objective of preparing the children for the second- and third-grade stages of the program, in which it is proposed that the children's final activity in a Listening lesson is not answering all the questions, but answering those that are possible to answer, and sorting out and revising the others for further investigation in other resources.

The spiral nature of the program allows for implicit familiarity during the first fifty lessons with the processes described by Bloom as comprehension skills. The processes are then recycled to provide explicit familiarity through naming them, as for example the paraphrase skills which are interpreted for first graders as ways to tell someone about a story. It is intended that by employing this implicit-to-explicit familiarity the children will, as Vygotsky suggested, come into possession of the processes before conscious control of them is expected. (Vygotsky, 1962)

The spiral projects into the second, third, and fourth grades with the introduction of the processes of analysis, synthesis, and evaluation. (Bloom, et al., 1956) This is not to say that these processes are not in use in some form from the beginning of the program. Nor is it to say that one school year is devoted to each of these processes. This projection is discussed more fully later in the paper. With respect to the spiral nature of the program, it suffices here to point out that these processes are planned for systematic introduction at approximately the time when the children are preparing to enter the stage Piaget describes as formal operations. The point in following the hierarchy of processes, which Bloom suggests is cumulative and sequential, is two-fold. First, a minimal guarantee is established that each skill will become familiar to the child in a useful order of abstraction. Secondly, through such familiarity with a system of processes, it is hoped that a proclivity is fostered in the child for continuing to use the processes, along with the tool of inquiry, all the more readily.

Background of the Problem and the Program

Considering the burgeoning influx of facts in this world, it is little wonder that in classroom practice the term "comprehension" has come to be equated with recognizing and recalling facts, as in reading comprehension, or as in testing for listening comprehension. (Sanders, 1966; Guszak, 1967)

As both the research and the editorializing in the area of inquiry education suggests, getting the facts for responsible scholars and citizens is just the beginning; comprehension of them is the next step, and the process should not stop here.

The notion that message-receiving is an active endeavor calling for many more processes beyond simply getting and recalling the facts is not new. But classroom practices which foster these processes are few and far between, as amply documented in the literature. (Duker, 1966; Bruner, 1971) While not all message-sending is intended for the listening mode alone, much of it in the classroom is. One study estimates that elementary-school children spend approximately sixty percent of their classroom day engaged in this activity, if we can consider thinking at the recognition-recall level as active engagement. (Wilt, 1966) Another study revealed it was this kind of thinking that was the main focus of teachers' questions to students about reading material in twelve randomly selected classrooms in Texas; about seventy percent of the teacher's questions required only that the children recall explicit facts from the material they had read. This relegated other thinking processes (e.g. interpretation, analysis, substantiated evaluation, etc.) to the remaining thirty percent of the questions. (Guszak, 1967) This kind of classroom message to children is probably responsible for the facts behind the lament of one graduate student who recently wrote to the editor of the *Los Angeles Times* "Too many students will do anything to avoid the real essence of education which takes place only when the student reacts to material after being exposed to it and personally thinking about it." (Lister, 1971)

The Listening program grew out of concern with such problems in message-receiving and processing, particularly as young learners of ESL face them now in their classrooms, and as they will face them in whatever media transmit the messages in their future.

The working hypothesis in the development of the Listening program is that these children will be better equipped as learners if they first receive systematic instruction in learning to use their new language as a medium for learning, learning used ·here as a paraphrase for thinking, particularly for thinking beyond the recognition and recall level to more abstract levels of cognition.

In terms of its general and specific objectives, the Listening program assumes the validity of Covington's point:

> . . .before the student can derive maximum benefits from a strong process-oriented approach to education, it will be necessary to develop a curriculum model which has as one of its fundamental objectives the fostering of intellectual processes in their own right, a goal which must be fully integrated and coordinated with other more traditional objectives such as mastery of content and assimilation of cultural values. (Covington, 1970)

The long-range goal in this program is the learner's active involvement first in thinking about the facts he listens to, then in applying language and thinking processes which help him comprehend and retain the salient features of a message which often exceed the explicit facts, then forming new questions about them.

The thinking processes fostered in this program are from those described in *A Taxonomy of Educational Objectives, Handbook 1: The Cognitive Domain.* (Bloom, et al., 1956) Beyond the knowledge level which emphasizes the processes of recognizing and recalling, they are comprehending, applying, analyzing, synthesizing, and evaluating. The stages of the Listening program developed in daily lesson plans to date focus on the sequence of comprehension level skills, extrapolated for the program as:

  i. Paraphrasing
   a. rephrasing the information from one symbolic form to another. The student can 'translate' verbal information to visual or spatial terms. For example, identifying or building a model which has been described verbally.
   b. rephrasing the information from one level of abstraction to another. The students can summarize a story, or 'translate' a general principle by giving an example of it.
   c. rephrasing the information from one verbal form to another, as in providing the literal meaning of figurative speech.
  ii. Interpreting
   a. comparative relationships. The student can distinguish related from unrelated ideas; he can distinguish identical, similar, and different ideas, etc.
   b. relationship of implication. The student understands the relationships between evidence presented and an implication.
   c. relationship of generalization to supporting evidence. The student can survey and find within it a characteristic common to each piece of evidence which leads to the generalization.
   d. relationship of a skill or definition to an example of its use. A skill or definition is described for the student and he can identify or compose an example of it.
   e. cause and effect relationships. The student can describe or identify the cause of specific effects.
  iii. Extrapolating
   a. **predicting** the continuation of a sequence. The student can accurately predict an event on the basis of established evidence.
   b. inferring, as in supplying data implied but not stated.
   c. distinguishing probable from improbable consequences.

These comprise the cognitive objectives for the first-grade lessons of stages one and two, approximately one hundred lessons. The outline projected for stages three through six incorporates the processes classified as applying, analyzing, synthesizing, and evaluating.

Inquiry is the language process by which these thinking processes are fostered in the course of each daily lesson. While much of the focus in inquiry education is on getting teachers to ask better questions (Sanders, 1966; Guszak, 1967), the power of inquiry as a learning-how-to-learn tool suggests that it should be at the disposal of the students, particularly in a program or curriculum which is heuristic in nature. The Listening program is designed with the optimistic expectation that curricula like that proposed by Covington and his colleagues will flourish increasingly, but also with a practical view toward what is actually the case in many classrooms today, if the research on teachers' questions can be generalized at all. This practical view is the basis for designing the Listening program in terms of explicit lesson plans through which the teacher becomes familiar with the specific thinking processes that various kinds of questions can trigger. In addition, the lesson plans specify the teaching steps that encourage the children to ask questions confidently.

Accepting the principle of appropriate practice of desired behavior as the best way to achieve that behavior and in addition the notion that "the critical content of any learning experience is the method or process through which the learning takes place" (Postman and Weingartner, 1969), it makes sense to have the children learn to ask relevant, appropriate, and substantial questions, and to value such inquiry, by actually engaging in this activity.

It is through this means — inquiry which triggers thinking beyond the recognition-recall level — that a transition can be effected from learning a second language to learning in a second language. For the benefit of children as maturing learners in a new language, the transition from basic language acquisition to a more sophisticated language-comprehension program must view the relationship between language and thinking as a process in which the two develop interdependently, and in which the relation of thought to word undergoes changes as the composite matures. (Vygotsky, 1962)

In the Listening program, question-asking acts as the pivot for the transition from second-language learning to learning in the second language. Question-asking is the constant language process used by the children for the communication tasks of their ESL program, and also for the higher level thinking tasks in the Listening program. The difference might grossly be illustrated as the difference in purpose between asking "Is Mary skipping? " (in a situation where one child is skipping and another is clapping her hands), to practice yes/no questions with the present progressive tense and two forms of verb phrase; and asking "Is Mary skipping? " because one infers from the strange noises behind his back that six-year-old Mary has finally learned to skip, and he wants to confirm or correct the inference.

Inquiry and thinking beyond the knowledge level are the major heuristic characteristics of the Listening program. By the nature of their presence as learner objectives in every lesson in the program they are at once both the means, or media, and the intended learning outcomes.

Inquiry, as it is used in the Listening program, not only includes seeking information that is readily available in the form of explicit facts, but also includes seeking other kinds of information, for example that which may be inferred on the basis of explicit facts, that which may be compared with the facts, and that which may be predicted on the basis of facts. In addition, inquiry is used for hypothesis-formation, a skill already familiar to the children as demonstrated by their preference for information-testing questions.

The ability of a listener to hypothesize while he is listening, that is, to provide himself with an anticipatory set about the material, appears to be a significant aid to listening comprehension. (Keller, 1966) The significance of the anticipatory set, as a strategy worth developing in the children, is additionally supported by its compatibility with the objectives of inquiry and cognitive processing beyond the recall level. It is a strategy the mass media have applied for years to keep listeners tuned-in and focused on the purpose of the message: "How will Tarzan rescue Jane from the man-eating tiger? Will the no-enzyme detergent get the wash as clean as the enzyme detergent? "

While the message senders of our mass media will continue providing the message-receivers with such ready-made anticipatory sets, it seems most useful in a learning-how-to-learn program to have the listeners learn to form their own hypotheses before and during a communication by asking questions about it. The listener's anticipatory questions provide him a focus, a frame of reference through which to consider the incoming data. These questions are also valuable in that they can trigger thinking processes relevant to the message and thus profitably exploit the thinking time made available by the differential between the speaking rate and the thinking rate, whether that is the estimate of approximately 200 words per minute one study showed (Toussaint, 1966), or the thousands of words per minute suggested by the accomplishments of some speed readers. Both the listener's attention to the material and his purpose in listening to it are fostered by his anticipatory questioning. This helps the listener get to his tasks of associating the ideas within the material and associating his related experiences to those ideas.

A Pre-Assessment

The Listening program was developed as a part of a comprehensive and innovative primary curriculum provided by Consultants in Total Education (CITE) for Navajo children in Bureau of Indian Affairs Schools on the Navajo Reservation, and for Mexican-American children in the public schools of Fresno, California. Language skills taught to pre-first graders in the ESL component of the CITE curriculum provided the prerequisite foundation for the Listening program.

The children, through their ESL lessons, learned to ask the range of question types available in English — the wh-questions, including simple how- and why-questions, and yes/no questions. They learned to ask such questions when cued by an indirect question or command, at first from the teacher and then from another child. They asked these questions in the context of situations designed by the program writers to place all the language-learning in a meaningful context. The children's facility grew through participation in a systematic presentation which included the major sentence patterns of English and the processes of substitution, deletion, expansion, and transformation. Teachers' regular reports on the children's achievement of the question-asking and answering objectives in the daily ESL lessons indicated when they had acquired the language foundation necessary for using inquiry in the Listening program.

The first step was to find out if first-grade children could switch from asking questions which were syntactically cued, as in the ESL program, to generating original questions independently of such specific indirect question cues. For example, in the ESL program the children's questions were cued by the teacher's command, e.g., "Joe, tell Susie to ask Jim what he has," and another child's subsequent question, e.g., "Susie, ask Jim. . ." In the Listening program the children's questions would be cued only by the teacher's minimal cue, "Who wants to ask a question? "

Before the Listening program was actually implemented, data were gathered in three Navajo first-grade classrooms to find out if the children could and would generalize their question-asking skills to new content and respond to such a minimal cue. The teachers were asked to show two filmstrips the children had not seen before, and were instructed to use only the cue "Who wants to ask a question? " as they showed the filmstrips. The children were told at the beginning that they could ask any questions they wished about any of the pictures, including asking them of the teacher. This was to insure that the children would feel free to ask questions that they might otherwise not ask out of consideration for their peers who might not know the answers. This built-in safeguard was particularly important because the children knew that responses were always readily available in the ESL lessons. In an ESL lesson a child could respond correctly to questions by making correct choices from a minimal situation in which other children and objects were "set up" to perform the action being asked about.

To summarize the data recorded by the teachers:

   i. All the children in each classroom volunteered to ask questions in response to the cue "Who wants to ask a question? "

   ii. All the questions were relevant to visual information presented in the frames about which they were asked.

   iii. All the questions were grammatically correct, that is, normal American English.

These data were taken as an indication that such first graders could be expected to have the question-asking facility, and the willingness to use it, prerequisite to the Listening program. Two other important features appeared in the children's questions recorded by the teachers. One feature was the nearly total focus on recognizing and recalling information, and the other was the predominant yes/no question pattern. Of the classroom average of sixty-five questions, sixty-three were questions like: "Are those chickens? Is that a man riding the horse? Are the foxes in the cave? " While preference for such specific information-testing questions might be interpreted as typical of the age group (Mosher and Hornsby, 1966), the more significant feature for development of the Listening program was the recognition-recall focus of the questions. The tentative implication was that, having learned to ask questions with this focus throughout the ESL program, perhaps the children could learn just as readily to ask questions for other purposes. Indeed, having learned to ask questions of the recognition-recall type so thoroughly, the children might need to practice asking other kinds of questions to expand the scope of their learning tools.

The Program

The long-range objectives in the entire Listening program are the development of learner skill in (a) comprehending a message (b) retaining the salient features of the message (through answering his anticipatory questions and summarizing the data), and then using other resources to answer (i) anticipatory questions which were not satisfactorily answered by the message, and (ii) other questions generated as a result of the message.

Acquisition of an anticipatory set and familiarization with the thought processes comprising the skills of comprehension are the general learner objectives for stage 1 of the program. Stage 1 is made up of fifty-four daily lessons of about one half hour each. The specific objectives for each lesson in stage 1 are for the child to ask questions before listening to a story and to answer such questions after listening to the story.

Each comprehension process is the focus for the stories in a sequence of several lessons. For example, in lessons sixteen through eighteen the children paraphrase from one symbolic form to another, through such activities as building simple models after listening to an oral description of them and selecting and sequencing illustrations appropriate to a story after listening to the story.

The general objectives for stage 1 are accomplished by (i) a cumulative sequence of cognitive objectives, (ii) the procedural content of basic lesson format, and (iii) the design of the oral messages in story form to focus on a particular cognitive objective for each lesson.

The cumulative and sequential nature of the hierarchy of cognitive objectives which comprise the outline might be simply illustrated by pointing out the need for a child to have knowledge of certain categories and classes before he can apply the comprehension process of comparing relationships among them.

Procedural content of stage 1 lessons provides a sequence of steps to insure learner success through observation and practice of the behavior specifically desired. A typical stage 1 lesson is composed of three short stories, each story constructed as a paragraph of seven or eight sentences at most, generalizing from the fund of language structure provided in the ESL program.

The function of the first story is to provide the learner a model analogous to his expected behavior. The teacher has a puppet ask anticipatory questions based on an introductory sentence she gives about the story to be read. She reads the story and then calls on volunteering children to respond to the questions the puppet asked in advance of the story. Children respond to the questions, and peers evaluate the responses for appropriateness, with the teacher assisting by confirming or correcting responses on the basis of the story.

The function of the second story is to provide the children practice in asking anticipatory questions based on an introductory sentence. Volunteers ask questions, and the teacher writes them on the chalkboard so they may be answered after she reads the story. As after the first story, the teacher again calls on volunteers to respond to one another's questions, and on other children to evaluate the responses.

The third story provides a final session in which the children ask questions before listening to the story and answer them after listening to it. After this third, and last, story all the children respond to the advance questions by circling pictures on a worksheet. This exercise tests the listening comprehension of all the children.

Each story in a lesson is designed to focus on a particular cognitive process, such as the extrapolation process of predicting the continuation of a sequence. Thus, the introductory sentence for each story is designed to elicit specific questions about the story, i.e., questions about the sequence of events in the story, questions about the causes and effects in a story, questions about the generalizations which might be made on the basis of evidence presented in the story, etc.

The children's questions which are related to the particular cognitive objective of a story are called "planned questions." To answer these questions, the children have to apply the thought process which is the focus of the story. For example, here are the introductory sentences, the children's questions, and the story for an early stage 1 lesson in which the focus is distinguishing related from unrelated objects, a preliminary to the later task of distinguishing related from unrelated ideas.

Teacher: I'm going to read you a story about Sammy. He saw his breakfast on the table, but he also saw something he didn't need for breakfast there, so he put it on the floor.

Joe: Did Sammy see a car?

Carl: Did Sammy have a truck?

Ervin: Did Sammy have a cat?

Ilene: What did Sammy eat for breakfast?

Leona: What did Sammy put on the floor?

Teacher: Sammy was getting ready for school. He was all dressed and ready to eat breakfast. He looked on the table. He saw a glass of orange juice. He saw his baby kitten, and he saw a piece of bread. "Good," said Sammy. "Everything I want for breakfast is right here on the table. But I don't need this for breakfast," Sammy laughed. "I'll put it on the floor." He picked something up from the table and put it on the floor. Then he ate his breakfast.

Here are additional examples of children's questions from the same Navajo class about another story in the same lesson, which had different content but the same focus on distinguishing related from unrelated objects:

Renee: What did Bobby find?

Leroy: What did Bobby take to play baseball?

Renee: What did he leave in the closet?

Carol: What did Bobby think?

Garry: What toy did Bobby want?

The children who ask, answer, and evaluate the planned questions and responses focus on distinguishing the related and unrelated objects in the stories. Children who ask, answer, and evaluate the other questions and responses also have a focused purpose while listening. The minimal set of planned questions focuses attention on the cognitive purpose of the message; the additional questions provide a broader perspective about the message. After the third story, when the children respond to the planned questions by marking pictures on a worksheet, application of the necessary thought process by all the children is tested.

The general objectives for stage 2 occur further along the continuum toward the long-range goal, with specific objectives for fifty more lessons. The comprehension processes are recycled in new stories, with some additions. For example, in stage 1 the children compare relationships only by distinguishing related and unrelated objects. During stage 2 the comparative relationship lesson sequence expands so the children distinguish objects then actions, and finally ideas, for their degree of relationship to each other.

The general objectives of stage 2 are to familiarize the children with strategies for increased retention of material and to foster question-asking during a message as well as before it, concomitant with the long-range goal of hypothesis-revision while listening. In addition, the implication of a message for further thinking and reaction is promoted by designing new activities to replace the picture worksheets at the end of each lesson. To provide for achievement of these goals through daily specific objectives, lesson procedures were adapted so that each lesson contains one longer story rather than the three short stories. This story is presented in two parts, a short introductory paragraph and a longer conclusion. The children's objectives are to ask questions after listening to the first paragraph, then to answer them after listening to the entire story. The children then contribute to an oral summarization of the story, which the teacher prints on large chart paper. The final lesson activity is playing a game, making models, dramatizing, or whatever activity results most naturally from the content of the story the children have listened to. For example, in a stage 2 lesson on paraphrasing, the children listen to a story about a child making his own picture book. The materials and the steps in the process are detailed in the story. After listening to the story, the children end the lesson by making their own picture books, following the same basic steps but using their own ideas for content and arrangement. These activities perform the testing function of the picture-worksheets of stage 1.

The objective of stage 3 is transfer of stage 1 and 2 skills to other areas of school study. Focused anticipatory questioning about science, math, social studies, etc. is a technique used by some teachers, but it stands in direct contrast to the technique used by others. "Read the chapter. Then you'll have a test on it." Not only the techniques, but the cognitive objectives as well, are concomitant with reading comprehension objectives of the elementary school.

But if the child is to benefit fully from the skills taught in stages 1 through 3, further development in listening comprehension skills is also suggested by the research.

Two pieces of evidence reveal a further direction for the Listening program in stages 4, 5, and 6. One indicates the significant difference in comprehension and retention of material by the listener who has a favorable anticipatory set in contrast with the listener who has an unfavorable bias at the outset. (Keller, 1966) The other indicates the temporary paralysis that occurs when a listener hears a "loaded word," that is, a term that is emotion-laden for him. (Toussaint, 1966) This might, indeed, cause a listener to "see red." While the practiced public speaker is aware of this, and uses it, school children are rarely taught how to handle the situation as listeners. If the learner can retain the relatively objective kind of anticipatory set practiced in the first three stages of the program and then become skilled in recognizing propaganda techniques, perhaps his chances of becoming a skilled, mature listener will be increased.

Toward this end, and others, general objectives for stages 4 through 6 are designed. They refer generally to curriculum development for late second grade through fifth grade for second language learners. In addition, maintenance of basic listening strategies from previous stages characterizes each new stage.

General objectives for stage 4 are further development of hypothesis-formation on the basis of a message; for example, asking questions initiated by information presented in the area of natural science; and familiarization with other resources for seeking answers to such questions; for example, dictionaries and other reference works, resource speakers, and experimentation. The cognitive processes for this stage are characterized by the application skills described by Bloom, in which the student learns to select the appropriate knowledge and comprehension skills for solving particular problems.

Stage 5 is characterized by transfer of the major strategies already learned to understanding persuasive messages, including familiarization with various propaganda techniques. Analysis, synthesis, and evaluation skills described by Bloom are introduced in this stage. An explicit objective here is maintenance of objectivity in message-receiving through awareness of the purpose of such messages and skill in individual hypothesis-formation, revision, and testing.

Stage 6 recycles analysis, synthesis, and evaluation processes in more explicit terms for a variety of purposes, including classifying messages by distinguishing between those whose value is self-contained (some humorous stories, fantasy, etc.), and those worthy of further investigation (some political rhetoric, traditional subject area studies, etc.). A main objective is for the students to evaluate messages for their major value, their critical contributions or errors in information and logic, and to demonstrate thoughtful reaction when this is both appropriate and of personal interest.

Some results

The formative evaluation supplied by teachers' responses on questionnaires about the first-grade program, the only portion implemented to date, indicated achievement of the affective as well as the cognitive and linguistic objectives. The teachers provided samples of the children's questions with every report. The teachers' and children's enthusiasm was substantiated in these samples, some of which are:

Did the boy do what Emily wanted him to do?
What kind of sounds did Jimmy hear?
Why did Danny put his clothes in one place and his toys in another?
Will Larry get a big balloon or a small balloon?
What did Mary Jane choose to play with?
What did Penelope make disappear?
How did she make it disappear?

Though these examples are presented here without association with the cognitive objectives of the lessons in which they were asked, they indicate the children's development in inquiry which is appropriate to the task at hand, relevant to their own curiosity as it was tapped by an introductory sentence, and substantial in the kinds of information it seeks from the stories.

Problems indicated in the teachers' reports for the first stage 1 unit of six lessons reflect primarily a period of pupil adjustment in becoming familiar with the procedures in this new kind of lesson.

By the third lesson, most of the children (on a scale of "all," "most," "about half," and "a fourth or less") in every classroom were volunteering to ask questions after listening to the teacher's introductory sentences about a story. Problems reported for the rest of stage 1 were a random assortment reflecting occasional difficulties caused by the size and accuracy of visual aids, inappropriate construction of introductory sentences for the objective of a story, and similar items which were remedied in revising the program for the second year of use.

On the positive effects of the program, the teachers reported in some of the following ways:

Unit 1: "Children didn't ask questions during Lesson 1, but by Lesson 3, they had no problems" (Fresno)

"By Lesson 3, the children had caught on to asking and answering questions" (Navajo)

"The Lesson 3 questions were asked with great enthusiasm, the first breakthrough in Listening." (Navajo)

Unit 6: "No difficulty achieving questioning objectives." (Fresno)

"No problems arose with respect to children's asking questions, planned or otherwise." (Fresno)

"Interesting, challenging. The children are apparently very satisfied after asking questions." (Fresno)

"The children got so much better at asking why-questions. I was pleased with their growth, especially with inference." (Navajo)

"Majority have made a great deal of progress." (Navajo)

Seventy-five percent were able to ask questions, all were able to read their own questions aloud from the chalkboard, as well as on the work-sheet." (Fresno)

On the problems encountered, here are some sample reports:

Unit 1: "At first, the children couldn't use an interrogative word to ask a question. However, this situation smoothed itself out." (Fresno)

"Some asked grammatically incorrect questions. I corrected this by saying it was a good question, then saying it correctly and having the child repeat it." (Fresno)

"The biggest problem is structure, using the wrong tense or pronoun. I'm very pleased with the children's ability to ask questions, and more relevant questions came out as the unit progressed." (Navajo)

Some teachers' affective reflections:

"I would like more lessons like this throughout the year." (Navajo)

"This is the first time in my four years of working with Navajo students in the first grade that they could ask good questions so easily. They know the difference between a question and an answer." (Navajo)

"Very effective." (Fresno)

While the intent of the questionnaires to the teachers was to gather data pertaining to the feasibility of the program, enough data were volunteered to indicate that other studies, pertaining to more than feasibility, will be possible. Among these will be a comparison of linguistic and cognitive features of questions from the rural Navajo-speaking children and the urban Spanish-speaking children.

Various aspects of the program suggest many more questions.

Conclusion

This paper has described some aspects of the background, the application, and some results of a program for primary-grade children who entered school as native speakers of Spanish or Navajo. Though the program is called "Listening," it serves several functions beyond that of fostering listening comprehension skills in the children's second language, English.

The program suggests a multitude of questions for further study. On the basis of Lambert's studies of young children being schooled in French as a second language, the potential seems likely for transfer of some skills taught in the Listening program to the children's native languages. What would be the results of testing in Navajo, in Spanish the skills taught in the second language in this program?

Does this program effect better second-language comprehension on the part of children participating in it than on the part of peers who do not participate in it?

What is the effect of the advance question-asking on children who ask the questions as contrasted with children who only listen to questions being generated by their peers?

What is the relationship of oral question-asking by the children to their inner speech?

Considering the potential for early intervention in the education of children, what would be the effects of introducing this program, or aspects of it, in the children's native language before first grade and continuing it in the second language once sufficient fluency is gained?

What would be the effects of applying some of the techniques of this program among native speakers of English in their first language?

The program's significance as a teacher education program for beginning inquiry education is suggested by the appraisals of teachers who have used it. What would be the effects of a condensed version of the Listening program for the purpose of helping teachers to recognize and encourage good questions on the part of children?

What would the learning results be like in a classroom where children spent alternate periods in practicing asking questions and in investigating a variety of resources for answers?

Summary

This paper describes the synthesis and application of research in linguistics, psychology, and pedagogy in a classroom program, a prototype model of which was successfully implemented in seven Navajo first grades during the past academic year. A revised version of the program will be implemented in twenty Navajo first grades and in six Fresno second grades during the coming year.

Bibliography

Bloom, Benjamin S., *et al. Taxonomy of Educational Objectives, Handbook 1: Cognitive Domain.* New York: David McKay Company, (1956).

Bruner, Jerome S. *The Relevance of Education.* New York: W.W. Norton and Company, (1971).

Covington, Martin V. "The Cognitive Curriculum: A Process-Oriented Approach to Education." In Jerome Helmuth, ed., New York: Brunner/Mazel, (1970), p. 491.

Duker, Sam. *Listening: Readings.* New York: The Scarecrow Press, (1966).

Guszak, Frank J. "Teacher Questioning and Reading." *The Reading Teacher* Vol. 21, No. 3 (1967), pp. 227-34.

Keller, Paul W. "Major Findings in Listening in the Past Ten Years." In Sam Duker, ed., *Listening: Readings.* New York: Scarecrow Press, (1966).

Lambert, Wallace E., M. Just, and N. Segalowitz. "Some Cognitive Consequences of Following the Curriculum of Grades One and Two in a Foreign Language." In James E. Alatis, eds., *Monograph Series on Languages and Linguistics*, No. 23. Washington, D.C.: Georgetown University Press, (1970).

Lister, E. Darlene. "The Public Speaks Out." *Los Angeles Times*, September 4, (1971), p. 4.

Mosher, Frederic A., and Joan Rigney Hornsby. "On Asking Questions." In Jerome S. Bruner *et al.*, eds., *Studies in Cognitive Growth.* New York: John Wiley and Sons, (1966), p. 86-102.

Postman, Neil, and Charles Weingartner. *Teaching as a Subversive Activity.* New York: Delacorte Press, (1969), p. 19-23.

Sanders, Norris M. *Classroom Questions, What Kinds?* New York: Harper and Row, 1966.

Toussaint, Isabella H. "A Classified Summary of Listening, 1950-1959." *Listening: Readings.* Ed. Sam Duker. New York: The Scarecrow Press, 1966, p. 157.

Vygotsky, L.S. *Thought and Language.* New York: John Wiley and Sons, 1962.

Wilson, Robert D. *Curricular Implications of the Relationship Between Language and Thought.* Paper delivered at the TESOL Conference, San Francisco, March 1970. Unpublished.

Wilt, Miriam. "Demands on the Listening Skills of Elementary School Children." *Listening: Readings.* Ed. Sam Duker. New York: Scarecrow Press. 1966.

21

Pre-Reading Skills in a Second Language or Dialect
Serafina Krear Colombani

Federally funded bilingual programs in the United States are rapidly multiplying across the nation as funds, expertise, and community interest increase. To shift from an ethnocentric monolingual curriculum to a bicentric bilingual curriculum implies a great deal more than doubling staff and efforts. Decision models for bilingual programs are nonexistent. Although Mackey (1969), Andersson and Boyer (1970), and Valencia (1969) have developed sophisticated descriptions of possible curriculum patterns, educators are still searching for clearly defined criteria for selecting a particular course of action. The most critical relationships needing clarification are in the areas of oral language, pre-reading skills, and developmental reading.

It is the purpose of this paper to suggest that there should be a relationship between the sociolinguistic reality of the school community, the satisfaction or dissatisfaction of community members with that reality, and decisions regarding the language or dialect for pre-reading and reading development. Decision models derived from a sociolinguistic perspective for biliteracy programs will be presented.

At the 1970 TESOL convention, Joshua Fishman's paper clearly presented the rationale for deriving bilingual programs from a sociolinguistic assessment of the community. His concept of using descriptions of communities in maintenance or language transfer patterns as a sound basis for curriculum development seems logical. This investigator's translation of Fishman's suggestion led to the development of a concept currently being field tested in a Title VII project in Sacramento, California, "The Valley Intercultural Project."

It was hypothesized that non-English speakers living in a community of language shift would find it difficult to meet their needs whereas non-English speakers living in a language-maintenance community could participate meaningfully within their respective communities without knowing English. It follows then that the bilingual reality in a community has a direct relationship to the urgency or lack of it for learning English to meet personal needs. That is to say, in a community of language transfer children need to learn English efficiently and immediately. A program designed to mirror the bilingual reality of such a community would give greater emphasis to English as a second language or dialect than to dialect or mother-tongue development. On the other hand, in a language-maintenance community, where there is no urgency to learn English, a greater emphasis can be given to dialect or mother tongue development. Pre-reading and reading skills, then, would be developed in English in a transfer community and in Language X or Dialect X in a maintenance community. The development of an oral language, pre-reading, and reading program as just described is both simplistic in nature and arrogant in spirit, for although it has a sociolinguistic base it is derived from the ivory tower.

A more sophisticated approach would consider the wishes of community members before making such curricular decisions. A grass-roots approach would involve community members not only in assessing the bilingual reality but also in deciding whether they wish to mirror that reality in the biliteracy program or not. The alternate decision would be based on dissatisfaction with the reality that there was an urgency to learn English or that there was no urgency and there should be. The Sociolinguistic Decision Model (Diagram I) indicates the alternate choices of maintenance or transfer programs either for maintenance or transfer communities. This model reflects the hypothesis that the bilingual curriculum may have a strong enough impact to change the bilingual reality within the community.

On the following pages four models (Diagrams II, III, IV, V) representing the four alternatives in Diagram I are presented. The models for transfer communities are delayed reading models; pre-reading skills being developed in English are extended into the middle of Grade I. Pre-reading skills developed in the native language for maintenance communities should preclude the need for delaying the introduction of the printed word. The last three diagrams are suggested models for the development of pre-reading skills and reading for dialect speakers. If print is to be introduced in the non-standard dialect, pre-reading skills must be developed in dialect. Again, there is no reason to delay the introduction to print. Models suggesting delayed reading for dialect speakers take into account the additional time needed to teach oral language skills and pre-reading skills in the standard dialect or new language.

In the models, attention is directed to the following premises:

SOCIOLINGUISTIC DECISION MODEL

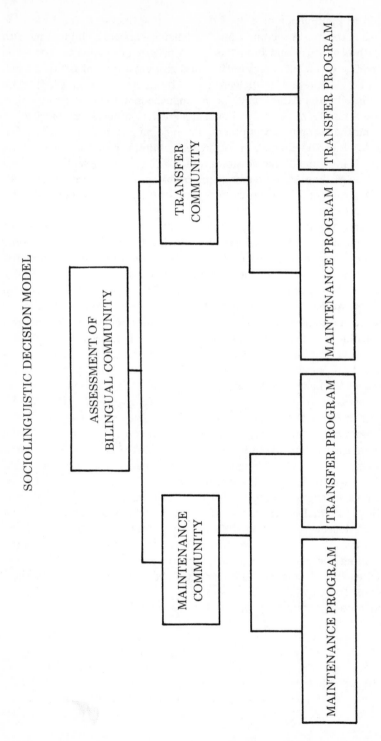

DIAGRAM I

1) A maintenance program results in equal time distribution; that is 50% of the school day will be spent in English and 50% in Language X or Dialect X.
2) A transfer program results in an increased emphasis in English; that is, approximately 75% of the school day will be spent in English and the remainder in Language X or Dialect X.
3) None of the models presented here transfer totally to English; such programs are not being discredited by omission. By Title VII guidelines they are not fundable at the point where the transition to English is complete.
4) All models adhere to the principle that pre-reading skills must be developed in the same language or dialect selected for the introduction of reading.
5) Models show transition patterns over a four-year period.
6) A basic principle underlying the models is that in a transfer community, the non-English speaker cannot meet his needs. The pressure to learn English in such a community must be reflected in the emphasis given to ESL.
7) All models adhere to the principle that during the first year of school, concepts must be presented in the student's native language or dialect. At least 75% of the time allotted for concept development is shown to be in the native language. The instructional model (Preview-Review — Diagram IX) presented later clarifies the relationship between second-language principles and concept development that must be considered in order to comply with USOE Title VII Guidelines which specify that at least one academic area must be presented in the second language.
8) All models in which reading is introduced in the second language or dialect are delayed reading models; this is indicated with an arrow drawn into the middle of first grade with a continuation of pre-reading skills supported by heavy emphasis on oral second-language development.
9) None of the models for English speakers show reading introduced in the second language. This possibility for experimental study is not discredited by omission; the models for X speakers may be applied to English speakers to validate or invalidate the following hypotheses:
   a) If the phoneme/grapheme correspondence of language X is better than English, English speakers might have greater success in learning to decode by being introduced to reading in language X in a delayed reading program.
   b) English speakers in the St. Lambert School near Montreal (d'Anglejan and Tucker, 1970) and Spanish speakers in the Hamilton School in Mexico City (Andersson and Boyer, 1970) learned to read in the second language successfully. English speakers in the United States having the "power" language and none of the identity problems of non-English speakers in this country may learn to read

successfully in the second language if the motivation is based on solidarity rather than power.

10) Models presented for E and X speakers are based on the assumption that the languages spoken natively are not non-standard dialects (Diagrams II, III, IV, V).

11) Models for non-standard dialect speakers are presented for X speakers only. However, the models should be applicable for bilingual programs where English as a Second Language is being taught (Diagrams VI, VII, VIII).

12) The alternatives presented in the dialect models are:

a) To introduce reading in dialect with a transition to reading the standard dialect before reading English. Decisions with respect to dialect reading materials must be made on the following possibilities:

1. Translations into dialect or existing materials representing dominant culture.

2. Materials written in dialect representing dominant culture, local culture or a combination, that is, heterocultural materials.

3. Materials elicited from the learners in a language experience approach representing ethnocentric, bicentric, or polycentric views depending on the students and the topics.

b) Delayed reading until the middle of the first grade with the following alternatives:

1. Reading in the standard dialect with heavy emphasis on oral second-dialect development.

2. Reading in the second language with heavy emphasis on ESL.

13) Teaching non-standard dialects to standard speakers is not discredited by omission. Such a bidialectal or biloquial program is based on the belief that if a student lives in a bidialectal community the most efficient approach to changing negative attitudes about non-standard dialects is to teach non-standard dialects to standard speakers where the non-standard dialect is functional. Again the models presented provide enough examples for adaptations to non-standard E or X for standard speakers of E and X.

The preceding models graphically describe the alternative routes for articulating oral-language development, pre-reading skills, and introduction to print in bilingual programs. Briefly the alternatives are:

I. For speakers of Standard X:

A. ESL; Pre-reading in E; Delayed introduction to print in E.

B. Native-language development; Pre-reading in X; Introduction to print at beginning of Grade I or earlier in X.

II. For speakers of Non-standard X:

A. ESL; Pre-reading in E; Delayed introduction to print in E.

B. XSD; Pre-reading in X; Delayed introduction to print in X.

C. Dialect development; Pre-reading in dialect; Introduction to print at beginning of Grade I or earlier in dialect.

Pre-reading skills for speakers of English are designed to prepare a child to meet the language which he speaks in print. Many of the activities designed to prepare a speaker of English to read English have little if anything to do with preparing a Spanish speaker to read Spanish. The grapheme/phoneme fit in Spanish precludes the necessity of many pre-reading activities for English. It is critical that when the decision is made to introduce reading in standard or non-standard dialects of non-English tongues that teachers be given in-service training specifically designed for the language or dialect to be taught.

The following models show a relationship between the amount of time used for language development and the amount of time used for concept development. The model which follows clarifies the relationship between language and concept development. (Diagram IX)

The Preview-Review Model is presented in graphic form as a method of grouping for instruction; the basic principle is to develop concepts in an introductory, brief preview lesson. The main lesson is pictured as a larger box to indicate a fuller development of the concepts presented in the preview lesson; the main lesson is presented to a mixed language group. The review lesson is taught in the second language; this implies a measure of linguistic control in the earliest stages of language development. The model is based on the assumption that the student learns best in his native language; it allows for either the English speaker or the X speaker to receive a preview lesson in his stronger language when the main lesson is in his weaker language. The model may be used for dialect speakers in bilingual programs.

MAINTENANCE Program

MAINTENANCE Community

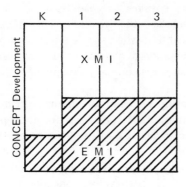

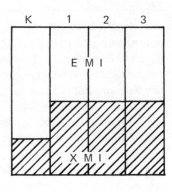

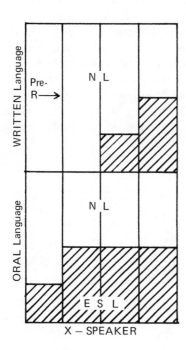

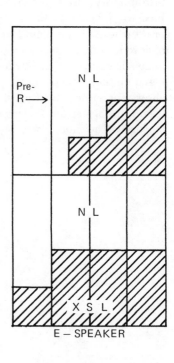

☐	Native Language	

▨	Second Language	

Pre-R	Pre-Reading Skills
ESL	English as a Second Language
XSL	X as a Second Language
EMI	English as a Medium of Instruction
XMI	Language X as a Medium of Instruction

DIAGRAM II

TRANSFER Program

MAINTENANCE Community

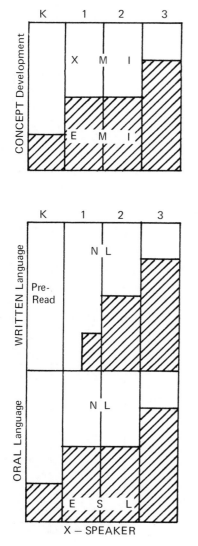

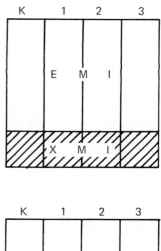

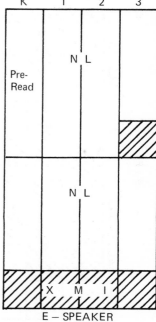

X — SPEAKER   E — SPEAKER

☐ Native Language	Pre-R	Pre-Reading Skills
	ESL	English as a Second Language
	XSL	X as a Second Language
▧ Second Language	EMI	English as a Medium of Instruction
	XMI	Language X as a Medium of Instruction

DIAGRAM III

MAINTENANCE Program

for

TRANSFER Community

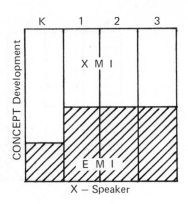

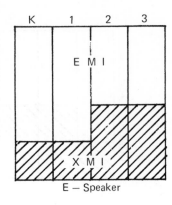

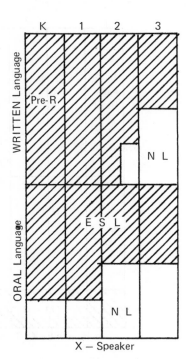

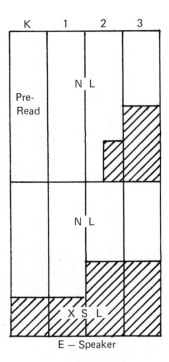

DELAYED READING

	Native Language

	Second Language

Pre-R	Pre-Reading Skills
ESL	English as a Second Language
XSL	X as a Second Language
EMI	English as a Medium of Instruction
XMI	Language X as a Medium of Instruction

DIAGRAM IV

TRANSFER Program

TRANSFER Community

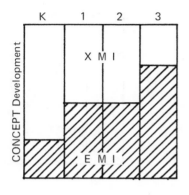

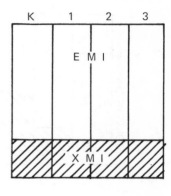

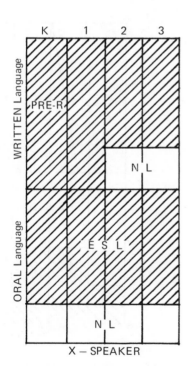

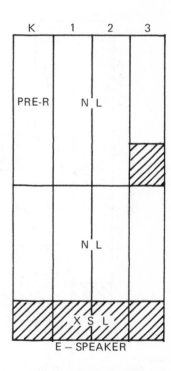

X – SPEAKER

E – SPEAKER

DELAYED READING

Native Language	
Second Language	

Pre-R	Pre-Reading Skills
ESL	English as a Second Language
XSL	X as a Second Language
EMI	English as a Medium of Instruction
XMI	Language X as a Medium of Instruction

DIAGRAM V

**MAINTENANCE Program
MAINTENANCE Community**

**TRANSFER Program
MAINTENANCE Community**

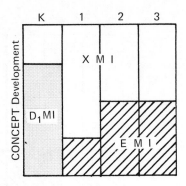

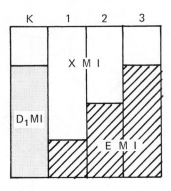

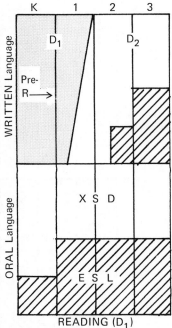

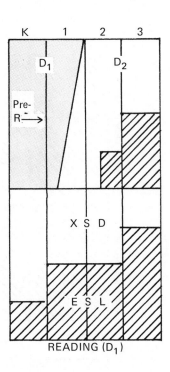

Non-Standard X (Dialect₁)

Standard X (Dialect₂)

Standard English

ESL	English as a Second Language
XSD	X as a Second Dialect
D₁MI	Dialect as a Medium of Instruction
XMI	X as a Medium of Instruction
EMI	English as a Medium of Instruction

DIAGRAM VI

MAINTENANCE Program
MAINTENANCE Community

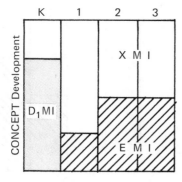

MAINTENANCE Program
TRANSFER Community

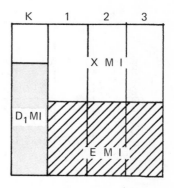

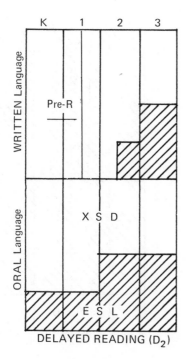

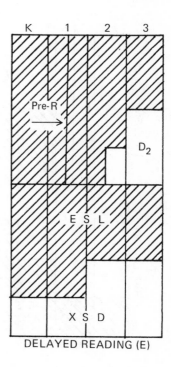

Non-Standard X (Dialect₁)

Standard X (Dialect₂)

Standard English

ESL	English as a Second Language
XSD	X as a Second Dialect
D₁MI	Dialect as a Medium of Instruction
XMI	X as a Medium of Instruction
EMI	English as a Medium of Instruction

DIAGRAM VII

TRANSFER Program
MAINTENANCE Community

TRANSFER Program
TRANSFER Community

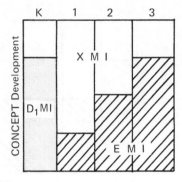

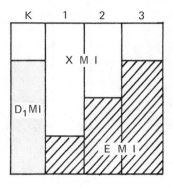

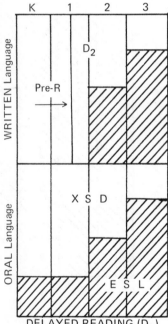

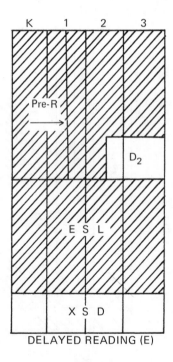

Non-Standard X (Dialect₁)

Standard X (Dialect₂)

Standard English

ESL	English as a Second Language
XSD	X as a Second Dialect
D_1MI	Dialect as a Medium of Instruction
XMI	X as a Medium of Instruction
EMI	English as a Medium of Instruction

DIAGRAM VIII

PREVIEW-REVIEW
INSTRUCTIONAL MODEL FOR CONCEPT DEVELOPMENT

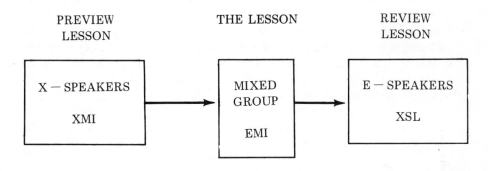

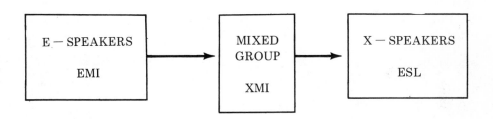

Preview: Concepts are introduced in student's mother tongue.

Review: At the earliest stage linguistic control is necessary when concepts are presented in the second language.

EMI: English as a Medium of Instruction.

XMI: Language X as a Medium of Instruction.

XSL: Language X as a Second Language.

ESL: English as a Second Language.

DIAGRAM IX

Summary

A sociolinguistic perspective for teaching reading in bilingual programs begins with an assessment of the bilingual reality of the school community and the community wishes for attempting to maintain or change that reality through the bilingual program. Decisions to introduce reading in the prestige dialect of a non-English tongue, the local dialect either of the English or non-English tongue, or of standard English affect the pre-reading program as well as the oral second language or dialect programs. Models will be presented for delayed reading and dialect reading programs based on sociolinguistic descriptions of the community and assessment of community wishes. Implications from the literature on the teaching of reading in non-standard English dialects as they relate to non-standard dialects of non-English tongues will be discussed.

There is a trend toward emphasis on the development of the receptive band of language for second-language learners which must be analyzed with respect to pre-reading skills.

GLOSSARY

Bicentric. The term "bicentric" is used to mean not ethnocentric. Although the word was not coined for this study, its use in describing a cultural viewpoint is presented here as a new term.

*Bicognitive. The term "bicognitive" refers to a person capable of thinking in two languages or dialects and solving problems in either language or dialect independently.

Bicultural. The term "bicultural" refers to a person who values the heritage represented in two language groups without preference and behaves appropriately in either situation.

Bidialectal. The term "bidialectal" refers to a person who understands and speaks two dialects of the same language. Biloquial is an equivalent term found in the literature.

Bilingual. For the purposes of this study, the term "bilingual" is used to describe a person who understands and speaks two different languages.

Bilingual Education. The term "bilingual education" is used to denote any educational program which includes bilingualism as a performance objective of instruction.

Biliterate. The term "biliterate" refers to a person who has the ability to read and write two languages.

*Heterocultural. The term "heterocultural" refers to a person who values the heritage represented in two dialect groups without preference and behaves appropriately in either situation.

*Heteroliterate. The term "heteroliterate" refers to a person who reads and writes two dialects of the same language and uses each appropriately.

Maintenance pattern. In this analysis, the term "maintenance pattern" (Mackey, 1969, p. 8) will be used to describe the time distribution, whether different or equal, of a bilingual school having the maintenance of both languages as an objective.

*Multicognitive. The term "multicognitive" refers to a person capable of thinking in several languages and/or dialects and solving problems in each independently.

Multicultural. The term "multicultural" refers to a person who values the heritage represented in several language and/or dialect groups and behaves appropriately in each situation.

Multilingual. The term "multilingual" refers to a person who understands and speaks several languages and/or dialects. Polyglot is an equivalent term found in the literature.

*Multiliterate. The term "multiliterate" refers to a person who reads and writes several language and/or dialects and uses each appropriately.

*Polycentric. The term "polycentric" is used to describe a non-ethnocentric viewpoint representative of several cultures.

Transfer pattern. In this analysis, in order to describe an abrupt or gradual shift from one medium of instruction to another, the term "transfer pattern" will be used. (Mackey 1969, p. 8)

---

*These terms were coined by the author for the purposes of this study.

Bibliography

Andersson, Theodore, and Mildred Boyer. "The Program" and "Needed Action and Research." Two chapters from *Bilingual Schooling in the United States.* An abstract from a document prepared under contract with the U.S. Office of Education. Austin: Southwest Educational Development Laboratory, (1970).

Baratz, Joan C. "Beginning Readers for Speakers of Divergent Dialects." In J. Allen Figurel, ed., *Reading Goals for the Disadvantaged.* Newark: International Reading Association, (1970).

Baratz, Joan C., and Roger W. Shuy (eds.). *Teaching Black Children to Read.* Washington, D.C.: Center for Applied Linguistics, (1969).

d'Anglejan, Alison, and G.R. Tucker. *The St. Lambert Program of Home-School Language Switch.* Montreal, Quebec: McGill University, (1970). (ERIC ED 040 631).

Fasold, Ralph W. "Orthography in Reading Materials for Black English Speaking Children." In Joan C. Baratz and Roger W. Shuy, eds., *Teaching Black Children to Read.* Washington, D.C.: Center for Applied Linguistics, (1969).

Fishman, Joshua A. "Bilingual Education in Sociolinguistic Perspective." Address at the Fourth Annual Convention of Teachers of English to Speakers of Other Languages. San Francisco, California, March 20, (1970).

Goodman, Kenneth S. "Dialect Barriers to Reading Comprehension." In Joan C. Baratz and Roger W. Shuy, eds., *Teaching Black Children to Read.* Washington, D.C.: Center for Applied Linguistics, (1969).

Hillerich, Robert L. "ERMAS: A Beginning Reading Program for Mexican-American Children." *National Elementary Principal,* 50 (1970), pp. 88-84.

Horn, Thomas D. "Three Methods of Developing Reading Readiness in Spanish-Speaking Children in First Grade." *Reading Teacher,* 20 (1966), pp. 38-42.

Krear, Serafina. "A Proposed Framework Derived from an Analysis of 1969-1970 Title VII Bilingual Education Proposals in California." Unpublished dissertation. Berkeley: University of California, (1971).

Mackey, William F. *Language Teaching Analysis.* London: Longmans, (1965).

——. *A Typology of Bilingual Education.* Prepared for a Research Conference on Bilingual Education, June 30, (1969).

Modiano, Nancy. *A Comparative Study of Two Approaches to the Teaching of Reading in the National Language.* New York University, (1966) (ERIC ED 010 049).

O'Donnell, C. Michael P. "The Effectiveness of an Informal Conceptual-Language Program in Developing Reading Readiness in the

Kindergarten." In Carl Braun, eds., *Language, Reading and the Communication Process.* Newark, Delaware: International Reading Association, (1971).

Rivers, Wilga M. *The Psychologist and the Foreign-Language Teacher.* Chicago: The University of Chicago Press, (1964).

Rosen, Carl L. "Needed Research in Language and Reading Instructional Problems of Spanish-Speaking Children." In J. Allen Figurel, ed., *Reading Goals for the Disadvantaged.* Newark International Reading Association, (1970).

Saville, Muriel R., and Rudolph C. Troike (eds.). *A Handbook for Bilingual Education.* Washington, D.C.: Center for Applied Linguistics, January, (1970).

Stewart, William A. "On the Use of Negro Dialect in the Teaching of Reading." In Joan C. Baratz and Roger W. Shuy, eds., *Teaching Black Children to Read.* Washington, D.C.: Center for Applied Linguistics, 1969.

Thonis, Eleanor. *Bilingual Education for Mexican-American Children.* California State Department of Education, (1967).

Ulibarrí, Horacio. *Bilingual Education: A Handbook for Education.* Dallas, Texas: Southern Methodist University, (1970).

UNESCO. *The Use of Vernacular Languages in Education.* Paris: UNESCO, (1953).

Valencia, Atilano A. *Bilingual/Bicultural Education.* Albuquerque: Southwest Cooperative Educational Laboratory, Inc., April, (1969).

Wolfram, Walt. "Sociolinguistic Alternatives in Teaching Reading to Non-Standard Speakers." *Reading Research Quarterly, 6 (1970), pp. 9-33.*

22

Developing Curriculum for Bilingual Education
Ralph Robinett

Emergence of a need

From 1963 when renewed interest in public bilingual education gave impetus to a handful of bilingual programs to 1967 when federal monies made it possible to subsidize more than 70 such experiments, the home language held a low position in curriculum priorities. In 1970, with nearly double the 1967 centers under Title VII ESEA and numerous others funded from various sources, the need for home language materials caused the Bilingual Education Programs Branch of the Office of Education to fund multiple efforts to provide curricular materials.

Materials Acquisition Project

One of three major efforts to provide curriculum support materials is the Materials Acquisition Project, located in San Diego. The function of this project is to identify commercially available materials and, with the help of cooperating centers, determine their suitability for dissemination on a larger scale.

This solution to material needs has the obvious advantage of immediate availability of a wide range of material which has been developed by specialists in countries where the home language is the medium of instruction.

Unfortunately from our point of view, such materials often assume a **socioeconomic and geopolitical background markedly different from those** of the target populations in bilingual programs in the United States. The underlying assumptions in such materials tend to make them the least relevant to the needs and interests of the pupils and communities we must serve.

Materials so acquired will serve to great advantage as supplementary resources, though they tend to be fragmentary in a situation which demands as well mutually supportive curricula. Limitations of such resources do not negate their potential contributions.

National Consortia for Bilingual Education

A second major effort to help fill the materials void centers around the refinement of curriculum produced at the local level in the many bilingual projects now in operation. Among the limitations of grass roots curriculum efforts in bilingual education thus far has been the built-in duplication of effort in areas which are not necessarily areas where uniqueness is a critical factor. A further problem in the long range aspirations for such materials stems from the limited resources local materials development components have had at their disposal in the production of their materials.

This second major effort has been undertaken in Fort Worth by the National Consortia for Bilingual Education, among whose functions is to identify promising local materials. Once identified, and with the help of cooperating centers, such materials can be further developed as necessary and made available to other centers seeking curriculum support.

As in the case of the Materials Acquisition Project, the National Consortia offers promise of early availability of a wide range of materials at all levels, and, in addition, the critical attribute of greater relevance to the target populations.

Spanish Curricula Development Center

A third major effort to provide home language resource materials is in the actual production of curriculum guides and support materials, and to this end the Bilingual Education Programs Branch funded the Spanish Curricula Development Center in Miami. The Center is charged with the development of multidisciplinary resource kits to help support the major areas of instruction in Spanish at the primary level.

Equally important to the product for which the Center is responsible is the process by which the product is developed. In this instance, as the product is being developed for national use, it became immediately important to build in credibility conditions to help ensure that the product would ultimately be acceptable as well as useful resource material for the three groups for whom it is being designed: Mexican-American, Puerto Rican, and Cuban. The first condition was to form an Advisory Council clearly representative of the populations to be served. The second was to recruit staff with similar ethnic and geographic qualifications. The third was to build in a feedback and revision process which would ensure that the final product was responsive to the ethnic and geographic needs of the pupils under widely varying conditions.

At present the Spanish Curricula Development Center is organized into ten teams. Five develop the basic instructional guides in Language Arts, Social Science, Science/Math, Fine Arts, and Spanish-Second Language. Three contribute directly to kit production in the development of assessment activities, the editing of manuscript, and in kit manufacture. Supporting the production effort is an administrative team, and responsible for dissemination and feedback is a field team. Evaluation is independent of other teams of the project, both in its formative and summative dimensions. In each team in which decisions are made relative to curriculum content, every effort has been made to maintain an ethnic balance in staff distribution.

During the first semester of operation in 1970-71, most of the time was devoted to staff development and to analysis of available curricula which might contribute to the development of materials by the Center. The second semester was devoted to the production of Curricula Kits 1-8, in order to have materials ready for field testing in the fall of 1971. During 1971-72, the Center will produce Kits 9-16 and 17-24, corresponding to the second half of the first grade and the first half of the second grade. Broadly speaking, the Center is committed to producing materials one semester ahead of their use in field trial centers, 48 kits in all.

CANBBE

The Curriculum Adaptation Network for Bilingual Bicultural Education (CANBBE) was funded in the summer of 1971 with monies from Title VII ESEA and from the Hearst Foundation. The function of CANBBE is two-fold: to facilitate the feedback process leading to the development of regional editions of the Curricula Kits, and to create supplementary and complementary materials which are beyond the resources and commitment of the Spanish Curricula Development Center.

With executive offices functioning through the National Urban Coalition and four regional offices attached to local education agencies in San Diego, Milwaukee, San Antonio, and New York, CANBBE is fiscally and administratively independent of the Spanish Curricula Development Center. However, the two projects do have interlocking Advisory Councils, and the success of the total effort requires a high degree of cooperation between both projects.

Contrary to the Spanish Curricula Development Center, which has a large full-time staff, CANBBE maintains a small staff in each regional center, leaving larger reserves for contracting on a short-term basis a wide range of highly specialized personnel in each region who would otherwise not be available.

Kit Components

Each of the curricula kits as projected is designed to serve as core resource material for approximately two weeks. Central to each kit are guides for five areas of instruction: Language Arts — Vernacular, Social Science, Science/Mathematics, Fine Arts, and Spanish-Second Language. To support the teachers in their evaluation of pupils' progress, each kit includes assessment activities.

As the instructional and assessment activities are carried out, the teachers will need a variety of audio-visual and manipulative materials. Those provided in each kit are a supplement of illustrations, a ditto packet for duplicating multiple copies of visuals and individual seatwork, and a tape cassette presenting songs and background music. Accompanying the first kit is a packet with two puppets for use in stimulating oral language development, and accompanying subsequent kits are multiple copies of pupils' books for use in the Language Arts and Spanish as a Second Language strands.

To facilitate the orientation of teachers and administrators involved in the field testing of the kits, a Product Design, or overview, is provided. To facilitate the feedback and revision process, a Field Review is supplied for each kit.

Summary

With the expansion of bilingual education, the need for curricular resource materials in the home language has increased proportionately. Neither curriculum components of bilingual projects nor commercial interests have been able to keep pace in curriculum development. To help meet the growing demand, the Bilingual Education Programs Branch of the U.S. Office of Education has set in motion acquisition and production projects of national scope. One such project is the Spanish Curricula Development Center, which is charged with producing Spanish curricula materials for the primary level. As the materials are written, they are piloted in local bilingual programs, then revised and prepared for distribution to other bilingual projects serving as field trial centers in various parts of the country. With the assistance of a curriculum adaptation network supported by federal and private foundation monies, these preliminary materials produced as a general edition will be converted to multiple editions which reflect the inputs of local and regional interests.

INSTRUCTIONAL GUIDES

1 — LANGUAGE ARTS STRAND

2 — SPANISH SL STRAND

3 — SOCIAL SCIENCE STRAND

4 — SCIENCE/MATH STRAND

5 — FINE ARTS STRAND

SUPPORT MATERIALS

6 — ASSESSMENT ACTIVITIES

7 — SUPPLEMENT

8 — DITTO PACKET

INSERVICE AND FEEDBACK

9 — PRODUCT DESIGN

10 — FIELD REVIEW

Organizing Threads

The instructional strands in the curricula kits are unified by four organizing threads: theme, basic concepts, processes, and strategies. There are four basic themes in the sixteen kits for Grade 1: classroom, family, school, and community. Spiraling questions guide the child in each thematic context.

The processes commonly associated with modern science programs are interwoven through all the instructional strands. These are: observing, using time/space relationships, classifying, using numbers, measuring, communicating, predicting, and inferring.

Strategies in "discovery learning" often associated with social science programs are also reflected in all the instructional strands. These are: concept development, interpretation of data, interpretation of feelings, attitudes, and values, and application of generalizations.

A limited number of high-level abstractions, or basic concepts, such as variability, interdependence, conflict, and change, drawn from social science and science, form the basic conceptual framework of the total program.

Language Arts Strand

The Language Arts-Vernacular Strand is designed to extend the language that Spanish-dominant children bring from their homes through structured and unstructured oral language experiences, at the same time recognizing and developing respect for regional dialects.

The strand also provides structured and unstructured reading experiences designed to develop systematically Spanish decoding skills, skills prerequisite to effective use of reading in the content areas, and habits and tastes in the reading of Spanish literary-type materials.

In each kit the activities are divided roughly into clusters of three, each cluster being planned for approximately sixty minutes of instruction. The first activity in each cluster focuses on oral language development and language experience reading. The second activity focuses on systematic treatment of the sound-symbol correspondences through the use of the chalkboard, pupils' books, and independent seatwork. The third activity presents orally a variety of folk tales and rhymes, and focuses on the development of skills of comprehension and interpretation on the oral level as well as in connection with the reading program.

Social Science Strand

The pupils' ability to understand their environment and in some measure influence it is a critical factor in developing success-oriented learners. From this premise, the Social Science Strand in each kit is designed to help pupils discover basic generalizations of the social sciences on an elementary level and to familiarize pupils with the process of inquiry so they may independently discover and order the rapidly changing world around them.

ORGANIZING THREADS — KITS 1-4

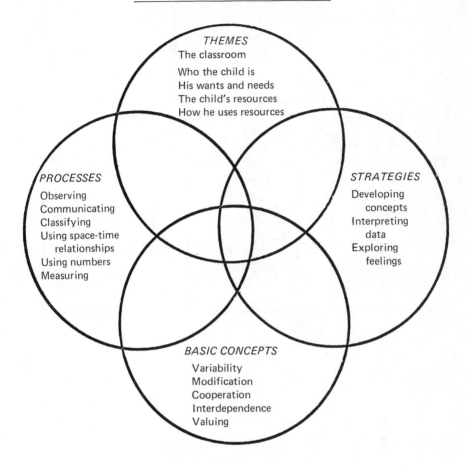

THEMES
The classroom

Who the child is
His wants and needs
The child's resources
How he uses resources

PROCESSES

Observing
Communicating
Classifying
Using space-time
  relationships
Using numbers
Measuring

STRATEGIES

Developing
  concepts
Interpreting
  data
Exploring
  feelings

BASIC CONCEPTS

Variability
Modification
Cooperation
Interdependence
Valuing

Themes:
such as classroom, family

Processes:
such as using time/space relationships

Strategies:
such as interpretation of feelings, attitudes, values

Basic Concepts:
such as variability

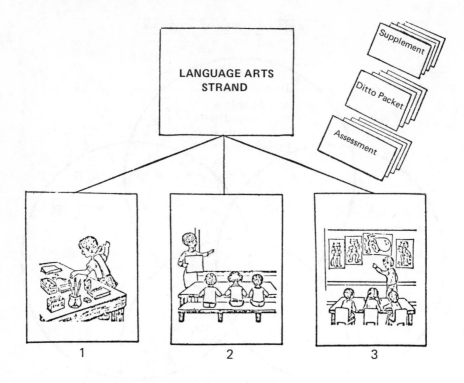

1   Oral Language Development
structured language practice
unstructured language practice

2   Reading
language experience reading
systematic practice in decoding
writing practice as reinforcement

3 Comprehension and Interpretation
with languages experience reading
with structured reading
as part of a listening program

The high level abstractions which serve as organizing threads throughout the strand connect important generalizations, or basic concepts. Specific facts are presented as illustrations of basic concepts rather than as ends in themselves.

Concepts are revisited, resulting in a spiral development. This spiral is exemplified in the Grade 1 kits by the recurring questions: *who the child is, what the wants and needs of the child are, what the resources of the child are,* and *how the child uses his resources,* in each thematic context: classroom, family, school, community.

Each guide in the Social Science Strand contains ten activities, designed for approximately twenty minutes of instruction each.

Science/Mathematics Strand

The Science/Mathematics Strand represents an attempt to blend two areas of study into an interdisciplinary program, each contributing to reinforce the other. The unifying elements are the basic processes common to both disciplines: observing, communicating, classifying, using time/space relationships, using numbers, measuring predicting, and inferring.

In the Science/Mathematics Strand, as in the Social Science Strand, specific facts and many concepts are presented as illustrations rather than ends in themselves. In this case they serve to develop the several processes enumerated previously. The conceptual content and learning behaviors of this strand, along with those of Social Science, form the conceptual foundation for all the strands in the Curricula Kit series.

Each guide in the Science/Mathematics Strand has twenty instructional activities, each planned for fifteen to twenty minutes of instruction. At appropriate points in each guide, review activities are provided to ensure needed reinforcement. The approach to these learning activities is pupil-centered, and provides abundant opportunities for doing as well as talking.

Fine Arts strand

The Fine Arts Strand is essentially a music program, designed to reflect a wide range of musical traditions. Many of the songs are of Hispanic-American origin, while others are of traditional international origin. However, the strand includes other dimensions, such as reinforcement of language arts through rhyme and dramatization, and reinforcement of the social science themes and concepts.

The music activities are usually eight in number, and are planned for twenty-minute periods of instruction. They focus on the basic music elements of rhythm, melody, form, and interpretation. The activities include experiences in music appreciation, singing, construction and use of simple musical instruments, rhythmic expression, creation of rhythms or movements in time with music, and simple folkloric dances.

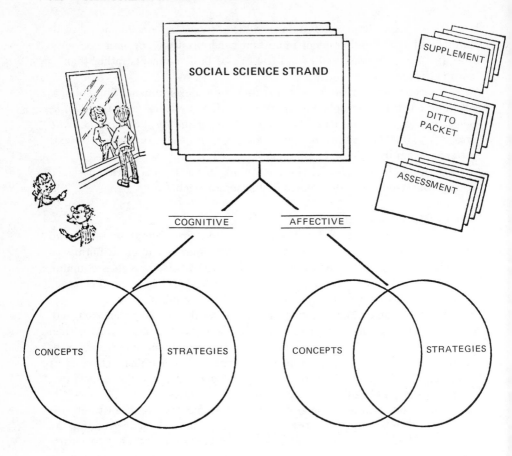

Basic Concepts

variability	differences	power
conflict	societal control	change
causality	interdependence	tradition
cooperation	modification	valuing

Strategies

concept development
interpretation of data
interpretation of feelings, attitudes, and values
application of generalizations

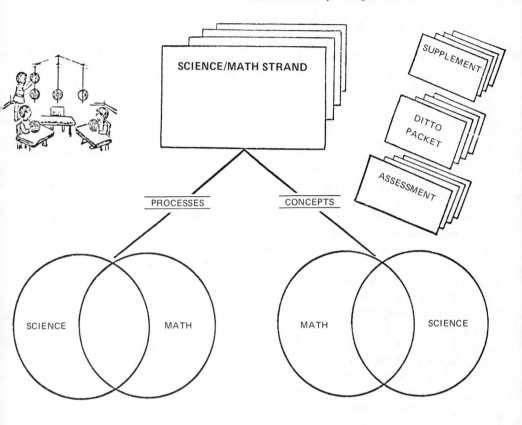

Processes
—————

observing   using time/space relationships
classifying   predicting
measuring   inferring
communicating
using numbers

Concepts
—————

from science, such as colors
from math, such as set

In the initial kits, art activities are included in the Fine Arts Guide. These art activities are designed primarily to familiarize the pupils with the materials they will be using in art activities throughout the day. In subsequent kits, art is included functionally in the development of all the instructional strands.

Spanish-Second Language Strand

The Spanish as a Second Language Strand is designed to help provide the English-dominant child the Spanish structures and vocabulary he will need for effective communication in a bilingual environment. The activities are designed to help the child build concepts in his new language through formal and informal language experiences. Initially all of the activities are oral, but as the child becomes familiar with decoding in his own language, he is introduced to reading in Spanish.

In the development of activities, the Spanish as a Second Language Strand draws heavily on and thus reinforces basic concepts and learning behaviors which are presented in other strands. As the learner gains minimum control over structures and vocabulary which can be utilized for this purpose, the second language begins to provide the child with an additional medium for learning.

In the early kits, the Spanish as a Second Language Strand has ten activities in each guide, planned for twenty to thirty minutes of instruction. As the child is introduced to Spanish reading, additional activities are provided, but with a balance maintained in favor of oral language development before reading.

Assessment Activities

The Assessment Activities are designed to sample pupils' progress and to reinforce previous learning.

In Language Arts — Vernacular, the categories sampled are oral language development, language experience reading, sound and letter recognition, word recognition, reading by structures, and comprehension and interpretation skiils.

In Social Science, the categories sampled are concepts from the affective domain and from the cognitive domain, as well as the learning strategies characteristic of discovery learning.

In Science/Mathematics, the categories sampled are concepts from science, concepts from mathematics, and the processes common to both disciplines.

In Fine Arts, the categories sampled are the recognition of musical elements: rhythm, form, melody and interpretation, and the production of music: singing and playing rhythm instruments.

In Spanish as a Second Language, the categories sampled are first structure and vocabulary. As the new language becomes a tool, cultural and

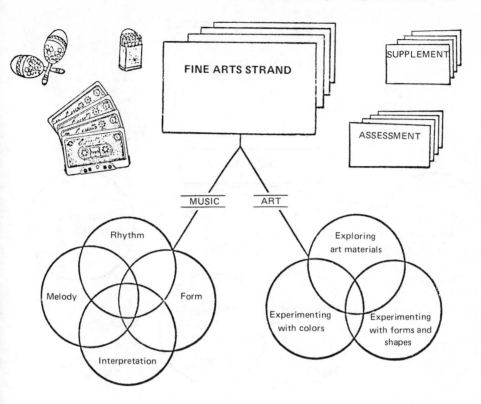

Music

Rhythm   Form
Melody   Interpretation

Concepts
----
from Language Arts
from Social Science

Learning Behaviors
----
processes
strategies

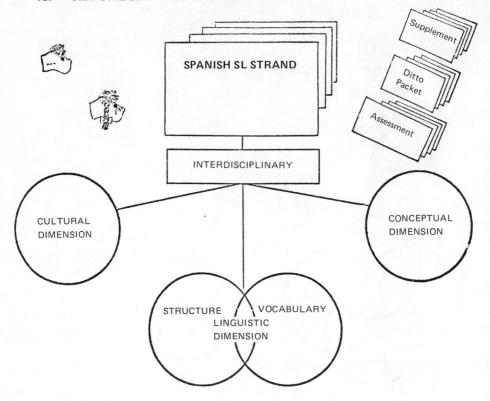

Language

aural-oral
reading
writing reinforcement

Concepts

for Social Science
from Science/Math
from Fine Arts

Learning Behaviors
processes
strategies

conceptual content are also tested.

Piloting, Field Testing

As the kits are produced, activities are piloted in local schools cooperating with the production teams. Either the writer or the classroom teacher may carry out the activity, the other serving as observer. Based on this experience, activities are modified, edited, and sent out to field trial centers.

The field trial centers are of two types, formal and informal. No regular visits are made to the informal centers by SCDC staff. To the twenty formal centers, four visits are made during the year. The visits provide opportunity to give orientation on the several strands in each unit of four kits, and opportunity to clarify doubts and receive preliminary reactions leading toward kit revision. The visits also provide opportunity to visit classrooms and gather direct impressions of teachers on strengths and weaknesses of kits which have already been used. And equally important, the visits provide the machinery through which the production team's associates assist local and Miami evaluation personnel in collecting data on the conditions under which the material is used and the results achieved under those conditions.

Approximately 150 teachers and 4,000 pupils are anticipated in field testing during 1971-72.

Revision, Regional Editions

In keeping with the Center's commitment to produce materials which will be responsive to local needs, the revision after the first year's field trial will be a process of converting the preliminary edition into regional editions. The result will be a Far West Edition reflecting feedback primarily from California, a Southwest Edition reflecting feedback from Texas, New Mexico, and Arizona, a Puerto Rican Edition reflecting feedback from the Northeast, and a revised General Edition reflecting feedback from the mixed populations in the Midwest.

The revision plan provides for primary input to be collected through the resources of CANBBE and from the Center's own feedback process as it interacts with the field trial centers. The data will be analyzed and proposals for changes for each edition reviewed by an appropriate ethnic review committee within the Center. Changes within the commitments and resources of the Center will then be made by the editing team and the new editions channeled back into the field trial centers for further use.

In addition to the regional editions mentioned above, the Center will develop a Cuban Edition for use in areas in which Cuban-background pupils are the dominant Spanish-speaking group to be served.

Project Evaluation

Evaluation in the Spanish Curricula Development Center has an internal

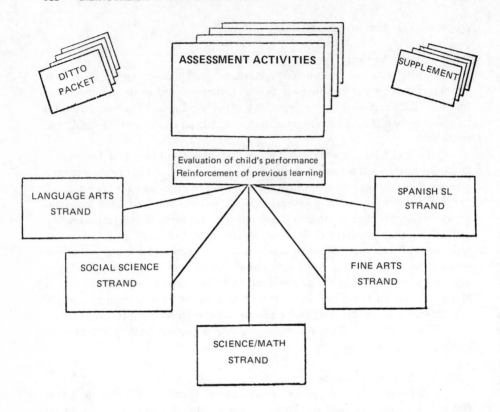

Language Arts
oral language
reading
comprehension
interpretation

Social Science
concept
strategies

Spanish SL
structure
vocabulary
culture
concepts

Fine Arts
recognition
production

Science/Math
concepts
processes

FORMAL FIELD TRIAL CENTERS

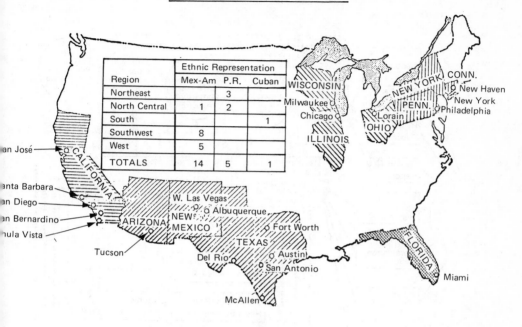

Region	Ethnic Representation		
	Mex-Am	P.R.	Cuban
Northeast		3	
North Central	1	2	
South			1
Southwest	8		
West	5		
TOTALS	14	5	1

San José
Santa Bárbara
San Diego and Chula Vista
San Bernardino
Riverside
Tucson
W. Las Vegas
Albuquerque
Del Río
McAllen

San Antonio
Austin
Fort Worth
Milwaukee
Chicago
Lorain
New Haven
New York
Philadelphia
Miami

FLOW IN DEVELOPMENT OF REGIONAL EDITIONS

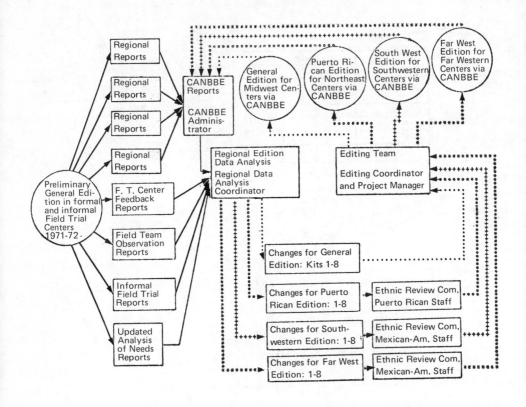

EXTERNAL INPUTS

from Curriculum Adaptation Network (CANBBE)
from special consultants
from formal field trial centers
from informal field trial centers

INTERNAL INPUTS

from direct observation by SCDC staff
from updated analysis of needs
from recommendations of ethnic review committees

function and is not responsible for determining quality of instruction in local projects cooperating with the Center.

Evaluation of the materials development process involves four objectives: monitoring the production of Kits 9-24, monitoring the field testing of Kits 1-16, **monitoring the** production of regional editions and monitoring production of the revised general edition. The monitoring and verification activities which proved functional during the first year will be utilized in 1971-72 to achieve these objectives.

Evaluation of the materials developed involves one objective aimed at determining the effectiveness of the materials as used under various conditions. Three field testing situations which represent optimal utilization of the Curricula Kits with the three target ethnic groups (Mexican-American, Puerto Rican, Cuban) will be selected in order to attain this objective.

The production of evaluation designs and reports also involves one objective. This dimension is an essential ingredient within the process of providing formative and summative evaluation for the Center.

Evaluation of materials development process

Monitor the production of Curricula Kits 9-24
Verify the collection of information
Verify the establishment of detailed projections
Verify the creation of Kits 9-24
Verify the piloting of Kits 9-24
Verify the revision of Kits 9-24, from piloting

Monitor field testing of Curricula Kits 1-16
Verify in-service orientation to field centers
Verify acquisition of feedback
Verify direct observation of classrooms
Produce general achievement tests for Kits 1-16
Analyze pupil responses on general achievement
tests and in assessment activities, Kits 1-16

Monitor production of regional editions
Verify creation of Northeast Edition, Kits 1-8
Verify creation of Southwest Edition, Kits 1-8
Verify creation of Far West Edition, Kits 1-8
Verify creation of Cuban Edition, Kits 1-16

Monitor revision of general edition
Verify revision of General Edition, Kits 1-8

Evaluation of materials developed

Evaluate Curricula Kits 1-16 in field situations
Analyze classroom utilization of Kits 1-16
Analyze pupil responses in Assessment Activities
Analyze responses on general achievement tests
Analyze correlation between (a) classroom use,
(b) performance in Assessment Activities, and
(c) performance on general achievement tests

Production of evaluation designs and reports

Create Evaluation Designs and Reports
Revise Evaluation Designs for 1971-72
Write Interim Evaluation Report for 1971-72
Write Evaluation Design for 1972-73
Write Final Evaluation Report for 1971-72

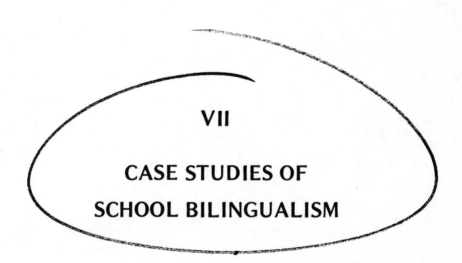

VII

CASE STUDIES OF

SCHOOL BILINGUALISM

23

A Home/School Language Switch Program
Wallace E. Lambert
and G. Richard Tucker

This paper describes a longitudinal, community-based study of two groups of English-Canadian children (a Pilot and a Follow-up class) who undertook their elementary schooling exclusively in French during kindergarten and Grade I. From Grades II through IV they studied mainly in French except for two 35 minute periods of English Language Arts, and in Grade V arithmetic was taught via English. This report focuses on the working hypotheses that guided the evaluation and on the measurement techniques used to assess the program's impact on the cognitive development of the children. This educational experiment has universal relevance since it touches on an educational matter faced also by minority groups in all countries and by most citizens in developing nations.

The parents of the children were concerned about the ineffectiveness of current methods of teaching foreign languages, and were impressed with recent accomplishments in teaching science and mathematics in the early elementary grades. They also realized that, as residents of a bicultural and bilingual society, they and their children are part of a much larger experiment in democratic co-existence that requires people of different cultures and languages to develop mutual understanding and respect. An essential first step for them was learning the other group's language thoroughly. The program which they have worked out may well serve as a model because the overall scheme (referred to as a home-school language switch) is simple enough to be tried out in other bi- or multicultural communities around the world, or, and perhaps of more importance, in essentially monocultural settings where a serious desire exists to develop second or foreign language proficiency. In any case, a basic educational issue is involved here: rather than estimating how many years of schooling should be provided in order to develop an undefined level of ability in a second language, the educator in this case asks how one goes about developing complete bilingual balance in the home and school languages (cf. Lambert and Tucker, 1972).

The hypotheses that guided us are given below along with a résumé of the types of measures used and the overall results obtained. We have compared the linguistic, cognitive, and attitudinal development of the Pilot and Follow-up experimental groups with control children carefully matched on non-verbal I.Q. and social class background, who followed normal English Canadian and French Canadian academic programs. The Experimental and English Control classes were also comparable as to parental attitudes toward French people and culture, and motivation to learn the other language; in fact if given the opportunity, the large majority of the control parents would have placed their children in experimental classes.

(1) What effect does such an educational program have on the Experimental children's progress in home language skills compared with the English Controls? The overall answer is that they are doing just as well as the Controls, showing no symptoms of retardation or negative transfer. On tests of English word knowledge, discrimination, and language usage, the Experimental Pilot Class falls above the 80th percentile on national norms as do the Controls, indicating that those in the experimental program do as well as the Controls and still perform at a very high level in terms of national norms. Their reading ability in English, their listening comprehension, and their knowledge of concepts in English (Peabody Picture Vocabulary) are all at the same level as those of the English Controls.

All signs are favorable also as to their progress in English expressive skills. When asked to retell or invent short stories in English they do so with as much comprehension and with as good or better command of rhythm, intonation, enunciation, and overall expression. Their spontaneous productions are as long and complex and their vocabulary as rich and diverse.

Their facility at decoding and utilizing descriptive English speech produced by children or adults is also at the same level as that of the Controls, and their word associations in English show as much maturity and appropriateness. Since they were at the same time reliably faster in making associations in English than the Controls, their speed of processing English may be advanced over that of the Controls.

(2) How well do children progress in developing second language skills under such a scheme when compared with French children who follow a normal all-French program of study? The answer is that they fare extremely well. Their French listening comprehension score was comparable to that of the Controls from Grade II on, and their knowledge of complex French concepts, measured with a French version of the Peabody Picture Vocabulary Test, is remarkably advanced. In fact, at the Grade IV level, they score at the same level as the French controls. From Grade I on, they have developed native-like control over the smaller units of French, but when asked to retell and invent short French stories, linguists rating their oral

proficiency find that their rhythm and intonation and their overall expression in French are noticeably inferior to that of the French Controls, even at Grade IV. Still, they have much better overall expression, enunciation, and rhythm and intonation when inventing stories of their own rather than simply retelling stories, suggesting that they are particularly motivated and clever when permitted to express their own flow of ideas with their own choice of expressions. The verbal content of their productions in French is as long and complex as that of the Controls and shows a similar degree of comprehension and vocabulary diversity. They make more errors in their French productions, especially errors of gender and contraction, but after Grade II, they do not make more mistakes involving word order or contractions. Their free associations in French are as rapid, mature, and appropriate as those of the Controls. They also show as much aptitude as the Controls in decoding spontaneous descriptions given by French adults or children their own age. By Grade IV, however, they are no longer as able as native speakers to decode the descriptions of children even though they are still as proficient as the controls when decoding adult descriptions. Amazing as this progress is when one considers their concurrent standing in English competence, there is room for improvement in their French expressive skill, assuming that it is desirable to become native-like in spoken aspects of the language. Imaginative changes could be introduced into the program as it now stands as to assure that a high level of skill is attained in the more passive skills while increasing expressive capacities. For example, this could easily be done by teaching physical education, music, and art (subjects that lend themselves naturally to social communication) in French. The teachers, new at this type of program as they all were, have perhaps overlooked the need to compensate for the lack of occasions outside school for improving skill in French expression. We believe now that attention can be directed to the content and fluency of the child's speech without sacrificing appropriate form, structure, and style. Greater interaction with French children would also improve the decoding abilities.

(3) How well do children following this program perform in comparison with Controls on tests of a content subject such as mathematics? The answer is that they perform at the same high level (both groups scoring beyond the 80th percentile) in both computational and problem-solving arithmetic tests. One can be confident that these children have been as able as the French Control groups to grasp, assimilate, and utilize mathematical principles through French, and that they are able to transfer this knowledge, acquired exclusively through French, to English when tested in arithmetic skills through English. The teachers in the Experimental program are not better trained in mathematics than those in the Control Classes nor is more time devoted to mathematics; their texts are French versions of those used in the English Control Classes.

(4) What effect does a bilingual program such as this, extended through

Grade V, have on the measured intelligence of the children involved? There is no sign at the end of Grade V of any intellectual deficit or retardation attributable to the bilingual experience judging from yearly retesting with Raven's Progressive Matrices and Lorge-Thorndike tests of intelligence. On standard measures of creativity, there is evidence that the Experimental children are also at the same level or slightly advanced in generating imaginative and unusual uses for everyday objects. This mental alertness is consonant with their generally faster rate of making free associations in English, noted earlier.

(5) What effect does the home-school language switch have on the children's self-concepts and their attitudes towards French people in general? At the Grade II and III levels their attitudes were much fairer and more charitable than those of the English and French Control children. They were less ethnocentric although at the same time they had healthy views of themselves as being particularly friendly, nice, tall, and big but not extreme in smartness or goodness. This suggests that suspicion and distrust between groups may be effectively reduced by means of this particular academic experience.

However, in the spring 1970 testing, we found that both the Grade IV and III level groups were essentially similar to the English Controls in their attitudes: neutral to slightly favorable toward European French people, more hostile toward French Canadians, and clearly favorable to their own group. We are not certain what caused this shift (e.g., French Canadian demands for separatism that were intense at this time; a realization that the few French Canadians they meet at school happen to be from a lower social class background and are academically poorer; or just wanting to be like others in their peer group as they grow older).

In the spring 1971 testing, when the Experimental groups had moved up to the grade IV and V levels, we surveyed their attitudes in greater detail and compared them with the English Control classes. Here it became very evident that the Experimental children are able to use the French language so effectively that they communicate with and establish satisfying friendship with French-speaking people. Thus, in contrast to the English Control children, they have developed sufficient language competence to enable them to enter into the French Canadian sphere of social activities, to understand and appreciate French people and French ways to a much greater degree, and to consider themselves as being both French and English Canadian in make-up. Furthermore, they are extremely satisfied with the French program offered them at school and reject the idea of switching now to an all-English program. In contrast, the Control pupils who have had no French training, other than a standard FLES program, feel they have had too much French, and react much more favorably to the idea of switching to a school program without any French at all.

Finally, there is no evidence that the self-concepts of the Experimental pupils are confused in any way.

In Perspective

Although the procedure described briefly above seems remarkably effective in this Canadian setting, permitting us to challenge various claims made about the harmful effects of early bilingual education, we do not propose this model as a universal solution for nations planning programs of bilingual education. Instead, a more general guiding principle is offered: in any social system where there is a serious widespread desire or need for a bilingual or multilingual citizenry, then priority for early schooling should be given to the language or languages least likely to be otherwise developed or most likely to be neglected. In the bilingual case, this will often call for the establishment of two elementary school streams: one conducted in language A and one in language B, with teachers who either are or who function as though they were monolingual. If A were the more prestigious language, then native speakers of A would start their schooling in B, and after they had attained functional bilingualism, they would use both languages for their schooling. Depending on the sociocultural setting, various options might be open for a linguistic minority group: for example, pre-kindergarten or very early schooling, with half of the day in B, half in A; concentration on B until reading and writing skills are certified, with switching delayed; or a completely bilingual program based on two monolingually organized streams. Rather than teaching languages A and B as languages, emphasis in all cases would be shifted from a linguistic focus to using the languages as vehicles for academic content.

The Province of Quebec provides a convenient illustrative example. Here the French Canadians — a national minority group but a clear majority group within the Province — have a fairly powerful political movement under way based on a desire to establish French as the "working language" and to separate politically from the rest of Canada. For English-speaking Canadians who see the value and importance of acquiring both of the national languages, the program of home-school language switch which we have described is an appropriate policy. French for them would otherwise be bypassed except in second-language training programs that have typically not produced the required proficiency. French Canadians, however, have reason to fear a loss of their language, faced as they are with the universal importance of English and the relatively low status attached to minority languages in North America.

French Canadians also may denigrate their dialect of French, which is at variance with that version given such high status in France. The home-school switch might worry them, as it would any North American minority group, who feared that English would easily swamp out their home language. In such circumstances, a valuable alternative would be to start a two-year preschool program at age 4 with half of the day in French and half of the day in English taught by two different teachers presenting themselves as monolinguals. Starting at Grade I, two separate academic streams could be offered, one fully French and the other fully English. Each student would have the option to move from one to the other for one or several courses until the two languages were brought to equivalent and high-level strengths. Such a program could, of course, integrate French and English Canadian children who so far have remained essentially strangers to one another because of separate schools based on religion and language.

In the Canadian setting, however, political decisions could have important counteracting consequences. For instance, a widespread movement for unilingualism and separatism among the French could postpone the thorough mastery of English beyond the receptive early years and all the advantages of being bilingual could easily pass from the minority group to the powerful English-speaking majority whose children now have the opportunity to become fully proficient in French and English.

Summary

This is a report on a longitudinal study of English Canadian children who undertook their elementary schooling exclusively in French except for two half-four daily periods of English Language Arts and part of their training in music, physical education, and plastic arts also taught via English. The experiment is referred to as a home-school language switch.

After five years it is evident that the children in Pilot and Follow-up Experimental classes perform at the same high level as English Control classes on all aspects of English language competence, have become functionally bilingual in French although certain nonnative features are still noted in their oral expression, have assimilated the mechanical and abstract aspects of arithmetic as well as the control children, have transferred readily their newly acquired competences (e.g., reading skill, verbal concepts) from French to English, and show no signs of intellectual or cognitive retardation. Their self-concepts, like those of the children in the control classes, are favorable and healthy in outlook and there are various signs that, with their attainment of such a high degree of competence in French, they have been able to cross more effectively than the English Controls the language barrier in the community, thereby improving their attitudes and feelings toward French-speaking people.

Bibliography

Lambert, W.E., and G.R. Tucker. *The Bilingual Education of Children.* Rowley, Mass.: Newbury House, (1972).

24

Free Language Alternation in School
William F. Mackey

Between the ages of three and eight in the bilingual upbringing of children the influence of the community, and in particular of the school, becomes stronger and stronger. Even at this early age, the school, which may include nursery classes, kindergarten and the early primary grades, can produce a long-lasting influence on the language competence of children.

Introduction

Bilingual education in early childhood has taken a number of different, and often contradictory, forms.[1] They range from the bilingual education of bilingual children in Wales to the unilingual education in another language of children from unilingual homes, as illustrated by the French schooling of children from Montreal English-speaking families in the remarkable St. Lambert experiment.[2]

The purposes of the various programs of bilingual education are not, however, always the same. In some cases, bilingual schooling may be simply a device to assure efficient foreign language learning.[3]

In others, it may be a means of assuring that minorities get at least part of their education in their mother tongue.[4] Or the purpose may be to transfer the medium of instruction from the foreign home language to the national language.[5] Or again, the objective may be the implementation of a national policy of bilingualism which gives the maximum possible chance of revival to a moribund national tongue.[6]

It would be nice to say that the formula adopted reflects the objectives to be attained. But this is unfortunately not always the case. The formulas are often either unenlightened or are based on inapplicable research conclusions arrived at under quite different and non-comparable conditions. By and large, early childhood bilingual education has been instituted as if there were a best formula applicable everywhere and under all circumstances.[7] One of these is based on the widespread belief that the two languages must be used and taught in different contexts, since the failure to do so would inevitably produce a single mixed language. And the greater the difference in contexts, the less the likelihood of mixture.[8] If the child addresses the same person indiscriminately in two languages, he may remain indifferent to their separate existence.[9] Such alternation is likely to lead to mixed word-associations.[10]

This widespread stricture against language alternation within the same context has determined the teaching pattern of many attempts throughout the world at early childhood bilingualism in school and kindergarten. As a result, elaborate and expensive precautions have sometimes been taken, including even the doubling of staff, to prevent the child from speaking two languages to the same person. The practice must go back more than half a century. In the early 1930s, for example, the multilingual international school in Madrid, which operated in two, three and sometimes four languages with children aged three to five years, required its teachers, in and outside the classroom, to use only one language with the children.[11]

Bilingual educators have blindly accepted the principle of language segregation without always inquiring into the reasons for its application, its relation to such important factors as the number of skills to be maintained, the order in which the languages have been acquired, the degree of control exercised by the teacher, and the age at which a second or third language was introduced.

The purpose of this paper is to question this claim that language alternation in education is universally harmful. I propose to do so, not by a series of controlled experiments, but by describing a single population which became bilingual through free language alternation in school, without apparent harm, at least over the ten-year period during which it has been observed.

I refer to a mixed population of children of American and German parentage in the city of Berlin. About 50% are children of Berlin residents most of whom speak German at home, about 40% are from American families living in Germany and about 10% from the international community — largely from the Commonwealth. In all, 62% of the children were born in Germany and about 48% make some use of both languages at home. As for the teachers, about half use only German at home, a third use only English and the remainder make some use of two or more languages.

The school, which in the 1960s was re-named after the ill-fated American president J.F. Kennedy, had a student population which passed the thousand mark in 1970. During the decade between 1960 and 1970, this bilingual school has been running an American-German curriculum through the free alternation of two languages — English and German. Although no final academic assessment is possible until the fate of the first graduates is known — after having completed their student careers in unilingual German or American universities — the effects of this type of bilingual instruction, even over a decade, do not seem to have been harmful, as far as anyone has been able to judge. If the reaction of the population is any indication, the educational formula used seems to have been successful, as indicated by the fact, that for 20 vacancies that occur every year in the primary grades, there are between 300 and 400 applications, especially from German families, some of whom apply for a place soon after their child is born.

Because the formula represents a type of bilingual education which has seldom been described, it might be useful here to outline how it has worked out in this particular case, especially at the kindergarten and early primary levels. Most of the material will be drawn from a study commissioned by the Ford Foundation and followed up by a full-length description which is to appear in a forthcoming book.[1][2] During this period free language alternation has been encouraged in a number of ways. The teachers, most of whom are in varying degrees bilingual, are free to use either language in their teaching, and in practice alternate considerably between languages within the same lesson. The pupils are also free to use either language in and outside of class, and for many of their activities are grouped in such a way as to promote bilingualism. Their other language is not called the second language or the foreign language, but rather the partner tongue.

The practice of free alternation of languages begins in the first year of kindergarten where a great many occasions are provided for the unilingual child to begin by listening to the partner tongue, before attempting to speak it, and in the early grades to read it and later write in it. Throughout his bilingual school years unobtrusive forces are at work which prevent his language alternation from developing into language mixture.

To understand how the formula works it is necessary to examine (1) how the context of free language alternation has been created, (2) how it is used in the teaching, (3) how the practice promotes learning, (4) the determinants of language alternation in the child's behavior, (5) the linguistic and (6) the educational effects of the formula.

Creating the context

In a primary school where children are expected to learn another language largely by associating with other children who speak it, it is important to create a social context which promotes such association.

If children of two different home languages are placed together in the same group, a condition is created in which at least some of the children may profit by the use of their second language. In the JFK School this is the most common type of grouping, promoted even out of class where parents are encouraged to organize outings, parties and picnics for the purpose of mixing the two language groups. The same is done for sports, in which the organizing of American groups to compete against German groups is not permitted; a German team is never opposed to an American team. Similarly, most classes outside mother tongue classes are bilingual in their grouping.

It is difficult, however, to prevent people with something in common — particularly children — from yielding to the natural tendency of birds of a feather to flock together. When this happens in bilingual schools, it creates language-based cliques and factions which work against the very reason for which some bilingual schools are created. To prevent this, the school encourages the creation of mixed friendship groups.

Much of this mixing is done in class, often through ingenious seating arrangements which break up unilingual conversation groups within the class and enable a learner to call on a partner for help in his second language. Some teachers use permanent arrangements originally arrived at on an informal basis. Others formalize the seating, alternating systematically between one language and the other. Some even change the pairing once a week so that every German child sits beside another English-speaking child at least for a week during the year. Other teachers have children sit where they wish at the beginning of the year and soon have them select the partners likely to help them most in their other language. This then becomes the permanent seating plan, for which a chart is made. Not only are the learners grouped in various possible ways, but each may be paired language-wise with teachers of different language backgrounds. There is also the question of the grouping of teachers among themselves.[1][2]

A bilingual group may be taught bilingually or unilingually by teachers who are dominant in either of the languages. Unilingual groups may also be taught by such teachers. In the JFK School all these combinations may be found — mixed language groups with American teachers, mixed language groups with German teachers, German groups with American teachers, German groups with German teachers, American groups with German teachers and American groups with American teachers. In some cases teachers group together to cover the syllabus, and experiments have been made in bilingual team teaching. The predominant grouping, however, is the mixed language class taught by either American or German teachers.[1][2]

It is possible that all children do not profit equally from free language alternation. That is why the school has prudently grouped children with language problems, children from broken bilingual homes, children unable to separate both languages and those with language blocks into special unilingual groups. Whether or not such a precaution proved to be necessary or desirable has not yet been determined.

Another exception to the practice of bilingual grouping is the organization of language classes in the home language and in the partner tongue. Since the objective is competence in at least one language comparable to that of a monolingual child of the same age, the school population in each grade is divided for purposes of language instruction into mother-tongue groups and partner-tongue groups according to level of competence, the highest level making no distinction between the two languages, that is, the child at this level follows both mother-tongue groups. In the other subjects children are grouped in such a way as to promote bilingualism through free language alternation.

Language Alternation in Teaching

The bilingual pattern is set from the first days of kindergarten, or as soon as the child enters the school and listens to the teacher alternating between languages. Since the alternation is free, however, it may take on any pattern or proportion, ranging from a single switch of language in mid-period to a continual sentence-by-sentence alternation.

The teacher may give part of the lesson in one language and part in another; he may give part of the material in one language and repeat the same thing in another language; or he may give only a summary in the other language. He may even have the bilingual students do the summary or repetition. He may alternate by period — giving one period in one language and one in the other. Or he may continually alternate between languages throughout the teaching. Although all these techniques are used in the JFK School, it is the latter that is predominant (See Table I).

The ways in which these techniques are used vary from teacher to teacher. Teachers who teach one period in one language and one in the other sometimes repeat the same material from a different point of view. Teachers who repeat the same material in the other language within the same class may do so in different ways. For example, in one arithmetic class all pupils, except four, are bilingual, with German as their dominant tongue. The teacher, whose home language is also German, does his teaching in German, but from time to time asks the four English-speaking students if they understood. He then switches entirely to English and all pupils both German and English-speaking automatically switch to English. The assignment is then given in German and completely translated by the teacher into English.[1 2]

Most teachers, however, prefer to alternate continually, and often freely, between languages. For example, in an elementary science class, with students divided about equally between German and English as home languages, the teacher, whose home language is German, constantly switches from German to English — often translating each question immediately into the other language. Definitions are translated and dictated in both languages; so are all technical terms. When a bilingual German student gives a correct answer to a question, the teacher may ask him to repeat it in English for the benefit of the English-speaking students.[1 2]

Another way of applying the technique of constant alternation may be seen in a social studies class. Here there is very little translation, but a constant alternation between English and German although the home language of the teacher is German. One day the teacher may begin the lesson in German, another day in English. After five minutes she may continue in the other language. In asking questions, the teacher will alternate irregularly between English and German. Students reply in either language — often the dominant one.

A third example of the technique of constant alternation may be seen in a first-grade music class. Here the home language of the teacher is English.

Much of the time is devoted to singing songs which have been translated into the other language. Songs are sung in each language, and sometimes alternate lines are sung in the other language, if the occasion permits.[1][2]

Language alternation in learning

The type and extent of free language alternation on the part of the children will greatly depend on their degree of bilingualism.

If they are still mostly monolingual they may eventually yield to the language of the teacher, even though their home language is the dominant one of the class. For example, in a kindergarten class an English-speaking teacher surrounded by monolingual Germans may be playing puppets with a single English-speaking child, who will eventually be joined by his German schoolmates in speaking in English about the puppets.[1][2]

Even in the early years of the primary school, pupils develop the habit of speaking in either language. For example, in an arithmetic class, where everything including the text is in English, several pupils will consistently ask questions in German, with both the assurance that they will be understood and that they can eventually understand the English replies. In one audio-visual class the lecture was entirely in English, all the student questions in German and all the teacher's answers in English.[1][2]

Many bilingual students may try consistently to ask and answer questions in the teacher's dominant language. They will not always succeed, however, and when the going gets difficult they will switch, even in mid-sentence, to their own dominant language. Other bilinguals reveal their language dominance by giving all their short questions and answers in their second language, but their longer ones in their mother tongue. Such transitional phenomena may be unconscious.

Some teachers try to structure the distribution of languages in the verbal behavior of the children. For example, in a geography class in the primary school each pupil pairs off with a pupil of the partner group to play a game which consists of finding places on a map.

As a result of all such bilingual activity reciprocal language alternation developed into a common practice, and it was not surprising to find that almost three quarters of the student population sometimes or often got a reply in a language other than the one in which they posed the question, and that 65% of the students stated that they had done the same (See Table II).

Behavioral determinants of language alternation

What determines this constant alternation between the two languages which is so typical of the whole school community?

There are several causes, stemming mostly from the natural dynamics of intercommunication. The pattern originates in the behavior of the teacher and is transmitted to the pupil, who extends it to his entire language behavior — in and out of school.

It starts in the kindergarten and extends right up to the final year. In the kindergarten, the bilingual teacher unconsciously tries to sense — to seek out — each child's dominant language in order better to communicate with him. In a kindergarten which may include 80% monolinguals — some 40% for each language — this means a continual alternation between languages. Later in the primary grades the teacher, in an effort to maintain the attention of the entire class, may have to switch languages with some frequency. When she notices, for example, that the four little American girls are not listening to her German explanation, she may unconsciously continue in English, to a point where she feels that she may be losing the attention of some of the German pupils. Or the switching may be the conscious result of a belief on the part of the teacher that a child should not entirely be deprived of his mother tongue.

The alternation may also depend on the choice of text. If the text is in one language, there may be either a certain amount of translation on the part of the teacher, or a conscious switch to the other language to redress the balance. For example, in a social studies class the bilingual German teacher taught in English because the text in the pupils' hands was German. She posed questions in English on pictures in the text having German captions and obtained replies in both languages. Contrariwise the language of the text may be reinforced by the teaching of the teacher.[1][2]

The degree of alternation is mostly affected by the presence of monolinguals — and as one goes up the grades these are mostly English-speaking. The arrival of a single monolingual pupil after the school year is already under way can suddenly alter the language distribution of the teaching. For example, an American child enters school in the primary grades a month after the beginning of the school year. In the social studies period the pupils who are now used to their German teacher's language pattern will, one morning, hear her begin the lesson in English and continue for some time. On her part, the teacher believes that this is necessary in order to make the unilingual newcomer feel at home. But because the newcomer may long remain unilingual, the teacher will continue to repeat herself in English for his benefit.

At the lower primary grades the change in emphasis may work in either direction. For example, in an arithmetic period the text and teaching are in English and the pupil's questions and answers bilingual. But for little Monika the teacher translates her questions into German and it is in German that Monika replies. One day, however, she may find that Monika is answering in English to her at all times. But when little Monika gets mixed up with her figures, the teacher switches back to German. She then continues in English for the benefit of the class. But toward the end of the lesson when she discovers the mischievious behavior of Kurt, Hans, and Trude, she will switch back to German.

What dominates most of this language alternation is the need to communicate, or the desire to please. This practice is then taken up by the students who have sometimes been the beneficiaries. Functionally bilingual children will soon know the dominant language of the teacher and use his language when speaking to him in or out of class. This respect or unconscious reaction to the other person's dominant language is transferred to the child's verbal behavior outside the class. In the street, such bilingual children even in a chance encounter, quickly sense the dominant language of their interlocutor and immediately use it. As soon as a newcomer opens his mouth these children know whether he is using his stronger or his weaker language. If he questions them in his weaker language (German or English) they will politely — and unhesitatingly respond in his other language. In school they will spend a certain amount of their time serving as handy resource persons to classmates whose German or English is not up to par.[1][2]

Many of these children, although they could pass for native speakers in either language and use both languages in their classroom questions, may still switch to their dominant language under stress, when tired at the end of class, or when technical words are involved. It is not unusual to listen for half an hour to a child one takes to be a native speaker of English only to find him asking the meaning of a word like *ivory*, which, he is told, means *Elfenbein* in his native German.

This pattern of free alternation is found not only in class; it also dominates all out-of-class activities — sports, meetings of the student council, meetings of the teachers and of the parents. It is, in fact, the bilingual pattern of the community; it is a form of receptive bilingualism in free variation.

One may ask what are the ultimate effects of such a pattern — its advantages and disadvantages. In order to find out, it is necessary to analyze the pattern into its two components. In the first place, there is the assumed freedom of being able at any time to express oneself in the language of one's choice with the assurance of being understood. In the second place, there is the assumption that one may hear the preferred language of the other person.[1][2]

Some persons see only disadvantages in this continual alternation between languages, claiming that it confuses the children and hinders their mental development. Others can see nothing but advantages, especially when a repetition of the same thing in the other language reinforces that redundancy which is essential to all communication. From the educational point of view of teaching, the crucial question may be whether concepts become clearer when they are expressed in more than one language.

Educational effects: comprehension and basic skills

What are the effects of this sort of teaching on the comprehension of subject-matter and the learning of the four basic language skills?

It is remarkable that out of a thousand students in all grades more than three quarters claim to understand everything in German or in English, and less than ten percent have stated that they understand very little of one of these languages. Since the investigation was conducted at the beginning of the school year (September to November), the latter category undoubtedly included a large percentage of newcomers (See Table III).

As for the acquisition of the four basic language skills of listening, speaking, reading and writing, each is given an early start.

In the kindergarten there is not only the great amount of incidental talk of the teacher and the other children, but also overt teaching of listening through the repeated hearing of stories, looking at puppet sketches, and participating in listening and guessing games with eyes closed. At this level the child is not forced to speak; he is helped to express himself when he wishes. If he is shy, he may put on a mask and play the role of an animal or hide in a box and become a radio or television. Or he may be the voice of the puppets or take part in the dramatization of a favorite story or in the solution of a riddle. If he is not too shy he may be invited to tell the teacher what he has done that morning, while the teacher repeats correctly the same thing. As for vocabulary development at that level, all new words are linked with the child's experience and explained from many angles. The important words, however, are those the child names himself.

In the kindergarten, although there is no teaching of reading as such, much that is done prepares the children for reading both in the mother tongue and in the second language. Stories are read to the children who care to listen as the teacher, who has prepared herself for the story, imitates the emotions it evokes. Some of these stories may even be read by visiting parents. Picture sequences forming a story are "read" by the children from left to right. Children cut out and group pictures of objects whose names begin with the same group of sounds. The children are encouraged to play with their languages — to form new words which rhyme, to find words that begin with the same sound as in their name, and to guess noises, for ear-training.

In the first grade, the children are taught to read in their mother tongue only, work in the second language being exclusively oral. They are also taught to read by a different method from that which is used in teaching them, the following year, to read their partner tongue; it will be global, if German, phonovisual if English, and it is likely to be taught by native primary school teachers.

Although most teachers give their lowest priority to writing, this is the most difficult skill to raise to the proficiency level of the mother tongue. As with reading, it starts with the mother tongue in the first grade, although most background work may be done in the kindergarten, where children sometimes have a wish to write words that mean much to them. Here they are encouraged to make signs with anything that is handy — even sticks and stones — regardless of size.

Writing in the mother tongue is taught in the first grade, the second grade being reserved for beginning writing in the second language. In the third grade the skill may, in a few cases, have developed to a point where the pupil may prefer to do his written work in the second language. The language of the textbook may also be a dominant factor in determining the language which the child will write. A student may always use English in class with a teacher whose dominant language is English; he may nevertheless systematically write his assignments in German.

One of the main functions of any primary school is the control of language — the teaching of the child to speak and write his mother tongue effectively and correctly. This is a difficult enough undertaking in itself; in a bilingual school it is doubly difficult, not only because there are two languages involved, but also because of the possibility of interference between them.

At the earliest school age, the problems of language mixture, in contradiction to language alternation, largely depend on the entering language behavior of the child, determined for the most part by his home environment. If the parents speak a mixed language, so will the child, for whom it is all one language. From this mixture the teacher has the job of creating two languages.

Real language mixture is the exception rather than the rule in the JFK School since most children come to school with a secure mother tongue. Any correction at the kindergarten level is mostly limited to the mother tongue. Even at that level there seems to be very little grammar mixture. At other levels newcomers will make mistakes in grammar — especially in word-order, but these are immediately corrected.

The area in which one does find a certain amount of interference is in vocabulary. And this should not be surprising, not only because there are so many words, but also because they convey the new concepts and ideas which the school transmits to the learner. Since these may be either in English or in German and not necessarily in both, it is not surprising that an English sentence may contain a German word from time to time, and vice versa.

If a German student uses an English textbook, he may there learn a word for an idea, thing or concept that is new to him. If he wishes to use this concept in an assignment written in German, it is the English word which he may use, since it is uppermost in his mind — the only one he knows. In such cases, some teachers require the students to put such words in quotation marks, indicating that they know it belongs to the other language. This same phenomenon may be observed in the spoken language used in class. A learner speaking nothing but English during the entire class may suddenly use German for one of the key words of the lesson, simply because the textbook in which he has been following happens to be German. It may be German not necessarily because a German text has been imposed but simply because this English-speaking learner — for one of many reasons — may have chosen it instead of the English text. The motivation is so strong for the pupil to fill in any blanks in his vocabulary that there is a continual process of lexical equalization which results in the steady growth of both languages.

It has often been said that all teachers are language teachers. This is not only because they teach new words and expressions along with the new ideas and concepts which they inculcate into the minds of the young, but also because they may exercise a certain control over the quality of the languages used. In the JFK School the great majority of teachers, no matter what they teach, do a certain amount of language correction — some only in class, a few only in the homework; but most of them correct mistakes when they see or hear them.

A practice which is widespread in the JFK School is that of having one pupil correct the language usage of another. This is usually done between pupils of different native languages — between native Germans and Americans for example, and it has seemingly been most successful. It is all done in a very friendly way. The practice is sometimes pushed a step further in some classes, when the teacher asks or encourages the students to correct her own second-language mistakes. The practice is most widespread when a newly-arrived American teacher tries to find the German word for something; the native German students are generally all too willing to oblige.[1][2]

Not all teachers correct language mistakes in the same way. Some simply repeat the form correctly or supply the right word; some give an explanation in the language they happen to be using; others do the explaining in the mother tongue of the learner. Finally, a number of teachers use a variety of "other techniques" such as having any of the other pupils supply the correct form, using student assistants for the purpose, having the pupils find the correct form in the dictionary or in previous lessons, or actually having them practice a remedial exercise in the language laboratory. The long term effect of these language correction practices is a modification in the degree of binguality of the instruction.

Linguistic effects: degrees of bilingualism

What has been the effect of this sort of free alternation in usage on the dominance and distribution of each of the languages involved?

In each of the various groupings, the languages may be distributed in varying amounts and varying patterns. Between the extremes of all German and all English, both languages may be used in any proportion. Some teachers teach mostly in one language; others try to maintain a balance. But the extent to which any one language is used may not depend entirely on the teacher; it also depends on the language behavior of the learners. Almost a third of the students use as much English in class as they do German, about a tenth use only one language, and all the others show some preference (See **Table IV**).

Except when teaching the language as a subject, most teachers either try to keep a balance between the two languages or use one of the languages most of the time, supplementing the lesson with remarks in the other language. Very few teachers completely exclude the other language in their teaching unless they are teaching language as such. But most teachers express either bilingual balance or marked dominance; few express weak dominance or unilingualism in their teaching.[1][2]

Teachers do not always use the same pattern of distribution, however, with all their classes. In some classes they may use mostly German as a counterweight to a textbook which is exclusively in English. Or because the textbook is English, the teacher may do most of her teaching in that language. Therefore, the appropriate measure for determining the distribution of the language throughout the entire classroom activity of the school is not the teacher but the class. By using this measure, we find that more than half the classes tend toward an equal use of both languages (57.4%) and that in more than 32% of the classes one language is dominant (16%) in each. In the remaining 10% of the classes, English dominates in a proportion of two to one, since 3.6% of these subject classes are exclusively English (as against 1.1% all German) and there are also more English classes with slight English dominance.

At all events, there is a clear pattern of language distribution in the teaching, and considering the fact that the choice and amount of each language used is left to the teacher, this pattern has turned out to be surprisingly symmetrical (See Table I).

Conclusion

From a study of the results achieved over a ten-year period, it would seem that, if at least one of the languages of the pre-school child is secure as a medium of communication, free language alternation in early childhood education can be used with mixed language populations as a means to promote bilingualism in the kindergarten and primary grades. If however the child is linguistically, emotionally or intellectually unprepared for such an adventure, it might seem wise to concentrate on the strengthening of one of his languages before aiming at the objective of a bilingual education.

TABLE I

Patterns of bilingual teaching
General and non-language subjects
Distribution of languages in teaching

TEXTS	G (1.1%)	G^e (16%)	eG (2.3%)	GE (57.4%)	gE (3.6%)	E^g (16%)	E (3.6%)
1 German							
English							
Both E&G					1		
None							
2 German				2			
English						4	
Both E&G		5				1	
None					4	3	
3 German							
English				4		4	
Both E&G		1		4		1	
None			2				
4 German		2		3			
English				14		3	
Both E&G		9	2	31		2	
None	1	6		18		3	4
5 German							
English						3	1
Both E&G				8	1		
None		1		2		1	
6 German		3					
English	1			2	1		
Both E&G				1			1
None				8		1	
TOTALS:	2	27	4	97	7	26	6

Number of classes using various techniques, combined with seven different patterns of language distribution in teaching and textbook use. Techniques: (1) Part of the lesson in one language, another part in the other language. (2) All material in one language, repetition of the same material in the other language. (3) All material in one language, summary in the other language. (4) Continual alternation from one language to the other. (5) Some periods in one language, some in the other language. (6) Other techniques including explanation by the students of some of material in other language. G (German), G^e (mostly), eG (more), E (English), E^g (mostly), gE (more), GE (equal).

TABLE II

Language alternation of a thousand students
(Replies given and received in the other language)

		Home	Neighborhood	Playground	Classroom
		%	%	%	%
Reply	Never:	47.7	57.5	33.0	32.1
given	Often:	10.6	6.4	13.9	18.1
in the	Sometimes:	38.7	32.3	48.6	44.7
other	Always:	2.2	2.4	2.0	2.2
language	No answer:	.8	1.4	2.5	2.8
Reply	Never:	41.4	46.7	23.2	21.2
received	Often:	16.6	11.1	21.0	26.9
in the	Sometimes:	39.8	39.4	51.7	46.7
other	Always:	1.5	2.0	1.8	2.3
language	No answer:	.7	.8	2.3	2.9

Percentage of students giving and receiving replies in one language in response to questions in the other.

TABLE III

Degrees of comprehension

	in German	in English
Everything	65.5%	40.6%
Mostly everything	16.8%	37.2%
Not everything	6.1%	10.7%
Very little	7.0%	9.9%
No answer	1.3%	1.6%

Answers of a thousand students to the question of whether they understand everything at school.

TABLE IV

Class language usage of a thousand students

	G %	G^e %	eG %	GE %	gE %	E^g %	E %
% of students	10.9	18.8	15.2	28.9	5.3	10.8	9.5
	all German	mostly German	more German	about equal	more English	mostly English	all English

NOTES

[1] Mackey, William F. "A Typology of Bilingual Education" *Foreign Language Annals*, Vol. 3, 4 (1970), pp. 596-608. Also in Andersson & Boyer (No. 4 below).

[2] Lambert, W.E., M. Just, and N. Segalowitz. "Some Cognitive Consequences of Following the Curricula of the Early School Grades in a Foreign Language." In James E. Alatis, ed., *Monograph Series on Languages and Linguistics*, 23 (1970), pp. 230-279.

[3] Mackey, W.F. "The Lesson to be Drawn from Bilingualism." *Applied Linguistics and the Teaching of French*. Montreal: Centre éducatif et culturel, (1967), pp. 53-63.

[4] Andersson, Theodore, and Mildred Boyer. *Bilingual Schooling in the United States*, 2 vols. Washington: U.S. Government Printing Office, (1970).

[5] Mackey, W.F., and J.A. Noonan. "An Experiment in Bilingual Education." *English Language Teaching*, Vol. 6, 1 (1951), pp. 112-132.

[6] Macnamara, John. *Bilingualism and Primary Education*. Edinburgh: Edinburgh University Press, (1966).

[7] Mackey, W.F. "Bilingualism and Education." *Pédagogie-Orientation*, Vol. 6, 2 (1952), pp. 135-147.

[8] Ittenbach, Max. "Zweisprachigkeit und organischer Grundbegriff." *Auslandsdeutsche Volksforschung*, 1 (1937), pp. 420-423.

[9] Smith, Madorah E. "A Study of the Speech of Eight Bilingual Children of the Same Family." *Child Development*, 6 (1935), pp. 19-25.

[10] Volkmer, August. "Die Zweisprachigkeit im Lichte der neueren Seelenkunde." *Der Oberschlesier*, 2 (1936).

[11] Castillejo, José, "Modern Languages in an International School." In *Home and School*, 14 (1933), pp. 7-10.

[12] Mackey, W.F. *Bilingual Education in a Binational School*. Rowley, Mass.: Newbury House (1972).

25

Cultural Contrasts in Bilingual Instruction
W. Harry Giles

According to Piaget, the sources of intellectual operations are to be found, not in language, but in the preverbal, sensori-motor period when schemas are elaborated which prefigure certain aspects of the structures of classes and relations, and the elementary forms of conservation and operative reversibility. The formation of representational thought is contemporaneous with the acquisition of language. Both of these are seen to be aspects of the symbolic function in general. In this, the first verbal utterances of the young child are intimately linked to, and contemporaneous with, symbolic play, deferred imitation, and mental images as interiorized imitation. Thought has its roots in action. Before the appearance of language, or of the symbolic function in general, the baby has overcome its initial perceptive and motor egocentrism by a series of decentrations and coordinations.

Language is seen as one of the instruments which enables the child through the symbolic function generally to represent reality through the intermediary of signifiers which are distinct from the objects or the actions that they signify. This capacity to represent reality by distinct signifiers had its roots in early imitation.

If, however, it is true that the first words the child uses are signifiers of the object or actions which they signify, it is equally true that children do not start with words. They start with syllables which are often ill pronounced, and are often an attempt to imitate either the whole or a part of the desired signifier. Thus, even the attempts at the first word retain the imitative character of the symbol, imitated in isolation. The child who uses the sounds in an attempt to replicate words usually does so as part of an expression of a possible action — an expression of a demand or a desire.

Much of the speech-learning done by the child immediately after birth is relatively independent of adult vocal stimulation. The crying and wailing of the young child, the methods of short sharp inhalation and prolonged exhalation are fundamental to the speech which is in the course of evolution. The lip, jaw, and tongue movements required in all languages are repeatedly practiced. This physical activity is fundamental to speech readiness. The non-crying sounds of grunts, gurgles, and sighs include most of the front vowels, the consonants /k/, /l/, /g/, and the glottal catch (a plosive sound made by suddenly releasing the air stream that has been held back by the closed glottis).

The effect of duck imprinting (Hess) where freshly hatched goslings were given a mechanical decoy which said "gock" led to the young goslings preferring the mechanical "gock" to the honk made by the adult goose. Even if geese are not human, we still know that institutionalized children learn more slowly than those who interact with their parents and with even two days of conditioning (Rheingold) three-month-old children have made substantial advances in sound production. The use of reflex sound tends to be followed by babbling, which starts about eight weeks after birth with little vowels such as /i/, /I/, /a/, and others made at the front of the mouth, a few m's, b's, and consonant sounds, juxtaposed with an assorted variety of gurgles and grunts.

At about the sixth month in a normal unprecipitated context (in the sense of Burton White's experiments) visual control over the hand resulting in a grasping and sucking schema, which is then coordinated with socialized vocal play, is characteristic of the average child. Such vocal exercises are customarily employed to obtain attention, to support rejection, and to express demands. This stage is often characterized by syllable repetition or the doubling of sounds (i.e., *da da*) which will be practiced to the exclusion of other sounds for weeks at a time. In fact, prelinguistic utterances during the first six months undergo parallel development for both deaf and for hearing children, thus indicating the importance of the physical structure of the human animal, or, as Chomsky might describe it, of inborn biological factors.

At about the eighth month the child begins to use inflections in the babbling. Until this period the repertoire of sounds could probably be that of any language group.

Between eight months and a year, the sound vocabulary increases, especially in the development of front vowels and consonants. Back vowels (u, ʉ , o, ɔ) are now used more extensively, and these appear to be fundamental in the development of early speech. It has been noted (Irwin & Curry) that 92 percent of all vowels uttered by babies are front vowels as opposed to 49 percent for adult speech. During this period babbling occupies a dramatically larger portion of the child's time as compared with crying. Speech sounds appear in meaningful words, singly, doubly, usually in a playful context. The first words of the child often resemble those of the adult. Many of them are of the "abracadabra" variety — such as when the child says "mama" and mama appears. Essentially the words used are words employed in a situation context as part of a total schema.

At about eighteen months the mythical average child has a vocabulary of from one to twenty-five words. Many of these are one sentence words of a sort expressing demands or desires. As the child experiences a particular sensori-motor schema by manipulating it, and an adult intervenes to provide the word, the child will, on repetition, come to recognize the words as part of the total experience. The child of this age employs a rich jargon in a seemingly purposive way, talking to people, animals, and toys. The child's new teeth enable him to produce new sounds, which must be practiced. Sometimes the child begins to parrot back what the parent has said.

At the age of two, the age chosen for beginning our formal consideration, the average child is talking. Language has become not only a safety valve, but also a tool. Simple and compound sentences have arrived and, even if the jargon has largely disappeared, his speech rhythm is uneven.

The verbal growth in the third and fourth years is especially important. The explorations of the child require an expanded vocabulary and a larger area of traditional syntax. He must expand his control of certain sounds, i.e., the tongue tip /l/ and /r/ sounds for the labial /w/, the use of the /k/ and /g/ plosives for /t/ and /d/, and many combinations and blends.

In the learning of one's mother tongue, the child proceeds through a coordination of sensori-motor schemas which have been actively built up during the first eighteen months of life, starting from hereditary reflexes, and which take place while language is being heard. The child's actions are often described in language terms with the young being conditioned to hearing certain sound patterns describing objects or activities. "By naming objects, and so defining their connections and relations, the adult creates new forms of reality in the child, incomparably deeper and more complex than those which he could have formed through individual experience" (Luria, 1966, p. 11). He acquires a verbal label as one of the multitude of sensory attributes of an object, and a bond develops between word and referant.

In the case of the Luria twins, children of five used their own private sounds and words to communicate. This "language" was phonetically impaired, as were their physical games. The same thing is true for the younger normal child whose ability to understand another person's normal speech is dependent, not on a simple accumulation of vocabulary, but rather on a process of gradual discrimination of the verbal signals from which words are made up, and the physical situation within which the verbal signals are first presented.

An examination of the role of generalization and classification of whole words tends to underline some of the inherent problems in the learning of one's mother tongue. First, we should note that words not only have many meanings but when juxtaposed with other words can be modified still further. Vygotsky's work has tended to show that changes in semantic structure are accompanied by changes in the inter-relationship among psychological processes comprising cognitive activity.

During the initial stages of development, discourse is understood by a child only within the limits of a specific concrete situation. Word meaning thus depends less on the relationship amongst the words than on the connection with a specific situation originating in the perception of some object which is recalled by a sentence.

In working with words differing by a single phoneme, Shvachkin showed that the general course of phonetic development in children aged eleven months to one year ten months, phonemic development in Russian for native speakers passed through the following stages:

1) differentiation of vowels,
2) differentiation of the presence of consonants,
3) differentiation of sonants (all sonants have one common feature: in articulating a sonant the organs of speech form an obstruction to the flow of outgoing air, but there always remains a free passage either in the mouth or in the nasal cavity. In Russian the consonants /r/, /x/ are sonants; in English the sonants are such sounds as /b/, /v/, /w/, and /d/, being sounds in the normal production of which the voice plays a part) and articulate plosives (in English any one of the six consonants /p/, /b/, /t/, /d/, /k/, /g/, characterized by the breath stream at some point in the speech mechanism followed by a sudden release),
4) differentiation of hard and soft consonants,
5) differentiation of sonants,
6) differentiation of plosives.

Put in another way, repeated exposure to particular kinds of perceptual discrimination problems greatly favors educability. As a consequence of inter-problem learning and the formation of learning sets, discriminations are made more rapidly (Harlow; Reese). Learning how to learn means learning how to perceive. The growth of phonemic hearing in preparing preschool children to read El 'Konin and Zharova, the development of children's abilities to discriminate pitch and rhythm (Vetlugina), follow this pattern.

A shift in judgmental activity between the ages of five and seven years seems to lead the child from simple dependence upon sensori-perceptual qualities to a reliance upon more inferential conceptual manipulations. This is reflected in social judgments (Gollin), conceptual styles (Kagan, Moss & Sigel), and in conservation (Piaget, 1960). It is argued by some that there are allegedly optimal periods of readiness for every type of cognitive skill, and the child who fails to learn the skill at the appropriate age is forever handicapped in acquiring such skills at a later date (Fowler).

Shvachkin also notes that hearing plays an important role in distinguishing nuances in both the earliest stages of phonetic perception and the latest. This was seen as being especially important in the differentiation of consonants whose articulation has a close resemblance (i.e., between voiced and unvoiced consonants). Gvozdev established that in Russian the assimilation of new sounds takes place as a gradual process through intermediate sounds. This classifying characteristic was carried further by El 'Konin and Zharova. They trained five- to six-year-old children to distinguish sounds in their mother tongue by classifying the phonemic nature of the words. Thus, by changing the "e" sound in the word *kët* (meaning catfish) to "o," the child sees the production of a new word, *kōt* (meaning cat). The child begins to recognize the role that patterns make, and the auditory discrimination which was taught produced significant advances resulting in earlier effective teaching of reading, writing, and the more complex types of oral speech.

This type of research has been continued in English and we have seen that, by the age of three, over 90 percent of native speakers of English have mastered the vowel sounds in English, even if the consonant sounds are normally not all mastered until about eight years of age. The nature of the progression of the learning of children's speech sounds in English seems to indicate that varied factors, such as socio-economic status, the number of siblings and adults in the immediate environment, parents' education, the physical, mental, and emotional growth of the child, all influence development. Indeed, in English, no single "developmental sequence" has been identified in the acquisition of articulatory skills. It seems likely that more than one sequence is possible (Healey) and, in any event, girls seem generally to pass boys at age three and during the years four and five.

At the age of five, it would appear that both boys and girls have in English acquired the consonants /p/, /b/, /m/, /h/, /w/, /d/, /n/, /k/, /t/, /g/, and /ʒ/, and that girls will have also acquired /l/, leaving the normal sounds of /j/, /ʒ/, /tr/ to be acquired during the year five, and /dʒ/, /wh/, /tr/ to be acquired by both boys and girls at six, with girls also acquiring /tʃ/, /ʃ/, /r/, and /ʒ/. At the age of seven, boys traditionally acquire /f/, /l/, /r/, /tʃ/, /ʃ/, /s/, /z/, /ð/, /v/, with girls acquiring the /s/, /z/, /ð/. The consonant blends /tr/, /bl/, /pr/, etc. develop between the ages of nine and ten, these usually arriving about one year after the single consonants have been acquired (Healey). Thus it is clear that in English, at least, the basis of the use of one's mother tongue is not fully formed until about the age of ten years. This is later than has been commonly thought but the data sample with which Healey has been working is very large. It is to be noted that Healey is not talking about phonemes per se, but most — if not all — of the sounds produced are phonemes. It could be that the 30,000 children in the sample have not been exposed to sufficient experiences involving discrimination; but they do constitute a large sample. It has also recently been observed that the earlier assumption that a child's whole grammar was acquired before the age of seven is substantially inaccurate in at least the area of syntax (C. Chomsky).

When one looks at the problem of positive transfer between one language and another in respect to development of phonemes, morphemes or syntax, or negative transfer, it would seem that special problems exist for the bilingual owing to the interference of the one language with the other, and it is at least a reasonable hypothesis that the late delay of English language development may perhaps lead to either a retardation in development or to a more enriched classificatory system of both syntax and sounds.

The mental processes which the child goes through during the stage of intuitive thinking (ages four to seven) are characterized for the most part by what Piaget calls "transductive thinking." That is, the child tends to link together neighboring events on the basis of what the individual situations have in common. If we had a collection of groups of materials differing in shape and color, then we might say that groups one and two could be linked by color, and two and three by shape, with three and four linked again by color.

One possible inference from this is that early reading and language learning in a bilingual school should be in the language with fewer exceptions, and one with more regular patterns. Thus we begin our first language of formal instruction in French, rather than in English. We recognize that early learning will reflect a kind of slow motion film state with the child moving from the particular to the particular. Variants in physical form, as in language, are introduced to ensure that when the child is mature enough to pass beyond the level of linear succession to a multiplicity of similarities and differences leading to hierarchical inclusions, he will have the experiences to be able to advance.

The movement of the child through the non-graphic state (in which the child is beginning to develop an understanding of logical classes) arrives during the learning of different ways of discriminating more and less, bigger and smaller, thicker and thinner, and, generally, the same or different. These concepts and the vocabulary associated with them are learned perceptually in action. If the child has a tendency to focus on only one aspect of a comparison, then a variety of physical interactions coupled with language may enable the child to acquire the experience necessary to go beyond this preliminary stage. Depending upon the child, it would seem that, between the ages of seven and eight, the child is able for the first time to coordinate representative relations, and to conserve the idea of sameness, and to reverse ideas. The differences in languages which are marked in the child of five and six begin to be separable on a developmental basis at seven and eight.

The development levels in English found by Carol Chomsky and William Healey respectively for syntax and for phoneme development may be the normal levels in average children learning only in English, given the types of environment, including the education, of the individual children. Knowing what we do about linguistic transfers, the juxtaposition of several languages is at least likely to cause initial confusion both in syntax and with respect to phonemes, and this is exactly what our experiences have indicated in our own school.

When the native speaker of English first comes to our school as a student, he has progressed, for the most part, through the development indicated. He brings to the school that chain of physical experience for sound making which is peculiar to native speakers of English. At the age of three to three and a half, he enters our nursery classes which are entirely conducted in French as they have been for some thirteen years. Since we know that passive learning devoid of sensori-motor involvement is relatively ineffectual in bringing about verbal assimilation, our program is structured about games of a sensori-motor character. Children in the third year learn the names of things two to three times more quickly if they are permitted to handle them while learning the names (Razran). Thus we attempt to make our learning situation imitative of real life, sensori-motor in character, and active in involvement. The use of mime and drama becomes a must in the context, as does the involvement of the child in games in which the child's choice of toys is of real importance. In our preschool classes, the language of instruction is French, and French becomes the obligatory medium of instruction after a short period of time, for the Nursery, Junior Kindergarten, and Grade I. In Grades II and III, the students have up to eight and a half hours a week in English to cover the normal program taught during Grades I, II, and III in all other all-English schools and to deal with at least some of the problems generated by the nature of the program.

The fact that we start reading in English only in Grade II produces a number of side effects. We succeed in creating high standards in reading in French, and in avoiding the confusion which would probably have resulted if we had taught both English and French reading in Grade I, at the same time. On the other hand, we may have delayed phoneme development in English by not providing instruction in the language at the Kindergarten and Grade I year levels. Thus, the child who knows how to read in French will have acquired a phoneme association with that language. Because of a variety of factors, including the methods employed to teach reading, a significant percentage of our children read in English before having had a specific program for English reading, albeit many do so with a French accent (see Table I). These results have been consistently achieved in the same 1,300-1,400 children who have passed through our Grade I. At the end of our Grade IV, our children have achieved equally interesting results (see Table II).

If our reading program, despite phoneme confusion, achieves exacting results, our spelling program produces results which are predictable for two reasons. First, creative writing is taught entirely apart from spelling, and the clash of phonemes produces a written form of English which is phonetically based, and confused as between English and French. The kinds of spelling errors typified by this type of approach would include those set out in Table III.

A typical mistake found in other material is the simple addition of an extra "e" at the end of a word. Of course, our basic problem in English spelling is that there are more vowel and consonant phonemes in English than there are vowels to represent them. The relations amongst stress, spelling, and pronunciation constitutes a further variable. In some areas of spelling difficulties, the sound patterns are normally acquired for the first time at ages seven and eight in an all-English school where reading is firmly established in the mother tongue. The failure to teach these sounds formally may be a contributing factor in the failure, if any, within the normal pattern of acquisition of such sounds, at the ages of five and six years. Equally, the higher levels of achievement at later stages might also be a by-product of the richer structural pattern of experiences within our school.

Striking problems in early spelling levels in English in The Toronto French School in Grades II and III, based on standardized tests, continue to ameliorate in Grades IV and V, in Grades VI and VII (see Table IV). We teach patterns in spelling early, and the exceptions somewhat later. This experience, like all bilingual experiences, is not really generalizable, because it probably depends upon the teachers, their linguistic training, the class size, the hidden curriculum of the home, the structure of the program, the extent to which the program is actually followed, the emotional environment of the classrooms, and a number of other significant variables, such as the economic use of what is being learned, the status of what is being done, the social content of the language, the juxtaposition of native speakers of the other language, cultural supports which exist apart from native speakers, etc. Our bilingual speakers in Toronto are not the same as the bilingual English-French speakers in the Province of Quebec. Developmental patterns probably are somewhat consistent, but it is questionable whether other aspects, in different situations, follow the same pattern.

In some ways our progression in spelling resembles one matched pair experiment which we ran with our Grade II children some years ago. We wished to explore the effect of teaching English children who had been entirely taught in English in Kindergarten and Grade I, again in French in Grade II. We were looking at progress in English for these children when they were deprived entirely of English throughout the Grade II year, as compared with their control group which received a regular seven-hour-a-week English program. We were looking at such questions as word recognition, vocabulary, reading, spelling, and creative writing to see what effect, if any, a total absence of instruction in English at school would have on English results. Tests were given at Christmas and at the year end. Differences to the .05 level of significance existed in every area at Christmas but by the year end, the deprived students were achieving results which were statistically equivalent except for spelling results and those in creative writing. In the spelling area, on the tests employed, our average child in the normal Grade II seems to move from the grade levels of 3.2 in Grade II, to

4.7 in Grade III, to 5.9 in Grade IV, to 7.9 in Grade V, to 9.2 in Grade VI. A systematic exposure to conflicting structures seems to provide the children with a better understanding of the phonetic base in both language — but not immediately. The immediate result is confusion and only when the child has developed the classificatory rules sufficiently can he separate English from French in this area. Having done that, the child seems to become much more aware of differences than the children reflected within the norms of the standardized tests.

Many types of linguistic confusion in syntax exist with English-French bilinguals. The kinds of confusion may be a product of age or the kinds of informal or formal learning patterns presented to the learner. As in other instances, our problems of confusion seem to be due to structural interference arising from parallel construction.

At the ages of five and six, the constructions most frequently confounded in our school are those set out in Table V. It will be noted that in the main they consist of idiomatic expressions which must simply be learned via pattern drills or generic games. The constructions are literal translations from English despite the fact that no translation from English to French is permitted at any time in the classes. What this seems to indicate is that native speakers of English who reside in an all-English environment, where no French is spoken in the home, still seem in many cases to have a tendency to impose English syntax upon the French language even when all of his formal instruction for one, or two, or even three years is entirely in French. Perhaps even so small a thing as the existence of a French TV station and the opportunity to obtain some reinforcement outside of class would modify the pattern. Our students do not seem to experience syntactical confusion in their English due to their learning in French. These two factors taken together might well be taken to lead to a conclusion that for the majority of our students, English is still dominant at the age of eight or nine.

We know that classificatory exercises of all kinds increase learning from the very first days. Thus experiments involving the verbal description of action and its visual depiction have increased the learning of paired pictures (Reese). In addition to the normal development of classification in mathematical areas, we can regularly see children grouping items according to perceptual properties, and the self-directed use of linguistic terms for characterizing objects demonstrates a gradual course of development (Olver and Hornsby). A researcher has found that a minimum amount of language is necessary for adequate performance on a sorting task (Stodolsky).

The age of five to six appears to be a transitional stage in orienting effectively against the suggestive power of strong stimuli. By the seventh year, it would seem that most children's motor systems have been sufficiently influenced by verbal classificatory experience that the systems themselves have become amenable to regulation by a verbal system of elective connections. Learning of this latter kind which conforms to prescribed criteria rather than to transductive associations must be initiated by an orienting or organizational process which is inherently complex, consisting of a preliminary representation of the product, then of the process itself, and finally of a system of reference points which allow the task to be performed (Gal'perin and Talyzina). The gradual replacement of concrete actions with verbal ones reflects the gradual advances of the child towards a generative form of language and structure. It seems clear both through published research and our own experience that a close linkage exists between verbal and non-verbal conceptual development and that the organizing of reading and spelling through patterns tends to accelerate development in the skills area by creating artificially the classificatory means which enable the child to advance. Generalizing of words and structures do lead to early confusion, but consistent approaches with regular rein-forcement **gradually ameliorate the problem.** Language by its nature is generalizing and thus ensures cognitive feedback from perception of response into stimulus, with the one concrete and sensorily disclosed, and the other verbal. Words are probably more amenable to exact definition than sensori-motor responses, with the result that verbal interaction inevitably seems to lead to greater classification and differentiation.

In a study which was done some years ago on children in the school which is shortly to be published it was found that the standard type of interference was not fully present (James). The most numerous phonemic faults appear to have been caused because of the similarity between the consonantal systems of English and French. The /i/ is well distinguished at all levels, and the nasals are better handled than the orals, due to the confusion between /õ/ and /ã/ and in the production of the vowels /e/ and /a/. Several instances were noted of interference of written English with pronounced French. One surprising observation was that little difficulty was experienced with the phoneme /y/ which most Anglophones find the sound difficult to pronounce. One of the interesting results of this study as well as the other spelling study is the fact that the results underline once again that classification and seriation do not come about by accident. There are differences, and the dominant language does influence the secondary language. In order to eliminate such interferences on English spelling a special spelling program was introduced which had as its objective the clear establishment of sound patterns so that both the usual patterns and then later the exceptions could be acquired. A more systematized approach to sound patterns and to syntax has since been established within the school, and hopefully the articulatory habits have been further ameliorated in this domain as well.

Teaching through a second language has proved to be an effective tool in eliminating poor teaching methods. After teaching through the medium of French we stopped using many traditional approaches because we found that the filter of teaching through the second language eliminated understanding unless the learning program was of a kind which would make up for an inadequate language control and hence inadequate ties between the language used and cognition. For instance, we have learned that children with visual perceptual handicaps, when taught to read in French, do not acquire reading skills in English in Grade I, whereas those who have no such problems generate reading skills in English on their own on the basis of the approach learned in French. This has necessitated special approaches for all children in Kindergarten. Since it is commonly said that nearly 20 percent of all children have either minimal or substantial perceptual difficulties (L. Shannon), the size of the problem cannot be ignored. Thus, while the filter aspect can be an advantage, it can also produce enormous human disasters unless honest evaluation constantly leads to the rejection of poor teachers, poor curriculum, and poor methods in bilingual schools.

It may be argued that in the long run exposure to broader classification of sounds through bilingual education will lead to greater classificatory understanding and hence greater cognitive development in that area. No doubt this may be true if the learning is well structured and effectively organized, but such results have not been achieved consistently in the bilingual schools for native speakers of French in Ontario and in New Brunswick where a French-English bilingualism has existed for over fifty years. It has also been suggested that there may be critical learning periods during which deliberate exposure to certain constructions would result in learning but denial of the teaching might inhibit the development for all time (C. Chomsky, p. 102). This has implications for second-language learning in general, and of course it has particular implications for the whole question of whether one should suppress the teaching of a second language until the first one is soundly acquired.

Summary

The paper analyzes the sensori-motor and cognitive basis of the phoneme development of a native speaker of English whose language has engrafted upon that development an immersion in French. An examination of phoneme confusion and linguistic practices in specific learning areas for native speakers of English learning French leads in turn to the consideration of phoneme development which is closely related in developmental terms to the Piagetian concepts of classification and seriation.

TABLE I

Reading and Language Achievement in Grades I (without English) and Grades II (with English) according to The Metropolitan Achievement Primary I Battery Tests with Regular Classes at The Toronto French School.

	Grade I	Grade II
Word Knowledge	1.8	3.9
Word Discrimination	2.8	3.7
Reading	2.4	3.6

TABLE II

Reading and Language Achievement in English in Grades III, IV, V, VI, VII, VIII with a variety of Tests, on the graded level.

Metropolitan Achievement Tests

	Word Knowledge	Word Discrimination	Reading	Language	Language Study Skills	Social Skills
Grade III	5.2	4.9	5.0	4.4	N/A	
Grade IV	6.8	5.7	6.4	6.1	N/A	
Grade V	8.8	N/A	8.3	7.7	7.2	7.1
Grade VI	8.8	8.3	9.5	8.4	8.4	9.3

TABLE III

should	chood — as in *ch*ê*ne*
share	cheir — as in *ch*e*r* or *ch*a*r*
other	ather — *a* as in m*a*l
my	mi — *i* equals *y*
mad	made — silent *e* at the end of a syllable in French to sound the syllable
because	bicose — *i* as in l*i*re
	ose as in ch*ose*
	s = *z*
hurts	herts — *er* as in h*er*be, t*er*miner
easy	isi — *i* = *y*
	s = *z*
does	das — *a* as in m*a*l or t*a*sse
always	allwes — non accentuated *e*
tease	tise — *i* as in l*i*tre or t*i*sse
	s = *z*
laugh	laf — *gh* = *f* *as in* m*a*l
	af as in *af*faire
class	classe — as in *classe*
friend	frent — hearing difficulty between *t* and *d*
make	mek — as in m*é*cano
to	tu — as in *tu*
lunch	luche — silent *e*
then	thenne — doubling of consonants between vowels as in e*nn*emi
sure	shur — *s* = *ch* as in *ch*oux
have	av — silent *e* removed as in English
mad	mat — hearing difficulty between *t* and *d*
gate	gait — as in g*a*îté
who	hoo, ho — *w* is silent, as in h*ou*x
why	wy, why — *i* = *y*
	h is silent letter
she	chee — as in *ch*at
sky	skaee, seky, skie, sei — influenced by *ski*
come	cam — *o* = *a* as in camarade
can	can, cane, cann, kane — *k* = *c* as in *c*anne
come	comme, kum, cum — as in *comme*
of	ov — *f* = *v*
blue	bleu — influence of French spelling
December	Desember — *s* = *c*

fish	fich — as in *fiche*
remembered	rememberd — *e* omitted because of French influence as in *perdre*
could	cold, cod — *l* omitted due to French influence of *code*
touch	tuch — English *ou* = French *u*
friend	frind — as in *pin*
their	there — as in *mère*
know	no — *k* and *w* are silent letters — *no* as in domi*no*
knew	new — silent *k*
like	lyke — *i* = *y*
corn	korn — *c* = *k*
we	wi — English *e* = French *i*
knife	nife — silent *k*
few	fiu — *fu* = French *i* and English u
lots	lottes — as in *botte*
math	mathe — *e* as added at end of French words
he	hi — as in hib*ou*
dentist	dentiste — influence of French spelling
soft	softe — *e* as added at end of French words
very	veri — as in *véri*table or *véri*té
towel	towl — silent *e*
can	kan — *c* = *k*
grey	grai — as in *grai*ne or *grai*sse
hair	her — as in *her*be
wait	wate — English *a* plus French *e* at end of word
she	che — as in *cher*

A number of errors are due to the interference of both English and French phonetics. For example:

$$s = z$$
$$i = y$$
$$rr = r$$
$$mm = m$$
$$i = é$$

Further errors may be due to hearing difficulties as in the case of $f = v$, and $t = d$, or to silent letters such as h and e.

It is to be noted that in an American school which is somewhat famous for its work with children who have visual perceptual difficulties — the Gowl school in South Wales, New York — children as a practice are not permitted to learn French because their ongoing experience is reputed to show that Romance Languages in general cause enormous problems in English, and the French problem is most acute. Latin, on the other hand, which might be defined as the mother of French, does not appear to cause such confusion.

TABLE IV

Spelling Results in The Toronto French School in English on The Metropolitan Achievement Tests, Primary II Battery, Elementary Battery and Intermediate Battery.

Actual Grade	Average Grade Level	Average Percentile level for each Grade
Grade II	3.2	65
Grade III	4.7	70
Grade IV	5.7	75
Grade V	7.8	85
Grade VI	9.2	87

TABLE V

Correct Usage	Typical Error
J'ai faim	Je suis faim
J'ai soif	Je suis soif
J'ai froid	Je suis froid
J'ai chaud	Je suis chaud
J'ai fini	Je suis fini
J'ai cinq ans	Je suis cinq ans
Je suis un garçon	J'ai un garçon
J'ai mal à la gorge	J'ai mal au cou
J'ai un crayon	J'ai a un crayon
Ma maison	Mon maison *ou* moi maison
C'est ma maison	C'est la maison de moi
C'est la plume de John	C'est John's plume *ou* La John plume
C'est à John	C'est John's
C'est à moi *ou* c'est le mien	C'est mon
J'attends John	J'attends pour John
Quelle heure est-il?	Quel temps est-il?
La robe rouge	La rouge robe
A la télévision	Sur le télévision

J'ai parlé à John au téléphone	J'ai parlé à John sur le téléphone
Je vais chez le docteur	Je vais au docteur
Je vais chez le coiffeur	Je vais au coiffeur
Je vais chez le dentiste	Je vais au dentiste
Je vais au cinéma	Je vais à le cinéma
Puis-je me laver les mains?	Puis-je laver mes mains?
Puis-je avoir un crayon?	Puis-je un crayon?
J'écris mon devoir	Moi écris mon devoir
Tu es joli	Tu regardes joli
Je l'ai vu (le chat)	J'ai vu le
Je t'aime	J'aime toi
Lundi c'est ma fête	Sur lundi c'est ma fête
Mes cheveux sont courts	Mon cheveu est court
Il s'est moqué de moi	Il a ri de moi
C'est pourquoi faire?	Qu'est-ce que c'est ça pour?
J'ai 8 ans, 9 ans	Je suis 8, 9
Le bonbon rouge, etc.	Le rouge bonbon, etc.
Samedi, j'irai	Sur samedi, j'irai
Le matin, je	Dans le matin, je
Je le donne à Jacques (la, les)	Je donne le à Jacques (la, les)
C'est mon cahier (ou c'est le mien, le tien, etc.)	C'est mon (ton, son, ma, etc.)
Je suis allé (tu, il, etc.) tombé	J'ai allé (tu, il, etc.) tombé
Tellement	Si beaucoup
Il ressemble à	Il regarde comme
Je viens de demander	J'ai juste demandé
Il fait chaud, froid, etc.	C'est chaud, froid, etc.
Il m'embête	Il embête moi
Il faut	Je faut
C'est ce que je voulais dire	C'est qu'est-ce-que je voulais dire
Je dois mettre	Je dois mis
Je peux apporter	Je peux porter
Je vais	Je vas
Ils se battent	Il bat (ou il batter)
Aux	à les
Au	à le
Des	de les
Du	de le

Bibliography

Brooks, Nelson. *Language and Language Learning.* 2nd edition. New York: Harcourt Brace & World, (1964).

Chomsky, Carol. *The Acquisition of Syntax in Children from 5 to 10.* Cambridge: M.I.T. Press, (1969).

Chomsky, Noam. "Language and the Mind," *Psychology Today,* I, No. 9 (1968).

Crothers, E., and P. Suppes. *Experiments in Second Language Learning.* New York: Academic Press, (1967).

El 'Konin, D.B., and L.E. Zharova. "A Contribution to the Problem Concerning the Development of Phonemic Perception in Preschool Children," *Sensory Training of Preschool Children.* Moscow: Izd, Akad, Pedog. Nauk RSFSR, (1963).

Fowler, W. "Dimensions and Directions in the Development of Affecto-Cognitive Systems," *Human Development,* 9 (1966), pp. 18-29.

Gesell, A. *The Psychology of Early Growth Including Norms for Infant Behaviour and a Method of Genetic Analysis.* New York: The Macmillan Co., 1938.

Gollin, E.S. "Developmental Approach in Learning and Cognition," in L.P. Lipsett and C.C. Spiker, eds., *Advances in Child Development and Behaviour,* New York: Academic Press, (1965), II, 159-186.

Gvozdev, A.N. *Mastery by the Infant of the Auditory Aspect of the Russian Language.* Moscow: Izd, Akad, Pedog. Nauk RSFSR, (1948).

Harlow, H.F. "The Formation of Learning Sets," *Psych. Bull.,* 56 (1949), pp. 51-65.

Hess, Eckhard Heinrich. *Inprinting: Early Experience and the Development Psychobiology of Attachment.* New York: Van Nostrand Reinhold Co., (1973).

Healey, William. *Speech Development in Children.* American Academy of Pediatrics, (1971).

Hebron, Miriam. *Motivated Learning.* London: Methuen & Co., (1966).

Irwin, O.C., and Y. Curry. "Vowel Elements in the Crying of Infants under Ten Days of Age," *Child Development,* Vol. 12 (1941).

James, E.F. "The Acquisition of French Habits by Young Anglophones at The Toronto French School," *Bulletin pédagogique I.U.T. Langue Vivante* (to appear).

John, Vera P., and Sarah Moskovitz. "Language Acquisition and Development in Early Childhood," in A.H. Marckwardt, ed., *Linguistics in School Programmes,* Chicago: NSSE, (1970), pp. 167-214.

Kagan, I., H.A. Moss, and I.E. Sigel. "Psychological Significance of Styles of Conceptualization." Monographs of the Society for Research in Child Development, Vol. 28, no. 2(1963), p. 73-112.

Luria, Alexander, R. *The Role of Speech in the Regulation of Normal and*

Abnormal Behaviour. New York: Liveright Publishing Corp., (1961).

Luria, Alexander R., and R. Yudavich. *Speech and the Development of Mental Processes in the Child.* London: Staples Press, (1966).

McNeil, David. "The Creation of Language by Children," in J. Lyons and R.J. Wales, eds., *Psycholinguistic Papers,* Edinburgh: Edinburgh University Press, (1967), pp. 99-115.

Olver, Rose, and Joan Hornsby. "On Equivalence," in J. Brenley *et al.,* eds., *Studies in Cognitive Growth,* pp. 68-85, New York: John Wiley & Sons, (1966).

Piaget, J. *The Language and Thought of the Child.* New York: Routledge & Kegan Paul, (1959).

———. *The Psychology of Intelligence.* New Jersey: Littlefield Adams, (1960).

———. *Structuralism.* London: Routledge & Kegan Paul, (1971).

Razran, G. "The Observable Unconscious and the Inferable Conscious in Current Soviet Psychophysiology," *Psych. Rev.,* 68, 2 (1961).

Reese, H.W. "Discrimination Learning Set in Children," in L.P. Lipsett and C.C. Spilcer, eds., in *Child Development and Behaviour,* New York: Academic Press, (1963), I, 115-145.

Rheingold Harriet Lange. *The Modification of Social Responsiveness in Institutional Babies.* Lafayette Indiana: Child Development Publications, (1956). (Monographs of the Society for Research in Child Development, Vol. 21, no. 2, Serial No. 63).

Shannon, L. *One Million Children.* Published by Leonard Craneford for the Commission on Emotional and Learning Disabilities in Children, Toronto, (1970).

Shvachkin, N.K. "Development of Phonemic Perception of Speech in Early Childhood." Moscow: Izd, Akad, Pedog, Nauk, RSFSR, (1948), No. 13.

Stodolsky, S. "Maternal Behavior and Language and Concept Formation in Negro Preschool Children: An Inquiry into Process." Unpublished Ph.D. dissertation, University of Chicago, (1965).

Venezky, Richard L. "Linguistics and Spelling," in A. H. Marckwardt, eds., *Linguistics in School Programmes,* Chicago: NSSE, (1970), pp. 264-274.

Vetlugina, N.A. "The Development of Perception of Pitch and Rhythm Relationships in the Process of Singing Instruction Offered to Preschool Children," in *Sensory Training of Preschool Children.* Moscow: Izd, Akad, Pedag., Nauk, RSFST, (1963).

Vygotsky, L.S. *Thought and Language.* Cambridge, Mass.: M.I.T. Press; New York: John Wiley & Sons, (1962).

White,Burton. "The Initial Coordination of Sensorimotor Schemas in Human Infants: Piaget's Ideas and the Role of Experience," in J. Hellmuth, ed., *Cognitive Studies,* New York: Brunner Mazel, (1970), I. 24-43.

26

Bilingual Schooling in Dade County

Rosa G. de Inclán

With the five administrative directives which the Dade County School Board has approved, (see Appendix I) the sixth largest school system of the U.S.A. has taken the initiative in bilingual education by becoming fully committed to it.[1] The directives and the newly revised *Bilingual Education Procedures Manual* is the System's response to a report on the educational needs of the bilingual community issued in the spring by an Ad Hoc Advisory Committee on the Education of Spanish Speakers in Dade County. The Committee was organized by invitation from the Associate Superintendent of Instruction as a result of expressed criticism by members of the Greater Miami Coalition as to the manner in which some instructional programs in Bilingual Education were being implemented in several schools. Its members were representative of various areas of the community — university, public and parochial school administrators, parent groups, teachers, aides, students, the news media, community relations agencies. It was charged with the responsibility of re-examining all components of the Bilingual Education Program in the schools and of making recommendations for their improvement to the Division.

Because the terms "bilingual schooling" and "bilingual education" mean so many different things to so many different people, it is probably pertinent to define what each means in Dade County. In re-examining our program to try to bring it into a Program Planning and Budgeting System structure (PPBS), we concluded that the term *Bilingual School Organization*[2] is a more accurate and meaningful means to define the kind of instructional program in which the two languages spoken by two different culture groups are used to mediate curriculum for both groups within a school. In Dade, a school is said to have a bilingual school organization if, in addition to offering the regular curriculum content in English, it also offers the four components of the Bilingual Education Program, i.e.:

1. Curriculum Content in Spanish (CCS)
2. Spanish for Spanish Speakers (Spanish-S)[3]

3. Spanish as a Second Language (SSL)[4]

4. English as a Second Language (ESL)[5]

A school does not necessarily have to be a bilingual school *in toto*, such as Coral Way, where all of its pupils are involved in a bilingual school organization. It may well be like Dade's Shenandoah Junior High School, or Miami Senior, in both of which the once Coral Way children study part of the curriculum in English and part in Spanish. A group of 47 tenth graders in Miami Senior (4 of them English language origin)[6] study biology in Spanish in addition to Spanish-S. Of the 3,766 Spanish language origin[7] students 1,403 are involved in Spanish-S and 421 in English SL. Since they do not study curriculum content in Spanish, these students are not considered to be in a Bilingual School Organization.

At Shenandoah Junior, with a total membership of 1,916 students, of which 1,348 are of Spanish Language Origin (SLO), 159 seventh, 66 eighth and 73 ninth graders are involved in a Bilingual School Organization. Of these, 58 are of English Language Origin (ELO) and 213 SLO. All of them take Spanish-S (or Spanish-SL if not yet bilingual ELO) and some curriculum content in Spanish, Science, and Social Studies. As in Miami High, the rest of the Shenandoah Junior Spanish language origin students may also be involved in one or two of the Bilingual Education Program components. At present 876 are taking Spanish-S courses and 243, English SL.

In Miami Beach, Leroy D. Fienberg Elementary had a total membership of 244 SLO and 215 ELO, all of whom took an extended program in Spanish-S, Spanish SL, and curriculum content in Spanish. ELO and SLO pupils separate for vernacular language arts and second language instruction. They come together again for curriculum content in Spanish and stay in mixed classes for the remainder of the day. Fienberg's feeder junior high school, Ida Fisher, has 24 SLO seventh graders and 13 ELO studying Social Studies, Language, and Culture core in Spanish.

A third elementary school in Key Biscayne has begun to evolve towards a bilingual school organization by offering Spanish-S, Spanish SL, and curriculum content in Spanish.

In all, there is one Bilingual School Organization in Dade County which involves the entire school population, Coral Way Elementary, one which involves part of the school membership, Shenandoah Junior, and five gradually evolving Bilingual School Organizations: Leroy D. Fienberg Elementary, South Beach Elementary, Key Biscayne Elementary, Ida Fisher Junior, and Miami Senior.

In the new quinmester[8] program, there are multidisciplinary quins in Spanish, among them a whole set in business education, which will enable secondary schools to offer more curriculum content in Spanish.

The elementary schools are already using the materials from the Spanish Curricula Development Center[9] as they are being produced.

On what grounds is a large public school system such as Dade County committing itself so definitely to bilingual education, and in particular, to bilingual schooling? The Richardson studies[10] of the years 1966, 67, and 68 verify the hypothesis that "there is no significant difference in achievement in the language arts and in arithmetic, at the same grade levels, between English and Spanish-speaking pupils in the experimental bilingual groups and English and Spanish-speaking pupils in the control groups." (Richardson, 1968, p. 61)

A study made in 1969 by Beulah Cypress while in the Research Training Program at the University of Miami further concludes that bilingual schooling does not "influence normal progress in language arts, or in arithmetic. Except for the language sub-test results for the Cuban groups, any significant differences favor the experimental groups."[11] In the Cypress study, the Cooperative Inter American Reading Tests in English and in Spanish were administered to 19 North American boys and girls and 17 Cubans in their sixth year at Coral Way. The Stanford Achievement tests in language and in arithmetic were also administered to these (experimental group) and to a similar control group in a neighboring school.

The table below, reproduced from Miss Cypress's report, shows the means of experimental and control groups, adjusted by I.Q. There is a significant difference in spelling between North American experimental and control groups in favor of the experimental group.

MEANS OF EXPERIMENTAL AND CONTROL GROUPS ADJUSTED BY IQ

| | NORTH AMERICAN | | CUBAN | |
	EXPER.	CONTROL	EXPER.	CONTROL
Word meaning	25.592	26.687	23.263	24.579
Paragraph meaning	43.171	39.392	37.736	37.001
Spelling	39.580	28.780	31.509	32.439
Language	91.609	88.127	83.030	90.812
Arithmetic computation	21.370	20.824	21.132	18.973
Arithmetic concepts	19.076	18.824	17.448	14.447
Arithmetic application	24.155	21.721	20.740	18.681

The hypothesis that by the sixth grade bilingual children are equally proficient in reading in two languages is tenable in reference to the Spanish language origin pupils, but not to the English language origin. If we consider that these children are in an English-speaking country, we will have to agree that this outcome is to be expected. Another of Cypress's tables shows this as it brings out the comparison of native and second language mean scores.

COMPARISON OF NATIVE AND SECOND LANGUAGES, BILINGUAL STUDENTS

	NORTH AMERICAN N = 17		CUBAN N =19	
	NATIVE	SECOND	NATIVE	SECOND
Mean	110.4	74.1	101.5	101.3
Std. Dev.	11.98	18.44	13.54	17.00
T =	12.1		0.85	
D.F.	16		18	
Prob.	Less than .05		Greater than 0.5	

Further studies were conducted by the Dade County Department of Program Evaluation in the spring of 1970[12]. The Cooperative Inter American tests of reading and general ability were used for grades 3-8 and, in addition, the science and social studies tests in both languages were administered in grade 8. Results indicate that the group of experimental Spanish language origin students perform as well in the English language as their counterparts in the control, "monolingual" English School. Interestingly enough, though, the control junior high school group — with the exception of eighth grade girls — performed better in the Spanish language. We had better add here also that the control junior high school has a particularly well structured Spanish-S program. Our hypothesis of skills transference seems to be tenable, for the students in the control school had not studied either science or social studies in Spanish as had been the case with the Shenandoah Junior (experimental) students. However, the instructional programs do not differ for girls and boys in any school.

In spite of these rather consistent results, some parents are still apprehensive about their children's competency in English when part of their school day is devoted to studying in Spanish. In response to this genuine concern — which is shared by some conscientious educators also — the Department of Program Evaluation conducted two other studies. In one of them, the performance of the ELO students in the county-wide testing program was analyzed.

The experimental group consisted of a random sample of 70 ELO students in Fienberg's and Coral Way's 4th and 5th grades who had been in either school for at least four years. Their grade equivalent scores in Paragraph Meaning and Arithmetic Computation (Stanford Achievement Tests) were considered as pre-tests, and a control group was selected at random from neighboring schools among children who had identical grade equivalent scores on one of the two subtests.

Scores attained by these same students during the following county-wide test in May of 1971 were then treated as post test scores.

> No significant difference emerged between the post-test results for the experimental group and the post-test results for the control group on either the Arithmetic Computation or the Paragraph Meaning subtests at either grade level. In terms of the Stanford Achievement Test, this

investigation indicated that "English Language Origin" students in an elementary "bilingual program" (Fienberg's) or in a "bilingual school" (Coral Way's) achieve as much in reading and arithmetic computation during the school year as they would in a school without a "bilingual program."[13]

Tables 1, 2, 3 and 4 (See Appendix II) show mean scores.

The second study recently done by the Program Evaluation Department assessed the transference of skills acquired in the first language. The hypothesis that a student who is a skilled reader in his vernacular is bound to be a skilled reader in his second language appears to be tenable also.

Performances of random samples of fourth, fifth, and sixth graders in the Spanish and in the English language forms of the Cooperative Inter American Reading tests were compared. All pupils had been in either Fienberg or Coral Way for at least three years. Results were as follows:

1. The SLO pupils from Coral Way were "approximately as proficient in their second language as they were in their first." (Evaluation Report, July 30, 1971)

2. Both groups of ELO's at Coral Way (the bilingual school) and at Fienberg (the extended Spanish-S and SL program) read significantly better in the English language at all three grade levels.

3. The SLO pupils at Coral Way attained approximately equal scores on the reading tests in both languages at all three levels.

It is pertinent to remember at this point that the bilingual school organization of instruction at Coral Way allows approximately equal time to instruction in both languages for all students. At Fienberg, different schedules have been in existence for different grade levels from year to year. The maximum time allowed for Spanish "core" and "enrichment" activities and for Spanish language instruction — either SL or first language — has been 90 minutes in all, at any grade level.

In conclusion, all studies conducted in Dade County, whether informally or with tighter statistical controls, seem to indicate that children and older students involved in a bilingual school organization of instruction lose absolutely nothing in terms of English language skills. If, in addition, we consider the enormous gains involved in bilingualism for the individual destined to live in a bilingual, or in a pluralistic society, the choice for educators in leadership positions appears to be obvious.

Summary

Both Spanish (SLO) and English-language-origin (ELO) pupils participating in the bilingual school program at the Coral Way Elementary School in Miami have "achieved as much in the way of skills, abilities, and understandings as they would have had they attended a monolingual school, and in addition have derived benefits which they could not have attained in a traditional school." The attainment of the primary objective originally proposed for the Dade County bilingual public school has been again ascertained by the 1970 evaluation of the performance of children in grades 3-8 in reading and general ability, as measured by paralled Spanish and English forms of the Cooperative Interamerican Tests. Further comparison in terms of the Stanford Achievement Test in English of a group of 17 English-language-origin sixth graders who had been in the program the entire six years with a similar control group from a monolingual school showed no statistically significant differences between the groups in Arithmetic Computation, Concepts, or Applications, nor in Word Meaning or Paragraph Meaning. The significant differences found ($p. < .002$) on the Spelling Test were in favor of the bilingual group. These findings should allay the apprehensions of the skeptics who fear that the bilingual program will cause a possible deficit in English language skills. Without suffering any such loss, both ELO and SLO children achieve a significant degree of bilingualism.

Appendix I

Five Administrative Directives for the Bilingual Education Program from the Dade County Superintendent of Schools.

"The Superintendent of Schools directs the Division of Instruction, districts, and schools to take the steps necessary to implement the following directives:

1. That each school provide instruction in English as a Second Language for those students entering the school who are either 'Nonindependent' or 'intermediate.' Schools not offering such a program must receive approval from the district superintendent and the Associate Superintendent for Instruction.[1]
2. That every school provide the opportunity for Spanish language origin and bilingual English language origin students to be involved in an instructional program in Spanish for Spanish speakers. Schools not offering such a program must receive approval from the district superintendent and the Associate Superintendent for Instruction.[2]
3. That a Spanish-as-a-Second-Language pilot program be implemented by the Division of Instruction in one or more districts in schools not functioning within a bilingual school organization for the 1971-72 school year; and that, based on the success of the Spanish SL pilot program or programs during the 1971-72 school year, a supplemental budget appropriation request be submitted for 1972-73 to provide funds for the expansion of the programs to all schools that identify the need for such a program.[3]
4. That each district, in cooperation with the Division of Instruction, develop a plan during the 1971-72 school year for establishing within the district a K-12 Bilingual School Organization.[4]
5. That an internal certification program in second language teaching and in Spanish-S for teachers and paraprofessionals be developed by the Division of Instruction, in cooperation with the Personnel Division. This certification program is to be developed since the state has no certification program for English SL, Spanish-S, or Bilingual Education. The definitions and procedures for implementation of these directives are found in *Procedures Manual*, Bilingual Education Program, Bulletin 1-C."

Division of Instruction (10-15-71)

Appendix II

Achievement of "English Language Origin" students in bilingual and non-bilingual elementary schools as indicated by the Arithmetic Computation Subtest of the Stanford Achievement Tests, grade 5-6.

Table 1

	Bilingual Schools		Non-Bilingual Schools
Mean	8.58		7.85
Std. Dev.		0.43	
T		1.70	
D.F.		32	
Prob		N.S.	

Achievement of "English Language Origin" students in bilingual and non-bilingual elementary schools as indicated by the Paragraph Meaning Subtest of the Stanford Achievement Tests, grades 4-5.

Table 2

	Bilingual Schools		Non-Bilingual Schools
Mean	7.60		7.08
Std. Dev.		0.38	
T		1.34	
D.F.		31	
Prob		N.S.	

Achievement of "English Language Origin" students in bilingual and non-bilingual elementary schools as indicated by the Arithmetic Computation Subtest of the Stanford Achievement Tests, grades 4-5.

Table 3

	Bilingual Schools	Non-Bilingual Schools
Mean	6.45	6.50
Std. Dev.	.195	
T	0.257	
D.F.	35	
Prob	N.S.	

Achievement of "English Language Origin" students in bilingual and non-bilingual elementary schools as indicated by the Paragraph Meaning Subtest of the Stanford Achievement Tests, grades 5-6.

Table 4

	Bilingual Schools	Non-Bilingual Schools
Mean	9.42	8.55
Std. Dev.	0.378	
T	2.30	
D.F.	34	
Prob	>.01	
	<.05	

NOTES

[1] The first public bilingual school to have been established after World War I in the U.S. is Coral Way Elementary in Miami, Dade County, as stated by Andersson and Boyer in *Bilingual Schooling in the United States*, vol. one, (Austin, Texas: Southwest Educational Laboratory, 1970), pp. 17-18.

[2] The criteria that define a bilingual school organization are:

a. SLO and ELO students being offered an organization of instruction which provides for
  1. Second-language programs in Spanish and in English that enable the average student to attain an independent classification in approximately three years; and
  2. Appropriate language arts programs in English and in Spanish (Spanish-S) which meet the county criteria.
b. Organization of instruction that provides for staged introduction of learning activities in Spanish in at least one subject in each of the two subject area groups below:
  1. Music, art, physical education, home economics, industrial arts; and
  2. Social studies, science, mathematics.
c. Utilization of teachers and aides trained in teaching second language and curriculum content in Spanish and in English.
d. Utilization of materials in English and in Spanish designed for native speakers of the language in their study of the various subject areas and of materials designed for second language learners.

[3] The criteria that define Spanish-S;

a. A class made up of SLO or bilingual ELO students.
b. A daily schedule of instruction during a block of 30-60 minutes at the elementary level and 45-60 minutes at the secondary level; a minimum of 150 minutes of instruction each week at the elementary level and of 225 at the secondary level.
c. Utilization of teachers and aides who are either native speakers of Spanish or can function effectively in Spanish and who are trained in teaching Spanish language arts.

[4] The criteria that define Spanish-SL are: In order to be defined as such, a Spanish SL class must meet the following criteria:

a. A class made up of ELO students for Spanish language instruction and conceivably including SLO students for content area instruction.
b. At the elementary level, a schedule providing daily instruction in Spanish for a minimum of 50 minutes, usually including 30 minutes in

structured language learning activities and an additional 20 minutes of activities reinforcing aspects of the regular curriculum (a minimum of 250 minutes of instruction in Spanish each week). At the secondary level, a schedule providing daily instruction in Spanish for a minimum of 90 minutes, usually including 45 minutes of structured language learning activities and an additional 45 minutes of activities reinforcing aspects of the regular curriculum, a minimum of 450 minutes of instruction in Spanish per week. For students whose Spanish language proficiency permits, a period of curriculum content in Spanish satisfies the requirement for the second period of instruction.

c. Utilization of teachers and/or aides specially trained for Spanish SL instruction at all levels.

d. Utilization of Spanish SL materials and interdisciplinary materials specially designed for Spanish SL for content area instruction at the secondary level; utilization also of materials designed for SLO students.

[5] The criteria that define an ESL class in Dade County's Bulletin 1C are as follows:

a. A class made up entirely of non-English language origin students.

b. A daily schedule of instruction in the elementary school of from one to three hours and in the secondary school of one to three class periods, determined by the language proficiency of the students, as defined in 2.62 on pages 10-11. (Bulletin 1C)

c. Utilization of **ELO teachers or bilingual teachers and aides who** demonstrate mastery of English comparable to the independent level of students, as measured by the Oral Language Proficiency Scale (see page 79).

d. Utilization of teachers and aides specially trained in teaching a second language.

[6] *English language origin (ELO)* is the term used by Dade County to refer to the native North Americans or "Anglos," that is, children who used English as their first language for communication at home *and* who still communicate effectively in English at the time of placement in an instructional program. (See *Procedures Manual, Bilingual Education Program, Bulletin 1C*, Revised 1971, Division of Instruction, Dade County Schools, Miami, Florida, p. 3.)

[7] *Spanish language origin (SLO)* refers to all students considered by themselves, their parents, their school, or their community to be of Spanish origin *and* who can communicate in Spanish with native proficiency at the time of placement in an instructional program.

[8] The Quinmester Plan divides the school year into five 9-week

segments. Courses of study specially written for each quinmester are called *quins.* Each course description provides objectives and indicators of success, which assist students in determining their own readiness for each quin as they make their selection.

[9] The Spanish Curricula Development Center is a federally funded Bilingual Education Act project designed to produce materials in Spanish for Spanish language origin children in grades 1-3. Materials cover the areas of Social Studies, Science and Math, Fine Arts, and Language Arts. In addition, the Center is producing a strand in Spanish SL designed for ELO pupils which is also multidisciplinary in its approach.

[10] Mabel W. Richardson, "An Evaluation of Certain Aspects of the Academic Achievement of Elementary Pupils in a Bilingual Program," Coral Gables, Florida: The University of Miami, (1968).

[11] Beulah Cypress, "Evaluation of the Academic Achievement of Sixth Grade Pupils in a Bilingual Education Program." Unpublished report presented while in the Research Training Program at the University of Miami, Coral Gables, Florida, (1969). It might be pertinent to remember that the Stanford subtest in language measures mechanics (capitalization, punctuation, dictionary skills, and sentence sense).

[12] Department of Program Evaluation, Dade County Public Schools, Miami, Florida, (April, 1970). "Evaluation Report: The Instructional Program for 'Spanish Language Origin' Students, (1970-71)," pp. 67-69, unpublished interim report.

[13] Department of Program Evaluation, Dade County Public Schools, Miami, Florida, (July 30, 1971). "Evaluation Report: The Instructional Program for 'Spanish Language Origin' Students, (1970-71)," unpublished draft.

Bibliography

Allen, Harold B. *TENES Report. A Survey of the Teaching of English to Non-English Speakers in the U.S.*, Champaign, Ill.: National Council of Teachers of English, (1966).

Andersson, T., and M. Boyer. *Bilingual Schooling in the United States*, Austin, Texas: Southwest Educational Laboratory, (1970).

Cypress, Beulah. "Evaluation of the Academic Achievement of Sixth Grade Pupils in a Bilingual Education Program," Unpublished report, (1969).

Dade County Public Schools, Department of Program Evaluation. "An Evaluation Report: The Instructional Program for 'Spanish Language Origin' Students, (1970-71)," Miami, Florida, (April 1970; July 30, 1971).

Dade County Public Schools, Division of Instruction. *Procedures Manual: Bilingual Education Program*, Bulletin 1C, Revised, Miami, Florida, (1971).

Richardson, Mabel W. "An Evaluation of Certain Aspects of the Academic Achievement of Elementary Pupils in a Bilingual Program," Coral Gables, Florida: The University of Miami, (1968).

VIII

POLICY AND RESEARCH

27

After Childhood, What?

Robert L. Muckley

The recent development of bilingual education programs for those groups whose native language is other than English has lent a new interest to the concept of ethnic language retention (ELRET). The question has been raised whether bilingual education (i.e., education through the medium of English together with some other language) is primarily a transitional device to help children of our ethnic minorities until they become fluent in English, or whether one aim is the retention of the vernacular even after (and in a sense independent of) the acquisition of fluency in English.

If the Bilingual Education Act is intended to conserve our language resources, then measures for the retention of the vernacular, or ethnic language, should be built into our bilingual programs. And measures should be taken not only within schools where formal bilingual programs are in progress but in all schools having ethnic speakers, and particularly in those schools where foreign languages are offered which are the ethnic languages of a number of the students. Thus time will not be wasted in teaching students things which they already know, and the ethnic speakers will make a contribution by making the language come alive for monolingual students interested in acquiring it.

For much of our foreign-language teaching is ethnic oriented. It is not by accident that Spanish has been widely taught in the Southwest, that French is popular in New England and Louisiana, or that Portuguese is taught in New Bedford, Massachusetts. Efforts directed towards ethnic language retention are certainly not new in the United States (most of our immigrant groups have formed organizations for this purpose), nor for that matter is bilingual education. German-English bilingual schools, both public and private, flourished during the nineteenth century and up until the First World War. Spanish and French were also used in bilingual schools in New Mexico and Louisiana respectively. Yet during the period after the First World War public school bilingual education ceased completely and the idea of any effort towards public school assistance in programs designed to

380

enhance ethnic language retention was so completely absent from the national scene that Brault could claim in 1962 that his "Bowdoin Institutes" (the first of which took place in 1961) sponsored by the National Defense Education Act in order to train teachers and prepare materials for teaching French to ethnic speakers, marked the first time in history that an ethnic group was accorded federal support in its struggle to preserve its linguistic heritage.[1] The rebirth of bilingual education in our times seems to have taken place in 1963 at the Coral Way School in Miami in response to the needs of Cuban refugees of that area, though the program has been so successful that monolingual speakers of English have been included and have benefited from it. Foreign-language instruction in the United States has, however, for the most part ignored the needs of the ethnic speaker; and, with the exception of a few materials to be mentioned later on, there is nothing commercially available for teaching ethnic languages, and there is no organized effort or formalized structure within which the teaching of ethnic languages can be planned and discussed.

Considering the fact that in the United States there may be nearly 20,000,000 people with some knowledge of an ethnic language,[2] this seems incredible, particularly since our federal government evidenced its belief that people with a knowledge of a foreign language constitute a valuable resource by making foreign-language study eligible for support under NDEA. In regard to these NDEA projects, A. Bruce Gaarder of the United States Office of Education has stated that "The Federal Government encourages a multi-million dollar expenditure annually for language development (in both the 'common' and 'neglected' languages) but no part of the effort is directed specifically to the further development of those same languages in the more than one in ten Americans who already have a measure of native competence in them."[3] Brault's Bowdoin Institutes constitute a unique exception. It is true that Gaarder made this statement before the passage of the Bilingual Education Act and some bilingual programs have attempted to remedy this anomaly. However, more recent studies by Gaarder have been highly critical of many bilingual programs precisely because of inadequate attention given to the ethnic language. In a recent essay on the subject, he points out that in the first seventy-six bilingual schooling projects supported by grants under the Bilingual Education Act there appears to be "such inadequate attention — time, resources, and understanding — to the other tongue, as compared to the attention paid to English that, on the whole, the concept of bilingual education represented by these plans of operation seems to be something less than the legislation and its advocates intended."[4] Gaarder also implies that foreign-language teachers should be much more involved in bilingual education than they are by mentioning, apparently as an exception, one program in which this involvement does occur: "Milwaukee sees the importance of uniting its bilingual schooling project with the efforts of its regular foreign-language teachers at the high school level, and will offer a history and culture course for both groups of students together."[5]

Long a staunch advocate of ethnic language retention, Gaarder has insisted that bilingual education should be something more than simply a transitional device to enable low-income groups to become more acculturated. Another outstanding scholar whose work has been primarily in support of ELRET is Joshua Fishman, who has made extensive studies of the linguistic resources of our country and of the tendency towards maintenance or shift among the various ethnic groups. Major projects which Fishman has directed for the Research Section of the United States Office of Education have produced reports such as *Language Loyalty in the United States* and, more recently, *Bilingualism in the Barrio*, which deals specifically with linguistic habits of Puerto Rican families living in the New York City area.[6] In order to make the climate for ethnic languages more favorable, Fishman suggests the establishment of a "'Commission on Biculturism (or Bilingualism) in American Life' with national, regional and local subdivisions." He also recommends financial and other aid to language maintenance organizations, and of more immediate interest, the "preparation of special teaching materials for the bilingual child" and the "granting of credit for out-of-school language mastery."[7]

The preparation of special teaching materials will be discussed in detail. Granting credit for out-of-school language mastery, however, is also extremely important because of the way our educational system is "credit point" and "basic requirement" oriented. One way we educators can show ethnic speakers that we feel it important that they have kept up their language is by giving credit for competence and not simply for patience. Let us hope that more high schools and colleges will allow competent ethnic speakers to receive credit through proficiency examinations and the College Board will extend its CLEP (College Level Examination Program) to include languages other than English.

In mentioning scholarly work in ELRET, the name of Einar Haugen should certainly not be passed over. He provides a somewhat heart-rending account of how a once vigorous ethnic language has succumbed to external and internal erosion.[8] He has also produced materials for teaching Norwegian. Another scholar, Uriel Weinreich, provides a framework for analyzing types of interference.[9] And the *Journal of Social Issues* devotes its April, 1967 issue to "Problems of Bilingualism," where, in addition to articles by Gaarder and Fishman, there are others by Susan Ervin-Tripp, John J. Gumperz, Dell Hymes, Heinz Kloss, Wallace Lambert, and John Macnamara. Lambert's research in particular has very positive implications for bilingual education and ethnic language retention programs. His experiments tend to show that the bilingual is less bound by rigid norms of a particular group and "may well start life with the enormous advantage of having a more open, receptive mind about himself and other people."[10] Gaarder refers to the Peal-Lambert study of bilingual ten-year-olds in

Montreal, which gives evidence that "if the children are equally well educated in both languages, i.e., [are] 'balanced' bilinguals, they are superior in both verbal and non-verbal intelligence to monolinguals."[11] This should give the ethnic speaker a powerful reason for maintaining his bilingual ability independent of the advantages to be derived from the knowledge of a particular language, although Lambert's experiments should be replicated with language combinations other than French and English.

It is impossible to report here all the findings of scholars which might have implications for ELRET programs. It seems to me, however, that the most important single factor to be gleaned from scholarly research can be stated quite simply and unequivocally, although the implications for teaching will tax the best efforts of material writers and curriculum planners who devote themselves to developing programs for teaching ethnic languages. The factor may be called the "domain stability" concept. That is, an ethnic language will be retained as long as it continues to be the preferred language within certain definite areas of activity. To again quote Fishman, ". . .If a strict domain separation becomes institutionalized such that each language is associated with a number of important but distinct domains, bilingualism can become both universal and stabilized even though an entire population consists of bilinguals interacting with other bilinguals."[12] In my own work with Spanish-speaking groups, I have noticed that the Mexican Americans conserve Spanish much better, even after generations of living in the United States, than do the "Neo-Ricans" or children of Puerto Rican parents living in New York and in other large urban areas of the East, because the Neo-Ricans tend to prefer English in all domains and speak Spanish only to older people. A questionnaire which a number of Neo-Rican students filled out for me indicated a preference for use of English among those of their own age group for all purposes. Cooper and Greenfield in examining a group of Puerto Rican background living in Jersey City conclude that "the finding that young people, in speaking among themselves, use English more often than Spanish in all domains, including family, suggests that bilingualism in the community under study is characterized by language shift."[13]

The problem, then, for those of us who write materials and plan programs designed to enhance ethnic language retention is whether these materials can be so contrived that they will induce ethnic speakers to stabilize certain domains in which the ethnic language will be used in their daily lives, particularly for groups like the "Neo-Ricans" for whom such domain stability does not appear to exist at the present time. The problem is not a simple one — it will, as I have said, tax our best efforts — yet it is quite possible that there is a good bit that we can do, particularly since our efforts now seem to go hand in hand with the designs of youth organizations among Spanish-speaking groups whose purposes, according to Gaarder, are to acquire an education and to reaffirm their ethnicity.[14] Certain clues as to how to approach the problem may be gathered from *Bilingualism in the*

Barrio, in which it is pointed out that Spanish does have an important role in the lives of the youth of Puerto Rican background living in the New York area. For example, it is imperative that a boy speak Spanish when he is first introduced to his girl friend's parents — that is, when he is requesting permission to be her formal *novio*.[15] Fishman points out that boys whose command of Spanish is poor look forward to this moment with dread and we can certainly imagine they would be grateful for some pointers as to how to handle the situation. Sample dialogs can be built into materials, and hopefully, the boy's future *suegro* will not discuss topics on which he is tongue-tied. Also, Spanish continued to be the language of the *piropo*. The ingeniously worded little compliment which the admiring male makes to female beauty simply would not come off in English. It has a tradition of its own which depends on Spanish. And Fishman points out that the ability to invent clever *piropos* is highly valued.

ELRET materials should, in short, take advantage of community and family relationships and should serve to bring the school and the community closer together. In complementation of Fishman's points, mentioned earlier, Gaarder insists that there should be:

(1) New, strong links between what the schools do and what the community is and wants;

(2) an end to the attitude of condescension on the part of foreign language teachers toward the language of the folk bilinguals.[16]

Regarding the first point, we might add that positive, understanding efforts should be made to sell the community on the ELRET concept. Are they aware, for example, of the results of Lambert's studies on the correlation of bilingualism and intelligence? Parents who desire that their children keep up the ethnic language often insist that it be spoken in the home. Lacking this, it can be suggested (and such suggestions can be built into the material) that the ethnic language should at least be conserved in certain situations. A favorite is at the dinner table. If this is accepted good-naturedly, it becomes a kind of game in which the person who accidentally utters a word in English must pay a fine or some other type of forfeit. Additional suggestions related to activities where the ethnic language might be used could involve club meetings, summer camps, and ethnic festivals. The important thing is to have a certain group of activities which will always be carried out in the ethnic language and on which its retention will be anchored. This does not mean that the ethnic language need always be limited to these activities, nor does it even mean, in my opinion, that there is anything wrong with mixing languages in certain domains as long as competence in both English and the ethnic language is assured by the existence of domains in which a single language must be used exclusively. Gaarder is not happy about mixing languages, but I feel that his exhortation that "every effort be made to avoid this mixing of Spanish and English"[17] is a bit too severe, having found in my own personal experience that one of the most enjoyable things about being bilingual is having two languages at my disposal instead of one and in being able to use either of them when in conversation with other bilinguals. It is fascinating to reflect on why certain things are said in one language and not the other. Being able to mix languages is really a bonus for being bilingual.

Regarding the second point, since it seems to be pretty much assumed that outside of formal bilingual programs, and particularly at the secondary level, ELRET efforts will fall to the foreign-language teacher, the question arises as to what special training such a teacher needs — special courses in methodology of teaching an ethnic language, social problems of minority groups, or possibly more work in applied linguistics with special reference to dialectology? It is crucial that the teacher take a positive attitude toward the ethnic group and its linguistic idiosyncracies. For if domain stability is a central concept to ELRET, then a corollary to this is that procedures for teaching ethnic speakers should certainly not imperil domains in which the ethnic language is already used, however imperfectly. In regard to this, Gaarder expresses the viewpoints of the AATSP Committee in the following manner:

> The dialect speaker must be accepted wholeheartedly as and where he is and must never be censured or subjected to pressure simply because he speaks the dialect. The position to be taken is that each style of speaking, each dialect, is appropriate to certain situations, and that the pupil, eventually, is to learn a world standard in order to increase his repertory of speech styles and so increase his versatility and power.[18]

In other words, the ethnic speaker should learn the standard language. But deviant forms should be considered matters of interest rather than matters of scorn.

In making a survey of materials now available, we find very little specifically designed for teaching ethnic speakers in the United States — either in their language or about their language. Bilingual programs often seek to make use of materials produced in other countries where the language is native. Gaarder, however, laments the fact that not enough attention is given to the development and procurement of materials in the ethnic language, and points out that instead, bilingual teachers "are expected in most of the projects to create or assist in the creation of teaching materials in the non-English tongue."[19] Since these teachers are usually untrained in writing materials in any language, the results can be disastrous.

What is being done is mainly at the primary level. The Spanish Curricula Development Center, located in Miami Beach, has been set up as part of a major effort of the Bilingual Education Programs Branch of the Office of Education, "for the purpose of creating primary bloc Spanish curricula to support Spanish-English bilingual education programs." The Center plans to develop "48 multidisciplinary, multimedia Spanish Curricula kits" for use in the first three grades. In addition to focusing on the language itself, these will include "strands" in social science, fine arts, science, and mathematics.[20] Final completion of these materials is scheduled for August 1974, and they will be available not only to formal bilingual programs but also "to interested school systems with relevant pupil populations."[21] Ralph Robinett, the director of this Center, had previously worked as director of the Michigan Migrant Primary Interdisciplinary Project, which developed special curricula for the children of migrant workers in the state of Michigan — The Michigan Oral Language Series. This included a "Spanish Guide" for use at the kindergarten level.

I might add here that it was my privilege to be contracted by the Philadelphia Public School System to write ELRET materials in Spanish for the 10-12 grade level.

Before going further into the matter of specialized materials for ethnic speakers at the secondary level, it might be convenient first to discuss characteristics of the target groups and typical problems in their language usage. It is not easy to make sharp cut-off points, of course; ethnic speakers differ in their linguistic abilities and many with ethnic surnames may have little or no knowledge of the language. Gaarder lists as minimal qualifications for participation in a program designed for ethnic speakers (in this case, Spanish), "the ability to understand ordinary conversation in the dialect of his parents and their peers plus the ability to follow simple instructions given in Spanish.[22] My comments at this point will be mainly limited to the group I have directly studied — the "Neo-Rican" college freshmen, children of Puerto Rican parents who have been reared and educated in the United States, for whom Spanish is the language spoken in the home but not at school. (They did not have the advantage of bilingual education programs.) In their use of and attitudes toward Spanish, this group evidences the following characteristics:

1. They control the mechanics of the spoken language quite well (their vocabulary is limited to terms that are common in everyday use).

2. However, they usually prefer to use English among themselves (with an occasional Spanish word or expression thrown in) though most state they would like to better their command of Spanish.

3. Their phonetic habits are characteristically Puerto Rican. That is, there is little evidence of deterioration through contact with English.

4. They can read when required to do so, though they do so slowly and are somewhat hampered by lack of vocabulary.

5. Their spelling of Spanish is very deficient. It is influenced by their pronunciation habits and by English spelling in the case of cognates. They usually refuse to use written accent marks.

6. They are aware of their Puerto Rican heritage, but do not feel they belong to Puerto Rico. As one once said, they prefer to associate "with people like me — Puerto Ricans who come from the United States or New York."

While different groups of ethnic speakers may differ somewhat in regard to some of these points (some, hopefully, still show more evidence of domain stability in the ethnic language), one feature which I feel they all have in common is the lack of ability in reading and writing, which requires special training, as opposed to the development of oral facility, which would come naturally from the environment. This fact has important implications for materials and procedures. Some pronunciation therapy may of course be needed, but basically ELRET materials should not be audio-lingually oriented.

The foreign-language teacher at the secondary level not involved in formal bilingual programs and seeking guidance and specialized materials for teaching ethnic speakers will find that such materials are almost nonexistent. A pioneering effort in this area was produced under the direction of Gerald J. Brault during his Bowdoin Institutes, already mentioned, whose purpose was the "formation and professional perfection of our Franco-American French teachers at the secondary level."[23] However, the text, entitled *Cours de langue française destiné aux jeunes franco-américains*, is not commercially available and is quite difficult to obtain. According to Elphège Roy, founder of the Franco-American Teachers Association, it is used in the largest public high school in Manchester, New Hampshire, and "in a few schools in New England."[24]

Since this is the pioneering effort in the ELRET field, some comments seem appropriate. According to the author, it is designed to be used by students who have already had "six or seven years of French at the Franco-American parochial school," who understand spoken French and who can read a passage of medium difficulty.[25] It consists of thirty units, whose format includes a short article, a dialog, an explanation of difficult vocabulary items, pronunciation exercises to correct typical Franco-American or French Canadian errors, oral exercises of the pattern practice type, and translation exercises to and from French. The pattern practice component occasionally attempts to correct errors which are typical in Franco-American although it may simply introduce a verb form or structural feature, with no reference to existing usage. The articles and dialogs involve points of social and historical interest to Franco-Americans and treat both French Canadian and French culture. For one who has not actually used the book in question or taught the target group, it is difficult to make a just criticism. Offhand, it seems to resemble too much a text for teaching French as a foreign language, and except for the exercises involving corrections in Franco-American usage, a casual glance would lead one to believe that it is exactly that. The extensive use of controlled oral pattern practice so characteristic of the audio-lingual method of foreign-language teaching would seem to be dull and wasteful when dealing with ethnic speakers who already control the basic mechanics of the language, who already understand spoken French, and can read passages of medium difficulty.

Independent of bilingual programs established under Title VII, most of the work done in ethnic language retention has been carried out with the Mexican Americans who appear to be somewhat ahead of the rest of the country in the formalization of ELRET efforts. Consequently, the experiences which they are having need to be observed carefully to determine their degree of applicability to other groups. For example, in June 1969 the Texas Education Agency published an unbound book *Español para alumnos hispanohablantes* to provide guidance to junior and senior high school teachers of the state in setting up special classes for the Spanish speaking. Although this publication includes sample lessons, it is not itself a textbook, is not sold commercially, and is not made available except to teachers. In the section on "Specialized Classes" it is pointed out that "Some school systems in Texas have been following now, for several years, the plan for accelerated classes" for native speakers of Spanish, and that "The Superintendent's Annual Report for 1967-68 shows 120 school systems which provide separate classes for native speakers of Spanish at the secondary level."[26] There is also a section recommending materials which might be used. These include a number of textbooks used in Latin America for native speakers of Spanish, a few texts produced for teaching Spanish in the United States (particularly in the literature area), and the only two textbooks published commercially (by National Textbook Company) for teaching an ethnic language in the continental United States — Paulline Baker's *Español para los hispanos*,[27] and Marie Esman Barker's *Español para el bilingüe.*[28]

Español para los hispanos is short and mainly designed to strengthen and correct the student's use of the language at a basic level and the author suggests that it be supplemented with literary texts. There are explanations and exercises designed to teach proper spelling and pronunciation, correct substandard usage, and increase vocabulary, as well as a section on letter writing and on parliamentary terminology.

Marie Esman Barker's text is much more complete. It is divided into twenty-one separate units, each centered about a particular point of linguistic, literary, or cultural interest. The format for each unit usually includes two articles or short stories on the particular topic in question, an explanation of some grammatical point, and a number of exercises involving vocabulary, morphemics, syntax, and pronunciation. The book would obviously be very useful at the high school or even at the beginning college level.

However, at this point a word of warning is necessary. Although the titles of these two texts use the general terms *hispano* and *bilingüe*, they are so obviously aimed, both culturally and linguistically, at the Mexican American of the Southwest that they are not appropriate for use among other Spanish-speaking groups, such as those of Cuban or Puerto Rican background. The cultural orientation of the articles in Mrs. Barker's text is all towards Mexico and is designed to enhance pride in the Mexican American cultural heritage. From the standpoint of linguistics, while it is true that, for example, Neo-Rican and Mexican American Spanish may share certain problem areas because of contact with English, there are also differences derived from corresponding differences in Puerto Rican and Mexican Spanish. In addition the Chicanos, living more in rural isolation and more determined to assert their identity linguistically, have evolved their own *caló* or *pachuco* dialect. *Español para los hispanos*, in particular, presents a wealth of *pachuquismos* and their equivalents in standard Spanish, along with translation exercises involving *pachuco*. A sentence such as "Anochi me jambaron mi huacha y todo mi jando" would be incomprehensible to a Neo-Rican.

And so we find that outside of Title VII bilingual programs, almost all formalized ELRET efforts, and the only two commercially available publications, are aimed at the Chicanos. Publishers of educational materials are naturally reluctant to enter a new field unless a demand for the material is supported by a formal curriculum structure. Even within the formal framework of bilingual education, it is interesting to note the extent to which the Chicanos are favored. Of the first seventy-six bilingual schooling projects supported by grants under the Bilingual Education Act, fifty-eight are for Mexican Americans. Sixty-eight of the total are for the Spanish-speaking, nine among these involving Puerto Ricans. It is true that a very few of the bilingual schooling projects which involve Spanish also involve one other language, but even taking this fact into consideration, there are only fourteen of the total seventy-six projects which deal with an ethnic language other than Spanish.[29] The reason for this of course involves the socio-economic status of the Spanish-speaking and the fact that bilingual education is aimed at the lowest income groups. Now there is nothing wrong with helping people who are disadvantaged in the socio-economic scale to better themselves by providing them with educational programs geared to their needs, but if knowledge of another language is really a resource, then efforts should be made to preserve it whether it is found among the lower, middle, or upper classes.

One is amazed to realize, for example, that Italian, the language which accounted for the largest number of non-English speakers according to the Census of 1960,[30] and German, which according to one report had the greatest number of speakers as late as 1964[31] are not even represented in bilingual education programs, and textbooks for teaching Italian and German in the United States make no allowances for the large number of ethnic speakers. Andersson and Boyer state that as far as their own research can ascertain, "no attempt has ever been made throughout the history of Italian immigration to the United States to instruct Italian Americans in the Italian language."[32] Italian is of course taught as a subject in most universities and in a number of high schools, and ethnicity is doubtless one reason why students choose to take it.[33] We can only hope that where a number of ethnic speakers are involved, the perceptive and imaginative teacher can improvise materials designed for their particular needs. One serious problem with Italian is dialectal difference. "Standard" Italian differs quite considerably from the home dialect of most Italo-Americans. Andersson and Boyer do not forecast a bright future for them, stating that it is "ironic that Neapolitan provinces and from Sicily, whereas those living in the West are from North Italy and that many Italo-Americans "were not even aware of the great cultural heritage associated with the standard Italian language and so they showed no desire to preserve it and perpetuate it."[34] An additional problem which Andersson and Boyer cite is the negative attitude, particularly among the South Italians, toward formal education in general.[35] At this point, needless to say, their attitude is drastically different from that of the Puerto Ricans, who see formal education as a kind of panacea. Since my own work has been with the Spanish-speaking, it is perhaps somewhat risky to venture an opinion regarding the dialect issue, but it would seem that where there is a large enough group speaking a single dialect, such as Neapolitan or Sicilian, material could be prepared for that group using comparisons between the dialect and the standard, in somewhat the same way that Paulline Baker compares *pachuco* with standard Spanish.

In regard to German, we have already mentioned earlier how the First World War brought an end to their vigorous system of bilingual education. Although there are still large German-speaking enclaves, Andersson and Boyer do not forecast a bright future for them, stating that it is "ironic that we spend so many thousands of dollars teaching German on the higher levels when a continuation of past language maintenance efforts on the part of the German community itself could have supplied us with a rich fund of teachers and educated speakers of German."[36]

There is not time here to discuss each ethnic group separately. Andersson and Boyer's *Bilingual Schooling in the United States* gives a brief overview of most of them along with a comment on the status and advisability of bilingual education and ELRET activities. And in my own conclusion of this paper, I can only express again my heart-felt conviction of the need for setting up more formal channels and organizations through which ELRET issues can be aired and discussed within the educational framework. The American Association of Teachers of Spanish and Portuguese has taken cognizance of the problem by devoting two sessions of its last annual meeting in December, 1970 to ELRET, and by setting up a committee of nine members, chaired by Bruce Gaarder, to prepare a report on teaching Spanish to ethnic speakers. In this paper I have frequently referred to a draft of this report, as yet unpublished. And TESOL (Teachers of English to Speakers of Other Languages) through its Committee on Socio-Political Concerns of Minority Groups in TESOL, has issued a position paper as yet not approved by the entire organization, which includes statements to the effect that the teaching of English should be carried out so that minority groups will not sacrifice "in the process of acquisition, at great emotional and psychological cost, their native languages and cultures." The paper further requests that the Committee be made a regular standing committee of the organization and that it have at least one annual meeting aside from the national annual meeting of TESOL.[37]

These are good beginnings, but more coordination of ELRET interested groups will be necessary. ELRET may still bring pride and power to ethnic groups who have been neglected. We are standing on the threshold of an era of unparalleled opportunities disguised as insoluble problems in which the dream of America of cultural diversity within political unity may yet be realized. Let us endeavor to exploit the possibilities fully and fairly so that all the strands in our coat of many colors will shine forth in their true brilliance.

Summary

Ethnic language retention (ELRET) is a special field requiring a formalized structure of its own. The present paper explores its present status, particularly in relation to the broader field of bilingual education: attitudes toward ELRET on the part of ethnic speakers themselves, the general public, teachers, and publishers of educational materials; special training needed for teachers; materials and procedures required; and the opportunity of cross fertilization between ELRET and foreign language classes.

NOTES

[1] Gerald J. Brault, "The Special NDEA Institute at Bowdoin College for French Teachers of Canadian Descent," PMLA, LXXVII (September, 1962), p. 1.

[2] Joshua A. Fishman, "The Status and Prospects of Bilingualism in the United States," *The Modern Language Journal*, XLIX (March, 1965), p. 143.

[3] A. Bruce Gaarder, "Teaching the Bilingual Child: Research, Development, and Policy," *The Modern Language Journal*, XLIX (March, 1965), p. 166.

[4] A. Bruce Gaarder, "The First Seventy-Six Bilingual Education Projects," in James E. Alatis, ed., *Monograph Series on Languages and Linguistics*, No. 23, Washington, D.C.: Georgetown University, (1970), p. 163.

[5] *Ibid.*, p. 173.

[6] The first of these was published by Mouton & Company in The Hague in 1966. The second is supposedly available from the Bureau of Research of the U.S. Department of Health, Education, and Welfare (Contract No. OEC-1-062817-0297), though copies are extremely difficult to obtain. Articles from *Bilingualism in the Barrio* appear in *The Modern Language Journal*, LIII, No. 3 and No. 4 (1969).

[7] Joshua A. Fishman, "The Status and Prospects of Bilingualism in the United States," *The Modern Language Journal*, XLIX (March, 1965), p. 153.

[8] Einar Haugen, *The Norwegian Language in America* (2 vols.); Philadelphia: University of Pennsylvania Press, (1953).

[9] Uriel Weinreich, *Languages in Contact.* The Hague: Mouton & Company, (1967).

[10] Wallace E. Lambert, "A Social Psychology of Bilingualism," *The Journal of Social Issues*, XXIII (April, 1967), p. 106.

[11] Gaarder, "Teaching the Bilingual Child," *op. cit.*, p. 173.

[12] As quoted in Gaarder, *ibid.*, p. 172.

[13] Robert L. Cooper and Lawrence Greenfield, "Language Use in a Bilingual Community," *The Modern Language Journal*, LIII (March, 1969), p. 172.

[14] A. Bruce Gaarder, "Teaching Spanish in School and College to Native Speakers of Spanish." Unpublished draft of a report commissioned by the Executive Council of the American Association of Teachers of Spanish and Portuguese, (1971), p. 8.

[15] Joshua A. Fishman *et al. Bilingualism in the Barrio*, I, p. 67.

[16] A. Bruce Gaarder, personal letter, (January 19, 1971).

[17] Gaarder, "Teaching Spanish in School and College to Native Speakers of Spanish," p. 16.

[18] *Ibid.*, p. 67.

[19] Gaarder, "The First Seventy-Six Bilingual Education Projects," p. 167.

[20] Ralph F. Robinett, "The Spanish Curricula Development Center," *The National Elementary Principal*, I (November, 1970), p. 72.

[21] *Ibid.*, p. 63.

[22] Gaarder, "Teaching Spanish in School and College to Native Speakers of Spanish," p. 3.

[23] Gerald J. Brault, *Livret du professeur de français franco-américain*. Brunswick, (1962), p. 1.

[24] Elphège Roy, personal letter, (November 8, 1969). Information regarding the text can be obtained from Mr. Roy at 103 Oak Street, Manchester, New Hampshire 03104.

[25] Gerald J. Brault, *Cours de langue française destiné aux jeunes franco-américains*. Manchester, (1965), p. 7.

[26] The Texas Education Agency, *Español para alumnos hispano-hablantes. Preliminary ed.*, n.p., *(1969), p. 4.*

[27] Paulline Baker, *Español para los hispanos*. Skokie, Ill., (1968), p. 50.

[28] Marie Esman Barker, *Español para el bilingüe*. Skokie, Ill., (1971).

[29] Gaarder, "The First Seventy-Six Bilingual Education Projects," p. 163.

[30] Theodore Andersson, "A New Focus on the Bilingual Child," *The Modern Language Journal*, XLIX (March, 1965), p. 156.

[31] Theodore Andersson and Mildred Boyer, *Bilingual Schooling in the United States* (2 vols.); Austin: Southwest Educational Development Laboratory, (1970); II, p. 22, quoting Siegfried H. Muller, *The World's Living Languages: Basic Facts of Their Structure, Kinship, Location and Number of Speakers*. New York, (1964).

[32] *Ibid.*, II, p. 141.

[33] Of the 33,038 total enrollment for Italian in public secondary schools in the fall of 1968, 6,795 were from New England and 15,610 from the state of New York. See Julia Gibson Kant, "Foreign Language Offerings and Enrollments in Public Secondary Schools, (Fall 1968)", *Foreign Language Annals*, III (March, 1970), p. 443.

[34] Andersson and Boyer, II, p. 139.

[35] *Ibid.*, p. 140.

[36] *Ibid.*, p. 126.

[37] "Position Paper by the Committee on Socio-Political Concerns of Minority Groups in TESOL, (February 1, 1970)", *TESOL Newsletter*, IV (September/December, 1970), pp. 8-9. This paper is reproduced and slightly amended in *TESOL Newsletter*, V (June, 1971), pp. 6-7.

28

American Education and Bilingual Education Research
Paul F. Streiff

Throughout most of the history of American education, the fact that children attending school were not native speakers of English was not accepted as a matter to be taken seriously when planning curriculum. If children did not speak English, there was felt to be something wrong in the background from which he came, and the quickest way to correct the condition was to teach at them as though they did indeed understand and speak English. No special instructional design was provided, and yet much of the American adult public became speakers of English within a relatively brief span of years. Of course there were islands of language users that seemed to resist replacing their language with English and failed in wholesale numbers in their school efforts, and the evidence became quite convincing that these populations just were not quite as well equipped intellectually as others. Only about a decade ago was a serious question raised concerning the fact that the prevailing approach did not seem to be working and that there might be some important relationships between language and thought that were being overlooked. Indeed, a new school of thought suggested that a whole new view of the problems of teaching and learning English be accepted; a view which would accept the fact that for the non-English speaking population English is really a second language requiring a whole new curriculum rationale and methodology. A period of feverish activity followed in which new and innovative programs were developed, institutes and workshops were held, and even national organizations founded to promote better education through English as a Second Language (ESL) for non-English speaking populations in American schools.

An almost simultaneous effort, sometimes carried on by overlapping task forces, suggested that there might be merit in using a child's first language as a medium for instruction while teaching English as a second

---

The views expressed in this paper are those of the author. No official support or endorsement of them by the Bureau of Indian Affairs, U.S. Department of Interior, is intended or should be inferred.

language, and within a short time the advocates of this notion uncovered an astounding background of experience in dual-language schooling programs from around the world. As early as 1910, a study of dual-language schooling cited more than 100 items of bibliography on the subject. (Weinreich, 1953)

But in the beginning studies of bilingualism were almost wholly concerned with the organization of schools in bilingual areas. Relatively little effort was made toward increased understanding of the complex psycholinguistic and sociolinguistic aspects of the phenomenon of second-language acquisition. Weinreich stated in 1953:

> It is a major task in research planning to promote the coordination of studies in this field. . .[in order that] new research will then become more systematic and the results more fully comparable. . .and useful. (p.121)

Dual-language instruction was introduced into American education and then given official support with the passage of the Bilingual Education Act of 1967 (Title VII of ESEA); and, in terms of resources and attention brought to bear on the subject, research in bilingualism and bilingual education through federally funded projects has taken on considerable importance. There is evidence, however, that little new and useful research data from bilingual schooling projects have resulted to date (Gaarder, 1970, Tucker and d'Anglejan, 1970), and many experts agree that bilingual education is not a well defined and well understood discipline amenable to investigation. (Mackey, 1970; Andersson and Boyer, 1970). What is still most needed, they feel, is a perspective in which the inter-relationships between component disciplines may be considered — an overall research policy within which the several disciplines, each with its legitimate interest, can be brought together into an overall plan for cooperative and non-overlapping research, (Mackey, 1970).

It is the purpose of this paper to present a preliminary outline for a plan to provide those involved in bilingual education research a framework within which they can more effectively undertake their tasks and thereby enhance their contributions to the field.

Assumptions underlying the plan

Underlying the task of developing such a plan are several important assumptions:

1. Federal legislation in support of bilingual education is intended to produce new information about bilingualism and dual-language instruction in American schools.

2. Measurable new information of value results from carefully conducted research.

3. Most bilingual education projects have proceeded on the basis of unquestioned yet unspecified assumptions derived from several component disciplines and unarticulated and untested hypotheses deriving from them.

4. Bilingual education is not a well defined and well understood

concept amenable to investigation.

The position I am taking is that a critical step in providing a plan through which researchable hypotheses can be generated is the preparation of a conceptual model, defined as a theoretical construct designed to place in appropriate relationship the fragments of knowledge presently existing in an academic field under consideration. (Goodlad, 1966)

It is suggested that the proposed conceptual model serve to bring about a unification of purpose in the conduct of projects and programs in bilingual education. Specifically, it is intended to provide a framework within which important contributions may be made by projects funded under the Bilingual Education Act, among others.

Functions of a conceptual model

The work of those presenting papers here, and that of their sponsoring organizations, gives testimony to the impressive increase in interest in the subject of bilingualism among scholars of quite diverse commitments and disciplines. We are aware of the existence of institutions whose purposes are specifically the study of bilingualism, and we are reminded at every turn of the complexity of the subject and of how that complexity is multiplied when we introduce bilingualism into American education.

We have experienced disappointments as we have become aware of the extent to which we are unable to agree on intended outcomes. In reality, we have approached the opportunities for serious study of bilingualism and bilingual education in America in such a way as to almost assure confusion. We have viewed bilingualism and bilingual education as both means and ends in the projects which have been funded, but usually as a simple matter easily understood and practiced by para-professionals, and the results have been, for the most part, a failure to establish researchable hypotheses as the bases for fruitful study. Gaarder has stated that "the Congress couched its extraordinarily generous and innovative legislation in support of dual-language public schooling in terms that permit both the ethnocentrists and the cultural pluralists to see what they want to see in the Act." (Gaarder, 1970) The Guidelines provided by the United States Office of Education do little to help clarify the range or limitations for project aims and activities with the official interpretation of bilingual education as "the use of two languages, one of which is English, as mediums of instruction. . .for the same student population, in a well-organized program which encompasses part or all of the curriculum, plus study of the history and culture associated with a student's mother tongue." With a whole continuum of language and culture combinations as possible curricular components, it is not surprising that most local education agencies would try to be all things to all men and for the most part this is precisely what has happened. The obvious disparity between aims and means has been enormous, as Gaarder has pointed out, and all too often in reading proposals one can find no rationale nor any clearly stated objectives on which project design is based. Yet we find that a research orientation is intended. The Guidelines specifically require "planning for and taking other steps leading to the development of...research projects; pilot projects to test the effectiveness of developed plans; projects that envision an imaginative solution to bilingual education problems over time; and projects that present a new and imaginative plan...which gives promise of developing into a model program." (*Guidelines*, Title VII ESEA, 1968)

Whatever activities project staffs may be engaged in, it is not likely that most of them accomplish any of these mandates or contribute substantively to better understanding of bilingualism and bilingual education. Expertise to do this is in short supply, usually not found where it is most needed. Assistance must be provided in an overall plan which can be followed confidently within local limitations and which provides a guard against operating on irrational and indefensible assumptions.

The model suggested here may best be considered as fulfilling the function of clarifying and at the same time simplifying the role of cultural and linguistic concepts which a prospective bilingual education project must be prepared to cope with as a part of the overall research effort. It may be thought of as a step which was omitted in the development of the Guidelines and as providing the means for detecting and avoiding gaps and overlaps.

Bilingual education research defined

I propose first that bilingual education research be defined as "An attempt in curriculum research and development to place unusual emphasis on the roles of language and culture in the education of American children from designated socio-cultural backgrounds and to measure the effect of that emphasis." While the language of the legislation leaves much to be specified concerning the place of two languages as either means or ends in the education of the child, it is perfectly clear on one point concerning outcomes: that is, improved learning is the overriding concern. This concern is, by definition, the domain of the curriculum theorist. The legitimate focus, then, for research in bilingual education is the curriculum, and the conceptual model for overall research in bilingual education will derive essentially from conceptual curricular systems. The system to be developed should point to the data source or sources most relevant in determining the research hypotheses to be investigated. An appropriate curriculum research model will reflect this capability. There is a need to specify clearly the purposes of individual bilingual education projects in order that defensible objectives may be selected and in order that judgments may be made about their feasibility and the capacity of the project to carry them out. In other words, an appropriate curriculum research model will result in carefully developed rationales for bilingual education proposals; rationales which will carefully specify and elaborate those theoretical assumptions from which derives the special focus of the project as a part of an overall research effort.

Development of a model

A conceptual system performs several functions essential to effective study of bilingualism in education: (1) it identifies problems and questions relevant to planning bilingual instructional programs; (2) it clarifies the types of inquiry that are likely to be productive in dealing with those problems and questions; (3) it reveals possible connections between those problems and questions; (4) it identifies promising data sources for dealing with those problems and questions; and (5) it facilitates the initiation of processes designed to show the relevance of these sources and of data extracted from them to the problems and questions classified by the system. (Goodlad, 1966)

In terms of our model for overall decision-making in bilingual education research, the basis, as has been stated, must be in curriculum theory; and the rationale developed by Ralph Tyler (1950) provides the key questions which any educational endeavor must be prepared to answer:

1. What educational purposes should the school seek to attain?

Efforts to answer this question constitute the greatest challenge to bilingual education projects. A very serious value judgment is called for involving questions of language and culture which have not been asked of American communities until recently, questions which have reversed long-held notions about the ends to be sought by and for the individual within his own sub-culture or within the larger society. The question of purpose must not be taken lightly but must be the focus of the most rigorous and conscientious examination. Herschel Manuel warned several years ago that "We should be very careful that, in our enthusiasm, we don't simply proliferate unproved and unwise programs which can only lead to disillusionment and delay." (Congressional Hearings on Bilingual Education, 1967)

2. What educational experiences can be provided that are likely to attain these purposes?

This question, of course, calls for deductions from the first one; and the answers to it, in terms of our definition of bilingual education, are likely to suggest a range of possible means. But the legitimacy and usefulness of any of those means, and the possibility of effectively comparing them depends on the degree of specificity with which answers to the first question have been derived. Assumptions must be stated as assumptions, and hypotheses must be derived which can be tested in the course of carefully selected experiences. We must not continue to ignore advice such as that of Gumperz when he warned that "the common assumption that uneducated speakers of minority languages learn better when instructed through the medium of their own vernacular is not necessarily always justified. Instructional materials in these vernaculars may rely on monolingual norms which are quite alien to the student and linguistically different from his home speech." (Gumperz, 1967)

3. How can these educational experiences be effectively organized?

This question can obviously have little meaning until the first two have been answered; but at this point in the discussion it should be pointed out that, while expertise from selected disciplines in the social and behavioral sciences (e.g., linguistics, psycholinguistics, sociology) is essential to adequately answering the first question as well as most of the second, it becomes the task of the educator and psychologist to provide proper guidance in answering the third.

4. How can we determine whether these purposes are being attained?

The process of evaluation has only recently been recognized as distinct in fundamental ways from that of research; but its major function, when appropriately and efficiently employed, is to assure that the entire system is self-correcting within the limits set by the answers given to the first question. In the model we propose for research in bilingual education it is imperative that the ground rules for evaluation be observed if rational decisions are to be made possible concerning the merit of alternative program hypotheses.

A broad curriculum model, representing the Tyler rationale, may be pictured as follows:

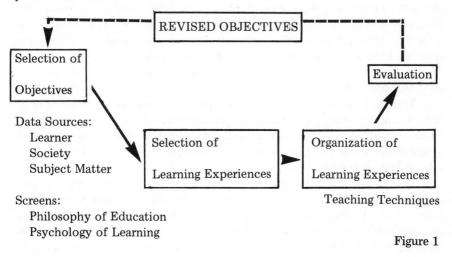

Figure 1

In proceeding toward the development of a conceptual framework through which we may make better decisions for investigating the many aspects of bilingualism relative to education, particularly education in American schools, we need a more detailed model. The position taken by any advocate of bilingual education is one of strong value preference; and while the Tyler model would have us wrestle first with the question of "What should [ought] the educational purposes of the school be? ," obviously a value decision, he turns first to three data sources, society, the learner, and subject matter. He leaves the decision (desirable, undesirable, feasible, unattainable, contradictory) to be handled by passing them through philosophical and psychological screens.

Goodlad, in elaborating on and modifying the Tyler rationale, developed a conceptual system which turns first to values as the primary data-source in selecting purposes for the school and in making all subsequent curricular decisions. Goodlad takes the position that in making any beginning one accepts certain assumptions and that values are imbedded in assumptions. From our position, we might profitably reverse the last statement and point out that assumptions are imbedded in values. The need is to identify and articulate those values and assumptions central to a given instructional situation. Several other clarifications and distinctions in the Goodlad model are appropriate to our present needs, especially the observation that curriculum planning occurs at several levels of remoteness from the learner, specifically, the instructional, the institutional, and the societal. In any society, the transactions conducted within these frames of reference are to a considerable degree political in character, in both the best and the worst sense of the word.

Transactions between sanctioning bodies and controlling agencies (e.g., the community and the school board), between controlling agencies and administrators (e.g., the board and the superintendent), and between administrators and teachers involve all manner of tactics and techniques for influencing, persuading, and compromising.

In a complex society such as we have in the United States, we find that decision-making is coming increasingly under the influence of powerful forces at the Federal level. Since educational decisions are deemed to be in the national interest, we have modified the notions of the past, which viewed local control of decision-making in education as sacred. This is particularly true of the influences which brought about legislation supporting bilingual-bicultural programs for American schools, which points up the great importance of a fourth level or data source for decision-making in curriculum, designated by Goodlad as the ideological. It is precisely at this level of decision-making that the determination of curricular ends and means must be accomplished in a rational manner and not through whim and speculation. Decisions must be based on careful consideration of alternative means based on alternative value premises.

It is essential and critical that definitions, assumptions, data sources, decisions, and rationales be rigorously analyzed by those involved in the conduct of programs intended as part of a serious ideological effort. Their plans and their work must reflect the substance of rationality, and in order that this may be accomplished they must have a carefully designed system or model to follow. Banathy remarks that

> In an age when problems seem to generate faster than we can identify them, and change appears to be the only certainty, we are eager to find ways to define and resolve our problems — complex as they may be — and to cope with change, perpetual though it may be. Evidence from various realms of our contemporary life indicates that in the systems concept we have available a way of thinking with which we can deal with complex problems and their changing relationships. (Banathy, 1968)

It is clear that the responsibility for refinement and application of a system or model toward a coordination of research in bilingual education cannot be assigned to the project (institutional and instructional) level. There are obvious reasons why this is true, most of which have to do with overall perspective, adequate staffing, and limited study design capabilities. Direction and decision-making for a program of this scope and complexity will, to a great extent, require the expert services of "subject matter specialists" as prime data sources, 'subject matter' here meaning those separate but related disciplines involved in the study of bilingualism. Ideological-level decision-making is at the heart of the task, and it is these specialists who must interpret the relevant, expressed societal values. They must refine statements of broad, ideologically based aims which were generated by an appropriate representation of the community to be involved, and our model must provide for efficient and valid procedures for ascertaining them.

It is important to note here that our "specialists" are not consulted at this point for the purpose of determining what the aims ought to be, but rather for purposes of refining aims that have already been selected.

Additional criteria must now be applied that will allow a proposed project to be included in the overall schema for research of significant problems in bilingualism and bilingual education, and particularly to place it in one of several major integrated study blocks. Analysis of information concerning the broad ideological aims and their translation into specific linguistic and/or sociocultural propositions must reveal comprehensiveness, consistency, and potential contribution to the field, all of which are in turn governed by criteria of attainability and feasibility.

Figure 2 represents stage one of the model, which serves primarily to represent the first step of the Tyler rationale: that of selection of the general educational aims; or, to use Goodlad's levels of data sources, it represents the marriage of the ideological and the societal levels of decision-making through the mediation of appropriate specialists from the component disciplines.

It should be noted here that I am not trying to deal with the question

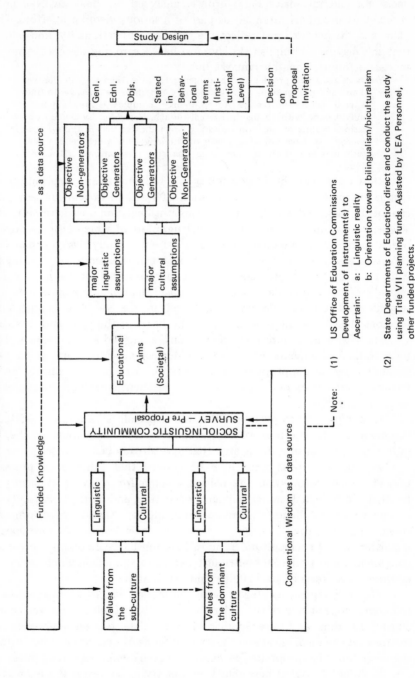

Figure 2

Stage 1

Determination of General Educational Objectives

of the master study design itself; that is, for example, how many projects should be undertaking the investigation of problems of reading in the first language (L1) prior to the second language (L2), etc. It has been well established that there is an almost endless variety of important questions that can be generated in several distinct bilingual-bicultural study domains. The important step that must be taken, possibly by the combined representation of the sponsoring organizations of this conference as an initial powerful contribution, is that of establishing those domains. Basically each domain must be a category with parameters sufficiently well defined to permit relatively easy assignment of a given project once stage one of the model has been implemented.

Input for stage one of decision-making based on this model includes what will hopefully be the best specialized knowledge available. The contribution of the 'specialist,' however, will be focused on the careful gathering and analysis of population data needed to ascertain the linguistic reality of the community and community attitudes toward aspects of bilingualism and biculturalism. The key inputs on which a given project study design will be based will be those provided by the student and citizen population. It is necessary to find out what these populations believe, what they want, and what they already know. A recording of their interests, wishes, and understandings is essential when translating ideological-level decisions to immediate societal and institutional decisions concerning bilingual education. This may be considered as assessment of conventional wisdom (Goodlad, 1966), from which derive the specific assumptions, the rationale, and the working hypotheses for those projects.

This stage of the development and implementation of an overall plan for research in bilingual education is clearly benefited by the contributions of Lambert and his associates (Lambert, 1967), Lambert, 1969, Lambert, Gardner, Olton, and Tunstall, 1962), and a recent study by Cohen suggests the process and instrumentation. (Cohen, 1970) The measurement of language use and attitudes toward language is obviously essential to any rational approach to the study of bilingual/bicultural education in any community, but it is only a first step. It does not tell us anything about the possible mix of curricular decisions (alternatives) that might be employed in trying to meet the educational needs of a specific population. What key questions will derive from the linguistic and cultural assumptions which will in turn determine the character of the learning opportunities to be provided?

The critical discipline as a primary data source now becomes pedagogy All of the components of learning theory, instructional principles, curriculum and evaluation design, etc., now come into prominence in the person of the curriculum theorist, and in company with other specialists in the social and behavioral sciences decisions must be systematically reached concerning the specification of educational objectives at the institutional and the instructional levels. Stage two of the model (Figure 3) illustrates the basic steps in this process.

Since each project involved constitutes potentially a component of a comprehensive research effort, it is important to point out that once the design is established, and for its duration as a study, new data input will be from evaluation of a formative nature. Summative evaluation procedures will ascertain whether the general education objectives have been attained and will involve the school and community populations in again expressing their views on sociolinguistic aspects of the question, "What educational purposes should the school seek to attain? "

Conclusions

Research into the phenomenon of second-language acquisition by children received tremendous potential impetus and support with the passage of the Bilingual Education Act by the United States Congress. At this time there are more than 150 projects receiving funding under this legislation, yet there is disappointment in many quarters that the significant resources made available have not resulted in more systematic study of bilingualism and dual-language instruction. It has been suggested that the subject is so complex and possible approaches to it so diverse as to make such systematic study impossible without a conceptual model by means of which a host of "complex, related, interacting phenomena may be identified, and relationships among them may be revealed." (Goodlad, 1966) The approach taken in this paper is that the proper theoretical basis for such a model is to be found in curriculum theory, and a preliminary two-stage model has been presented. The model suggests that the following elements can be part of an effort to undertake more effective research in bilingualism in American schools:

1. Establishment of a limited number of component study domains and delineation of their parameters.
2. Sociolinguistic assessment of all potential participant communities, utilizing methodology and instrumentation already developed in order to determine:
   a. Linguistic reality.
   b. Orientation toward bilingualism and biculturalism as valued educational aims.
3. Definition of bilingual education research as curriculum research, and thereby assigning the curriculum theorist a key role in the development of study design and project specifications.
4. Provision for more effective pre-proposal (planning) procedures involving guidance and assistance from State and Federal levels.
5. Limitation of operational hypotheses in any project in accordance with derived assumptions, as well as criteria of feasibility and attainability of objectives.

Stage 2

Figure 3

Project Development as Bilingual Education Research Component

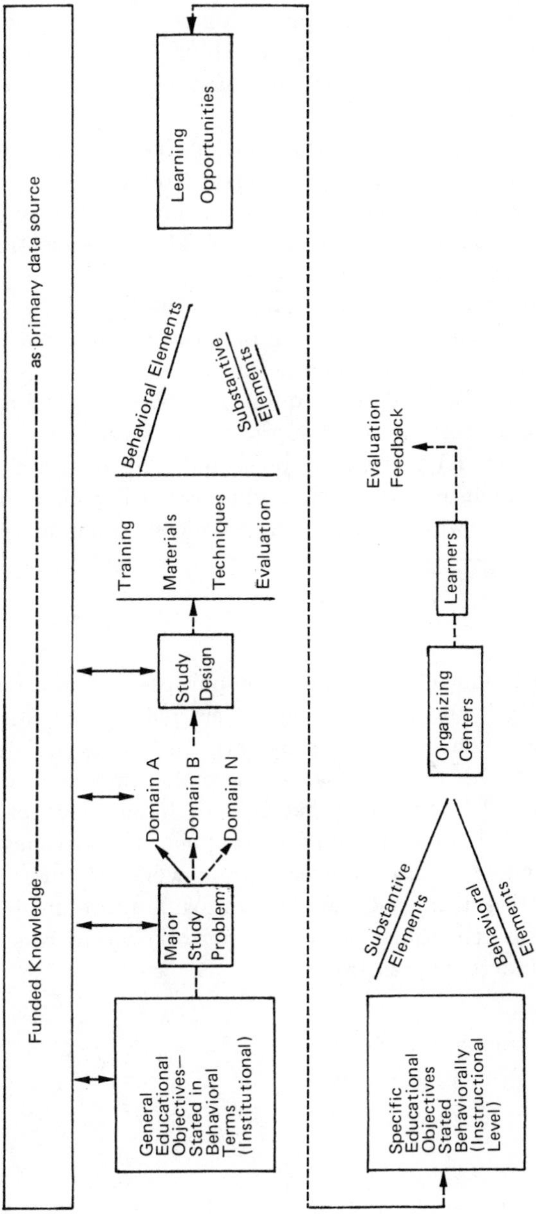

There is no intention in what has been presented of overlooking or ignoring several realities confronting those who would attempt to literally change the entire approach to bilingual education research at this point in time. It is obvious, for example, that a very complex organizational arrangement has grown up in the four-year history of the Bilingual Education Act; an arrangement in which roles and functions have become rooted and resistant to modification.

It is also obvious that many decisions having to do with distribution of funds for bilingual education programs are politically determined or are not really intended to make a contribution to the field. It may not be possible to include more than a small percentage of Bilingual Education Act projects as participants in a unified research effort.

Another hurdle to be considered is the general negative tendency in attitude toward innovative ideas and approaches which often follows initial bursts of enthusiastic involvement.

In conclusion, a serious question concerning bilingualism and the national interest may be more approachable through the establishment and use of such a model as has been presented. This question is whether or not societal bilingualism and cultural pluralism are valued aims for American education, aims which people in American communities are willing to support.

Summary

Bilingual education is not, for purposes of research, a single well defined and well understood discipline amenable to investigation although it is treated as such in many programs. It derives its definition from a composite of theoretical bases of several component disciplines, but a conceptual model for overall research of bilingual education problems in American schools does not now exist. Such a model must elaborate those theoretical cases within an overall framework of curricular theory. This paper will present one such model to provide those involved with bilingual education research efforts with a framework within which they can more effectively undertake their tasks.

Bibliography

Andersson, Theodore, and Mildred Boyer. *Bilingual Schooling in the United States* (2 vols.) Washington, D.C.: U.S. Government Printing Office, (1970).

Banathy, Bela. *Instructional Systems*, Palo Alto: Pearson Publishing, (1968).

Bilingual Education Act. *Section 701, Elementary and Secondary Education Amendments*, House of Representatives 90th Congress Report No. 1049. Washington, D.C.: U.S. Printing Office, (1967).

Cohen, Andrew D. *A Sociolinguistic Approach to Bilingual Education.* Unpublished paper. Committee on Linguistics, Stanford University, (1970).

Gaarder, Bruce A. "The First Seventy-Six Bilingual Education Projects." In James E. Alatis, Ed., *Monograph Series on Language and Linguistics*, No. 23, Washington, D.C.: Georgetown University Press, (1970).

Goodlad, John I., with M. N. Richter, Jr. *The Development of a Conceptual System for Dealing with Problems of Curriculum and Instruction.* University of California at Los Angeles, (1966).

Gumperz, John J. "On the Linguistic Markers of Bilingual Communication." *Journal of Social Issues*, Vol. XXIII, No. 2, p. 56. Yeshiva University, New York, (April 1967).

Johnson, Mauritz Jr. "Definitions and Models in Curriculum Theory." In Edmund C. Short and George D. Marconnit, eds., *Contemporary Thought on Public School Curriculum*, New York: William C. Brown, (1968).

Lambert, Wallace E. "A Social Psychology of Bilingualism." *Journal of Social Issues*, vol. XXIII, No. 2, pp. 91-109. Yeshiva University. New York, (April 1967).

——. "Psychological Aspects of Motivation in Language Learning." *The Florida Foreign Language Reporter*, Miami, (1969).

Lambert, W.E., *et al. A Study of the Roles of Attitudes and Motivation in Second Language Learning.* Unpublished. Montreal, McGill University, (1962).

Mackey, William F. "A Typology of Bilingual Education." *Report of Research Conference on Bilingual Education.* Washington, D.C.: U.S. Office of Education, Bureau of Research, (1969).

Manuel, Herschel. Report. *Congressional Hearings on Bilingual Education.* Carl D. Perkins, Chairman. Washington, D.C.: U.S. Printing Office, (1967).

Popham, W. James. *The Teacher-Empiricist.* Los Angeles: Tinnon-Brown, (1965).

Roeming, Robert F. "Bilingualism and the National Interest." In James E. Alatis, ed., *Monograph Series on Language and Linguistics*, No. 23, Washington, D.C.: Georgetown University Press, (1970).

Tucker, G.R., and Alison d'Anglejan. *Some Thoughts Concerning Bilingual Education Programs.* Unpublished manuscript. McGill University, (1970).

Tyler, Ralph. W. *Basic Principles of Curriculum and Instruction.* Chicago: University of Chicago Press, (1950).

U.S. Office of Education. *Guidelines to the Bilingual Education Program.* Under Title VII Elementary and Secondary Education Act of 1965, as amended in 1967.

Weinreich, Uriel. *Languages in Contact.* The Hague: Mouton, (1967).

29

Language Maintenance or Language Shift [1]
A. Bruce Gaarder

> One might be tempted to define bilingualism as divided linguistic allegiance.
>
> André Martinet [2]

Introduction

What is the likelihood that Spanish will endure as a language of the people in the United States with increased prestige and usefulness, or that its uses, users, and importance will quickly decrease in extent and number? Can it be maintained or will there be a widespread shift to English? This essay will not answer the question, but it will examine many of the factors which are even now determining the answer. Beginning with its title, which follows Uriel Weinreich and Joshua Fishman, the essay is conceived as the best available substitute for a conference of experts on the subject. The role of the author is to keep the world-ranging discussion focused on Spanish in the United States.

Social justice and cultural pluralism

The difference between these two is essential to the discussion, because it is at the base of the ambivalence among the Spanish speakers themselves regarding their language and culture. The two main groups of Spanish speakers in the United States — the Mexican Americans and the Puerto Ricans — are engaged in an increasingly intense and successful struggle for social justice. In a score and more of different ways they are pressing for an end to discriminatory practices which have given them much less than the full rights and privileges of citizenship. But social justice can be achieved within a context of social, cultural, and ethnic assimilation to the dominant culture of the majority. Witness the Swedes, who once were immigrants in this country and whose achievement of social justice now includes only nostalgic vestiges of their own language and original culture. Social justice means treatment as equals: equal opportunities, freedom from discrimination, unrestricted intermarriage, etc.

Cultural pluralism, on the other hand, implies social justice, but goes far beyond. It means co-existence in a status of at least mutual respect and tolerance, preferably mutual respect and encouragement, within the same state or nation, of two or more cultures which are significantly distinct one from the other in their patterns of belief and behavior, including, in the present case, different languages. The espousal of cultural pluralism is not an assimilative posture; it is a negation of assimilation. It is a posture which asserts that there is more than one legitimate way of being human without paying the penalty of second-class citizenship, and that such pluralism would enrich the quality of life for all people in the nation.

Mere social justice calls for a fair share of the pie and is, in effect, assimilative. Cultural pluralism calls for that fair share plus the right not to assimilate. Both postures are legitimate and worthy of respect, but in essential respects they are contradictory. In their thinking about these matters the Spanish speakers are ambivalent and at times seemingly confused.

It is not a simple two-way division, with some favoring assimilation and preferring English while the others reject assimilation and want a continuing and increasing role for Spanish. Rather, even as all clamor for social justice, all want English and few would happily forego Spanish. The ambivalence lies in seeking the closest possible integration with the "Anglo"[3] majority and at the same time insistently defining themselves as a distinct, identifiable minority group, the "brown" in contrast to the "black" and the "white," with a distinct culture and language which must be preserved. The confusion comes from the same insistence on preservation of that culture and language without regard for the contradictions implied and without a vision either of the new sociolinguistic pattern that would result or of the means required to secure it.

Certain lawsuits and court rulings in Texas are revealing in this respect. The specific problem was that although Mexican Americans had gone to court in 1954 to establish that they are white (to protect themselves from the discriminatory segregation suffered by the blacks), in some Texas cities, notably Houston, the school authorities attempted in 1970 to meet the requirements of the Civil Rights Act for the elimination of segregated schools by combining Blacks and Mexican American. Relief from this new kind of discrimination was sought and secured in the courts. Mario Obledo, Director and General Counsel of the Mexican American Legal Defense and Education Fund, remarked in this connection, "To facilitate the enforcement of these remedies, the Mexican American should be classified as a class apart, as a significant identifiable group, as the brown in contrast to the black and the white" (MAE, p. 2524). In the same discussion Mr. Obledo said, "The Mexican American was lost because we are part of the white race, so to speak. That is why it is very important. . .that the brown be classified as a class apart. . ." (MAE, p. 2533). Regarding a similar case in Austin, Mr. Jesús J. Rubio, Research Director, Mexican American Development

Corporation, remarked, "Austin supposedly has a beautiful integration plan, but the whites turned out to be brown. . ." (MAE, p. 2510). Abraham Ramírez, Jr., one of three lawyers representing the Fund, asked, "For instance, if a school is to have 555 Negroes and 395 whites, we want to know — whites or Mexican Americans? " (MAE, p. 2560).

Dr. Hector García, distinguished champion of civil rights and founder of the G.I. Forum, a nation-wide veterans' organization for Mexican Americans, in testimony before a U.S. Senate committee was discussing the history of the conflict between this country and Mexico and the grievances of Texans and Mexican Americans against Mexico. Ambivalence is plain in the following paragraph of his text, to which parenthetical explanations have been added.

> They complained (both Texans and Mexicans in what is now Texas) about the Mexican military, they talked about being quartered in their houses and being tyrannical. Then the hate against us (Mexican Americans) started. By 1845, we (the entire U.S. people or its government) knew we wanted the Northwest Mexican Territory. We had to make a *cause célèbre*. We had to have a scapegoat. This is where history was perverted and distorted, by making the Texas Revolution completely an English, Anglo fight against Mexicans, when it was never so. We (again the Mexican Americans) become the scapegoats. We became the "hate symbol." (MAE, p. 2567)

In the same discussion Dr. García said, "Of course, we were always white, legally we were white, but it didn't make any difference" (MAE, p. 2567). Later he spoke of the great importance of the *Pete Hernández, Petitioner v. The State of Texas*, case in 1954, by which... "it was legally established that we were Caucasians" (MAE, p. 2570).

Armando Rodríguez, at that time head of the Mexican American Affairs Unit, U.S. Office of Education, an ardent supporter of bilingual-bicultural education and opponent of segregated schooling, testified against the monocultural and monolingual educational philosophy of the American school "that confuses homogenous [sic] learning environment with 'providing for individual differences' which results in ethnic and linguistic isolation." It is not at all clear in what way such a learning environment in unsegregated schools for all children would produce such isolation, nor how ethnic and linguistic isolation would be lessened by recognition of and provision for those ethnic and linguistic differences (MAE, p. 2595).

While the linguistic position of the Spanish speakers is notably unlike that of any other non-English minority in the United States and in some ways notably stronger, there are many similarities and no few disadvantages which in the end may be overriding. Briefly, the strength rests on nine points:

1. They were here first. This goes far beyond such facts as colonization in the Southwest before the landing of the Pilgrims. The brown-white point referred to above is buttressed by a growing inclination among Mexican Americans to see their own origins in common with those of the American Indian 20,000 or more years ago in that same Southwest. Dr. George I.

Sánchez, illustrious defender of the Mexican American, has said, "After all, we are not immigrants. As Indians, we have been here since time immemorial and as Spanish speakers, since the sixteenth century (TNEP, p.103). Dr. Sergio D. Elizondo, professor at California State College, San Bernardino, writing on the curriculum of Chicano studies programs, says, "An introductory course in Mexican American history must have its beginnings in Pre-Columbian Mesoamerica."[4]

2. The proximity and easy accessibility of Mexico and Puerto Rico.

3. The constant in-migrant and immigrant streams from Puerto Rico, Mexico, and other Spanish-speaking countries.

4. The large numbers involved: roughly six million Mexican Americans, two million Puerto Ricans, one million Cubans, one million other Latin Americans and Spaniards.

5. The relative isolation — hence linguistic solidarity — of the rural, or segregated, uneducated poor.

6. The similarities of religion and folkways among all Spanish speakers.

7. The fact of their being, in large measure, a "visible minority."

8. The inter-generational stability of the extended family (Hayden, LLUS, p. 205).

9. The present-day climate in the United States of tolerance — even encouragement — of cultural diversity. For example, Congressman Roman Pucinski, at the hearings on the proposed Ethnic Heritage Studies Act, said, "Experience has taught us that the pressure toward homogeneity has been superficial and counter-productive; that the spirit of ethnicity, now lying dormant in our national soul, begs for reawakening in a time of fundamental national needs."[5]

The similarities and contrasts with other ethnic groups in the United States and other tongues are even more instructive. For example — and too briefly to give anything approaching a clear picture — German Americans at one time, 1910, counted close to nine million who spoke German natively; many lived in "language islands" or in monolingual urban settings; they published extensively in German, "books on poetry, local history, theology, philosophy, . . .also some non-narrative prose covering various branches of the sciences and humanities, such as zoology, archaeology, medicine, general history, linguistics, etc."[6] There was a steady influx of immigrants including highly cultured intellectuals. Daily newspapers in German by 1904 had a circulation of nearly 800,000. German American clubs once numbered close to 10,000. Close to four millions attended church services in German. In 1900, 4,127 public and private schools used German as the language of instruction. Theological and teachers seminaries and colleges were numerous. Yet despite the immense prestige of German and the vigor of its speakers, their efforts were largely swept aside, only in part because of World War I. And the Germans were not in any sense disadvantaged.

Comparison with Norwegian Americans

Those who know the situation of Spanish and its speakers in the United States may find several parallels with an experience that they might suppose to be different in every way: that of Norwegian, told by Einar Haugen in his monumental study, *The Norwegian Language in America* (TNLIA). It took roughly a century for that people — almost a million immigrants from Norway — to live through it all, from the early years when the permanence of Norwegian in this country was never questioned, until — somehow by the very nature of things — the shift had taken place and the few remaining speakers were like museum pieces.

> Bilingualism began as a marginal phenomenon mediating between two groups of monolinguals. . .most of them could read Norwegian, many could write but there were few books. . .distance cut them off from renewal from the old country. . .the bilinguals were almost all of Norwegian mother tongue, for the English speakers did not learn Norwegian. . .the accommodation was all in one direction. . .among the bilinguals there was ever more facile switching from Norwegian to English to address the major society and back to Norwegian. . .and the number of these borrowings grew constantly. . .borrowing from English while speaking Norwegian ("mixing") increased: "it is so easy and practical a way of getting along". . .all in all, the learning of English had a disastrous effect on their Norwegian. . .the immigrants were scorned, made fun of, patronized, and exploited. . .their feelings of shame of being Norwegian and their sence of inferiority are recorded over and over. . .the solid, usually rural enclaves of Norwegian monolinguals sustained the language; their dispersal hastened its disappearance. . .educated people from Norway did not understand the "underlying necessity in the process" of "mixing"; they found the Norwegian spoken here offensive, which created a barrier of misunderstanding and resentment between them and the immigrants. . .their hyphenated state[says Haugen] played the role of a "home in passage". . .in no less measure their "mixed" Norwegian was a half-way house on the road to English.

Norwegian Americans — most of them — cherished their mother tongue, but Haugen found that they "stoutly resisted those who advocated parochial or other schools that would have segregated their children from other Americans."

Finally, with the Norwegian Lutheran churches beginning to shift their services to English and the number of newspapers (they too were notably "mixed" — how better could they communicate with their readers?) decreasing, came the anxiety to "preserve" Norwegian. Uncounted organizations were formed with that as a main goal. In 1917 there were supplementary Norwegian schools with 1,796 teachers and 41,716 pupils; there was widespread abhorrence of the melting pot and impassioned pleas arose to preserve the language or lose the "Norwegian soul." Haugen quotes an eminent Norwegian American author and editor, Waldemar Ager: ". . .the so-called American does not himself wish to be assimilated with the foreigners; he does not wish either to assimilate or take up in himself the Russian, the Pole, or the Jew: but he wants these to be absorbed in each other" (TNLIA, p. 251). Meanwhile, teachers in the public schools were threatening the pupils with punishment for speaking Norwegian on the playgrounds; children rebelled against their parents: when addressed in Norwegian they replied in English. But the monolingual Norwegian group was no more; the reason for bilingualism had ceased to exist; the shift to English had run its course.[7]

Restatement of the problem

To equal or excel the German-Americans' language maintenance efforts (if that is indeed required for Spanish to survive) would not be easy. It might be impossible even to reverse and avoid the kind of slow, then ever-faster linguistic interference which changed Norwegian in the United States into a pastiche before the shift to English was complete. Yet it may be that neither of these is the most essential factor. Rather, the fundamental issues seem to be: (1) If all the group becomes bilingual there is no further need for bilinguality; and (2) No people needs two languages for the same set of purposes.

The first of these propositions recalls the essential marginality of bilingualism. Two human communities come in extended, long-term contact, each speaking a different language. From that contact there develops a marginal group of bilingual persons, intermediaries. As Einar Haugen says, "Those who learn the language of the other group become carriers of intergroup relations, but from the point of view of the group their behavior is marginal rather than central." They are not indulging in an activity that all can share (TNLIA, p. 5). Haugen finds that ". . .it appears to require considerable social pressure for such a group to remain bilingual for any length of time. As long as the group is a true link between monolinguals, this pressure exists. But if the monolinguals on the one side disappear, becoming bilinguals or going over to the other language entirely, the reason for bilingualism disappears and its functional importance is reduced" (TNLIA, p. 7). He is saying in effect that societal bilingualism is inseparable from this marginality and that if all the Spanish speakers become bilingual, one language (Spanish) must go. In this view it is only to the extent that the monolingual Spanish speakers exist as a group apart from their bilingual element that bilingualism can continue.

William F. Mackey, speaking to the same point, says "An individual's use of two languages supposes the existence of two different language communities; it does not suppose the existence of a bilingual community. The bilingual community can only be regarded as a dependent collection of individuals who have reasons for being bilingual. A self-sufficient bilingual community has no reason to remain bilingual, since a closed community in which everyone is fluent in two languages could get along just as well with one language" (RITSOL, pp. 554-555).

E.G. Malherbe (TBS, p. 46; DMB, p. 326), reporting on

English-Afrikaans bilingualism and bilingual schooling in South Africa notes that "the percentage of people speaking both English and Afrikaans dropped from 73 percent in 1951 to 66 percent in 1960 as a result of separating Afrikaans and English-speaking children at school and students at Universities in separate institutions." This policy of segregation imposed by the Nationalist (Afrikaans) regime reflects the proposition of marginality. Socio-cultural pressures had always caused more Afrikaans speakers to learn English than they caused English speakers to learn Afrikaans. If the entire population became bilingual, there would be no reason for two languages; Afrikaans would be abandoned in favor of the more useful world language, and the Afrikaners' identity as a group would be severely threatened, perhaps even destroyed. Thus the Afrikaans speakers seek to defend their language by reducing the number of bilingual individuals in their country.

It should be noted that many countries popularly believed to be bilingual are only marginally so. Only 11 percent of Finns reported a knowledge of both Finnish and Swedish in Finland's 1950 census and in the 1960 census this percentage dropped to 7. In Belgium only 18 percent spoke Flemish and French in 1947 (DMB, p. 318). In Paraguay slightly more than half of the population is bilingual. In all of Canada "only about 12 percent of the population reported a knowledge of both official languages in 1961; three-quarters of these were of French mother tongue," according to K.D. Macrae (DMB, p. 318). In the Quebec capital, as Everett Hughes points out (DMB, p. 322), three-quarters of the people are of French mother tongue and ethnic identity and of the remainder most are of English mother tongue. Although some of the latter are also bilingual, their bilingualism becomes functional mainly at limited points of contact, e.g., the foreman passing orders from the English monolingual industrialist to his French-speaking workmen, or in large department stores among sales-people, but there are in Montreal completely separate religious and educational systems with one or the other language used exclusively. "From Kindergarten," says Hughes, "to the doctorate of law, medicine or philosophy one may be taught in one language [exclusively] or the other, so far as the daily contact of pupil with pupil, and of teacher with teacher are concerned." Again we see that, within the totality of the two ethnic groups in contact, bilinguals and their bilingualism are marginal.

The second fundamental proposition is, as Joshua Fishman has said, that no people needs two languages for the same set of purposes. It would be difficult to find a case of bilingualism at the societal (as opposed to the individual) level in which both languages serve the same general purposes. Stated otherwise, it is probably true that societal bilingualism is stable to the extent that the purposes served by the two languages are different (distinct, compartmentalized, complementary, in Fishman's terms) and it is unstable — hence tending toward or verging on shift — to the extent that they are the same. The term "diglossia" was coined (Ferguson 1959) to specify a situation such as that in Arabic countries, where an H(igh) language, classical, Koranic Arabic, and a very divergent L(ow) language, any one of the Arabic vernaculars, stand in a relatively stable relationship to each other, each being used by bilingual persons in distinct domains of their lives. Diglossia has since been extended (Fishman 1967) to embrace a relatively stable relationship of distinct, compartmentalized, complementary functions between two or more related languages such as the example above, between unrelated ones such as Spanish and Guaraní in Paraguay, and even between two or more code varieties or registers within a single language, e.g., standard and non-standard native United States speech in English (Stewart 1967, Labov 1966, Hymes 1967).

The case of Paraguay (Rubin 1962, 1963; Garvin and Mathiot 1956) is particularly illuminating. There in 1951 about 52 percent of the people, of all social classes, including city dwellers, spoke both Spanish and Guaraní, but not usually for the same purposes. The 1951 census also showed for the nation as a whole 4 percent monolingual in Spanish and 40 percent monolingual in Guaraní. However, in Asunción 90 percent were bilingual; in Laque, a nearby town, 60 percent; and in all of the interior, 48 percent.

Rubin's study shows that among bilingual Paraguayans Spanish is used in the domains of public administration, schooling, between doctor and patient, lawyer and client, and in general for most formal, non-intimate functions. Guaraní is associated with the domains of informality, intimacy, jokes, love. Rubin found that the sociolinguistic system which determines the uses of Spanish and Guaraní closely parallels the system found by Brown and Gilman to determine the choice between the formal and informal pronouns of address in certain European languages, e.g., *vous* and *tu* in French (Brown and Gilman).

Bilingualism is increasing in Paraguay and with it, according to Rubin, comes a trend toward greater alternate use of both languages. Garvin and Mathiot, writing almost a decade earlier than Rubin, found a concerted, government-backed effort among Paraguayans to have the two languages coexist as equals. An Academia de Cultura Guaraní had been founded for the purpose of codifying Guaraní and was preparing "normative orthographic, grammatical and lexical materials preparatory to an expected and hoped-for introduction of the teaching of Guaraní in the schools" (RITSOL, p. 367). These two investigators found among Paraguayans an increasing pride in and loyalty to Guaraní. Most significantly, they report that immigrants, whether or not they know Spanish, commonly learn Guaraní. Paraguayans make of the language a treasured symbol of their nationality and adopt a puristic, prescriptive attitude toward its use. "Many Paraguayans," say Garvin and Mathiot, "are bilingual and would like to speak both Spanish and Guaraní elegantly; they feel that mixing them, expecially introducing unnecessary Spanish loans into Guaraní, is sloppy" (RITSOL, p. 373).

Robert Di Pietro has gone so far as to propose as a "universal" "the presence of multilingualism [he includes bilingualism in this term] in a speech community depends on the association of each language involved with specific domains of social interaction." He finds "at the base of the matter. . .a criterion of simplicity, statable as follows: Given two or more codes (i.e., languages) to convey the same set of messages, all but one will be abandoned." In Di Pietro's view "a perfect balance of multilingualism in which, say, English and Spanish would be used equally as well for all domains of interaction is highly transitory and represents the step just before a new stage of monolingualism in one or the other language" (LALS, pp. 18-19).

A quotation from Kroeber used by Weinreich in a discussion of the relative stability of cultural practices (including language) is highly pertinent here:

> That a cultural practice is invested with emotion is an important thing about it, but is not decisive for its stability or lability. What decides between continuance or change seems to be whether or not a practice has become involved in an organized system of ideas and sentiments: how much it is inter-woven with other items of culture into a larger pattern. If it is thus connected. . .it has good expectations of persisting, since large systems tend to endure. But a trait that is only loosely connected and essentially free-floating can be superseded very quickly.[8]

Are the uses made of Spanish in the United States part of an organized system, a larger pattern, or are they loosely connected and essentially free-floating?

Another example of bilingualism elsewhere is instructive. Uriel Weinreich (LC, pp. 84-110 and passim) described in 1950 the relationships of the Raetoroman language, of the Schwyzertutsch German dialect vernacular, and of standard German in the Swiss territory of Romansh. The Raetoromans without a unilingual hinterland (Mexico is the Mexican Americans' hinterland) were becoming, all of them, bilingual in their mother tongue and Schwyzertutsch and the functions of the two tongues were overlapping. Weinreich found the overlapping aggravated by the fact that many children learn both languages from the same persons, their parents, and thus tend to use both languages with the same interlocutors and the distinction between the two tongues is blurred. This is in contrast to more stable situations, where children learn each language from different speakers, use them with different speakers and for complementary purposes. Weinreich described the Raetoromans (in the Sutselva area he was studying) as largely a peasant population with little schooling. He found most bilingual speakers to be of Romansh mother tongue, since few native speakers of Schwyzertutsch would learn the less prestigious tongue.

Needless to say, Weinreich found the Romansh population of the Sutselva was undergoing a language shift. German elements in Romansh speech were tolerated practically without limit. Knowledge of German was considered essential to acculturation and social advance. When speaking

German, the bilingual guarded against Romansh borrowings. On the contrary, no value was attached to purity or correctness in Romansh.

Factors tending to weaken Spanish and lead to shift

Weinreich (LC, p. 5) distinguishes between (1) purely structural or linguistic mechanisms which promote or impede interference in the speech of bilinguals and contribute to or impede the abandonment of one of the languages, and (2) the socio-cultural, non-structural factors which have the same effects. The former, which he says are "to a considerable degree independent of non-linguistic experience and behavior," will not be considered in this discussion, which focuses solely on the latter, the socio-cultural factors amenable to control.

We saw in the previous section how the relative status of Schwyzertutsch and Romansh worked to encourage interference and borrowings in Romansh and protected the Germanic tongue. A different order of values obtains in western Switzerland, Weinreich points out (LC, pp. 86, 88), where Schwyzertutsch is in contact with French, "a standardized language with zealously guarded norms propagated by the schools." He notes that in that area of Switzerland, "the functional 'inferiority' of Schwyzertutsch (predominantly a spoken language) as against French — a language of unrestricted functions — is so deeply felt by many bilinguals of both mother tongues that the flow of borrowings from French to Schwyzertutsch in border areas is considered as natural as the inhospitality of French to loanwords from Schwyzertutsch." The difference between the two cases stems primarily from the status ascribed to the languages involved.

Consider a moment some related facts about Spanish in the United States. The Spanish-English bilinguals here are virtually all mother tongue speakers of Spanish. Although children are all remarkably facile learners of second languages, contact among mixed groups on the schools' playgrounds in the United States teaches only English as a second language. Very few Anglo children learn Spanish. Although, as we pointed out above, linguistic interference is notable in the English of many Spanish-English bilinguals, the English language itself remains untouched by the seven score years of contact in the Southwest except for a few lexical items. It is notable that although linguistic borrowing and switching commonly go unhampered when Spanish-speaking bilinguals address each other, when addressing monolingual speakers of English they do not borrow from Spanish and interference is avoided entirely or as much as possible.

One frequently hears the plaint that bilingualism should be reciprocal: "the Anglos — especially schoolchildren — should learn Spanish too." The notion is cruelly illusory because — apart from college and university departments of foreign language — Spanish in the United States has virtually no prestige, especially among its own native-born speakers.

Since Spanish is one of the great world languages, the reasons for its lack of prestige in this country must be sought in its cultural setting here: the relationships between the two groups in contact, the uses to which Spanish is put, and the attitudes of its speakers toward their language. Notable among those attitudes is a widespread "disdain for correctness," and an even more widespread seeming unawareness that language norms serve any purpose beyond pedantry, or as Weinreich says, "an intellectualistic affliction" (LC, p. 102). Spanish speakers as a whole are loyal — often fiercely loyal — to Spanish. Those whose family traditions or personal experience include — even indirectly or vicariously — schooling, high literacy and professional activity in Spanish probably see it as the symbol of Hispanic culture in the "great tradition." Those whose traditions and experience are largely or exclusively with oral Spanish see it simply as a symbol of *la raza*.

The result — at least among Mexican Americans — is that neither in their struggle for social justice nor in their yearning for cultural pluralism does one find evidence of regard for Spanish as the ideologized symbol of ethnic group identity replete with aesthetic and emotional overtones, to be defended from every encroachment by English, to be cultivated by the poet and the scholar and taught assiduously to the young. Haugen (BLCIL, p. 94) reported on a reflection of this in a study of Puerto Rican intellectuals in New York by Fishman. When asked, "What makes you a Puerto Rican? " ordinary people simply pointed to the facts of birthplace and parentage, but the intellectuals stressed their attitudes, knowledge, sentiments, and behaviors (Fishman 1968).

Among the Chicanos, rare is the writer on *Chicanismo*, education, or any other aspect of the *movimiento* who does not extol "bilingual-bicultural education." The Chicano half of the second part of this dichotomy is well and often described. What is to be done about Spanish is not specified. "The educated Spanish-speaking person who has survived the (American) school system is likely to be one who has been stripped of his native language, or, at least, speaks and writes it imperfectly," says Dr. David Ballesteros, Chicano activist and University of Texas professor (TNEP, pp. 26-27). "We are desperately trying to retain what we have, or regain what we have lost. . .," says Marcela Trujillo, director of a Chicano studies program at the University of Denver (TNEP, p. 90).

But in no Chicano publication or public statement known to me (e.g., the November 1970 special edition of *The National Elementary Principal on Education for the Spanish Speaking; El Plan de Santa Bárbara*, by the Chicano Coordinating Council on Higher Education; the issues to date of the Chicano journals, *El Grito, Aztlán, Con Safos, Regeneración*; the volume of proceedings of the first Texas Conference for the Mexican-American, April 1967, *Improving Educational Opportunities of the Mexican-American*, Austin: SEDL 1967; the volume of *Proceedings of the National Conference on Educational Opportunities for Mexican Americans* (April 1968); the

Congressional testimony in support of the Bilingual Education Act; the dozen scholarly papers in the Chicano Studies Institutes series (1970) with support from the National Endowment for the Humanities; those issues which I have seen of the newspapers in the Chicano Press Association; etc.) is there so much as an allusion to the problems of language maintenance or the imminence of language shift. The closest thing to such an allusion that I have found is a statement by Joseph Fitzpatrick, in a study of education for Puerto Ricans in New York Commissioned by the Puerto Rican Forum, that the Spanish language might be a rallying point to unite the Puerto Ricans (TNEP, pp. 70-71).

In the published curricula of three score "Chicano studies programs" there are courses in "Barrio Spanish," "Chicano Spanish," "Bilingual Communication Skills," and such Spanish language requirements as "proficiency equivalent to completion of the fourth semester college course"; and some courses are taught "bilingually." Several programs include Mexican literature in translation and children's literature of Latin America in translation. Among the proposed courses at one college was one on "Chicano Poetry: Creative Writing. Reading and Writing of Spanish/English macaronic verse. . .bilingual poetry. . ."

The position taken in 1970 by Marcela Trujillo, then an instructor in the Chicano studies program, University of Denver, rejects world standard Spanish but is somewhat stronger and may be widely shared: "For I believe that language is the mirror that reflects the soul of a culture. Language and culture are so interwoven that one cannot exist without the other. Although some of our Chicano students no longer speak Spanish, they have inherited the attributes and characteristics of the ancestors who spoke Spanish. . .but they are in danger of losing those qualities if the language is not learned. . .It is necessary for the professor to be bilingual and bicultural. . .The Chicano professor does not need to be proficient in the standard Spanish of Spain or Latin America."

Linguistic interference. In the speech of bilinguals, deviations from the norms of either language are called linguistic interference (LC, p. 1). It has not been proved that interference — often loosely referred to as "mixing" — is the cause of language shift, i.e., in the final abandonment of one language (Spanish) and its replacement by another (English). Nevertheless, Haugen reports (BLCIL, pp. 53-54) that the research of Morgan E. Jones found borrowing from English to Spanish was an index of acculturation to the dominant English language culture in Puerto Rico; and that Stanley M. Tsuzaki's study "showed how the acculturation of Puerto Ricans in Detroit was correlated (a) to the incidence of borrowing from English, up to the time when the shift to English occurred and (b) after that time, to the use of English." At the same point Haugen reports John J. Bodine's finding about Taos, New Mexico, Indians that "the adaptation of names was another clue to acculturation."

It is unquestioned that gradual increase of interference phenomena in the recipient language (Spanish) and increase in the kinds of stimuli which result in switching (temporary or momentary change from the use of one language to that of another) are sure indicators of increased distance from the original language and of the likelihood of complete shift.

Haugen found "an underlying necessity" in the process of interference (TNLIA, p. 71). As he put it, "To save themselves effort bilinguals in speaking to each other take shortcuts that collapse distinctions which have no communicatory value. The result is a more or less gradual shift from two codes towards one. . ." (BLCIL, p. 28). Weinreich's explanation is that "a partial identification of the systems is to the bilingual a reduction of his linguistic burden" (LC, pp. 8, 24). He also makes an important distinction between the kinds of interference which are purely linguistic and can be analyzed in terms of descriptive linguistics, and the extra-linguistic factors — psychological and socio-cultural — which also determine the nature and extent of interference (LC, p. 3, and chapters 3 and 4).

For the purposes of this essay it will suffice to consider only the extra-linguistic factors, which, according to Weinreich, are the ones that determine whether language shift will occur (LC, p. 107). Leaning further on Weinreich (who does not deal in any way specifically with Spanish) the following table gives the principal socio-cultural factors and my best effort to indicate whether each factor contributes to an eventual shift to English or contributes to the resistance of that shift. Each reader is, of course, encouraged to correct these judgments.

Extra-linguistic, socio-cultural factors	Favors shift to English	Resists shift to English
1. Size and homo-geneity of bilingual group		Powerful resistance.
2. Historic priority of bilingual group		Powerful resistance.
3. Access and resource to renewal from a hinterland		(Potentially powerful factor of resistance but is in fact unexploited.)
4. Reinforcement by in-migration and immigration		Powerful resistance.

Extra-linguistic socio-cultural factors	Favors shift to English	Resists shift to English
5. Relative social isolation, including racist attitudes toward a visible minority	The struggle for integration in schools, in housing, etc., favors shift, as does the assimilative bridge-to-English orientation of bilingual schooling.	Differentiation as culturally distinct "brown" people. Pluralistic orientation to bilingual education and resistance to integration also resist shift to English.
6. Inter-generational stability of the extended family		Close-knit, extended family, especially grandparents and other elders living with grandchildren.
7. Order and age of learning		Spanish mother tongue and language of childhood is powerful psychological fact of resistance.
8. Relative proficiency in both tongues	Education solely through English favors shift; bilingual education is presently too weak to offset this.	
9. Specialized use by topics, domains, and interlocutors	Use of both languages for the same purposes favors shift. Absence of socio-cultural divisions to reinforce the difference in mother tongues facilitates shift (LC, p. 98).	Use of each language exclusively for certain topics and domains of life resists shift.
10. Manner of learning each language	Learning both from same persons in some situations facilitates switching and shift.	Learning from different persons in different situations resists shift.
11. Status of the bilingual groups	Except to the extent that the bilinguals' status favors Nos. 5 and 9 above, that status at present facilitates shift.	(Improved status, if made congruent with Nos. 3, 8, 9, 17-22, would resist shift.)
12. Disappearance of the Spanish monolingual group	Powerful force toward complete shift.	(Establishment of diglossia, No. 9 could forestall shift.)

Extra-linguistic socio-cultural factors	Favors shift to English	Resists shift to English
13. Attitudes toward cultural pluralism	Present absence of appropriate action by Spanish speakers facilitates shift. See Nos. 5, 7, and 9.	Overall national attitude of relative tolerance favors cultural pluralism.
14. Attitudes toward both cultures	Prevailing attitudes of both groups favor shift.	
15. Attitudes toward each language; emotional attachment	Other attitudes favor shift. See Nos. 17, 18, 19, 20.	Emotional attachment to Spanish resists shift. (Language loyalty.)
16. Attitudes toward bilingualism		Resist shift.
17. Attitudes toward correctness	Powerfully facilitate shift.	(Emphasis on standardization, purism, would resist shift.)
18. Attitudes toward "mixing" the languages	Powerfully facilitate shift.	
19. Modes of use of each language	Virtual absence of reading and writing of Spanish by adults powerfully facilitates shift.	
20. Relative usefulness of each language	Limitation of Spanish to oral, intimate, informal uses limits prestige, facilitates "mixing" and shift.	
21. Function of each language in social advance	Powerfully facilitates shift.	
22. Literary-cultural value	Absence of emphasis reduces prestige, facilitates "mixing" and shift.	

Factors that could support Spanish and resist shift

The preceding chart has indicated, if only by implication, some of what would be required to maintain Spanish and forestall a widespread shift to English. The sum of these indications is that it probably cannot be maintained — the shift for most speakers would be inevitable — at its present level of status, function, and interference from English. All of the evidence suggests that the potentially advantageous position of Spanish cannot be realized without certain affirmative actions.

Spanish as a "world language" The indigenous languages of the Americas, whatever their equality in purely linguistic terms with all others, are at a severe disadvantage in terms of usefulness and prestige compared to the great "world languages" such as English, Russian, Spanish, and French. The mark of a world language is not simply its extensive spread but also its use in all domains of human activity and the consequent vast body of printed material available to its users. It follows that to the extent that Spanish in the United States is anything but world standard Spanish — *el español común* — it will be unable to benefit from the prestige of Spanish and draw on that vast treasure of writing in every field.

Two typical statements by prominent Chicanos suggest that this judgment about *el español común* is not widely known or shared or is considered of no consequence. Lionel Sánchez, director of "Farm Workers United" in Lupton, Colorado, was writing of the relationship of Chicano studies programs to the Chicano cummunity: "There is no doubt that the Chicano of today must learn Spanish, but it must be the word usage that is continued in the Barrios. Too often a Chicano learns the Castillian [sic] Spanish which is of little or no benefit in his work with Chicanos who speak only the barrio Spanish." (Sánchez)

René Núñez, of the Centro de Estudios Chicanos at San Diego State College, in a similar formal paper on the qualifications of teachers for such centers had this to say of Chicano studies: "It speaks in a language that is at once English and Spanish — caló. . ." (Núñez)

There is a broader view — that the farm worker, the barrio dweller, and the school child could be met and served at their own language levels while the society as a whole, in its schools and other institutions, in its mass communications and in its aspirations would see itself as part of the world community of Spanish speakers. I have not yet found that broader view represented in the literature.

Renewal from the hinterlands. Unlike all other non-English languages in the United States except French in New England, Spanish could easily draw strength and continuous renewal from Puerto Rico and Mexico. Given the strong and unquestioned tradition of standardization among the *boricuas,* there is virtual unanimity on island and continent alike regarding the Spanish language — hence nothing to impede such cooperation.

Among Chicanos there is a continuum of attitudes ranging from the other-worldly purism of a few university professor-scholars in departments of romance languages to the *bato loco* in the barrio who may control a dialect marked only slightly by interference but who disdains it and flaunts the *pachuco caló* in contempt for all norms. The continuum is markedly skewed toward disdain for standardization.

Any attitude short of full respect for *el español común*, world standard Spanish, is virtually certain to give rise to disdain and even hostility on the part of Mexicans, even Mexican intellectuals. That attitude is already impeding the use of visiting teachers from Mexico in programs of bilingual education and the establishment in Mexico of centers for training Chicano teachers for employment in bilingual schools in the Southwest.

The potential of renewal from the hinterlands is incalculable: teacher and student exchange relationships, dual-campus arrangements between American and Puerto Rican or American and Mexican universities to facilitate work in residence at both sites; establishment by Puerto Rico and Mexico of a system of teaching centers in continental United States on the order of the *Alliance Française*; greater access to the flood of printed matter in Spanish; extended exchange visits by children at the individual home level for language learning, etc.

Difference as a source of strength. What was said above about ambivalence relates directly to our subject. The hypothesis is that any factor which serves to differentiate Spanish speakers from non-Spanish speakers is also likely to favor maintenance of the language and to resist the shift to English. A corollary of the hypothesis is that factors which assimilate (cause to resemble or be like) the Spanish speakers to other Spanish speakers in other areas of the world also favor maintenance and resist shift to English.

The propositions can be expressed as three continua, the first poles of which strongly favor maintenance, with the opposites strongly favoring shift:

1) A distinct, identifiable "visible" group ("brown," "bronze," with indigenous roots in the New World)

An undifferentiated group, "the same as everybody else."

2) Settlement, housing, and schooling patterns to form strong enclaves.[9]

Wide dispersal among the English-only majority.

3) A pluralistic orientation,
   including diglossia (sep-
   arate language domains
   for Spanish)

An assimilative orientation,
including use of both lan-
guages for all purposes.

It is apparent immediately that the choices are at the heart of the ambivalence referred to earlier.

Language planning. Such planning may be concerned with diverse matters: the choice of one or more languages among many in "developing" countries; choice and standardization of one dialect among many; systematic, intensive expansion of the lexicon of a language to make it more widely useful; relationship and use of two or more languages for school purposes; and above all, manifestations of language loyalty and activity of any kind to enhance and use the prestige of a language as symbolic of the integrity and prestige of the people who speak it and thus resist encroachment against the language and the people. Encroach means "to intrude usurpingly, by insidious or gradual advance, on the territory or rights of another."

Peoples under threat of encroachment have very commonly seized upon their language as the previous, ideologized symbol of their people-hood and have fought to defend it.[10] The defense has not always been successful — certainly not when undertaken too late.

In view of the histories of language planning efforts elsewhere, and very briefly, the remainder of the report on this simulated conference of experts will suggest a few limited approaches to language maintenance which are presently most accessible.

Reform of the teaching of Spanish to Spanish speakers in schools, colleges, and universities. It is widely reported and conceded that the least "successful" students of Spanish in the United States, especially at the secondary school level, are its native speakers. The explanation of this embarrassing incongruity is also widely known: the predominance of "Anglo" teachers with little functional competence in Spanish; use of materials and methods designed to teach English monolinguals; exaggeratedly prescriptive attitudes toward "correctness"; ignorance and fear of and disdain for the learners' dialect (which may indeed be close to the cultivated standards of Puerto Rico or Mexico); failure to build on the learners' strengths; insistence upon combining native speakers with ordinary foreign language learners on the basis of grade level instead of the basis of proficiency, etc.

The American Association of Teachers of Spanish and Portuguese has commissioned a study of this matter[11] which recommends strategies for correction of the anomalies by institution of a limited form of "bilingual education": special classes or sections for Spanish speakers at all levels, with competent (preferably native speaking) teachers using the language as an exclusive medium to reinforce all other areas of the curriculum rather than limited to teaching the language per se. The recommendations emphasize and specify ways to build strongly on the learner's dialect, and emphasize strong rapport with the struggle of Spanish speakers in the United States for a greater measure of social justice and cultural pluralism.

Strengthening the effectiveness of bilingual education. In a study of the orientation of some bilingual schooling in the Southwest, Rolf Kjolseth, University of Colorado sociologist, used the construct of a continuum running from the most assimilative orientation to the most pluralistic. Both orientations are, of course, equally defensible, but only the latter favors language maintenance. Kjolseth's findings indicated not only that the tendency in the schools he studied was markedly assimilative but that the projects' administrators tended to assume and claim a pluralistic orientation which the analysis showed to be otherwise (Kjolseth).

In a study of the explicit objectives, organization, and curriculum of twenty-three bilingual schools in California, Tay Lesley found that the general objective most supportive of Spanish was "to improve the academic achievement of non-English mother tongue students by using the mother tongue to further concept development." There was a notable absence in the study of any explicit intention to preserve or maintain Spanish or to increase its prestige or to develop in its native speakers a high degree of literacy and other competence. For monolingual speakers of English in the programs "mastery of Spanish" ranked in importance after "appreciation of the other culture" and "development of an impartial attitude toward one's own and the second language and culture" (Lesley, pp. 55-56).

Lesley found little correspondence "between factors in the curriculum and stated objectives" (p. 108) and noted a marked shift during the programs' periods of operation toward the predominant use of English.

Gaarder studied documentation on seventy-six federally-supported projects of bilingual schooling in the United States and found a notable absence of regard — especially in those projects serving Mexican American children — for teacher competence in respect to either speech or literacy in the Spanish language or its use as a medium of instruction (Gaarder 1970).

In 1970 thirty-odd teachers regularly employed for Spanish-medium work in public school bilingual schooling projects in New Mexico and Colorado — all of them native speakers of Spanish — were asked what books they had read in Spanish. Only one of them had read such a book. In 1971 most of a similar group of bilingual teachers were found to be unaware that there are differences between the alphabets of English and Spanish. In both cases the bilinguality was largely limited to speech. In respect to reading and writing they were virtually English monolinguals.

Malherbe, in his thorough study of English-Afrikaans bilingual schooling in South Africa (TBS, pp. 19-25) was very specific about the linguistic competence required of the teachers. He distinguished six stages of bilingual competence: (1) ability to follow intelligently an ordinary conversation, speech, or sermon, and read the newspapers; (2) in addition to the above, to converse intelligibly with fair fluency and read "literature"; (3) in addition to all the above, to write correctly, "free from grammatical and spelling errors and without gross violations of idiom"; (4) in addition to all the above, "a correct and convincing power of expression both in writing and speaking. . .[serving] as fit models for growing minds to imitate." "This stage," says Malherbe, "represents the minimum requirements for being a bilingual teacher or the principal of a bilingual school."

Malherbe's stage five is attained by only those who command the languages better than 90 percent of their native speakers. Stage six is the unapproachable ideal: perfection in both tongues. Needless to say, Malherbe found many teachers below stage four.

The specialists meeting under UNESCO sponsorship to discuss the use of vernacular languages in education noted (RITSOL, p. 696) that

> Teachers who have themselves received their education and professional training in a second language have real difficulty in learning to teach in the mother tongue. The main reasons for this difficulty are of two kinds. First: they have to teach subjects in a language which is not the language in which they are accustomed to think about them; and some of what they have to teach involves concepts which are alien to their pupils' culture and therefore have to be interpreted in a tongue to which they are alien. Secondly, there is often a lack of suitable books to guide or help them both in teaching and in teaching through their mother tongue; they have to depend, therefore, more on their own initiative and skill than when teaching through the second language in which they themselves have been trained. In those regions where a mother tongue is spoken by a large population, it should not be difficult to give teachers much of their theoretical training and all their practice teaching in the mother tongue. [added.]

There have been numerous references in the discussion to the effect of associating (or failing to associate) each of the languages with specific domains of usage. The consensus seems to be that bilingualism is stabilized and language shift resisted if the languages are kept apart and not used for the same purposes. Malherbe's research (DNB, p. 44) convinced him that in the young child becoming bilingual the "differentiation or realisation that [the two sets of] symbols constitute different languages is facilitated when these are consistently associated with different persons or sets of persons, for example, where the infant hears different members of the family or friends consistently speak different languages. . .[In] a bilingual country like South Africa a child has no difficulty in operating linguistically in different universes of discourse. It becomes naturally bilingual because it finds out very soon that certain persons are 'persons-to-whom-English-is-spoken,' that other persons are 'persons-to-whom-Afrikaans-is-spoken.'. . ." It follows that if bilingual schooling is not to aggravate what Haugen calls "the basic problem of the bilingual, that of keeping his language apart" (BLCIL, p. 70), the times, places, and persons for each language should be kept separate. Indeed Malherbe recommends that bilingual schools have "where possible specialist teachers for the language instruction in the case of both the first and the second languages" (TBS, p. 24).

Another major factor in the organization of bilingual schooling is whether or not to teach the young Spanish-speaking learners separately when such separation would make their learning more effective or to prefer a policy of combining them when possible with equal numbers of monolingual Anglos. The problem does not arise in two-way bilingual schools when, after the first three or so years of instruction, the Anglos have enough command of Spanish to permit its free use as a medium. It arises seriously in two other situations: (1) during the first years of elementary school instruction, when to combine Spanish speakers with Anglo monolinguals prevents the teacher from working with full force and authenticity in Spanish because the others would be unable to understand; and (2) in those cases where less than half of the day is devoted to Spanish, e.g., a single class period; in these cases, in addition to the weakness just described the practice of combining the two kinds of learners means that while the Hispanos get watered-down Spanish-medium instruction the Anglos get nothing but FLES, foreign language instruction. Teaching a language as a subject is entirely different from using it as a medium. The two are strongly incompatible.

Here again the ambivalence described above causes the confusion. Special classes for Spanish speakers in English as a second language are "homogeneous grouping." Special Spanish-medium class work for them is likely to be viewed as "segregation."

Language maintenance efforts elsewhere in Spanish America. For centuries Spanish speakers have cherished their language, and in every country the motto of the Royal Spanish Academy, *limpia, fija, y da esplendor*, has had strong adherents. Guillermo L. Guitarte and Rafael Torres Quintero have summarized formal and official efforts in support of the uniformity of Spanish, and the following account is drawn from that summary (CTL, pp. 562-604). The Royal Spanish Academy and its former corresponding academies were a major force since 1870 in combatting the linguistic nationalism and other centrifugal tendencies that threatened to fragment the Spanish language following the wars of independence in Latin America. They have been organized since 1951 in an *Asociación de Academias de la Lengua Española* "whose purpose is to work assiduously for the defense, unity, and integrity of our common language, and to see that its natural growth follows the traditional paths of the Spanish language." Related to that *Asociación*, an *Oficina Internacional de Información and Observación del Español* made up of linguists from the Spanish-speaking countries has been established in Madrid. Guitarte and Torres Quintero report that in its efforts to assure that every region with a large population of Spanish speakers will have a means of working for the control and defense of the language, the Association is considering the establishment of branches in such cities as Los Angeles, San Antonio, Chicago, and New York (CTL, p. 570).

In a number of Latin American countries the efforts to develop pride and respect for Spanish include holding literary and philological contests, the celebration of an annual "language day," special lectures and regular newspaper articles dealing with language, and in some countries laws which seek to encourage correctness of language in all media of mass communication including public signs (CTL, pp. 586-587).

Summation

The 400-year drama of Spanish in the United States is still far from its dénouement. The evidence presented and weighed by our "conference of experts" is that there are extraordinary potential advantages that favor the maintenance of Spanish. They are as yet an almost totally unrealized potential. In the face of this we have found no evidence to contravene one of the overall conclusions from Fishman's study of six separate cultural-linguistic groups in the United States, three of high prestige (French, Spanish, German) and three of low prestige (Ukrainian, Hungarian, Yiddish): that language maintenance and language shift have proceeded along quite similar lines in the six cases despite seemingly essential differences among them (LLUS, pp. 394-395). "The drift has been consistently toward Anglification and has become accelerated in recent years."

The most significant disclosure is the seemingly obvious one (developed in detail by U. Weinreich and others) that language, and languages in contact, are primarily and overwhelmingly social phenomena subject irremissibly to other social phenomena which in some measure can be controlled. A kind of corrollary of this is the disclosure that there seems to be something like rules which lend a measure of predictability to the interaction of languages and peoples. The two fundamental issues set forth above as a "restatement of the problem," are unavoidable. The disdain for correctness implies abandonment of the language that Hispanic peoples have in common. The ambivalencies will be resolved.

Spanish speakers in the United States may choose a kind of stable diglossia with English by dividing the domains of usage, and irrespective of the extent to which their mother tongue becomes dialectized. Or they may aspire to be the marginal bilingual group mediating between the Spanish monolinguals of Latin America and the English monolinguals of the United States and Canada. To function on this larger stage would require allegiance and adherence to standard Spanish, *el español común*. There are other choices, including the preference not to choose at all.

Let the conference conclude by noting that in purely linguistic terms the speech habits of all peoples (with whatever repertory of varieties of usage from whatever number of "languages") are equally adequate in service of the purposes for which they were developed. When new purposes are envisaged and factors beyond the purely linguistic must be considered, the matter becomes more complicated.

Summary

The paper discusses factors which contribute to the maintenance of Spanish as a language of common, everyday communication in the United States as opposed to factors which hasten the displacement of Spanish by English. An attempt will be made to draw parallels with similar cases at other times and places in the world. The aim of the paper is to raise pertinent questions and to demonstrate the urgency of language planning as a means of answering them.

NOTES

[1] This paper was written in the author's private capacity. No official support or endorsement by the U.S. Office of Education or the Department of Health, Education and Welfare is intended or should be inferred.

[2] Preface to Uriel Weinreich, *Languages in Contact.* The Hague: Mouton, (1968).

[3] This term, in the Spanish speakers' vocabulary, designates their fellow citizens who are not of *"la raza,"* usually (but not always!) excepting the Blacks, American Indians, and those of Oriental ancestry.

[4] "Critical Areas of Need for Research and Scholastic Study." In the series *Chicano Studies Institutes,* Summer 1970. Washington, D.C.: Montal Systems, 600 Federal Building, 1522 K Street N.W.

[5] Roman Pucinski's statements in Hearings on Ethnic Studies Act.

[6] Heinz Kloss, "German-American Language Maintenance Efforts." In LLUS, pp. 206-252.

[7] All of the above section on Norwegian is from Haugen's two-volume work *The Norwegian Language in America: A Study in Bilingual Behavior.* Bloomington: Indiana University Press, (1969). This comprehensive history and analysis, both sociological and linguistic, is indispensable to an understanding of the immigrant languages in this country.

[8] A. L. Kroeber, *Anthropology.* New York: Harcourt, Brace & World, (1948), p. 402; and LC, pp. 5-6.

[9] Witness, for example, the South African policy in this regard.

[10] Fishman's LLUS, and Sections VI and VII of RITSOL, and chapter 10 of TNLIA are concerned with language planning.

[11] The report and recommendations, available from Eugene Savaiano, Secretary-Treasurer, AATSP, Wichita State University, was prepared by Hernán LaFontaine, Adalberto Guerrero, Alonso Perales, Marie Esman Parker, Olivia Muñoz, Herminia Cantero, Charles Olstad, Donald Walsh, and Bruce Gaarder.

Key Works Consulted

BLCIL   Einar Haugen. *Bilingualism, Language Contact and Immigrant Languages in the United States: A Research Report, 1956-1970.* Cambridge, Mass.: Boylston Hall, Harvard University (preprint stenciled version). Scheduled for publication in Thomas A. Sebeok, ed., *Current Trends in Linguistics*, Vol. 10. The Hague: Mouton.

CTL   Thomas A. Sebeok (ed.). *Current Trends in Linguistics — Ibero-American and Caribbean Linguistics.* The Hague: Mouton, (1968).

DMB   L.G. Kelly (ed.). *Description and Measurement of Bilingualism: An International Seminar.* Toronto: University of Toronto Press, (1969).

LALS   James Alatis (ed.). *Linguistics and Language Study* (21st Annual Round Table Meeting). Washington, D.C.: Georgetown University Press, (1970).

LC   Uriel Weinreich. *Languages in Contact.* The Hague: Mouton, (1968).

LLUS   Joshua A. Fishman, *et al. Language Loyalty in the United States.* The Hague: Mouton, (1966).

MAE   Anon. *Equal Educational Opportunity, Part 4 — Mexican American Education.* (Hearings Before the Select Committee on Equal Educational Opportunity of the United States Senate, Ninety-first Congress, Second Session, August 18-21, 1970). Washington, D.C.: Government Printing Office, (1971).

RITSOL Joshua A. Fishman (ed.). *Readings in the Sociology of Language.* The Hague: Mouton, (1970).

TBS   E.G. Malherbe. *The Bilingual School.* London: Longmans, (1946).

TNEP   *The National Elementary Principal,* Vol. 50, No.2 (1970).

TNLIA   Einar Haugen. *The Norwegian Language in America.* Bloomington, Indiana: Indiana University Press, (1969).

Bibliography

Ballesteros, David. "Toward an Advantaged Society: Bilingual Education in the 70's," In TNEP, pp. 25-28.

Bodine, John J. "Taos Names: A Clue to Linguistic Acculturation," *Anthropological Linguistics*, Vol. 5, No. 2, pp. 23-27. (BLCIL)

Brown, Roger, and Albert Gilman. "The Pronouns of Power and Solidarity," in Thomas A. Sebeok, ed., *Style in Language.* Cambridge: Technology Press, (1960), pp. 253-276. (RITSOL)

Di Pietro, Robert J. "The Discovery of Universals in Multilingualism." In LALS, pp. 13-23.

Elizondo, Sergio D. "Critical Areas of Need for Research and Scholastic Study." In the series *Chicano Studies Institutes — Summer 1970.* Washington, D.C.: Montal Systems, 600 Federal Bldg., 1522 K Street, N.W., (1970).

Ferguson, Charles A. "Diglossia." *Word*, XV (1959), pp. 325-340.

Fishman, Joshua A. "Bilingualism with and without Diglossia; Diglossia with and without Bilingualism," *The Journal of Social Issues*, XXIII, No. 2 (1967), pp. 29-38.

Fishman, Joshua A., Robert L. Cooper, Roxana Ma, *et al. Bilingualism in the Barrio*, (2 vols.). Final Report, U.S. Office of Education. New York: Yeshiva University, (1968), pp. 124-145.

Fitzpatrick, Joseph P. "Educational Experience of the Puerto Rican Community in New York City: A Review Paper." Unpublished study commissioned by the Puerto Rican Institute for School and Community interaction of the Puerto Rican Forum, Inc., p. 67. (Cited by Hector I. Vázquez.)

Gaarder. A. Bruce. "The First Seventy-Six Bilingual Education Projects." In James E. Alatis, eds., *Monograph Series on Languages and Linguistics*, No. 23, (1970). Washington, D.C.: Georgetown University, pp. 163-178.

Garvin, Paul L., and Madeleine Mathiot. "The Urbanization of the Guaraní Language: A Problem in Language and Culture." In A.F.C. Wallace, ed., *Men and Cultures: Selected Papers of the Fifth International Congress of Anthropological and Ethnological Sciences.* Philadelphia: University of Pennsylvania Press, (1956). (RITSOL)

Guitarte, Guillermo L., and Rafael Torres Quintero. "Linguistic Correctness and the Role of the Academies." In CTL, pp. 562-604.

Hayden, Robert G. "Some Community Dynamics of Language Maintenance." in LLUS, p. 205.

Hughes, Everett C. Commentary in DMB, p. 322.

Hymes, Dell. "Models of the Interaction of Language and Social Setting." *The Journal of Social Issues*, XXIII, No. 2 (1967), pp. 8-28.

Jones, Morgan Emory. *A Phonological Study of English as Spoken by Puerto Ricans Contrasted with Puerto Rican Spanish and American English.*

Dissertation, University of Michigan, (1962). (BLCIL)

Kjolseth, Rolf. "Bilingual Education Programs in the United States: For Assimilation or Pluralism? " Paper presented in the section on Sociological Perspectives on Bilingual Education of the Socio-linguistics Program at the 7th World Congress of Sociology held in Varna, Bulgaria, September 14-19, (1971).

Kloss, Heinz. "German-American Language Maintenance Efforts." In LLUS, pp. 206-252.

Kroeber, A.L. *Anthropology.* New York: Harcourt, Brace & World, (1948), pp. 402. (LC, pp. 5-6)

Labov, William. *The Social Stratification of English in New York City.* Washington, D.C.: Center for Applied Linguistics, (1966).

Lesley, Tay. *Bilingual Education in California.* Master's thesis, University of California, Los Angeles, (1971).

Mackey, William F. "The Description of Bilingualism." In RITSOL, pp. 554-584.

Macrae, K.D. Commentary in DMB, p. 318.

Malherbe, E.G. Commentary in DMB, pp. 46, 326.

Núñez, René. *Criteria for Employment of Chicano Studies Staff.* In the series *Chicano Studies Institutes — Summer 1970.* Washington, D.C.: Montal Systems, 600 Federal Bldg., 1522 K Street, N.W., (1970).

Rubin, Joan. "Bilingualism in Paraguay." *Anthropological Linguistics,* IV, No. 1 (1962), pp. 52-58.

——. *National Bilingualism in Paraguay.* Doctoral dissertation, Yale University, (1963). Chapter 7, pp. 200-235. (Chapter 7 appeared in RITSOL, pp. 512-530.)

Sánchez, George I. "An Interview with George I. Sánchez." TNEP, p. 103.

Sánchez, Lionel. *La Raza Community and Chicano Studies.* In the series *Chicano Studies Institutes — Summer 1970.* Washington, D.C.: Montal Systems, 600 Federal Bldg., 1522 K Street, N.W., (1970).

Stewart, William. "Sociolinguistic Factors in the History of American Negro Dialects." *Florida FL Reporter,* V, No. 2 (Spring 1967).

Trujillo, Marcela L. *Guidelines for Employment in Chicano Studies.* In the series *Chicano Studies Institutes — Summer 1970.* Washington, D.C.: Montal Systems, 600 Federal Bldg., 1522 K Street, N.W., (1970).

——. Review of Thomas P. Carter, *Mexican Americans in School: A History of Educational Neglect.* New York: College Entrance Examination Board, (1970). In TNEP, pp. 88-92.

Tsuzaki, Stanley Mamoru. *English Influences in the Phonology and Morphology of the Spanish Spoken in the Mexican Colony in Detroit, Michigan.* Doctoral dissertation, University of Michigan, (1963). (BCLIL)

UNESCO. *The Use of Vernacular Languages in Education.* Monographs on Fundamental Education, VIII. Paris: UNESCO, (1953).

Conclusion

G. Richard Tucker

The purpose of the Conference was (a) to contribute to the work of the International Association of Applied Linguistics by seeking the collaboration of researchers in child language on this side of the Atlantic. Hopefully in future conferences it will be possible to elicit even broader representation and there will be people from areas which are not represented here at this meeting. The organizers wished (b) to identify researchers and to stimulate further research, especially in the learning of two or more languages or dialects by young children. We might perhaps add a corollary to that. One of the purposes of the Conference could be phrased a little differently, "to identify researchers who are interested in doing these things and also who are willing to communicate with the classroom teacher, with the people who are developing programs, to phrase their results in language that is intelligible to everyone," and (c) to seek ways of applying the results of such research to schooling with a view to improving our educational practices, especially in the rapidly developing field of bilingual education. Of course the third is not something that will appear as a finished product of this Conference, but I hope it is a direction in which we are moving. That's where we are. This is the consensus which was reflected by you people. The consensus may reflect things that you would like to talk about. What has become quite obvious on the basis of this conference is that such communication as this is both desirable and welcome; that researchers want very much to learn what teachers or supervisors are doing or thinking. They are interested in finding ways in which they can translate educators' questions into experimental paradigms. The converse is also true. Both research and the application of research results to teaching and learning are essential.

Let me very briefly summarize for you the ideas that emerged as a consensus from those of you who completed the questionnaires distributed during the conference.

1. Should the results of research in early language acquisition be made more accessible at the grass roots level? I interpret this to mean, "Should the classroom teacher be informed about, be brought up to date about new techniques, new advances, new knowledge concerning language acquisition?" There's been a big change, as you know, in the last decade, not only in the amount of research but in data-collecting techniques. Is this

something that should be communicated to the elementary-school teachers?

2. Are first- and second-language learning the same or not? How do they differ; how are they similar?

3. To what extent should we treat black English as a second dialect and to what extent should we apply to it techniques of bilingual education?

4. What is the Conference's recommendation regarding the role of the monolingual English-speaking child in a bilingual program? How does he fit into this program?

5. How can a bilingual program be designed on the basis of free alternation of languages such as that described by William Mackey?

6. What needs to be done to emphasize the affective domain in language teaching, whether it's first-language teaching, second-language teaching, conventional education, or bilingual education?

7. What steps should be taken to develop more adequate cultural materials in the minority languages?

8. What specifically can be done for ethnic language retention programs? What could be done, for example, to continue or to build up programs in areas other than Spanish or French or Portuguese?

9. How do we deal with the physically handicapped bilingual child or with the one who has severe language perceptual or motor disabilities?

10. Should there not be more communication among bilingual projects and training programs? We simply do not know what others are doing.

These represent ten of the recurring themes in the document which you returned to us. Each of these was expressed, not in the same words, by four or five or six or seven of the participants. This is an impressive consensus.

INDEX